I0138953

THE STORY OF MY CAMPAIGN

THE STORY OF MY CAMPAIGN

The Civil War Memoir of Captain Francis T. Moore, Second Illinois Cavalry

EDITED BY

Thomas Bahde

With a Foreword by Michael Fellman

NORTHERN ILLINOIS UNIVERSITY PRESS *DeKalb*

Published by the Northern Illinois University Press, DeKalb, Illinois 60115

Design by Shaun Allshouse

Library of Congress Cataloging-in-Publication Data
Moore, Francis T., 1838–1912.
The story of my campaign : the Civil War memoir of Captain Francis T. Moore, Second Illinois Cavalry / edited by Thomas Bahde.
p. cm.
Includes bibliographical references and index.
ISBN 978-0-87580-441-5 (clothbound : acid-free paper)
1. Moore, Francis T., 1838–1912. 2. United States. Army. Illinois Cavalry Regiment, 2nd (1861–1865) 3. United States. Army—Military life—History—19th century. 4. Soldiers—Illinois—Biography. 5. Illinois—History—Civil War, 1861–1865—Personal narratives. 6. United States—History—Civil War, 1861–1865—Personal narratives. 7. United States—History—Civil War, 1861–1865—Cavalry operations. 8. Illinois—History—Civil War, 1861–1865—Regimental histories. 9. United States—History—Civil War, 1861–1865—Regimental histories. I. Bahde, Thomas William. II. Title.
E505.62nd .M66 2011
973.7'8092—dc23
[B]
2011016757

Title page image courtesy of Special Collections and University Archives, San Diego State University Library & Information Access

CONTENTS

List of Images *vii*

Acknowledgments *ix*

Foreword by Michael Fellman *xi*

INTRODUCTION—Francis Moore's Memoir and the Construction of Civil War Memory *3*

MOORE'S PREFACE *15*

CHAPTER ONE—1861 *17*

CHAPTER TWO—1862 *64*

CHAPTER THREE—1863 *117*

CHAPTER FOUR—1864 *164*

CHAPTER FIVE—1865 *214*

EPILOGUE—Francis Moore, Civil War Veteran *257*

Appendix A
Roster of Company L, "Delano's Dragoons," Second Illinois Cavalry *265*

Appendix B
Letter of Francis C. Moore to Mary Moore, October 5, 1862 *277*

Appendix C
Letter of Francis C. Moore to Mary Moore, October 7, 1862 *279*

Appendix D
Captain Francis Moore to Adjutant-General Lorenzo Thomas Requesting Permission to Raise a Black Cavalry Regiment *281*

Notes *283*

Bibliography *297*

Index *303*

IMAGES

Map of Francis Moore's War 2

Title page of Francis Moore's memoir 11

Sketch of Bird's Point & Cairo, 1861 35

"Our Special Correspondent," Fort Holt, Kentucky, October 1861 37

"On the Outpost," Fort Holt, Kentucky, October 1861 46

"Gun Boat 'Lexington'" at Fort Holt, Kentucky, 1861 48

Sketch of Celebration at Fort Holt, Kentucky, 1861 55

Portrait of Francis Moore after he moved to National City 259

ACKNOWLEDGMENTS

In addition to the debts of gratitude Francis Moore no doubt accrued in the compilation of his memoir, I must acknowledge my own. At the Special Collections and University Archives at the San Diego State University Library, I am especially grateful to the librarians for bringing Moore's work to my attention and encouraging me to seek publication. At the National City Public Library, local history librarian Philip Kendall Price helped me piece together Moore's later life. Jane Kenealy at the San Diego History Center pointed me toward their Grand Army of the Republic Collection, where I found Moore on the roll books. At Northern Illinois University Press, Sara Hoerdeman enthusiastically guided this project to publication. Michael Fellman cheerfully added his significant expertise and insight to the foreword. My father, Bill, came out of retirement to draw the map of Moore's war, and my wife, Anne, helped index the volume. Of course, Francis Moore was my most significant collaborator, and I hope he would be pleased with the result. He is responsible for the book's virtues, and I for its shortcomings.

FOREWORD

Michael Fellman

In 1861, Francis Moore appeared to be a perfectly ordinary middle-class twenty-three-year-old man, settling into a secure and dull life as a carriage maker in his bustling Mississippi River hometown of Quincy, Illinois, population 14,000 and growing fast. There he well might have lived out his life in unadventurous comfort; but then the Civil War burst out, and Moore, along with most of his chums, like young men everywhere, both north and south, rushed to enlist in the army, in his case in a brand-new volunteer cavalry regiment. Moore's company set off almost immediately for what proved to be four years of nasty warfare, plunging into shattering experiences that would have been unimaginable back in small-town Illinois and that uprooted him, body and mind, for the remainder of his life.

As he neared the end of his days—he would die in Southern California at age seventy-four, in 1912, following many restless moves across the United States—Moore wrote a memoir of his war service. Guided by his wartime diaries and by newspaper clippings and other contemporary evidence, he recalled the great adventure of his life, and that of his whole generation, in vivid detail, not in the glorifying abstract, but in often gritty, up-close realism.

After Moore's death, his memoir found its way into the archives at San Diego State University. Bahde's wife, a special collections librarian at the university, suggested that he might find the manuscript interesting, but neither of them expected the rich memoir they discovered. As Moore had considerable literary flair, a shrewd mind, an irreverent sense of humor, and a sense for the telling detail, his Civil War account jumps out at the reader in a way few others approach. In his introduction and conclusion Bahde gives us a careful and often poignant biography of the prewar and postwar life of Captain Francis Moore.

Many of Moore's experiences were common to thousands of soldiers, and so his memoir is representative as well as distinctly individual. Even as they had been swept into this maelstrom, the young men who fought, as well as their families behind the lines (who sometimes were caught inside the war themselves), knew that this would be the biggest event of their lives. With the passing decades after the war, this sensibility only grew as they returned to the lesser problems of negotiating everyday life in the bustling republic. They retained a sense of astonishment about much of what they had seen and the acts they had observed and sometimes committed.

Unlike later American wars, the Civil War was almost entirely free from censorship, and so in reams of letters and diaries, soldiers and civilians alike reported and reflected on events more fully and openly than would be the case later on. Thousands saved those documents as cherished family keepsakes, later depositing them in the university, state, and local historical societies that flourished in the late nineteenth century, in considerable measure driven by the widespread impulse to save those war records. As Bahde's discovery in the San Diego archives demonstrates, even as we celebrate the 150th anniversary of the Civil War, vivid new evidence continues to emerge.

Moore's unit spent most of its service in the still understudied western theater, fighting guerrillas, who were particularly elusive and nasty enemies, and serving in garrison units rather than in the grand battles that garner the most attention of Civil War scholars and their readers. Such warfare was characterized by endless boredom, feckless chasing of almost always unseen enemies, and moments of stark terror when the guerrillas suddenly emerged from the bush. Moore constructs a vivid account of this tedious and fearsome ebb and flow of irregular warfare.

But this memoir is far more than a narrative of the disorganized guerrilla warfare in the American West. Francis Moore was a real live wire, and he made no effort in his memoir to gloss over his complex personality and the fun and games and hot water he experienced as a youthful junior officer. He had a sneaky and subtle sense of humor, and a readiness to party as well as to search out and destroy his enemies. He had a hot temper as well, as evidenced by his courts-martial for shooting off his mouth. He also carried grudges not only during the war but also into his memoir, written decades later, especially against the colonel who brought charges against him during the war. His own courts-martial, combined with his accounts of trials of other soldiers on which Moore sat as a judge, demonstrate much of the nasty, petty political edge of military unit life, and the cussed interpersonal punctiliousness to which the code of manly honor led Civil War soldiers.

This sort of feuding in part resulted from the unbelievable boredom that characterized much of garrison duty. Most soldiers' lives had little to do with stirring battles and dashing action, for which soldiers longed until they got there. And guerrilla war had its special frustrations, which Moore demonstrates. The civilians could never be trusted, and the dangers from the lurking enemy fighters could come from any quarter, at any moment.

Although he could be thoughtful as he attempted to understand the psychological and behavioral consequences of war, Moore was also quite conventional in his judgments about women and comrades, quite the typical cultural chauvinist in his responses to the jumped-up "aristocrats" whom he blamed for what he believed to be the degraded condition of poor whites in a slave society. Although sympathetic toward the desire of enslaved blacks to be free, Moore also reflected the racial condescension typical of Northerners like himself.

As Moore also illustrates vividly, endless illnesses and accidents carried away far more of his comrades than did combat. I have no doubt that malaria and other illnesses nearly killed Moore several times, and that they undermined his health in later life. These were indirect costs of the wartime experience that were not exactly the same as physical war wounds. When it came time to apply for pensions—the first big American use of the state for welfare purposes—the causal connections between illness and military wounding were hard to prove. On the other side of the equation, many veterans gamed the system, as Bahde hints was true in Moore's case with the connivance of his physician brother.

Moore also resented war profiteering and other forms of corruption by soldiers and civilians on his side. But did he have his moments of pillaging too? And were the relations with the girls strictly limited to flirtation, as the memoir insists? After all, as well as frightening and boring, war is sexy in many ways. How many impulses were acted out, how many constrained? As he was such a fun-seeking young man, with his buddies and with the people he met, the contradiction between asserted restraint and likely acting-out lay at the core of this document as it did in the lives of all these mid-Victorian Americans walking on the wild side.

Moore had a considerable talent for telling stories. His narrative of four years of fighting moves through a varied "warscape" with energy and intelligence, reflecting memories of hope and exasperation, fear and courage. The veteran who emerges in this story, though always proud of his defense of the Union, remains a very human personage, not a paragon of bravery. Moore was no hero, nor was he a coward or a fool. He was just a young man from the Midwest who served his nation for four long years of brutal human conflict, always remaining aware of the appalling waste that characterized his long season as a warrior, upon which he looked back with a kind of wonder.

The war also exacted a great permanent price from Francis Moore. As Bahde suggests in his biographical analysis, Moore suffered from chronic and often incapacitating ill health for the remainder of his life, doubtless in considerable measure due to the typhoid fever and malaria that he contracted during the war. And he also moved frequently, took up and dropped any number of careers—many of which seem to have amounted to dry wells and dead ends. Of course, we cannot know what Moore's life might have resembled if the Civil War had never occurred. And yet it seems likely that not only Moore's physical problems but also his mental health were permanently undermined by the impact of his long, trying service. Although one can never diagnosis mental or physical illness at such a remove, it would at least not be implausible, given the evidence of his chronic kidney and liver problems, that, along with countless thousands of other war veterans, Moore attempted self-medication with alcohol. He suffered terribly in the long decades of his postwar life, perhaps in part from what we now call post-combat stress disorder. One of the great mysteries of the Civil War era is that one never can reconstruct those grievous psychological injuries that remained under the surface of what turned out to be difficult lives.

In these troubled circumstances, when he sat down to write his memoirs as an aging veteran, Moore felt compelled to sort out his military experiences as calmly and honestly as he could. His memoir is both fun and troubling, evidence of a hard war in the context of the long, hard life that followed. *The Story of My Campaign* demonstrates damage and resiliency, an ordinary life that was difficult and tragic, and also, in sheer perseverance, quite heroic. Moore never believed his war was in vain, and he never stopped striving to make sense of his battles, for his nation as well as for himself.

THE STORY OF MY CAMPAIGN

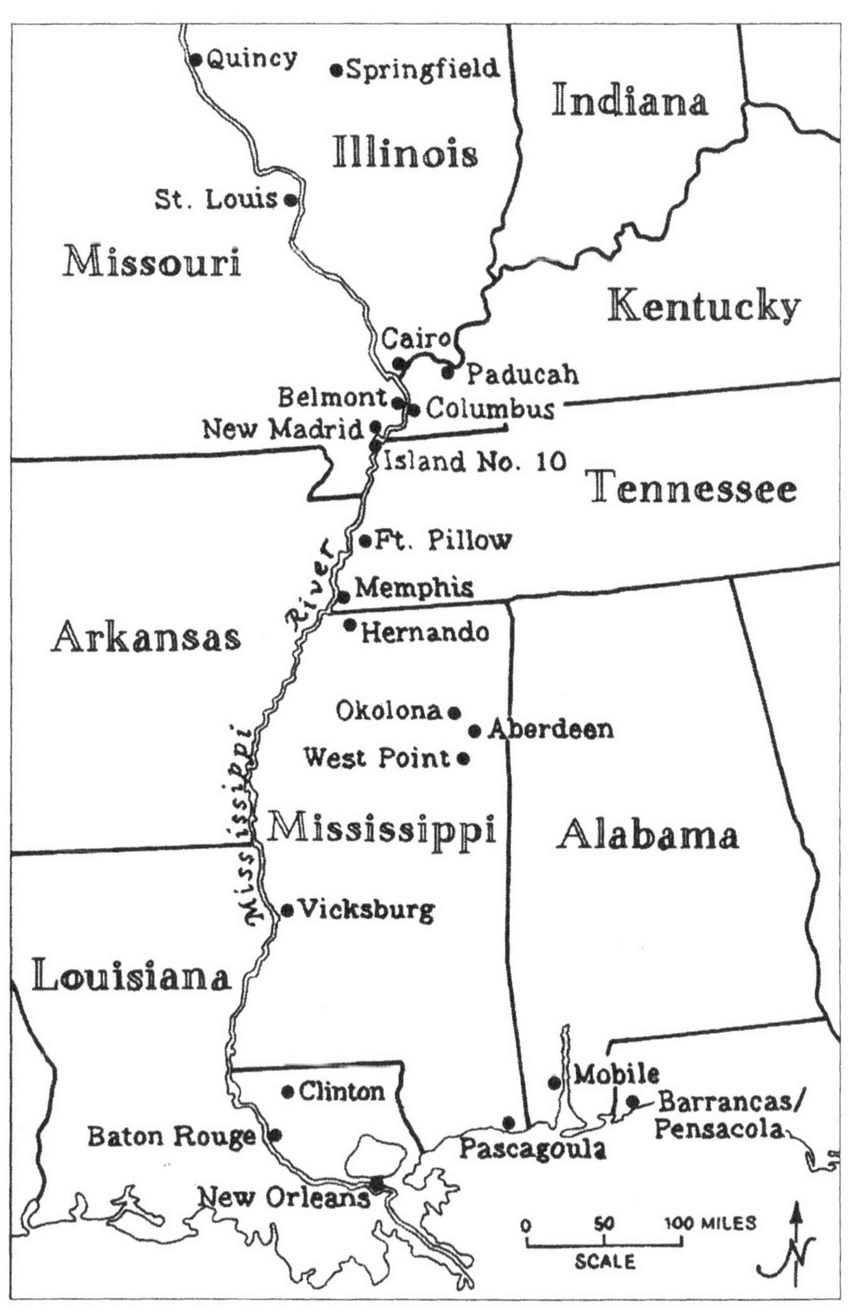

Map of Francis Moore's War

FRANCIS MOORE'S MEMOIR AND THE CONSTRUCTION OF CIVIL WAR MEMORY

Francis Moore was twenty-three years old in the summer of 1861 when he joined a volunteer company of cavalrymen in the Mississippi River town of Quincy, Illinois. He was working as a carriage maker when he enlisted, but just a year earlier, the federal census taker had listed him as a student. After a brief period of drill and preparation at Quincy's Camp Flagg, Francis and his company marched to Camp Butler, near Springfield, where they mustered into federal service in August as Company L of the Second Illinois Cavalry. Francis entered the army as a private but was elected lieutenant that fall, after one of the company officers became ill. After the accidental shooting death of Captain Sterling Delano in the spring of 1862, Francis was elected captain, a position he held until the end of the war.

Francis was the elder son of Francis Childs Moore and Mary Grant Moore of Quincy. His father, a veteran of the War of 1812, came to Illinois from New York in the 1830s to work as a land agent, a position he still held when the war started. The elder Francis married Mary Grant in 1837, and young Francis was born a year later. Sister Lydia was born in 1840, and brother Richard Channing Moore (affectionately, "Chan" in the memoir) in 1842. By 1860, Lydia was already married to a bank clerk named Ferdinand Sherman and had a young son. Eighteen-year-old Richard was still a student and was close friends with Julian Sherman, Ferdinand's younger brother. Patriarch Seth Sherman was also a land agent, and seventeen-year-old daughter Louisa Sherman was a likely marriage prospect for either Francis or Richard. In the spring of 1861 Francis faced a prosperous and predictable, if somewhat dreary, future as a carriage maker, family man, and upstanding member of the Quincy middle class. But as Francis tells us, the assault on Fort Sumter in April 1861 changed whatever plans he may have had, as "the entire country was now in a blaze of excitement—recruiting offices and camps were established in every town."

As captain of a western theater cavalry company, Francis participated in a demanding series of campaigns and prolonged guerilla warfare throughout Missouri, Kentucky, Tennessee, Mississippi, Louisiana, and Florida. From his company's first expedition in Missouri to its final combat actions in Louisiana, Francis and his men fought guerillas, bushwhackers, and irregular troops, and engaged regular Confederate forces under General Leonidas Polk, M. Jeff Thompson, and Nathan Bedford Forrest.

Although theirs was not always a war of dashing cavalry charges and dramatic pitched battles, the men of Company L endured the unflinching rigors of warfare against irregular troops, hunting bands of guerillas in swamplands, canebrakes, and woodlands. The populace of the countryside in which they operated was typically hostile, and while they may not have been always at the front lines, Francis and his men were occupiers in a rebellious land. Theirs was an intimate and intense war, chasing guerillas through the swamps, quartering within occupied cities and towns, and riding over miles of contested territory in which every stand of trees or country inn might conceal an enemy ambush.

Although much of this irregular campaigning involved chasing rumors, Francis presents the frustrating and wearing duty of guerilla warfare in vivid detail. His company was involved in dramatic running fights through Missouri swamps, skirmishes with larger forces of irregular troops, routing out guerillas in civilian settlements, administering the oath of allegiance to obstinate civilians, and attempting to disrupt clandestine supply networks to guerilla forces. This was not the kind of warfare later glorified by the shapers of Civil War memory, but it was perhaps a more trying sort of war than the pitched battles and extended campaigns that later became the standard by which wartime experiences were judged.

Francis Moore's Civil War

In his own brief preface to the memoir, Francis states that his wartime experience "was not very eventful, nor in any respect different from that of hundreds and thousands of others." But despite his modesty, Francis's memoir is remarkable for how comprehensively and lucidly he touches on all of the major themes we might expect, and some that we might not, infusing his observations with a combination of humor, wisdom, and impetuousness. Like many other western theater veterans, Francis tended not to sentimentalize his wartime experience, including the mundane, disturbing, and contradictory equally alongside more typical themes of patriotism, militarism, and feats of bravery. These frank observations of his service, along with Francis's hot temper and incisive wit ensured both a lively wartime experience and a remarkable postwar reflection.[1]

On the subject of Union, the Confederacy, and the righteousness of his cause, Francis has relatively little to say, but he is consistent throughout, even in subtle ways. He steadfastly refuses to capitalize "rebel" and frequently puts "Confederacy" in deprecating quotation marks, both features that have been retained in the edited version. For Francis, the army of the Union was as an "avalanche" bearing down on the rebellious South, with the inevitable result, but he spends little time extolling the virtues of the Union cause or celebrating the nation he believed he was defending. Instead of glorifying his own cause, Francis more often denigrates the ideology, people, and government of the Southern states and the Confederacy. His favorite expression of contempt for the Confederate military is to reference sarcastically the Southern assertion that they would fight until the "last ditch." He continually points out Confederate failures to live up to this dramatic prophecy and makes the joke so often it becomes tiresome. At other times, Francis admires the ability and tenacity of some Confederate soldiers but laments that they are wasted on such a wicked cause.

Francis's more detailed criticisms of the South and its people are of greater significance than his observations about the Confederate military. He is unapologetic in his observation that the people of the South are generally ignorant, lazy, and impoverished, all of which he blames on the slave aristocracy. His reflections on the connection between Southern ignorance and slavery are particularly acute articulations of how ordinary Northerners perceived the social and cultural stakes of the contest. Francis was glad to be an agent of the destruction of slavery, but more for the sake of the white American polity than for the sake of the slaves themselves.

In his racial views, Francis was a product of his time. The Moore family belonged to the Episcopal Church in Quincy, where Francis would have been exposed to abolitionist teachings and philosophy, and the family employed a black servant in 1860. These influences were not enough to convince Francis that blacks were equal to whites, and he was skeptical of former slaves as potential citizens. One of his major criticisms of the South is that slavery tended to produce admixture of blacks and whites, and he judged Louisiana's large mixed-race population "a sad commentary on the morals of Southern society." His religious views may have disposed him to view blacks more judiciously than some, but Francis also shared most Illinoisans' dim view of the future of slaves after emancipation. Expressing a common concern, Francis muses that former slaves have "the muscles and sinews of oxen, but I fear they have not the hearts and nerves of men."[2]

But while he bore significant racial prejudices, Francis was also willing to have his opinions altered by personal experiences and relationships. As he says, his religious faith taught him that all creatures strive to be free, and he believed that enslaved blacks were no exception. Although he was deeply wary of what would come with emancipation, Francis believed that the "experiment" should be tried. He sent his black camp cook back to Illinois with his father during the war, the elder Francis asking his wife to give her a chance as a domestic servant (his letters on the subject are included in Appendices B and C). Also, near the end of the memoir, Francis tells us in passing that his black hostler, Wash, accompanied him back to Quincy from the army at the end of the war, but we never learn what became of him.

In his actions, then, Francis was more liberal than in his written speculations on the future of blacks after emancipation. He believed that the best way to test the fitness of former slaves for citizenship was to make soldiers of them. He was so interested in the creation of black regiments that after hearing a speech by Adjutant-General Lorenzo Thomas in early 1863, he attempted to raise a regiment of black cavalry. Although his request was turned down by the War Department, Francis maintained an interest in black soldiers, commenting on them whenever he encountered them in the field or in camp. But although he thought well of black soldiers, he did not approve of "making pets and associates of them."

On military matters, Francis presents the views of an enthusiastic volunteer and occasionally alludes to his contempt for regular army "hirelings," as well as conscripts brought in on the draft. His view of military life is complex, for although he takes great pride in the hardy and adventurous image of the dashing volunteer cavalry soldier, he also laments the regulations and red tape of the military establishment, as well as the incompetence and corruption of his fellow volunteers. He rails against war profiteers, quartermasters, paymasters, sutlers, speculators, political generals, and dandies with equal venom, and he sets himself and his command apart as *real* soldiers, facing sacrifice, hardship, and danger at every turn. He excuses his own occasional lapses in good behavior (as when he pillages a bottle of quinine for his own use or participates in stealing sutlers' stores) by citing his record of hard service and by appealing to a broader ethic of justice that validates the indiscretions of well-meaning and hard-serving volunteers. The other side of this coin is a virulent unwillingness to excuse the lapses of those he perceives as disloyal or corrupt. He resents the rhetoric of Copperheads in the North, which he describes as outright treason, and he is ever suspicious of Southerners who claimed to be Unionists.

Despite his many friendships with Southerners in every region in which he campaigned, Francis quickly grew impatient with orders to respect the property of Confederate sympathizers and chaffed under commanders who would not sanction action against disloyal citizens, believing that the civilian population gave material and moral support to the bushwhackers that constantly pestered his command. In his recent study of Confederate guerilla warfare and Union reprisals, Clay Mountcastle has referred to this kind of action as punitive warfare, and for Francis Moore it was exactly that. When he was finally given the opportunity to engage in a more aggressive form of destructive warfare during the Smith-Grierson Raid into Mississippi in February 1864, he was jubilant and proud to chronicle the extent of the destruction he participated in, and disappointed that the raid did not accomplish more.[3]

Francis was also an almost constant observer of the river war that took place on the Mississippi River. From "tinclad" riverboats lightly retrofitted for martial purposes to the more specialized amphibious landing craft devised by the "Mississippi Marine Brigade," Francis was always interested in the traffic that passed his posts on the river. He spent a great deal of time aboard the boats as well, describing many trips up and down the river and complaining of the notoriously unreliable riverboat schedules. His descriptions of river craft, military travel behind the lines, and his experiences with the frontline river war (see especially the battle of Belmont, described by Francis in chapter 1) provide rich details of an important aspect of western theater warfare.[4]

Francis did not write only about the martial side of war. Although much of the memoir is rich with military content, other parts read like a curious young man's travel journal. He was an inveterate sightseer, always finding excuses to visit interesting landmarks or to catch a variety show at a local theater in Memphis or Baton Rouge. He found the French and Creole girls of the New Orleans street markets to be especially charming, and the ladies of Memphis he judged to be the prettiest he had ever seen. In Paducah, Kentucky, and Madrid Bend, Tennessee, Francis and his men formed such close relationships with the locals that they almost felt a part of those communities. Indeed, after leaving Paducah, Francis often made excuses to make flying visits back to the town to see his many friends there.

As the war progressed, and as Francis pushed farther south with his company, he observed the troubled transition from a slave economy to a free market. His observations about cotton speculation in Louisiana in 1864 and 1865 are among the memoir's most valuable sections, showing Southerners engaging in a vigorous trade in hoarded cotton, sometimes even with general officers of the Union Army. Likewise, his description of the dangers faced by northern leasers trying to operate seized cotton plantations with hired black labor sheds light on the vigilante violence of the wartime South.

With the end of the war, Francis makes the significant observation that he was "reduced, or elevated, to the rank of citizenship" upon receiving his discharge from the service. Although this line was probably composed long after the war, it likely reflects accurately the sense of ambiguity that confronted Francis at the end of his service. Although he had never quite abandoned his identity as a citizen first and a soldier second, Francis had embraced his role as a volunteer soldier fighting for a righteous cause. If he had viewed the ladies, or the variety shows, or the fields and orchards, or the cities and towns, with the interest of a citizen tourist, he had also witnessed and participated in pitched battles, violent deaths, and deep personal losses with the apparently unshakable resolve of a soldier. In his memoir, we see both identities expressed throughout the war, and in the end we are left wondering what Francis went on to make of his experiences as a citizen soldier, and how they shaped his later life. His memoir as an artifact of memory begins to offer some clues.

"Neither Historian nor Novelist"—Constructing the Memoir

"My object in writing the following pages is chiefly to amuse myself," wrote Francis Moore in the brief prologue to his memoir. But when Francis assembled the memoir that comprises this volume, he was likely well aware that his words carried greater import than merely his own amusement. The story of how Francis's memoir came to be is not altogether clear. Although we do not know precisely when Francis began his work, it was likely after 1880, and he had already embraced the roles of veteran and guardian of Civil War memory.

Francis probably did the majority of his writing after his arrival in National City, California, when he entered a sort of retirement after years of moving about the West (see the epilogue for Francis's postwar life).[5] He was then in the midst of a long-distance struggle to receive a veteran's pension from the federal government. His original application was denied, and he encountered substantial amounts of the same red tape he complained about during the war. It is possible that in compiling the evidence of his service for his pension application and appeals, he began also to "trail back . . . and in my mind live over again" his memories of the war and wish for some more comprehensive and comprehensible narrative of his service, a testament for posterity, not a testimony for a pension. To this end, he assembled an impressive collection of his own documents, including his diaries and letters from the war, and supplemented them with other documents from his service.[6]

Francis's extensive wartime diary forms the basis for his narrative, supplemented with letters he wrote to friends and family. He combined these into a single continuous narrative, to which he added his wartime drawings, and a wide range of handwritten official documents from the war, published printed material, and others' personal letters, all of which bore on his own service. Moore pasted these into his memoir at the appropriate places within his narrative, as if to bring his already vivid prose some greater immediacy or authority, and making his work as much a scrapbook as a memoir.

When he began the work of recopying his wartime diaries and collecting the documents he would paste into his book, Francis was no doubt familiar with the genre of memoir, and specifically Civil War memoir. By the 1880s, veterans' reminiscences of wartime service had appeared in national magazines, local newspapers, and in book form, written by rank-and-file soldiers as well as prominent generals and other officers. Private soldiers and noncommissioned officers frequently wrote folksy anecdotes of camp and field, or dramatic descriptions of the smoke and fury of battle, while officers tended to compose self-serving and grandiose memoirs concerned primarily with rehashing or attempting to settle wartime controversies. For both, the act of memorializing or reminiscing about the war helped imbue their experiences with meaning.

Francis Moore's impulse to write his own memoir no doubt originated from the same desire to sort through the remembered chaos and confusion of the war, and in the midst of an uneasy postwar peace, to construct a narrative of success and purpose. His work combined both of the major trends in Civil War memoir: an intense focus on the minutiae of daily camp and field experience as well as a broader nationalistic or moralistic purpose.

If the postwar and postemancipation nation was itself a chaotic and troubled time in which the sacrifices of war seemed to fade quickly from public memory, Northern veterans could reconstruct their wartime experiences as principled action directed toward two interrelated and noble causes: the preservation of the Union, and the destruction of slavery. If they could show that their war was a noble one, veterans could distance themselves from the failed promises of Reconstruction and the mad, moneyed rush of the later nineteenth century. Whatever problems had come in the postwar era, veterans, through the recasting of their memories, could disclaim responsibility for the troubles and assert that they had acted resolutely to put down the evils of secession and slavery.[7]

Memoir and memorial also played a didactic role, as organizations like the Grand Army of the Republic tried to keep the moral, patriotic, and nationalistic lessons of the war before a public that with each generation grew increasingly distant from the wartime experience. Published narratives and reminiscences of wartime service, public memorials and processions, and periodic encampments defined the symbols of Civil War memory and kept them before the public gaze. As Stuart McConnell has observed of these practices, "the men who had fought the war on the Union side first explained to themselves what it meant to be veterans, then tried to tell civilians what it meant to belong to the nation the war had preserved."[8]

As a member of the GAR almost from its inception, Francis was attuned to the active role memory played in shaping the lessons Americans should learn from veterans' sacrifices. While still in Quincy after the war, Francis joined his local GAR post in 1867, and he later joined posts in other cities in which he lived. Although we do not know how active he was in the organization, he maintained his membership despite frequent long-distance relocations. For Francis Moore and other Union veterans, membership in the GAR not only meant a means of extending their personal identification with the sacrifices and principles of their youth but also provided a means to carry the worthwhile ideals of the war era into the problematic postwar period. Although Francis ostensibly wrote his memoir only "to amuse" himself, he assembled his work with full awareness that his own humble memories composed a part of the national memory of the war, and that by writing he participated in a larger effort of making and remaking Civil War memory.

Francis was familiar enough with the publishing conventions of contemporary Civil War memoirs to make some attempt to copy their stylistic elements into his handwritten memoir. His book bears a frontispiece, a GAR memorial ribbon with the likeness of U. S. Grant, and his title page is a collage of items, arranged to frame his title: the outline of a maple leaf from Lincoln's tomb, a bit of poetry snipped from a newspaper, the signature of Captain Delano, a portrait of Abraham Lincoln.

His choice to write a brief preface was also a stylistic element borrowed from published memoirs, and his self-deprecating apology for being "neither historian nor novelist," repeated in slightly different form near the end of the memoir, conformed to nineteenth-century norms for the genre of life writing. The text of the narrative itself is augmented with page headings, marginal subtitles, illustrations, and documents. Although he produced his work for no other audience than himself, Francis self-consciously constructed a book that not only met many of the narrative conventions of the genre of nineteenth-century memoir but also included many of its physical and stylistic elements.

Although much of the narrative retains the structure and verb tense of Francis's wartime diary, his work is indeed a memoir in several important respects, not least of which is the fact that he undertook the work of compiling and recopying his wartime writing as a self-conscious act of memory. His project was specifically to "remember and relate," essential features of memoir. Indeed, Francis's heavy reliance on his diaries, rather than on official documents or other histories of the war, reveals the "presentness" of the past as he remembered it. As the reader progresses through the narrative, it is helpful to keep in mind the dualistic nature of the composition, product of both a soldier and a veteran.

The Story of my campaign.

Four Years
in the
Union Army

By
F. T. Moore
Late Capt. Co. "L" 2nd Regt. Illinois Cavalry Vols.

Commanding Company.

Abraham Lincoln

Title page of Francis Moore's memoir. Courtesy of Special Collections and University Archives, San Diego State University Library & Information Access

But Francis Moore's text is also a more complex artifact than simply a narrative memoir. The collection and insertion of the other wartime material, including his own sketches, memoranda, official orders, and other correspondence, made his work essentially a scrapbook, a multimedia memory tool, an artifact in and of itself. Carefully curated, arranged, and with its supplementary documents, Francis's memoir-as-scrapbook is an item that Tamar Katriel and Thomas Farrell have referred to as both an "art of memory" and "a rhetorical practice of construction and performance of self."[9] In a similar vein, Patricia Buckler and C. Kay Leeper refer to scrapbooks as "expressive discourse . . . a type of rhetoric that expresses social as well as individual personalities."[10] As both a social and an individual text, Francis presented himself through the memoir/scrapbook in multiple concurrent roles: soldier, diarist, memoirist, and veteran. This made Francis's work both a personal record "to amuse myself" and a consciously constructed artifact of broader social and historical significance.

The personal function of the memoir and its creation takes on a deeper significance when considered alongside the time line of Francis's later life. By the late 1880s, Francis was an increasingly sick man, suffering from a variety of chronic and recurring ailments caused by his war service (or so he claimed in his pension file). He was chronically underweight, suffered from liver problems, was weakened by arthritis, and was plagued by recurrent attacks of typhoid and malarial fever. To his brother, Richard, who was also a physician, Francis seemed "broken down and prematurely old," and his sister, Lydia, wrote that "although not old in years his body was bent and had the appearance of a man of 70."[11]

In failing health, unable to ride a horse, and with enough—perhaps too much—leisure to write, Francis engaged in a task that was meant, if not to recapture his lost youth, at least to "in my mind live over again" a time in his life in which he seemed able to do anything. In this sense, the moral or nationalistic imperative of the narrative becomes almost secondary to the physical memoir or scrapbook, which provided a tangible form through which Francis engaged the more personal task of reclaiming a sense of purpose for his own life. This is a different sort of subjectivity than concerns the content of the memoir's narrative, for the physically constructed book—and its act of construction—was also a deeply subjective and contingent process that relied on Francis Moore the veteran as much as it did on Francis Moore the soldier.

In editing and presenting his work, I have necessarily made a number of interventions that have altered the form of the memoir in fundamental ways. Most significantly, the work is no longer the mélange of documents Francis originally created. There are simply too many to reproduce or insert within the edited text. I have reproduced some of his best original drawings, and a few of the additional documents will be found in the appendices, but there are many more pasted within the pages of his handwritten narrative. In this sense, the volume presented here is not at all what Francis intended his memoir to be, for in crafting the narrative into a work for broader consumption, I have necessarily stripped away its artifactual nature. In transforming his work, however, I have tried to supplement the narrative core of the memoir to provide a volume that will be useful to modern readers and perhaps also elicit a larger conversation regarding the literal, physical construction of Civil War memoir and memory. If Francis himself had no such lofty goal in mind, I hope at least that he would not object.

Francis's spelling, grammar, and sentence construction have been lightly edited for clarity and to remove redundancies. In very few places I have removed short passages that seemed inconsequential to the larger narrative, were repetitive, or referenced documents or portions of documents that Francis did not include elsewhere in his memoir. All parenthetical notes and marks were made by Francis, including the (?) marks he sometimes used after certain words to convey sarcasm or doubt. I have felt it important to retain these marks to preserve the intended meaning of the words.

Francis divided his narrative by year, but he did not create or describe chapters as I have done. This intervention was made for the sake of clarity, accessibility, and readability, and it is one I believe a contemporary editor would also have made. I have added historical and historiographical notes and a biographical epilogue that takes up Francis Moore's life after the war and considers his postwar experiences through the lens of veteranhood.

As a last word, I will echo the sentiments expressed by Francis Moore at the beginning of his memoir: this is not a history of the war, nor is it comprehensive in any sense. It is a collection of one man's experiences and his reflections on a complex, momentous, tragic, and hopeful period in the history of the United States. Whatever insights or broader perspectives it allows us 150 years later, I would also suggest that the following pages are best viewed, at least momentarily, through the eyes of a young carriage maker from western Illinois, who in 1861 succumbed to the sense of excitement and duty that compelled hundreds of thousands of other Americans to take up arms against each other.

The rest of the story belongs to Francis Moore; it is his to tell.

MOORE'S PREFACE

My object in writing the following pages is chiefly to amuse myself. I do not propose to write a history of the "great rebellion." But I have leisure and find it convenient to "trail back" through my late campaign, and in my mind live over again "the times we had in the army." There were many little incidents and events, however important and interesting they may have appeared to those participating in them, that will never find a place in any general history of the war. Of such "trifles" is my story chiefly composed.

Although my experience was not very eventful, nor in any respect different from that of hundreds and thousands of others, there were many little incidents pleasant to me to remember and relate, and I shall endeavor to note them down as I remember them, assisted by a few scattering notes and memoranda, official papers, and letters to family and friends written at the time. For one better skilled at the "pen drill" there is material enough to be derived from the services and experiences of a company of volunteer cavalry during four years of active warfare to fill a large volume. But being neither historian nor novelist I shall confine myself chiefly to my own experiences and observations and the movements of the company to which I belonged.

Chapter One

1861

Outbreak of War—Quincy & Camp Flagg—Springfield & Camp Butler—Saint Louis & Southeastern Missouri—Punishments in Camp—Cairo, Bird's Point, & Fort Holt—A False Alarm—Observations of Fort Jefferson—The "Pork Battery"—Battle of Belmont, Missouri—Promoted to Lieutenant—Gunboats on the Mississippi—Fugitive Slaves & Slave Hunters in Camp—Christmas in Camp —Special Correspondents

When the rebellion first assumed a live warlike appearance, by the rebels bombarding and compelling the evacuation of Fort Sumter on the coast of South Carolina early in the month of April 1861, a proclamation was issued by President Lincoln calling for 75,000 volunteers to suppress the insurrection. I never believed that Mr. Lincoln really thought he could quench the flames of rebellion after they had once broken out with the insignificant army of 75,000 men, but it was necessary for him to say and do something, and he commenced in that way. The 75,000 men were soon enrolled for "three months" and sent to the front, where they found more insurrection than they could well take care of, and it was at once found necessary to call out more troops. I thought I saw from the first that we had a big job on hand that would require many thousands of men several years to finish, but I never had the least doubt as to the final result of the war. I expected another and a longer call when a great internal war would be commenced on a regular business foundation.

The entire country was now in a blaze of excitement—recruiting offices and camps were established in every town, and many more than the 75,000 called for presented themselves for enrollment. Another call was soon made for 300,000 men to serve for "three years or during the war." This now began to look like solid serious work, but our young men were ready for it, and enrolling officers were kept busy early and late examining and enrolling the thousands of eager patriots.

While many young men were enlisting in infantry regiments, there were many others equally patriotic and anxious to serve their country, but who could not reconcile themselves to the idea of doing so under the weight of a heavy musket and heavier knapsack. This latter class was composed chiefly of young farmers, who being accustomed to the use of horses, and many of them owning good horses, preferred serving as cavalry, but as no cavalry had yet been called for, they had to bide their time.

I had by this time fully decided to go into the army, and after carefully considering the matter, chose the cavalry arm of the service. Although in perfect health, I was not strong bodily, being only about five feet five or six inches tall and weighing not over 125 pounds, and I feared I would not be able to endure the marching and hard labor that I supposed an infantry soldier would be subjected to. I had also from a child been accustomed to the use of horses, was very fond of a horse and was a good rider, and I thought if fight I must, it would be easier and pleasanter to do so on the back of a good horse. I had previously belonged to a militia company of cavalry in Quincy, commanded by Captain Charles W. Mead, and had thus obtained a little insight into the mysteries of the cavalry drill and tactics, which proved to be of considerable benefit to me afterwards.

I was a little lame in my right foot, having cut the instep several years before, but this I was careful to say nothing about, for had it been known, I would have been at once rejected. At this early stage of the war, so great was the rush of volunteers, the mustering officers (all of whom belonged to the regular army) were very particular and would accept none but perfectly sound men. They had soon to abandon their rigid adherence to "army regulations," and by the time the third or fourth call was made, were glad to take anything that at all resembled the outside shape of a man.

Early in the month of July 1861, Silas Noble of Dixon, Illinois, was commissioned by the governor to raise a regiment of cavalry to report at Camp Butler near Springfield sometime in August. A roll was at once opened in Quincy by Sterling P. Delano, who used every effort to raise what he said should be the "crack company of the regiment." He was a young lawyer of excellent reputation and favorably known throughout the adjacent country, and but a few days elapsed before a sufficient number to form a minimum company had signed the roll. I enlisted on the 15th of July, my name being number seventeen on the roll. I had been to the camp several times "viewing the situation" and getting acquainted with some of the men before I signed the roll.[1]

We were yet without organization or discipline, new names were daily being added to the list, while a few, wishing either to back out before it was too late or to join some other company, "scratched" their names. The papers were full of sensational reports and telegrams from the "front" or "seat of war," and quite a number who had worked themselves up to a fever heat of patriotism and were red hot for war and ready to swallow a dozen or two of rebels, suddenly found their fiery enthusiasm cool down to about zero on reading a long list of the "killed and wounded" in some engagement in Virginia or Maryland, and would all at once discover that they "couldn't very well leave home just now.Don't feel altogether strong you know, boys," etc. Such fellows generally "scratched" and finally came in on the draft or as accomplished "bounty-jumpers."[2]

The 15th of July was appointed for a general rendezvous at Camp Flagg, on the old fair grounds east of Woodland Cemetery, for the purpose of organizing and electing company officers.[3] That first day in camp will never be forgotten by any who were present. It was the beginning of a new life to all of us—with very few exceptions none of us had ever before seen a military encampment. The first day was consumed in dividing off into messes of six men each, issuing cooking utensils and rations, and pitching our tents. Many of the squads or messes formed that day continued together throughout the service.

Our tents were of the common "A" pattern, each tent according to "army regulations" calculated to accommodate six men, but as every man brought with him "camp and garrison equipage" enough for a dozen, and many of them a trunk, box, or carpet bag, it seemed quite impossible for more than two to occupy the same tent. Some actually thought that a tent should be allowed to every two men, and each man be allowed a pack mule or a one-horse wagon to transport his baggage.

Pitching a tent, when you know just how the thing is done, is a very simple operation, in fact, "no trick at all." Any two old soldiers can set up and pin down in a storm or the darkest night in a few minutes, but to a lot of raw recruits, many of whom had never before seen a tent, it was a very serious undertaking, a task not to be undertaken thoughtlessly, nor without mature consideration. It would take five or six men, in daylight, with everything new and in order, an hour or two to set up a tent, and then likely it would be so loose that it would fall of its own weight, or so tight that the edges could not come within a foot of the ground, and so crooked that a man could not lay straight in it. But by persevering, we worried through the day, and before night our first camp presented a very respectable and military appearance.

At an informal meeting held in camp it was decided to meet that evening at the armory of the "Quincy City Guards" on the southwest corner of Main and 4th Streets, for the purpose of filling up the roll and electing officers. As soon as the roll was opened, a rush was made for the table, and in a short time, it was filled to the maximum number of 100. On being called to order, Sterling P. Delano was nominated, and by acclimation, unanimously elected captain. After considerable debate as to the election of lieutenants, it was decided that the captain should appoint two lieutenants to serve until we should become better acquainted with each other so as to be able to make a selection when another election should be held. The captain then appointed Ed Prince of Quincy First Lieutenant and James K. Catlin of Augusta Second Lieutenant, after which we dispersed, some to go back to camp, and others who lived in or near the city, to their homes. A. T. Murdock accompanied me home to my father's house, where we stayed that night.[4] The next day we entered upon regular military duty. A detail was made for camp guard and all hands were set to work erecting stables for our horses.

In appointing the noncommissioned officers, the captain endeavored to have each "clique" or squad from any one neighborhood represented by one or more members. This course gave general satisfaction, although there were, of course, some few "sore heads" who felt slighted and who thought they could much better serve their country in some more exalted position than that of "high private." But notwithstanding Captain Delano's entire ignorance of the qualifications of his men, his appointments happily proved very good ones.[5]

In a few days, an election was held in camp for two lieutenants. Party spirit ran pretty high and considerable wire-pulling and log rolling were indulged in. James K. Catlin of Augusta, Joseph L. Sawyer of Camp Point, and Ed Prince of Quincy were presented by their respective friends as candidates for First Lieutenant. After the first ballot, the name of Mr. Prince (having received the least number of votes) was dropped. The second ballot resulted in the election of Mr. Catlin by a large majority. Prince and Sawyer being the only candidates for Second Lieutenant, but one ballot was required, Sawyer leading with a small majority.[6]

The interval between now and the time of our departure for Camp Butler was occupied in drilling, both mounted and foot, and otherwise improving ourselves in our new duties. Two or three companies of the 1st Illinois Cavalry that had been some time in Camp Flagg with us, having received their arms and equipments, were now ordered to Missouri, where trouble was anticipated from "bush whackers" on the line of the Hannibal and St. Joseph Railroad, leaving us and Captain B. F. Marsh's company from Warsaw as the only defenders of Camp Flagg and Quincy.[7] We endeavored to realize the great responsibility thus thrust upon us, but when it is considered that our two companies numbered less than 200 men unarmed and undisciplined, the "protection" we were expected to afford the citizens of Quincy was certainly quite visionary, if not ludicrous in the extreme.

A few days after the departure of the companies of the First Illinois, a startling rumor was brought into camp by a "reliable gentleman" ("intelligent contraband" not having yet made their appearance) to the effect that a squad of rebels from Missouri were preparing to cross the river and give us battle. A picket guard was at once detailed and posted on the river bank, armed with old muskets, musketoons, or anything that could be procured. The whole camp was on the qui vive until a late hour in the night. Nearly everyone had some suggestions to offer as to the proper distribution of our forces when the fight should commence, but as we were quite unarmed except with some half dozen old weapons of the most disapproved class, no one had any very clear idea as to the best method of continuing a fight (on our part) once commenced. Each one having, in turn, expressed his views on the proper mode of conducting an extensive campaign, and all remaining quiet on the front, we retired to our quarters, those who had been fortunate enough to procure an old musket, pistol, or sword, to "sleep on their arms."

The only uniforms to be obtained at that time, and with which our company was now supplied, consisted of a red flannel shirt and a pair of top boots, clad in which we presented a novel, if not a strictly military appearance. We looked much more like firemen than soldiers. Every spare moment was occupied in drill, either in camp or on Alstyne's Prairie, and before we took our departure from Camp Flagg we were as well drilled and disciplined as many companies that had had months of experience. Captain Delano's time was much occupied with other business, so that the command of the company devolved almost entirely on Lieutenant Catlin, who proved himself to be an energetic, hard-working officer. Lieutenant Catlin entered upon the discharge of his new duties with great energy and took great pride in drilling and otherwise preparing the company for its future duties.

On Saturday evening, August 3rd, the company marched on foot from camp to the "Concert Hall" where we were met by the "Sisters of the Good Samaritan," a society of charitable and patriotic ladies, who presented the company with a beautiful silk guidon, and each member of the company with a pocket needle case, well-supplied with pins, needles, thread, and buttons.[8] The presentation speech was made by Miss Christy H. Tillson and was, as such little affairs always are, or supposed to be, very "neat and appropriate." The guidon was received by Captain Delano, who gracefully delivered himself of another "neat and appropriate" in which spread eagles, blood, hearthstones, ladies, and traitors were prominent features. After cheering for the Union and the ladies, and the singing of the Star Spangled Banner by Mr. M. B. Denman, the soldiers returned to camp to dream of pretty needle cases and pocket girls with the owner's name stuck in the back with pins.

The next evening, Sunday, August 4th, we went by invitation to the Presbyterian Church to hear a sermon prepared expressly for us by Reverend George T. King. We returned to Camp Flagg that night for the last time, as the captain had decided to start for Springfield early next morning. After reporting at camp I rode out home, accompanied by A. T. Murdock, who stayed with me that night, I wishing to spend my last night at home.

Early next morning, Monday, August 5th, I bid my parents goodbye and returned to camp. At seven o'clock the company formed, and with our new guidon at the head of the column, we marched through the city en route for Camp Butler. The streets were thronged with people who had turned out to see the boys off, and we were saluted on every side with the waving of hats and handkerchiefs and shouts of "goodbye boys" and "God bless you boys." It was a day to be long remembered. To read the thoughts of every soldier in that company and describe the many conflicting emotions is beyond the power of mortal man. The noise, music, speeches, and consequent excitement attending our enlistment and camp life were all over, and now quietly, without music or excitement of any kind, we were marching away from home—where to, or for how long, God only knew. We were leaving behind us homes, businesses, wives, sweethearts, everything that a man holds dear on earth, in response to our country's call for help. Each man knows what anxious thoughts and emotions filled his own heart, but cannot speak for his fellows.

Having no wagons, all of our baggage (enough, as we afterwards learned, for a whole regiment) was shipped to Springfield by rail in charge of Quartermaster Sergeant Wilks, and Corporal Gilpin. While in Camp Flagg, we lived more like royal guests than soldiers, having every possible convenience and being almost surfeited with all manner of delicacies provided by our friends in the city, by whom—especially ladies—our camp was daily thronged to such an extent that it was almost impossible to perform any other duty than paying attention to them and answering, or pretending to answer, a multitude of questions concerning the trials, hardships, and dangers (of which we certainly yet knew nothing) of a soldier's life. And now to start off on a march of 100 miles, without tents or baggage of any kind, certainly appeared rather rough, and began to look like regular business. We had now, in fact, exchanged all the necessaries, comforts, and restrictions of home for the severities, hardships, and uncertainties of a soldier's life.

While passing out Broadway through the "Institute," my old friend and pastor Reverend Alexander Capron came out to the road to greet us. The good old man bid me an affectionate farewell, and with tears in his eyes, bid me God's speed. He said, "my son, this is but the beginning of a long and terrible war, but if there can be any right in war, you are on the side of right."[9]

Arriving at Camp Point, twenty-one miles from Quincy, where a large number of our men resided, we were met by a general turnout of the citizens, who had assembled to bid their boys and the rest of us a last goodbye. We were here presented by Miss Mary Bowman with a second guidon, a beautiful little star-spangled banner in behalf of the patriotic ladies of Camp Point, by whose fair hands it was made. Captain Delano, receiving the guidon, made a few brief but pointed remarks. I exceedingly regret being unable to give the presentation speech of our fair patriot, but remember well that, though short, it was an exceedingly happy effort, well-timed, and delivered with calm, yet spirited enthusiasm, seldom witnessed in more experienced stump speakers.

The proceedings were somewhat interrupted by the falling of a shower of rain. The morning having been very hot and dusty, the rain was most welcome. It also afforded an excellent opportunity for many of the boys to be "led away captive," for when the roll was called before resuming our march, scarcely a Camp Pointer answered to his name. Soon after leaving town, however, the "captives" began dropping into their places in the column. They offered no excuse, nor was any required of them. We all knew "what's the matter."

About three miles from Clayton, another town largely represented in the company, we were met by a delegation of about three hundred ladies, "mounted and equipped," who escorted us into town, where we had another reception where "appropriate" remarks were made and responded to, after which we were conducted by a guard of ladies to a neighboring grove, where we found a bountiful repast spread for us by the lovely patriots of Clayton. Each soldier being the willing captive of one or more vigilant and attentive ladies, who it would seem, had made an oath to fill him or burst him, abandoned himself to a "feast of chicken and a flow of coffee" and other kindred pleasures and passions. The meal at last being finished, or rather the boys being filled, the Reverend Mr. Biggins in behalf of the ladies of Clayton, presented the "Adams County Dragoons" with a small leather-bound Bible, which was received by our captain in a few "neat and appropriate."

Supper, presentation, and all the attendant "few appropriate remarks" by some half dozen long-winded patriots who were willing to sacrifice, if necessary, every relative they had in this great and holy cause, having been appreciated or otherwise disposed of, our saddle-tired boys scattered in all directions; some to sleep, some to ponder over the events of the day and speculate on the future, while a few, doubtless with a view to accustoming themselves to the duties of "chain guard," might have been seen stepping in time with some fair partner to a late hour. I thought it was a pretty nice thing to be a Clayton boy that night. We certainly had not encountered many of the "hardships" of a soldier's life—yet.

While preparing to leave early the next morning, one of our men, Ed Hurd, was thrown from his horse and so severely injured by spraining an ankle that we were obliged to leave him behind.[10] Just before reaching Mount Sterling, the next town on our route, we were met by the "Mount Sterling Horse Guards," who escorted us into the town, where we found dinner already prepared for us by the citizens of that place. There being no presentations nor speeches here, we continued our march immediately after dinner, and that evening arrived at the Illinois River opposite the town of Meredosia.

Our saddles were of the old "Grimsley" pattern, and both saddles and men being new and unaccustomed to hard service, it was found necessary toward the end of the second day to dismount frequently and rest by walking a mile or two at a time, so that by the time the Illinois River was reached, the company was strung out a mile or two along the road. Those who reached the river first were fortunate(?) enough to secure the services of a crazy little ferry boat officered and manned by a half-witted chap who alternately, as occasion required, filled all the different positions of captain, pilot, engineer, and crew. The motive power which was to make our vessel "walk the waters like a thing of life" consisted of a blind horse and a lame mule, whose energies were nearly exhausted in their vain efforts to climb an endless platform that rolled under their feet. The engines(?) were awakened and beaten into a state of activity, and the boat, which was laden to her utmost capacity, "walked the waters" a little more than half way across the river when a cavalry horse stuck his foot through the bottom of the boat and blocked the game by sinking it in about two feet of water, when it was abandoned and all hands made the best of their way to the nearest land. The balance of the company, guided by fires on shore, succeeded in fording the stream without accident.

Late that night we obtained supper at a hotel. Some took beds in the hotel, while others slept on the porch or on the ground in a neighboring orchard. At Meredosia we were allowed the privilege of paying our own expenses, which we thought were out of proportion to the quality of the accommodations afforded. The liberality and patriotism of the Meredosians were in keeping with the general appearance and character of their town, it being sandy, lazy, fishy, and poverty-stricken generally.

At Jacksonville, where we arrived the next evening, we found a very good supper awaiting us at the hotel into which we were cordially invited to "pitch" without the tiresome formality of receptions and speech making, but as no forage had been provided for our horses, nor arrangements made for keeping us all night, we continued our march twelve miles farther to the farm of Mr. Alexander, where we encamped. Our experience as "raiders" began to date from that night. The old gentleman, not expecting such a perfect deluge of visitors, and being roused from his peaceful slumber to find his dooryard full of noisy "invaders," evinced a little more ill humor than we thought the circumstances of the case justified. The boys mistaking the true cause of his apparent inhospitality, unhesitatingly pronounced him a "Secesh" (the name of "Copperhead" had not then been coined), and honestly believing themselves bound by their oath to harass and discomfit the enemy wherever found, at once proceeded to "harass" etc., by laying violent hands on all the corn, fruit, and poultry required for their immediate consumption.

I am free to confess that it looked like very rough treatment at that time, and felt not a little shame and remorse for the active part I took in the affair, but when compared with what I have since witnessed, it was a very trivial affair indeed, little more than a harmless practical joke, and if our venerable host still thinks, as he said that night, that he was "the worse-used man in the world," let him follow our trail through Missouri, Kentucky, Tennessee, Mississippi, and Louisiana, and I will guarantee him a sure and lasting cure, and he will see how we kindly spared him to the neglect of our own personal comfort and convenience.

Leaving Alexander's before sunrise the next morning, Thursday, August 8th, we breakfasted in squads along the road wherever we could procure provisions. We reached Springfield about sundown that evening, and after parading around the State House Square and through the principle streets, proceeded to the never-to-be-forgotten Camp Butler on Clear Lake, seven miles from Springfield, where we arrived about nine o'clock. We found Sergeant Wilks there with our tents and baggage, but we were too tired to pitch tents that night, and so, after a hasty supper of raw ham and dry bread issued to us by the post commissary, we laid down under the trees and bushes and were soon all sound asleep.

The next morning, we pitched our tents on the ground assigned to us, having first cleared the ground of a heavy growth of bushes and briers with which it was covered. The camp was large and full of troops organizing and preparing for war; regiments and batteries were being daily sent to the front to make room for fresh arrivals, who, as fast as they were organized and equipped, were in turn sent to that mysterious and unknown country from which no soldier had yet returned, the "front."

We were not long in making the discovery that a soldier away from home and in a large camp is a very unimportant personage. At Camp Flagg, while yet unarmed, un-uniformed, and with little or no discipline, every individual man was considered, and indeed considered himself, a hero. But in Camp Butler amongst thousands of others already armed and uniformed who had been in camp several days or a week and considered themselves old troops, we were looked upon as "raw recruits" scarcely worth a passing notice, while the hundreds of gaily uniformed officers, dashing here and there on their "brass mounted war horses," put our company officers quite in the shade. But our boys soon experienced a feeling of relief and pride when our own officers appeared in new regulation uniforms, elevating us to a position from which we could look down with pity on raw recruits, whose officers wore only common clothes and straw hats.

We were kept busy every day cleaning up camp, grubbing roots and brush off the parade ground, and drilling. When not at work, our spare time was occupied in digging a well. As we needed a large supply of water, we dug a large well, about ten feet square and fifteen or twenty feet deep. Although there were several such wells in the camp, so great was the demand for water that they were kept nearly dry and the water muddy nearly all the time.

We here received a package of small straw-stuffed pillows, one for each man, that had been sent, a present from our thoughtful "Sisters of the Good Samaritan." At a meeting of the company a series of "whereas's" and appropriate "resolveds" were adopted and sent to the aforesaid "S. of G. S."

On the 12th of August, a day long to be remembered by us, we underwent a very critical medical examination (at which two of our men were rejected), immediately after which we were mustered into the United States service for "three years or during the war" by Captain Pitcher, 3rd U.S. Infantry, mustering officer. Our company, as accepted and mustered, numbered just one hundred: three officers and ninety-seven enlisted men. Captain Pitcher and the examining surgeon objected to me on account of my height, or rather want of height, and were on the point of rejecting me, but on a closer and more severe examination, finding me perfectly sound in limb and wind, finally accepted and passed me. The next day our horses were "sworn in" as the boys termed the examination and appraisal they underwent. All were accepted and passed at fair prices. Our regiment, when filled, was to be the 2nd Illinois Cavalry, but not knowing what letter would be given us, we organized under the name of the "Adams County Dragoons," by which name our company was pretty generally known until after the death of Captain Delano.

We expected to remain in Camp Butler several weeks, or until we should be armed and equipped and the regiment fully made up. Although we had as yet received neither arms nor uniforms, we were destined to begin our "career" sooner than we anticipated. Wednesday night, August 14th at eleven o'clock, orders were received for our company to proceed immediately to Springfield. Although quite unexpected, it did not find us unprepared. Camp was struck, wagons loaded, and by half-past twelve, we were marching out of camp under command of Lieutenant Catlin, Captain Delano having gone to Quincy the day previous on business. At Springfield we found a special train waiting to take us to St. Louis, for which place we now learned we were destined. We left Springfield at six o'clock the next morning, arriving at Alton about noon. At every village, station, and farm house along the line of the road, we were greeted with cheers and the waving of handkerchiefs, to which our men, riding on top of the freight cars, responded with a hearty good will, not omitting to throw kisses to all the ladies.

At Alton we embarked on the steamer *David Tatum* and at two o'clock were landed at St. Louis, somewhere I think, near the foot of Market Street, where after being detained sometime on the levee, we were marched to the Abbey race track, where we encamped at five o'clock, only seventeen hours from the time of receiving marching orders in Camp Butler.

We were now for the first time on what the rebels were pleased to call "their soil."[11] Everything and everybody about us here bore a sneaking "secesh" appearance, what little loyal sentiment may have existed in the city was pretty effectually muzzled. The glad shouts of welcome and waving of hats and handkerchiefs that greeted us on every hand in our native state were all wanting as we marched through the city of St. Louis. Our appearance on that memorable occasion was certainly not very attractive, nor calculated to inspire the hearts of our probable enemies with very intense feelings of patriotic enthusiasm. We were all tired, dusty, hungry, and when occasion offered, not a little saucy. During our halt on the levee, each man had provided himself with a loaf of bread and a piece of cheese or link of smoked sausage, and as we rode through the streets busily engaged in refreshing the inner man, we must have borne a strong resemblance to a traveling boarding house.

Captain Delano rejoined the company while in camp on the Abbey track. During the three days we remained here the weather was too hot and the ground too dusty for us to do much drilling, so we employed our time chiefly in reading the "startling rumors" with which the papers were filled, writing letters home, and wondering "what's next."

Monday morning, August 19th, we were ordered to proceed by railroad to Pilot Knob. Arriving at the depot early in the morning, we found that no provision had been made for our transportation, nor did we get off until five o'clock that evening. Our captain had been busy all day about General Fremont's headquarters endeavoring to procure arms for us, and was so far successful that just before embarking on the train, we were furnished with sabers and Colt's revolvers, which put an end to a good deal of grumbling, as our men began to think they were to be sent to war with such arms only as nature had given them. With our bright blades and six-shooters we felt more like real soldiers and were now willing to embrace an opportunity to try the metal and range of our new arms.

Our trip from St. Louis to Pilot Knob was not marked by any incident nor accident of interest, except a delay of a few hours occasioned by running over some cows on the track, which threw a freight car off the track and did some little injury to the engine. We improved the time occupied in repairing damages by skinning the cattle, taking with us the hides and one carcass. The meat was taken charge of by our commissary sergeant, and the hides we traded off to a sutler at Pilot Knob. I remember receiving as my share of the proceeds of one hide in which I was a partner, a plug of tobacco, a pocket comb, and a small bottle of "pain killer."

We arrived at Pilot Knob about noon the next day and marched three miles to Ironton, where we encamped. Ironton is a small village at the foot of Iron Mountain. We here met Brigadier General B. M. Prentiss of Quincy in command of some three or four thousand men, and of whose brigade we were now a part.[12] From him, through our captain, we learned the reason of our sudden departure from Camp Butler. General Fremont, commanding at St. Louis, complained that he could get no cavalry to operate in southern Missouri. He had been promised cavalry by the governors of several states, but none had yet reported and his troops were ready to move. General Prentiss promised to have a company of cavalry in St. Louis within twenty-four hours. He asked for Delano's company to be sent immediately, and the result was we were in the field several weeks in advance of the balance of the regiment.

General Prentiss' brigade at that time consisted of the 7th Illinois Infantry, commanded by Colonel John Cook (and which soon earned for itself the appropriate name of "Cook's Crampers" from the peculiar fact of their fingers becoming suddenly "cramped" or closed the moment they placed their hands on any little article not their own, and which "cramp" could only be relieved by thrusting the hand afflicted into the owner's pocket or knapsack); the "bloody" 19th Illinois Infantry, Colonel Turchin; 28th Illinois Infantry, Colonel A. K. Johnson; 2nd Iowa Infantry; Buell's and Taylor's Batteries; and two companies of cavalry (the Benton Hussars and our company).[13]

During our stay at Ironton, August 20th–28th, we were kept very busy, having been selected by General Prentiss as his bodyguard, and besides furnishing orderlies and guards for headquarters, we were required to fill heavy details for scouting and escorting supply trains to the neighboring camps and outposts, this place being the terminus of the railroad from St. Louis.

Friday morning, August 23rd, a detail of twenty men under command of Lieutenant Sawyer was sent to escort a commissary train to Fredericktown, twenty miles distant. Towards evening, we reached the St. Francis River, where we found a German lieutenant with a company of infantry guarding the bridge. Scouting parties of the enemy having been seen in the neighborhood lately, our lieutenant decided to camp that night at the bridge. The mules were properly corralled, pickets thrown out, and our little force disposed of to the best advantage. Our train consisted of nine large charcoal wagons, heavily laden with ammunition and commissary supplies, and would have been a valuable prize for Jeff Thompson, who commanded a rather large force of the enemy in southern Missouri.[14]

In the detail for picket, I came on the first relief. I came off guard at ten o'clock and turned in under one of the wagons, and in a few minutes was sound asleep. At midnight there was a cry raised: "Fall in boys. Fall in, lively now." This was our first alarm and I cannot refrain from taking considerable credit to ourselves for the very prompt and orderly manner in which we responded to this, our first order to "fall in." Our line was at once formed, told off, and deployed as skirmishers. Concealing ourselves behind trees and bushes, we resolved to give the enemy a warm reception and make our first shots tell, and to fall back to the wagons only when compelled to do so.

The chill night air had somewhat cooled our first excitement, and our nerves were coming down to a business level, when one of the pickets came in and reported it a false alarm. A stray mule, doubtless hearing or seeing his kindred eating at the wagons, and with a view to their better acquaintance, came mule-like, carefully picking his way through the brush, stopping every few steps to listen and acting generally in a suspicious manner, well-calculated to alarm the sentinel, Guy Lonnsbury, whose post he was approaching.[15] He promptly halted when commanded to do so, but failing to respond to the challenge, "who goes there?" was fired upon. Of course everybody was disappointed(?). The boys had made up their minds to have a fight and it was certainly provoking to have to turn in again without one. But we soon became accustomed to such things and thought little or nothing a month or two later of being turned out two or three times in a single night.

We reached Fredericktown about noon the next day, and after dinner started on our return to Ironton. The wagons being now empty and the roads in good condition, the drivers plied the lash lively, and away we went at a cracking rate, reaching the St. Francis River again before night, where we encamped. The bridge here is a very good wooden one, covered, a single span crossing the river, and guarded by a squad of forty men of the 17th Illinois Infantry, commanded by a young German lieutenant. They were a jolly-good set of fellows and had a very nice camp on the bank of the river.

The next morning, Sunday, August 25th, we returned to our camp at Ironton and found the rest of the company just returning from a scouting expedition to Farmington, twenty-five miles distant. This morning, in company with three or four comrades, I rode to the foot of Pilot Knob, where we tied our horses and climbed to the top. A narrow railroad track runs from the mines near the top of the knob to the furnace below. The cars are hauled up and let down by means of a long chain, passing over a pulley at the top and worked by an engine at the furnace. The ties of the railroad make a very convenient stairway. The mines were not now being worked, and the furnaces were idle. I visited this place once before in (I think) 1857, when they were in full blast.

The Knob is said to be about 780 feet above the valley in which it stands and about 1,200 feet above the Mississippi River, from which it can be seen by the pilots on steam boats, hence its name. The view from the top is beautiful, but not very extensive, as it is surrounded by mountains nearly as high. The Knob, like its fellow Iron Mountain, which stands in plain view a few miles distant, is composed of huge boulders of solid and nearly pure iron ore. For some distance up, the sides of the mountain are covered with a growth of small, stunted timber, but the top is quite naked, destitute of any vegetation.

While encamped at Ironton, I quite unexpectedly met my old friend Tom Hollowbush, a private in the 2nd Iowa Infantry. He said he had run away from home (Warsaw, Illinois) and that his father knew nothing of his whereabouts.[16]

Tuesday morning, August 27th, the entire brigade struck camp about daylight, but the column did not begin to move until about ten o'clock. While we were waiting, quite a brisk traffic was carried on in boxes, grain sacks, boards, etc., between the soldiers and the store keepers in the village. As many of the troops had received their arms here, the camps were full of ordnance packing cases. Each mess had two or three of these boxes, and as the boys were all keen for a little speculation, honest or otherwise, a pretty strong "corner" on boxes was gotten up. A soldier would start out and find a purchaser who would come and look at the lot, and a price "in trade" would be agreed on, the stuff to be removed as soon as we left camp. Seller and buyer would then go to the latter's store and settle, when another soldier would find another purchaser for the same lot on the same terms, and so on ad infinitum until every different lot of boxes or old boards in camp had been sold to not less than six different purchasers. Sometimes a single soldier would succeed in effecting three or four good sales of the same stuff. From my purchaser of a lot of boxes belonging(?) to my mess, I received tobacco enough to last me several weeks. No tax had yet been imposed on tobacco, nor had "war prices" yet been established, and a large plug of good tobacco could be bought for fifteen or twenty cents that a few years later cost a dollar.

We were very reasonable in our prices (considering that the boxes belonged to the government and cost us nothing), and but few minutes were consumed in making a trade. As the chain guard would not permit the mob of wagons, carts, and drays that soon made its appearance to enter camp until the column should move, we were denied the pleasure of hearing ourselves eulogized by our late customers. How such a little lot of camp debris was ever divided amongst so many owners, we never knew, nor cared. We were the first Yankee soldiers they had ever had the pleasure(?) of dealing with, and I think I may safely assert that that day's transactions are yet fresh in their memories. The next troops were doubtless looked upon with suspicion, and probably found considerable difficulty in disposing of their camp rubbish.

Ten o'clock found us en route, together with about 8,000 infantry and Buell's field battery of six-pounders. The men were all well uniformed and in high spirits, and with their new rifles and muskets glistening in the morning sun, presented a splendid appearance as they stepped off to the inspiring music of fife and drum. The horses of the artillery and cavalry were "fat and saucy" and unwilling to come down to the slow march of the infantry.

The whole brigade was under the immediate command of General Prentiss. The road from Ironton to the St. Francis River, like Jordan, is a hard one to travel, being very rough, up and down hill and crossed by many small streams. We reached the St. Francis River about the middle of the afternoon, by which time many of the infantry boys, not yet accustomed to marching under a heavy knapsack and musket, were completely "played out." As soon as we had cared for our horses, we plunged into the river, which is a clear, cold mountain stream, and had a most refreshing bath. The weather being warm and clear, we did not pitch our tents, but slept that night on the ground under the trees.

A detail of about twenty men was made to go in search of forage. About two miles from camp we found a log barn full of sheaf oats, the owner of which, we learned, was a major in the rebel army. In a few minutes we had the entire crop tied to our saddles and on our way back to camp. A special artist of *Harper's Weekly*, who was present, made a sketch of the scene at the barn, which shortly afterwards appeared in that paper.[17]

We left the river early the next morning and arrived at Fredericktown about 2pm, and encamped on a small stream just outside the town. It is without exception the prettiest and most convenient camp we have yet been in. This afternoon the boys had a regular cleaning up. The camp looks like a country tavern on wash day. Red and grey shirts, drawers, stockings, etc. are suspended from bushes, tent poles, and guy ropes in all directions, while here and there could be seen some shirtless soldier "up to his eyes in suds" scrubbing away on his only shirt in a bucket of cold water. I improved the opportunity and played the "Irish washer woman" for a short time, retiring to the privacy of my tent until my wardrobe was dry enough to be resumed. This, I believe, was my first venture in the retail laundry business, and for a novice I flatter myself I did pretty well.

It is reported (everything goes by "report" or "rumor" or "they say") that Hardee is at Greenville with a force variously estimated, according to the scare of the informer, from 12,000 to 30,000.[18] General Sigel is expected soon to join us, when we will probably advance to attack Hardee. Two companies of 4th Missouri Cavalry have just joined our brigade, they are all Dutch.[19] Our boys are cleaning up their pistols and sharpening their sabers in anticipation of the coming(?) fight.

We left Fredericktown about five o'clock Thursday afternoon, August 29th, as the advance guard of General Prentiss' brigade. The general has chosen the "Adams County Dragoons" for his bodyguard and says he means to keep us with him during the whole war. The general is a man of "great expectations." He is very popular with his troops. We bivouacked that night on the farm of an old rebel about eight miles from Fredericktown. I slept that night under the bushes near my horse, who I found lying down beside me like a dog when I awoke early next morning.

The next night we encamped on a small stream about eight miles from the town of Dallas. A detail was sent to a barn on a neighboring plantation to forage, and another to the orchard for fruit. Everything that will sustain or comfort life is considered "contraband of war" and treated accordingly. This plantation I afterwards learned belonged to Colonel David Dougherty, who was one of the representatives to the secession convention held in this state. I also learned that he was with Claiborne Jackson when he made his celebrated run out of St. Louis.[20]

The next day, passing through the town of Dallas, we picked up a few rebel soldiers, or rather bushwhackers, belonging to Jeff Thompson's command, who were enjoying "French leave" at home.[21] They were not hard to capture, and were, in fact, very willing captives, saying they had been "forced into the rebel army," which we knew to be all nonsense. They were willing to give all the information they possessed and tell all they knew, which, to say the most, was not a great deal. Another victim gobbled up at Dallas was a Doctor Carpenter, who had been stumping the country, making secession speeches and enlisting recruits for the rebel army. He was recognized by some of our men as Dr. Cassady, formerly of Augusta, Illinois, from which place he ran away several years before with another man's wife.

We reached the town of Jackson on Sunday afternoon, September 1st. Here the brigade went into camp while we continued with General Prentiss to Cape Girardeau, about twelve miles beyond on the Mississippi River, where we bivouacked on the bluffs just north of town. The road from Fredericktown to Dallas is a blind kind of track through the hills and timber, at many places almost impassable for wagons, but from Dallas to Cape Girardeau, it is one of the finest gravel roads I ever saw, as smooth and hard as a pavement.

Cape Girardeau is a little old-fashioned town that looks as if it had commenced going to decay and ruin a century ago. The streets are narrow, dirty, and unpaved. There are many log and stone houses, all old and presenting every stage of neglect and decay. About the only white male inhabitants of the place are a few Dutch mechanics and gardeners. The negroes are all here—idle, dirty, and supremely happy. On the bluff commanding both the town and river is a large fort, built of earth, well-entrenched, and mounted with six large guns.

Having no camp equipage with us, our rations were drawn at the post commissary and taken to a hotel to be cooked and served. The rebel cook at that hotel must have done his level best to make that supper as nasty and unpalatable as possible. The meat, beans, dried fruit, and coffee tasted as if boiled all in the same pot, and at the same time, and the pot been previously used in the manufacture of soap or some fertilizing compound for the kitchen garden. A half-starved Indian without the power of tasting or smelling and provided with an iron-clad, copper-bottomed stomach, might possibly have worried through that meal, but we soldiers couldn't. So, with a taste and a smell, we walked back to where our horses were picketed on the bluff and, rolling ourselves in our blankets, went hungrily to sleep.

The next morning we returned to Jackson and pitched our tents in a field on the banks of a small muddy creek, where we remained until Saturday, September 7th. The tents of our army (about 10,000 men) cover at least 200 acres and, from a little rise where our company is camped, look like quite a large city. At night when there is a light in every tent the camp presents a beautiful and novel appearance.

Yesterday some stragglers from the train guard were fired on from the bushes near Colonel Dougherty's mill and one man killed and four wounded. Orders, I understand, have been issued to the rear guard (when we leave here) to burn Dougherty's mill and house. This will about wind up his business. The advance guard took all the horses and mules, the commissary train took all the beef cattle, sheep and provisions, the negroes followed of their own accord, and now the rear guard will destroy all that is left. The colonel has certainly struck a streak of bad luck.

Two of our prisoners captured at Dallas, Dr. Carpenter and Baker, were this morning interviewed by Colonel John Cook. Baker was released upon taking the oath of allegiance to the United States. He is a poor, ignorant "white trash" unable either to read or write, and declares he did not volunteer, but was scared into the state (rebel) service. I have no doubt such was the case, and I think scare had a good deal to do with convincing him of the error of his ways and winning back his allegiance to the government. The doctor, being considered a much less harmless character, is kept a prisoner. A furlough from General Jackson (rebel) was found on him. He is also accused of being a spy.

It was during our stay at Jackson that General Prentiss was superseded in the command of southeastern Missouri by Brigadier General U.S. Grant, late colonel of the 21st Illinois Infantry. Not having seen a paper since leaving Ironton, we know little or nothing of what is going on in the world outside of camp. I don't know why he should resign or be superseded. He is well-liked by the entire command, and we shall be sorry to lose him. With a change of commanders, our company will doubtless lose its honorable position as bodyguard to the general commanding. What he may have done or left undone in his official capacity, we of course know nothing. Certainly, he has not been removed from such an important command without some good reason that is, perhaps, none of our business to know. General Grant we know little or nothing of. He was an officer in the Mexican War and belongs to the regular army.[22]

At this time, the enemy under Pillow was in strong force at Sikeston, Missouri, for which place it was generally believed by our men that General Prentiss was marching at the time he was superseded. His object appears to have been to capture the post of New Madrid and thus cut off Columbus, Hickman, and Island Number 10, all of which were then occupied by the enemy.

While at Jackson awaiting the settlement of the question of ranks between the rival generals, we were kept pretty busy drilling and scouting over the adjacent country. We picked up a good many rebel scouts and stragglers, and if we left anything that we thought could possibly in any way give "aid and comfort" to the enemy, it was because we did not find it.

I here witnessed a sight that I never saw again during four years of service. A soldier belonging to one of the infantry regiments was sentenced by a "drum head court martial" for stealing, to be "drummed out of camp." His regiment was formed for dress parade and the culprit, without coat, hat, or boots, and with a rope halter around his neck, was led by a corporal down the line, the band following playing the rogue's march. He was then led outside the line of guards and turned loose. What became of him, or what moral effect his treatment had on his after life, I have never learned. His offense was, I believe, stealing from and insulting some defenseless women. I also saw here for the first time soldiers punished by being tied to the gun wheels. This is done by spreading a man's legs and arms as far apart as he can and tying his feet and hands to the rim of a gun carriage wheel. It must of course be of short duration, but is pretty rough while it lasts.

On Saturday, September 7th, the whole brigade struck camp at Jackson and marched to Cape Girardeau, where we arrived about 5pm. After several hours' delay we were ferried across the Mississippi River, together with the "Benton Hussars," and stepped once more on the free soil of Illinois. The infantry and artillery embarked on steamers for Cairo. We remained that night on the riverbank, and early next morning took up our line of march for Cairo, where we arrived the next morning, Monday, September 9th at ten o'clock. Our march from Cape Girardeau to Cairo will be long and pleasantly remembered. Pawpaws, grapes, and other wild fruits were ripe and abundant, and there being no occasion to hurry, we marched slowly and at will, halting occasionally to pick the wild fruit. We passed through several towns, at all of which were troops either en route or recruiting. We remained at Cairo only about two hours, when we crossed the Ohio River to Kentucky.

Cairo was at that time a very important strategic point, commanding as it did the mouth of the Ohio River and its tributaries, the Cumberland and Tennessee,

Sketch of Bird's Point & Cairo, 1861. Courtesy of Special Collections and University Archives, San Diego State University Library & Information Access

on the banks of both of which the enemy had strong works. It was also the most southern point on the Mississippi River in possession of Union troops. It continued to be during the war the chief base of supplies for our army and fleet in the South and Southwest. Immediately south of the town and commanding both rivers was Fort Prentiss, built by General Ben Prentiss in the three months' service. Its name, I know not why, was afterwards changed to Fort Defiance.[23]

On the Kentucky shore, we found a regiment of infantry at work erecting fortifications, mounting guns, etc. A few days' labor gave the place a very formidable appearance, when it was named Fort Holt in honor of the Honorable Joe Holt of Kentucky.[24] We little thought on landing at Fort Holt that it was destined to be our home for nearly six months. Having started out so brash, we naturally supposed we were to continue on the rampage for "three years or during the war."

We pitched our tents on the bank of the Ohio a short distance above the fort, but a heavy storm of rain coming on next day, we found ourselves in danger of being drowned out, and were obliged to move to a ridge of sand farther up the river. In the rear, or east, of our camp was a large extent of low bottomland or swamp in which were a number of small lakes. In wet weather or during high water, this swamp is quite impassable, but at other times the ground is quite hard and firm. In this swamp were a great many pecan trees from which we reaped an abundant harvest of nuts. As it was necessary to cut down the trees in order to obtain the nuts, it was not long before the owner of the property, Mr. Hawes, began to lay complaints before the commanding officer, who issued a special order forbidding the cutting of any more trees, but not until hundreds of fine large pecan trees had been laid low in the sacred mud of Kentucky.

The boys, continuing to practice some of their sleight of hand tricks acquired in their Missouri campaign, it was found necessary to issue more "specials" forbidding the capturing or killing of pigs or other domestic animals, but notwithstanding the severe penalties attending the violation of these orders, I did not observe any decrease in our supply of fresh pork. As no one could be found to acknowledge the depredation, it was presumed that the unfortunate porkers were kicked to death by our horses while nosing around the stables at night. Our neighbors the infantry, having no horses to provide for them, were consequently deprived of many of the luxuries of the season. Their colonel's horse might occasionally bag a pig, but they could hardly require of him to furnish a whole regiment with steaks and spare ribs several times a week.

Our chief duties now consisted of picket and scouting, and writing letters home. We drilled, mounted occasionally, in an open field a mile or two from camp, but on account of the great distance from camp and the softness of the ground, these drills were soon discontinued.

An accident occurred here on drill one morning, which very nearly terminated fatally. While charging by platoons towards each other with open ranks, platoons to meet and pass, two horses, William Bell's and James Spence's, came together with a shock that burst both saddle girths, throwing one horse and both riders to the ground, and dislocating a shoulder of one of the horses. As we were charging with drawn sabers, it is a wonder that so little damage was done.

Captain Delano, accompanied by Sergeant John Cayton, went to St. Louis for the purpose of procuring carbines for the company.[25] Our pickets and scouts frequently encounter small scouting parties of the enemy, but as the latter are very careful to keep at a safe distance from our pistols, we want a more powerful weapon with which to interview them at a greater distance. The enemy's scouts are most generally armed with shotguns and rifles. However, Captain Delano returned from St. Louis without the carbines. So great has been the demand for infantry arms, that very few cavalry arms had yet been sent from the arsenal. The captain got his name on the list and was promised the carbines as soon as they could be obtained.

Lieutenant Catlin, while scouting down towards Columbus, found where a rebel picket had recently stood and where he had cut a rebel flag in the smooth bark of a large beech tree. The lieutenant with his knife soon changed it to the

"Our Special Correspondent," Fort Holt, Kentucky, October 1861. Courtesy of Special Collections and University Archives, San Diego State University Library & Information Access

"stars and stripes." Also about this time a small rebel flag was found by our scouts on the Columbus road, attached to which was a proclamation by the rebel General Pillow, giving Union soldiers three days in which to vacate the sacred soil of Kentucky, and threatening a terrible visitation of his official displeasure on all who shall be found here after the expiration of three days from the date thereof. As the three days of grace mercifully granted us in this wonderful proclamation had already expired before we discovered it, and as no General Pillow with his executioner had yet appeared, it is fair to presume that that officer had relented and concluded to let us remain a little longer. Anyhow, that's what we did.

The town of Columbus, twenty miles below Cairo, is occupied by the enemy in strong force under command of General Pillow. General Jeff Thompson, formerly mayor of St. Joseph, Missouri, is encamped with a considerable force somewhere in the vicinity of Sikeston, Missouri, about twenty-five miles southwest from Cairo.

Fort Holt is what is called a "sand battery." It is made of large gabions (a tall willow basket having no bottom, the stakes of which are driven into the ground) filled with sand, on top of which are placed bags of sand. The whole is then thickly covered and banked with sand and earth. Long green cottonwood logs are built in with the sand bags to strengthen and bind them together. It is built in the form of a half-circle. The armament consists of four 32-pounders that have a range of at least six miles down the river. Lying at anchor in the Ohio River, just above the fort, are a number of ironclad and wooden gunboats, which make frequent expeditions up and down the river in search of adventure. One day last week, one of our gunboats had an engagement with a small rebel gunboat and a battery that had been planted on the Kentucky shore, a few miles down the river. The rebel boat escaped and the battery was soon silenced. The firing was distinctly heard in camp.

About noon on Saturday, September 14th, the whole brigade at Fort Holt struck camp and moved southward. Troops could also be seen in movement at Cairo and Bird's Point, and it was the prevailing opinion among the troops that a general advance was about to be made on Columbus. Not being admitted to the councils of the general commanding, we were not thoroughly—in fact, not at all—informed of the object of the expedition, but as it affords soldiers a great comfort to guess and form conclusions, we decided that the time for the fall of Columbus, the "Gibraltar of the West," had come.

We marched south about eight miles to Mayfield Creek and encamped at Elliott's Mill, near old Fort Jefferson, and about two miles from the Mississippi River. The place is now called Camp Crittenden and is occupied by three regiments of infantry: the 17th Illinois under Colonel Ross, the 2nd Iowa under Colonel Tuttle, and the 7th Iowa under Colonel Lauman. The cavalry consists of two companies of Benton Hussars (German) and our Company L.[26]

The next day, some of our sick, and others of our company who had remained behind, came down by boat. Fort Holt is now nearly deserted, the only troops there being a small force of artillerists in the fort and one company of infantry sent over from Cairo by Colonel Morgan. The road from Fort Holt to this place is so very muddy and crooked that the wagons did not get through until this morning, and as a consequence we had no tents last night and many of our men were obliged to go hungry to sleep.

The morning of Sunday, September 15th, I was detailed as orderly to report to Colonel Ross, brigade commander. I rode with the colonel to the house of William Mercer, about two miles from camp. Mr. Mercer is one of the very few loyal men to be found in this country. He has been much persecuted and annoyed by the rebels, on account of his Union sentiment and adherence to the old flag. After feeding our horses and treating us to all the peaches and melons we could eat, he invited us in to dinner. We had an excellent substantial country meal, and for the first time since leaving home, I sat down to and ate off a table. Colonel Leonard Ross is an old friend of my father's.

Captain Delano with forty men and two companies of infantry under command of Colonel Ross, while out scouting today, approached within two or three miles of Columbus. Finding no pickets nor scouts of the enemy at that short distance from his camp, they went no nearer, fearing to fall into an ambuscade. The enemy is certainly lying very close within his works, for our cavalry, picketing all the roads and scouting the country in every direction, seldom encounter his scouts. Our presence here so near their stronghold is doubtless very annoying to the rebels, but if they know anything of the object of our presence here, they are better posted in our affairs than I am.

The "bloody 19th" left us this morning, September 16th. They are going east, they think to Virginia. Being a very rough, quarrelsome set of men, nobody regrets their departure, and their room will doubtless be more agreeable than their company. The colonel's wife accompanies her husband. She is a very rough, masculine-looking woman, and carries in her belt a revolver and knife. She certainly overestimates her attractions if she thinks she possesses charms that require the protection of so many deadly weapons.[27]

About noon today, September 18th, the pickets of our company were relieved by the Hussars, from whose officer we learned that the brigade had left Camp Crittenden and returned as far as old Fort Jefferson, about three miles toward Fort Holt, to which place we at once marched and found the infantry already in camp. We pitched our tents near a long woodpile at the foot of the bluff, on the top of which are the remains of old Fort Jefferson and a few old soldiers' graves.

We had only just cooked and eaten our dinner when one of the squad of Hussars that had been left on picket at Camp Crittenden came tearing up the road into camp at full speed, shouting at the top of his voice: "The rebels are coming, a whole damn regiment." We sprang to our horses and hardly had the bugle's sound "to arms" died away before we were mounted and in line, ready to move. "By twos—head of column to the right—gallop—march," and away we went, with Captain Delano at the head, and my old friend Tom Woodruff and I riding together, as we nearly always did.

The infantry, about 3,000 strong, were in line of battle along the road on which the enemy was expected. At Elliott's Mill, we learned that a troop of about 100 rebel cavalry had appeared and fired on our pickets, but without doing any damage, and immediately retreated on their fire being returned by the sentinel on post. Some of the relief guard became so confused(?) by the firing and the sudden appearance of so many rebels, that in the excitement of the moment, they forgot all about their horses, and took to the brush on foot, and where from their place of concealment, they had an opportunity of watching the movements of the enemy. From their somewhat confused and not very intelligible report, I made out that the rebels appeared quite as much surprised as our guards, and from the hasty manner in which they wheeled and galloped back towards Columbus, they evidently thought they had stumbled onto our whole brigade. The vidette did not stop to see the rebels retreat, but started at once for camp, and supposing they were closely following him, increased his speed at every jump until by the time he reached camp, his horse was touching ground but once in every twenty or thirty feet.

This is the first time our pickets have been molested here, although the enemy was certainly aware of the presence of our brigade at Elliott's Mill and Camp Crittenden. Now that he knows we have left there, our pickets and scouts may look out for frequent encounters. This sudden alarm was a good test of the dependence to be placed in our boys. Although we honestly believed the enemy was approaching, and that we would soon have more fighting than we could get away with, not one flinched, all were cool and in earnest, and it was gratifying to hear the general opinion expressed by our infantry comrades that "Delano's boys will do to tie to."

An amusing little incident occurred on the occasion of the above alarm. One of our corporals had hastily saddled and mounted his horse before he discovered that he had not untied his halter from the tree to which his horse was hitched. The line was already forming, and fearing he would not have time to dismount and untie his halter, and it probably not occurring to him that he had a sharp saber with which he could cut the halter, he began shouting lustily for help: "Somebody cut me loose!" But as everyone was just then fully occupied with his own affairs, he failed to obtain the required assistance. How he got loose, I don't know, but he was in his place when we started.

Fort Jefferson was once a small stockade with earthwork defenses, occupying a commanding position on the top of a high bluff, but by whom it was built or occupied, I was unable to learn.[28] It was probably built to protect the early settlers and emigrants from the Indians who occupied this country many years ago. It is certainly very old. The stockade and block house are all rotted away, and the trenches and walls are thickly covered with vines and bushes. Nearby are several graves—two or three of which are marked by headstones—of soldiers who died or were killed here many years ago. The stones are rough, unhewn slabs, and the names thereon rudely cut, as if done with an iron picket pin or the point of a bayonet, doubtless the last kind act of some old friend and comrade. A large and beautiful weeping willow droops over and shades these lonely graves. Little did the men of that little frontier garrison think, when their mission here having been accomplished, and they hauled down their flag and marched away, that their old campground would again be occupied by soldiers, fighting for that same flag, but under far different circumstances. Some of the same men perhaps who were then fighting for that flag are now fighting against it.

It having been reported that the rebels had planted a battery on the riverbank about five miles below, an expedition of about 2,000 men on three steamers, accompanied by two gunboats, started from here today to "go for it." Captain Delano with thirty men went with it. I could not go, being on the detail for picket. They all returned in three or four hours, having failed to find any battery.

On September 20th, our company received from "The Sisters of the Good Samaritan" a box of hospital stores consisting of bandages, lint, canned fruits, etc., all very nice for wounded and sick men, but not the most agreeable subjects for sound and well soldiers to look at and contemplate. It was, however, very kind and thoughtful of our dear Sisters, and the men all felt very thankful to them, but each one hoped that he might not be placed under further obligations to them by being obliged to wear any of their nice little rolls of bandages and lint on his limbs or body. Doctor Kendall took charge of the stores and says it will afford him pleasure to attend any who may require his professional services. A draft was made on our Sisters' present much sooner than any of us expected. Gideon Seldon, a private of our company, while unsaddling his horse, was accidentally shot through one arm by his revolver falling out of his saddle holster, or in some way becoming entangled in the straps of the saddle. He was promptly cared for, and the doctor thinks he will soon again be fit for duty.

Our German friends the "Hussars" appear to be in or out of luck a good deal. We have the outposts one day and they the next, and while our men seldom see anything of the rebels, the Hussars are attacked or driven in nearly every time they go out. It is no uncommon thing as we ride out on duty to hear the infantry say, "there'll be no alarm tonight, Delano's boys are on picket." This morning, the Hussars on the outposts were attacked by about 100 rebel cavalry and driven back to the line of infantry pickets, where a sharp skirmish ensued, in which one rebel was killed and several prisoners captured. Later in the day, information was brought in by some scouts or spies that a large force of the enemy was moving up from Columbus to attack us. I only wonder that so small a force has been permitted to remain here so long unmolested. Reinforcements were sent down to the advance guard at Elliott's Mill, the pickets and outposts were doubled, and that night we slept on our arms. The fight this morning took place directly in front of young Mercer's house on the Columbus Road.

Sergeant Hill and I stood together mounted on one post for the last twenty-four hours. The road was full of rebel cavalry tracks, and we frequently heard shots fired in their camps at Columbus. Returning to camp at Fort Jefferson, we were soon ordered back to reinforce the pickets on the lower Columbus road. The road through the bottom was very crooked and muddy and the night so dark that we could not see the ground. I rode in the advance and acted as guide. Being unable to see either sky, trees, or ground, I threw the reins across Ned's neck and, trusting to his good sense and my good luck, I waded in. At the infantry lines, we were promptly halted by the sentinel, who could hear but not see us, and who made me dismount and wade about a hundred yards through the brush and mire to give him the countersign.

On the extreme outpost I had a very agreeable companion, William McMurray, and we wiled away the watches of the night talking and laughing in a whisper. There were no mosquitoes to annoy us, but the owls—of which the forest was full—kept up an incessant hooting and calling. A very slight stretch of imagination was sufficient to make their hooting resemble the voices of men, or of all the different known or unknown animals of the earth, air, or water. We were slightly anticipating an attack; just enough to make the watch interesting and keep us wide awake.

The camp at Fort Jefferson is to be abandoned. The 2nd and 17th Iowa have gone across the river to Norfolk, and the balance of the troops are to return to Fort Holt tomorrow. During our encampment here our company had done a great deal of scouting, thoroughly scouring the country and becoming familiar with all the roads. I have several times been within a mile or two of the great rebel camps at Columbus, but never encountered their pickets and very seldom met their scouts. I frequently stood picket all night so near their camps that I could plainly hear their morning drums and bugle calls.

One day, being on the outpost under Sergeant Murdock at a point on the main Columbus road where the Hussars had been several times attacked and driven in, we concluded to fortify ourselves, so that if attacked, we could defend ourselves until reinforced by the infantry pickets instead of falling back to them. While arranging a barricade of logs and brush, we were annoyed by a drove of hungry hogs rooting around and stealing our horses' feed. One of them, a miserable half-starved wretch that looked as if he had been born hungry and never yet experienced the pleasure of a tight skin, attracted by the savory smell of frying bacon and hardtack, made bold to seize and run off with one of our haversacks, containing a day's rations. Without going through the formality of swearing out a warrant, or even arresting him, he was instantly tried and sentenced to death, and the whole relief (Frederick Turner, Jim Spence, William McMurray, and myself) with drawn sabers—for we dared not fire our pistols—rushed to execute the sentence of the court. He could run and dodge like a rabbit, and being apparently extremely desirous of saving his bacon, he led us a lively chase for a half-hour when he took refuge between the logs of our new barricade, where he was quickly dispatched by a saber thrust "in tierce" between his ribs. He was skinned, roasted (being too lean to fry) and his bones picked for dinner. In memory of the event, we named our fortification "Pork Battery."

We are all ordered back to Fort Holt. The great "March to Columbus" has terminated. The country has been pretty well ransacked, a few skirmishes had with the enemy's scouts and videttes, and that's about all. I don't know what grand object was in view when the expedition started, but being now all ordered back, I suppose it has been accomplished. Our company left about nine o'clock this morning, September 24th, as rear guard, and marched to Fort Holt, where we pitched out tents on the riverbank.

We learned today, September 25th, that the 1st Illinois Cavalry, which left Camp Flagg at Quincy a few days before we did, has been all captured by the rebel General Price at Lexington, Missouri.[29]

Captain Delano with fifty men went today, September 26th, to the village of Blandville, Kentucky, where he arrested a young man named Blake, charged with recruiting for the rebel army, and two citizens: Corbitt, the county clerk, and Vaughan, a merchant. The company halted outside the village while one of our men (dressed in butternut) and young Mercer rode up to the tavern, where they dismounted and called for whiskey. This looked so perfectly natural that no one suspected nor noticed anything remarkable about them. Had they called for something to eat or a drink of water, they would doubtless have aroused suspicion and been at once shot down. They listened to the conversation a few minutes, and by the time the company arrived had spotted their men, who were promptly arrested. A small rebel flag was flying on the courthouse, which the boys were anxious to secure, but the captain fearing any further delay would be dangerous, would not stop for it, but hastily returned with his prisoners to camp. The two men, Blake and Vaughan, were sent to Cairo to be held as hostages for the release and safe return of our old friend Mercer, living near Camp Crittenden, who was taken prisoner a few days ago by the rebels for being a Union man, and charged with having given "aid and comfort" in the form of sundry compotes and canteens of buttermilk, to our scouts and pickets whenever they chanced to pass his house. Mercer was released by the rebels at Columbus, and passed through camp on September 28th on his way to Cairo to solicit the release of his hostages.

Private William C. Stokes, our "company chaplain" as the boys are pleased to call him, held divine service in camp today, September 29th. After prayers and singing of familiar hymns, in which all could and did join, Mr. Stokes delivered a short, earnest sermon in which he particularly exhorted his comrades to guard against the many sins and vices of camp life, to which, unrestrained by the good influences of home and friends, they might be tempted. He dwelt at length, and with much feeling and earnestness, on the sin of profanity. The good old man's ears are often offended by the reckless, thoughtless blasts of profanity heard on all sides in every camp. "Parson Stokes" as he is familiarly—though respectfully—called by the men, is a great favorite and much thought of by all the company, and his teaching and counsel, both privately and in "meeting," are respectfully listened to and are, I think, productive of much good.

The "church call" this morning, October 6th, was well responded to, nearly the entire company assembling in front of the captain's quarters. The services were conducted by "Parson" Stokes, who after prayers and singing several old and well-known tunes, took for his text "ask and it shall be given unto you" (Matthew VII.7.). During his discourse, speaking of prayer, he said, "Every day I pray to God that the hearts of our enemies may be turned and that peace and union may be restored without the sacrifice of another life, but if, in his wisdom, he sees fit that we should fight for the Union, I pray Him to direct every saber stroke and that every ball may take effect. I pray Him to strengthen my arm and steady my aim." It was truly a pleasing sight to see those hardy men sitting or lounging in the shade that bright Sunday morning, all attentively listening to honest old Mr. Stokes. I have often listened to more eloquent, carefully prepared sermons, but never, I am sure, to one delivered with more sincerity and hearty honesty. Stokes not only preaches, but works and practices. In him are combined, I truly believe, the principles of a humble, faithful Christian, an honest man, and a brave soldier.

With the exception of our wonderful strategic movement to Camp Crittenden and our recent little expedition to Blandville, little of interest has occurred since our landing on this "foreign shore" a month ago; nothing but our regular camp and picket duties, with occasionally a little unimportant scout. Our pickets now and then bring in a straggler or a deserter from Columbus, or a runaway "contraband" sometimes comes in, all with long-winded contradictory stories from the enemy, all of which we have become so accustomed to that their repetition fails to create even a ripple on the surface of the minds of our quiet little community. Indeed, if one chances now and then to come in without a tale of horror to unfold, or some startling revelations to make, he is at once looked upon with suspicion and locked up in the guardhouse as a dangerous character.

This evening, October 11th, the Reverend Dr. McMasters, chaplain of Colonel Buford's 27th Illinois regiment, stationed at Cairo, visited our camp. He formerly resided in Palmyra, Missouri, and I have often heard him preach in Quincy. The next afternoon, John Whitbread and Albert Peabody from Quincy visited our camp. They both have relatives in the company. They say there is much more excitement at home about the war than they see or hear in camp.

On October 12th, a small sternwheel steamboat bearing a white flag came up the river and, passing under the guns of Fort Holt, landed at Cairo. I was standing on the walls of the fort when she passed. The walls of the fort and the riverbank were soon covered with soldiers to see what was, to them, a strange sight. A few rebel officers in full uniform were on the upper deck, viewing us with their field glasses. This was the first flag of truce we had seen. The boat (the *Grampus*) remained at Cairo but a few minutes, when she was taken in tow by the *Aleck Scott*, one of our largest transports, and escorted down the river. The *Scott* returned in about an hour, and that's about all any of us ever knew of the matter. The officer in command of the battery at Fort Holt, I understand, was reprimanded by General Grant, commanding at Cairo, for permitting the rebel boat to pass his post. All boats are hereafter to be brought to us as soon as they come within range of the guns of our fort.

The ground being now dry and the roads in good condition, we do a great deal of drilling and scouting. We have practiced with saber and pistol until our horses, as well as men, are well-trained and drilled. The drilling and practicing is done almost entirely by Lieutenant Catlin. Our captain is an excellent executive officer and attends to all official business (receiving and returning official calls, etc.), and makes an occasional scout into the country. Catlin is much the best drill master, and as he takes particular pride in drilling and exercising the company, the captain willingly lets him do the work. Lieutenant Sawyer has lately been in poor health and keeps in his quarters most of the time.

We have visited nearly every house and made the acquaintance of nearly every man, woman, and child within six or eight miles of camp. The natives here are not a very "highly intellectual" class. Some know enough to chew gum, while occasionally one can be found possessing sufficient intelligence to drive a goose to water. There are very few if any young men at home, they having nearly all gone off to the rebel army. There are plenty of old men, and both old and young women. The former of the last-named are all old, ugly, ignorant, and crass, while the latter are neither beautiful nor accomplished, nor in any way attractive, even to a soldier. I frequently go over to Cairo on the quartermaster's or commissary's detail, and sometimes on Sunday to church, but it is so hot, dirty, and generally disagreeable there, that I am always glad to get back to our clean, quiet camp.

There has been little activity among the troops at this point for several weeks. Most of the troops must have been sent east from the recruiting camps, and those arriving at Cairo by boat or rail are generally sent up the Ohio River. There is quite a strong force at Bird's Point, opposite here, on the Missouri shore. There is also a garrison at Paducah some forty or fifty miles up the Ohio.

Lieutenant Sawyer has gone home, having resigned his commission. His health has for some time been failing; he has consumption and cannot stand the damp night air of these swamps.

Having received orders to prepare winter quarters, we commenced the erection of a long row of log cabins a short distance below the fort. Cottonwood trees were cut and hauled in by our mule teams, and all hands, when not on other duty, were required to work in squads under noncommissioned officers. The work goes on gently and quietly, nobody straining nor overworking himself. We have been soldiers long enough to be pretty thoroughly weaned from all love of hard work.

"On the Outpost." Fort Holt, Kentucky, October 1861. Courtesy of Special Collections and University Archives, San Diego State University Library & Information Access

The ordinary quiet and monotony of camp has been interrupted by the battle of Belmont, which was fought on Thursday, November 7th. This is the first battle in which we have participated, and the first fought on the Mississippi River, and with the exception of a few battles in Missouri, it was the first fought in the West.[30] Wednesday evening, November 6th, our company under command of Lieutenant Catlin (Captain Delano having gone to St. Louis) embarked on the steamer *Keystone* together with a company of cavalry from Cairo. Our sick list was unfortunately quite large, only fifty-eight of our men being able to go. No one, of course, knew anything of our destination nor the object of the expedition, although the general impression prevailed that Columbus was our objective point and that a big fight was in the prospective.

Our entire force consisted of 2,700 men embarked on five steamers: the *Aleck Scott*, having on board Generals Grant and McClernand, the *Montgomery*, the *Chancellor* with a battery of flying artillery, the *Keystone*, and the *Belle Memphis*, the latter having on board Commodore Graham.[31]

The fleet started at ten o'clock at night, preceded by two gunboats, the *Lexington* and the *Tyler*. We steamed down the river about ten miles and tied up to the Kentucky shore, the gunboats coming to anchor just below us. Twenty men of our company were then detailed to go on shore and picket the approaches to the landing. The night passed quietly and at six o'clock the next morning we re-embarked and proceeded down the river.

About three miles from Columbus, but in a bend of the river which prevented us from seeing the town, the troops were all landed on the Missouri side and marched through a corn field into the swamp beyond. Immediately after landing, our company was ordered to the right of the infantry to reconnoiter and watch the movement of the enemy and await further orders. In a few minutes, we heard a few musket shots as the enemy's pickets were driven in. Word now came from Colonel Buford for us to return and charge a company of cavalry that had just appeared. We returned at a gallop, but too late, the rebel cavalry having fallen back. We then advanced into the swamp, deployed as skirmishers, closely followed by Lieutenant Colonel White with the 27th Illinois Infantry. We passed through the timber and formed in an open field.

Our gunboats now began by opening a heavy fire on the fort and batteries at Columbus. Their fire was promptly returned, and for a short time little could be heard save the thunder of cannon and the hissing of balls and shells. Many of the latter from Columbus burst high in the air over our heads, their fragments falling all around us, and filling the air with smoke.

A circumstance here occurred as strange and novel as it was interesting: I heard music under circumstances most peculiar. As our company was advancing in line of skirmishers, cautiously feeling our way and momentarily expecting to encounter the enemy, our troops a few hundred yards behind us were advancing in line of battle, the brass band of the 27th Illinois playing "Dixie," while the enemy, about the same distance in front of us, were also advancing in line of battle with their band playing the same tune at the same time. Neither band could hear the other, but we could hear both. It was certainly a very singular coincidence, and I have never since heard the tune of "Dixie" without vividly recalling the stirring events of that, to us, ever-memorable day, particularly so as it was the first time we had ever met the enemy in force, or witnessed a battle.

Pretty sharp firing was now heard on our right, where Colonel White had advanced. Just as I came to a turn in the road, on which I chanced at that moment to be riding in the skirmish line, I saw a short distance in front of me a rebel field officer with his staff, riding some distance in front of his troops. He was doubtless looking for me, for the moment he saw me—and I was the only one he could see—he turned and galloped back. He was an elderly man, handsomely dressed in a grey uniform with gold epaulets and a long black plume in his hat. By describing him to some prisoners afterwards, I learned that I had had the honor of seeing General and ex-bishop Polk, the commanding officer at Columbus. Although he appeared

"Gun Boat 'Lexington,'" at Fort Holt, 1861. Courtesy of Special Collections and University Archives, San Diego State University Library & Information Access

considerably interested in my appearance, he did not give me an opportunity of presenting my compliments or sending up my card, and consequently he never knew the name and rank of the first Yankee soldier he saw that day.[32]

The opposing lines were now approaching so near each other that we were ordered to form in a ditch, a dry watercourse, so the infantry could pass us. In a few minutes Colonel White crossed the ditch, and with his regiment pushed on into the swamp. The balls now began to fly thick and fast, several passing so near me that I felt their breath on my cheek. Colonel Buford soon followed with the balance of the 27th Illinois, and the firing became general and heavy all along the line, but particularly so immediately in front of us. I can liken the noise to nothing I have ever heard, except the noise made by a steamboat "blowing off" under water; it was one continual roar. I had no means of knowing how long the firing continued, but it seemed to me several hours. For a moment it ceases and a long, loud cheer from our men tells they are driving or charging the enemy. The firing again commences and roars with renewed fury. Little squads of two or three now begin to come from the front bearing their dead and wounded comrades; others, wounded, but yet able to walk, come limping by leaning on their muskets.

Up to this time, the fight had been altogether with the infantry, but now a sharp heavy boom from the enemy tells that his artillery is at work. Balls and shells fly thick and fast, branches are torn from the trees, and little clouds of dust show where the balls are ricocheting along the ground all around us.

During all this time our company was held in reserve in the ditch, idle spectators of the fight raging all around us. The fight being altogether in the woods, cavalry could be of no service, except as scouts and messengers, for which latter service many of our men were detailed to different parts of the field.

We had as yet used no artillery, while the enemy had been working his for an hour or two, but now an orderly was sent to the rear, and in a few minutes our field battery of six pieces, that had been held in reserve, came flying past us to the front with fearful speed, as fast as both whip and spur could drive the horses. They unlimbered a short distance beyond us, and in another moment were responding to the enemy's guns. It was a regular artillery duel, volley of canister, grape, and shell were exchanged as fast as the men could load and fire, and continued unabated for at least two hours.

I knew by the sound of the musketry that the enemy had more men than we had. Many of our wounded kept passing to the rear, and in reply to our question, "How goes the fight boys?" all replied, "We are getting the best of them." The firing now gradually diminished and finally ceased. That we were not beaten I well knew, and hoped we were victorious and that the battle might be over. Our troops had, in fact, beaten the enemy back, driving him into and through his camp, where they destroyed all the tents and camp equipage, capturing several field pieces and destroying a large amount of ammunition.

Our company was ordered around a small slough on the west of us to cut off the retreat of the enemy in that direction. We proceeded at a gallop about a mile when we dismounted and ambushed near a ford. Just before reaching the ford, a rebel soldier who was hidden in the bushes broke cover, but was soon captured by Lieutenant Catlin, who was mounted. He said his captain was killed and his company cut to pieces, and that he with some others had thrown down their arms and were taking the best care they could of themselves.

We had been concealed but a few minutes when a small party of rebel soldiers, without arms, came to the ford to cross. We fired a few shots at them, hoping to capture them, but the whole party escaped into the swamp.

Firing at the front now recommenced and was continued fiercely for some time. Shot and shell from the heavy guns in Columbus fell all around and beyond us. The firing again ceased for a few minutes and all was quiet, save the occasional crack of a musket or the bursting of a bomb high in the air, when we remounted and started back towards the battlefield.

Very heavy firing and shouting were again heard, and as we galloped down the road, we soon met our troops in retreat. It was a very disorderly retreat, in fact, a stampede. Not wishing to run until we knew what we were running from, and it being quite impossible to proceed farther towards the front, we drew out on one side and halted. The demoralization was nearly perfect; such as could be prevailed upon to stop long enough to say a word or two reported the most alarming and exaggerated stories of the number and fury of the enemy, and the complete annihilation that in a few minutes would be visited upon us all.

From the very wild stories, I gleaned the fact that the enemy had received heavy reinforcements of fresh troops from Columbus, and were now driving our exhausted men before them. Horsemen, infantry, and artillery went rushing past us in one excited, disordered mass, all making the best time they could for the boats. Many of the artillery horses were wounded, and it required the constant use of spur and whip to keep them up to their work. Some of the guns were drawn by single or spike teams, while other teams, in addition to their own loads, had a captured cannon hitched on behind.

We were then ordered to picket the approaches to the boats, to prevent the retreat being cut off. As the crowd arrived at the landing, the officers succeeded in reforming their commands and marching in order on board the boats. The dead and wounded that had been brought away were first taken on board and cared for. While the troops were embarking, our company was deployed as skirmishers below and about 200 or 300 yards from the boats. We had been in this position about a half-hour, when I heard shouting and the noise of cavalry approaching, and on raising in my stirrups, could plainly see a troop of cavalry charging towards us through the timber. We were at once ordered to fall back to the boats, which we did quickly, but in good order. The infantry and artillery were fortunately on board, leaving the way clear for us.

We had only just got on board, and before the stage was hauled in or the boat left the shore, a tremendous fire of musketry was opened on us from the bank, which at this place was about as high as the cabin of the boat, and which appeared to be literally covered with rebel soldiers. Their fire was principally directed towards the boats containing the infantry, who were more exposed, being crowded on the guards and upper decks, although many balls came through the sides of our boat. The pilots especially had a very hot time of it, as they were the principle objects of attraction, and being but partially protected by iron shields, it is a wonder and blessing they were not all killed. On them now solely depended the safety of our retreat. Had they been killed or disabled, the boats would have drifted helplessly at the mercy of the enemy, who was not just then in a very amiable state of mind.

The infantry and our field battery returned the enemy's fire with interest, and for a few minutes the battle raged almost as fiercely as it had done on shore. The enemy had several field pieces on the bank, with which they endeavored to disable our boats. I was standing on the guards of our boat, the *Keystone,* when a six-pound ball passed through her larboard wheel, but fortunately without doing any damage. Many musket balls struck and flattened against the boiler. So thick did the bullets come through the side of the boat next to the shore, that the engineer on that side had to keep himself hid, crouching behind his engine, springing up to work his valves in response to the pilot's bells, and quickly dodging down again.

A six-pounder on the bow of our boat was brought to bear on the rebel gun that fired into us, and just as the rebel gunners were loading for another shot, the ball from our piece struck their carriage, filling the air with fragments of gun carriage, gunners, and dirt. It was about as quick and thorough a case of "silencing a battery" as was possible. After landing our troops in the morning, the transports came to anchor in the middle of the river, when they were fired on by two small masked batteries on the Kentucky shore. Both batteries were silenced by one of the gunboats before they had inflicted any damage on the transports.

As soon as the transports could get away from the shore, the gunboats steamed in between them and the shore and opened a tremendous fire on the enemy. The bank being higher than the portholes, and the gunboats being close to it, the guns were elevated and many of the shots, striking the bank obliquely below the surface, tore up immense quantities of earth, effectually scattering or destroying everything on the top. After a few broadsides, the smoke became so dense that neither gunboats nor shore could be seen. They continued throwing shell and canister until it was certain no living thing could remain on the bank.

In the retreat and confusion of embarking, Colonel Buford with part of his regiment became separated from the brigade. He was about a mile from the river and in direct range of the gunboats when they opened fire, but fortunately escaped without loss, although it required some pretty lively scattering and marching to get out of range of the shot and shell that fell all around them. They were taken on board the *Chancellor* and *Keystone* some two or three miles up the river. Doctor Kendall of our company, who was left behind at the field hospital, also escaped with Colonel Buford.

There were many interesting incidents connected with the battle, many little trifles that were full of interest and excitement at that time, and under those circumstances, but which would appear dull and stupid on paper or if repeated elsewhere. I shall mention only a few that came to my knowledge or under my observation. At the commencement of the fight, a young infantry soldier near me received a ball in his thigh. "There now," he said, "that's too bad, and I've had only one shot at the d——d rebels." I asked him if he could walk back to the boats. "I don't know, but I'll have to try it. I'm of no use here," and leaning on his musket for a crutch, he started limping to the rear without a word or sign of pain, only regretting that he had been wounded too soon.

Lieutenant Colonel White, commanding a detachment of the 27th Illinois Infantry and the left wing, rode up and down his line encouraging his men: "Steady boys steady, don't get excited, keep cool, don't fire 'til you see something to shoot at, keep behind the trees all you can, don't load too fast, make every shot tell," etc. He was everywhere in the thickest of the fight. Once when near me he held up his arm and showed where a bullet had cut off one of his sleeve buttons. "That was pretty close," said he, "but I've been called louder than that before now."

A young mulatto, servant to some officer, passed near me with a six-pound ball in his hand. I asked him where he got it. "O, I picked it out of a bank down yonder, the darned thing liked to took my head off," and negro-like, he sat down on the ground and laughed as if it was a good joke.

"There," said a soldier a little pettishly, "some careless rebel has shot a hole through my canteen and spilled all my coffee."

Among the dead carried off the field, I saw one young fellow with his back cut open and one arm cut off by a cannon ball. He was laid across two muskets and carried by two men.

Part of the day, during the heaviest firing, was very hot, with not breeze enough to carry off the smoke, which became blinding and suffocating. I fortunately thought to fill my canteen with water before leaving the boat, and well that I did so, for I believe I should have nearly, if not quite, choked without it. I divided with some of my comrades who had lost their canteens.

Our faces were black and streaked, and our eyes, noses, and mouths filled with powder smoke. Every time a soldier rubbed his eyes or blew his nose (handkerchiefs being an unknown luxury with us), he would relieve the monotony of his countenance by a variegated blot or stream across his face, so that we soon resembled a party of Indians.

One fellow of the 7th Iowa discovered a caisson full of cartridges concealed in the bushes in the rebel camp. As he could not haul it away himself, and there was no time to hunt up a team, he resolved to destroy it. Catching up a brand from a camp fire, he threw it into the open box, and dodged behind a large cottonwood tree. The next instant, the whole thing went to smash, leaving the brave fellow uninjured, but covered with dirt and smoke.

Captain William Schmidt of Quincy was slightly wounded and Lieutenant William Shipley of the former's company was killed. Both were Quincy boys and former schoolmates of mine. I saw Shipley's body the next day in Cairo, he had two bullets through his bowels. Not one of our company was injured, the only company in the battle that did not suffer some loss in killed or wounded.

The soldiers, of course, had a great deal to say, and many opinions to give, concerning the fight. Everyone knew better than anyone else what ought and what ought not have been done. That we were badly beaten, no one offered to contradict. The real object of the expedition was not then known, but we all supposed it was to capture Columbus, and General Grant was severely censured for attempting with less than three thousand men to attack a strongly fortified place containing from 10,000 to 20,000 troops. He also committed the terrible blunder of landing his forces on the wrong side of the river.

The Northern papers were loud in their praises of Grant and his generalship as displayed on that occasion. That much brave fighting was done by both officers and men was very plain, but where so much strategy and generalship was displayed, we could not see, and for several weeks we considered ourselves a much-abused and badly beaten lot of fellows. But when we learned the true object of the expedition and fight, and the good accomplished by it, we saw things in quite another light, and began to hold up our heads again and felt much relieved in knowing that our defeat and loss had not been in vain.

The rebel General Price was at that time hard-pressed by our General Sigel in Missouri. Grant learned that a reinforcement of about 10,000 men were to leave Columbus to join Price. To prevent these troops going to Price and destroying Sigel's whole army, Grant decided to engage their attention nearer home. Hence, the battle of Belmont. Our attack was entirely unexpected, and although we were finally repulsed and driven to our boats, we first drove the enemy off the field, destroyed his camp, and brought away a number of prisoners and several field pieces of artillery, besides attaining the real object of the expedition, that of preventing reinforcements going to the assistance of Price.[33]

Our loss, considering the superior force we encountered, and the furious attack on the boats, was light. Killed, wounded, and missing did not exceed one hundred.[34] The next day, a boat went down under flag of truce to remove or bury our dead and with hospital supplies for our wounded. I have not attempted to give a correct or detailed account of the battle of Belmont. I have only spoken of events connected with it, so far as I saw or had knowledge of.

Several days were occupied by our boys in cleaning up and writing long letters home, then work was resumed on our cabins. They have been planned and commenced in such a grand scale that the work progresses very slowly so that we begin to think we shall not occupy them much before spring. The work is superintended principally by Lieutenant Catlin, but architectural honors(?), I believe, rest entirely with the captain, whose shoulders are fortunately broad and strong enough to withstand the pressure.

Considerable "log rolling" and "wire-pulling" has been going on in camp for some time, with a view to the election of a second lieutenant to fill the vacancy occasioned by the resignation of Lieutenant Sawyer. The boys have finally talked themselves into three "reliefs," the several candidates being Sergeant Fred Turner, Sergeant John Cayton, and Private Moore (myself). This afternoon, November 15th, in obedience to orders from Captain Delano, the company assembled in front of the captain's tent and proceeded to ballot without nominations, Lieutenant Catlin and company clerk Woodruff acting as tellers. On the first ballot, Sergeant Turner, having received the least number of votes, was dropped. The second ballot resulted in my election by a majority of 19 out of 85 votes cast.

The result, however gratifying, was to me entirely unexpected. Besides having very little desire for the office, I could not expect to successfully compete for the honor with two noncommissioned officers, who had had every advantage of me in drill and training, and each of whom I had reason to suppose had many more friends in the company than I had. Both my opponents were good men and brave soldiers and had earnest friends and supporters.

As soon as the result of the last ballot was announced by the captain, my friends, after indulging in the customary cheer for the successful candidate, demanded a speech. Now, having never made a speech in my life, and not anticipating the necessity of making one today, I was altogether unprepared with any "few appropriate remarks" and begged to be excused, but they were bound to hear from me and wouldn't take no for an answer, so with a spasmodic effort that made my heart go pit-a-pat and nearly choked me, I stepped to the front, and facing the line, was delivered of my mouse about this size: "Comrades, you have seen fit by your votes to impose on me, over other better-qualified men, the responsibilities of an office I neither expected nor desired. I thank you for the confidence reposed in me and hope you will never have occasion to repent this day's work."

I wished to remain with my mess until I should be commissioned by the governor of Illinois, but the men insisted that I should at once enter upon the discharge of my duties. So the next day, I moved my baggage (two blankets) to company headquarters. Our headquarters mess consisted of Captain Delano, Lieutenant Catlin, Orderly Sergeant Turner, company clerk Tom Woodruff, and myself.

Lieutenant Catlin does most of the drilling and scouting. He is an excellent drillmaster, and under his instruction the company is becoming very proficient in all details of cavalry drill. Guard, picket, fatigue, and some scouting duties keep me constantly employed. While Catlin superintends most of the work at

Sketch of Celebration at Fort Holt, Kentucky, 1861. Courtesy of Special Collections and University Archives, San Diego State University Library & Information Access

the cabins, much of my time is spent in the timber in charge of fatigue squads, chopping and hauling logs.

On the last day of November, we moved into our new winter quarters, and tonight for the third time since leaving home, I slept under a roof. On our march from Quincy to Springfield, I slept one night in a school house at Clayton, and one night in the tavern at Meredosia. Since then I have either slept in a tent or the open air.

Our room (headquarters) is twenty feet square and eight feet high, ceiled with rough boards, which gives a large attic or loft in which to store tents, etc., and where our cook and hostlers sleep. In the rear is a small shed kitchen in which we have a new cook stove, the possession of which latter article elevated our black cook "Marcellus" to the highest notch of human happiness. We take less ashes and dirt in our food now than formerly.

Our front room is warmed by a coal stove, which we find a great improvement over a smoky, scorching camp fire. We have also a table, and the captain has invested in a big easy camp chair, which during his temporary absence, is always occupied by whoever is fortunate enough to obtain possession, and much valuable time is consumed and much pleasure taken in burning our boot heels on top of the stove.

The men's quarters, of which there are eight, are the same size, and are warmed by large old-fashioned fireplaces, capable of containing a half-cord of wood each. Each room is occupied by a mess of twelve (more or less) men. Next to headquarters is the doctor's room, making in all ten rooms under one roof. The entire building is twenty feet wide by two hundred feet long, built of large rough logs, chinked and daubed with clay. It is almost two hundred yards below the fort, and the same distance from the river. In front, the bank slopes gently down to the water's edge, and being of hard, clean sand, forms an excellent drill and parade ground. In the rear are our stables, and immediately behind them, heavy timber.

This afternoon, Sunday, December 1st, three rebel gunboats made their appearance down the river. They were permitted to come within about three miles, when a shot from a sixty-four-pounder in Fort Holt warned them that a nearer approach was not desirable, and might, if persisted in, be attended by some inconvenience to them. The long roll was sounded, and in a few minutes the whole garrison was under arms. The gunboats promptly opened fire on us, firing in all but nine shots, all of which fell short in the river. Finding they could not reach us, and the balls from our fort falling all around and beyond them, and coming closer as the gunners got their range, they abandoned their siege and returned down the river without inflicting or receiving any damage. The boats were in a bend of the river and could not be seen from Cairo, nor could our telegraph operator be found to notify the commander at Cairo. The gunners in Fort Prentiss could see the firing from Fort Holt, and taking their range by the sound of the enemy's guns, fired a few shots at random over Bird's Point and across the bend. Could our operator have been found so as to notify our gunboats at Cairo of the approach of the rebels, we would have been favored with a fine view of a small naval engagement.

As soon as the firing was over, I was sent down the river with twenty men to reconnoiter, as it was thought perhaps the enemy might be landing troops under cover of their gunboats. I went as far as the Fort Jefferson landing, but found all quiet and no boats in sight. They probably came only for a Sunday afternoon call and an exchange of courtesies. It was quite interesting and somewhat exciting to watch the flash and hear the ball whistling from the rebel boats and speculate how near us it would strike.

A few days afterwards, a glowing account of the bombardment of Fort Holt and Cairo, and the destruction of the former by Commodore Hollins's fleet, appeared in the Memphis papers.[35] It was copied by the northern papers and caused much anxiety amongst our friends at home. It was also the occasion of much rejoicing among the northern "Copperheads" before they discovered their mistake and how badly they had been sold.

Ironclad gunboats are constantly arriving at Cairo until quite a large fleet is now at anchor in the stream. They are formidable-looking things, are quite low, with sloping sides and heavily plated with railroad iron. Troops are also daily arriving at Cairo, Bird's Point, and Mound City. Extensive preparations are evidently being made for an advance on some of the enemy's strongholds—either Columbus or some of their forts on the Tennessee or Cumberland rivers. The enemy is also in strong force at Island Number 10 and New Madrid. A sixty-four-pounder "Long Tom" has been mounted on the riverbank, some distance below our quarters.

On the night of December 13th, we received orders to double the guards and sleep on our arms. I was on duty as officer of the guard. As there was a prospect of some little excitement, my friend Tom Woodruff, our company clerk, desired to accompany me on guard, so together we made the grand rounds, riding from post to post through the entire night. The night was bright, clear, and quite cold, and to Tom, who was out all night for the first time, it was unusually long. No enemy, however, made his appearance and I never learned the cause of the alarm.

The guidon at company headquarters is today draped in mourning for the first time. One of our men, Corporal Warner D. Elliott, of La Prairie, Illinois, died in quarters this Saturday morning of quinsy.[36] Warner was a good soldier, very quiet in his manners, brave and cautious and always ready for any duty. He was conscious to the last and died as he had lived, a Christian. He had many warm friends in the company, and his loss is mourned by all. W. C. Stokes was appointed corporal to fill the vacancy occasioned by the death of Elliott.

The general health of the company is worse at present than at any time since we have been in the service. Twenty-six men were reported on the sick list this morning. Lieutenant Catlin, who has been sick several weeks with ague, is worse today. The climate and weather here is very trying on us. The days are generally warm and sultry and the nights cold and misty. We have neither the cold weather of the North, nor the heat of the South, but are between the two—have all the bad of both and the good of neither. As there now appears to be but little prospect of an immediate advance southward, our men are all anxious to be sent north into Missouri. They would gladly give up their comfortable quarters here and take the field, cold as it may be, in Missouri or any more healthy climate.

About this time, we received a large box of books, magazines, and papers from our very thoughtful and considerate friends, our dear "Sisters of the Good Samaritan" in Quincy. A series of resolutions appropriate to the subject and occasion were, of course, at once adopted and forwarded to them by the next mail. My father, who is my regular correspondent, frequently sends me Quincy and Chicago papers, so that we keep pretty well posted on all matters at the North.

On Tuesday, December 16th, all the troops at Cairo, Bird's Point, and Fort Holt were reviewed by General Van Rensselaer, who or what he was, I was unable to learn.[37] The Fort Holt troops, consisting of the 7th Illinois Infantry, Colonel Cook; 28th Illinois Infantry, Colonel Johnson; the heavy artillery; and Delano's Cavalry, were reviewed at four o'clock in the afternoon. The reviewing general, accompanied by some fifteen or twenty colonels, majors, and captains, dashed around a while on borrowed horses, displayed their fine uniforms and poor horsemanship and went back to Cairo, where they ought to stay or be hung with a piece of red tape.

Gunboats and mortar boats continue to arrive almost daily. There are now here lying at Cairo, or at anchor in the Ohio River, two wooden gunboats carrying nine guns each, seven ironclads of twelve to eighteen guns each, and about thirty-five mortar boats carrying each one sixteen-inch mortar. The latter are square, flat-bottomed boats protected by a wall of boiler iron about five feet high, and are towed by steamers, having no motive power of their own.

This afternoon, while scouting down the river with Adjutant Muller of the 7th Illinois Infantry and a small squad of my own men, we discovered a small rebel steamer coming up with a white flag flying at her jack staff. When about opposite us, and three or four miles from camp, she was brought to by a shot from our Long Tom at the fort. Advancing to the shore, I was soon discovered by those on board, and was at once the target for a score of field glasses. I asked, "Have you any communication for the commander at Cairo?" After some little delay, during which time they were probably electing a speaker, I was answered by a short, fat officer in a gray uniform, "We have ten prisoners to exchange." "Anything more?" "No sir." I dispatched a messenger to report the fact to Colonel Cook, commanding at Fort Holt. The boat was the *Prince*. There appeared to be at least thirty officers on board. Rather a large commission, I thought, to negotiate for the exchange of ten prisoners. These flag of truce boats always try to come as near to Cairo as they can, and always come well provided with telescopes and field glasses. While a few of those on board were examining Fort Holt with their telescopes, the rest kept us under a steady fire of field glasses. They appeared to have nothing more to say, and when I thought they had counted me about often enough, I terminated the interview by going about my business. When we returned the same way about sundown the boat had gone back.

Dr. Douglass of Quincy was in camp a few days ago, and spent the night at company headquarters. I sent home by him some ambrotypes I had taken in Cairo to father and Ned Manson.

Since Lieutenant Catlin's sickness I have had all the drilling of the company to attend to. Captain Delano's ambition not being satisfied with the command of a single company, he is working diligently to get a regiment, or at least a battalion, and in his endeavor to do so, finds so much "outside work," as he calls it, that he has little or no time to devote to drilling, and leaves that, as well as all other details of camp duties, to Lieutenant Catlin and myself. Captain Delano started for Springfield, Illinois, today for the purpose of recruiting another company to form an independent squadron.

We recently received sixteen muzzle-loading carbines or musketoons to use until we get our long-promised breech-loading carbines. A rifle squad has been formed and turned over to me to drill.

I have traded horses with Sergeant Murdock, paying him forty-five dollars. My old horse cost me in Quincy $110. I think I have now the best horse in the company. He is jet black, powerful, well-made, and active. My old horse, although a very good one, was too heavy and clumsy for me.

Captain Frank Moore's Company D of our regiment has been here a short time and is encamped a short distance above the fort. In the absence of Captain Delano, Captain Moore commands the squadron. He comes from Alton, Illinois, where his company was raised.[38]

The slaves in this part of Kentucky are continually running off and coming into our camps. Notwithstanding all that is told them by their masters and the rebels generally to the contrary, and the very little encouragement or inducement that is offered them by our government and military commanders, they persist in thinking that we are their friends and have come to deliver them from bondage. The great desire of their lives is to get into our camps. What they are to do, how they are to live, or what will become of them, are subjects far beyond the range of their mental vision, and concerning which they neither know nor care. A "Yankee camp" is in their minds a haven of rest, a sure place of refuge from all their troubles.

So great is the rush of "contrabands" becoming into our border camps, and so anxious are they to give information concerning the enemy, and to be of service to us in any capacity, so that they may escape from the bondage to which they were born and have all their lives been subject, that I can plainly foresee that our government must before long do something with them, by either forming them into camps of refuge and providing for them, or by making of them soldiers or laborers. Much, if not all, of the hard labor now performed by soldiers in trenches and on fortifications or in the commissary or quartermaster departments, might better be done by them, thus leaving more effective troops for camp and field duties. It is a problem that is forcing itself upon us and as it won't down at our bidding, must—however knotty—be solved, and the sooner the better.[39]

A few nights ago, a wench with three little children walked all night to get to our lower pickets, who brought her into camp next morning. Her husband has been working for me for some time, taking care of my horse, etc. He is very happy in the society of his wife and pickaninnies, but they constitute a larger company than I feel able to entertain. Nearly every morning the advance pickets bring in one or more contrabands. Every mess in camp has its black cook. They consider it quite a privilege to be permitted to cook, clean horses, chop wood, and do anything they are bid for their board and a few cast off clothes, and as they are content to eat what is left (for no rations can be drawn for them), and as soldiers' clothes are generally "cast off" only in time to prevent their falling off, their wages are not very exorbitant.

This afternoon, December 24th, Mr. Mercer, Judge Marshall, brother of the brave(?) Colonel Marshall, 1st Illinois Cavalry of Lexington, Missouri, notoriety, and —— Utteback, the owner of the woman and children above mentioned, visited our camp, with a paper from General Grant authorizing them to search our quarters for the lost property. Lieutenant Catlin, who was in command, told them he could not resist General Grant's orders, but would not assist them nor be responsible for the behavior of the men towards them. They might search the quarters, but must take their own risks in so doing.

Not seeing the objects of their search in headquarters, they next proceeded to the doctor's quarters, then occupied by Mrs. Cook, our company laundress. The runaways were all in this room, scared nearly to death, but Mrs. Cook was forewarned, and before admitting the searchers, hustled the nigs all into her bunk and drew down the curtains, before which Cook, otherwise known as "Uncle Hiram," took his seat on a stove. Failing to discover their property, one of the party proposed searching the bed, and was proceeding to do so when "Uncle Hi" filed remonstrance by saying that was his old woman's bed and he didn't want any men fooling about it. If they must search that bed, they would have to get away with him first, but before attempting that they had better send for reinforcements, as he felt pretty mad and in good fighting condition. Not responding as promptly as Uncle Hi thought proper to his invitation to "get out and go about their business," he with gentle(?) force put them all out and locked the door.

The whole company had by this time resolved itself into an indignation meeting, with each individual member an independent committee of one on resolutions and addresses, and their "few and appropriate remarks" as they gathered around the "nigger-hunters" were not of a nature calculated to rouse the drooping spirits, nor cheer the hearts of said "hunters," nor greatly encourage them in the further prosecution of their search. Such remarks as, "why don't you find your niggers?," "They're in my quarters, come and get them," "We've sold your niggers," "Why don't you offer a reward?," "If every man was at home, you'd be in hell," were amongst the mildest and best-natured. Our captain's darkey "Marcellus," a huge

Missouri contraband, and a very quiet, harmless fellow generally, introduced himself to Utteback by generously volunteering to "punch his damned Secesh head and throw him into the river." The men encouraged him until he was on the point of executing his threat, when they interfered and obliged him to forego his anticipated pleasure. The rather confused state of Mr. Utteback's mental faculties just then, when momentarily anticipating a pounding, and perhaps a ducking, at the hands of a "run-away nigger," and obliged to submit to the taunts and insults of the hated "Yankee soldiers," was certainly unenviable. I greatly feared the soldiers would do them some harm, and thus get us all into trouble, but they finally allowed them to depart without inflicting on them any bodily injury.

Quiet being once more restored in camp, the next question that came up for consideration was, "What shall be done with the wench and children?" It was, in itself, a very simple little question, that any child might ask, but one requiring diplomacy and statesmanship of a higher order than could be found ready-made in company headquarters. It is not to be wondered at that a few inexperienced soldiers could not "on sight" dispose of a conundrum that a few months later tangled the wisest minds in the nation. We could not keep her in camp and we would not return her to slavery.

The Gordian knot was finally untied by giving the woman a few days' rations and putting her across the Ohio River into Illinois, there to seek her fortune.[40] This proved to be the best means at our command of dealing with this vexed question, and thereafter whenever contrabands got too thick in camp, the men would muster a squad, and with a great show of secrecy, take them across the river some dark night with instructions, as soon as they landed, to jump ashore and run for dear life, and to keep running all night, and for several nights. It was always necessary to choose dark or stormy nights for these expeditions and to go some distance up the river before attempting to cross in order to avoid the watch on the gunboats.[41]

Mrs. Davis, wife of E. M. Davis of Quincy, was at company headquarters today. She came up by river from New Orleans, where she says her husband was broken up in business and all his goods and property confiscated by the rebels, to Columbus, Kentucky, where she saw General Polk and from him obtained a pass through his lines to Blandville, from which latter place she came in a wagon to our lines. She had a pretty hard time amongst the rebs, from whom she was happy to escape without imprisonment or bodily injury. She is on her way to Quincy accompanied by her little boy, three or four years of age.

This evening, a fatigue party that had been working all day in Cairo, loading forage on a boat, returned with their skins and canteens full of contraband whiskey. Hearing sounds of revelry in the lower end of the quarters, I went down to investigate the cause thereof and found the boys having a regular jollification. Francis Weaver and Charley Craine, our two buglers, with their violins, were doing the music. A "stag" set was on the floor, the "ladies" being distinguished from the other men by a handkerchief tied around one arm. Some of the latter having lost their insignia of sex, the set was in a bewildering state of entanglement, from which the caller was endeavoring to unwind them as I entered. I at once took a share of stock in the enterprise, with Miss(?) Billy Gilpin for a partner. The boys were all very jolly and noisy, but at the sound of "taps," the lights were extinguished and all retired quietly to quarters.

This is our first Christmas spent in camp. We have no drills nor fatigue duties, nothing but necessary picket and guard duties, and they are made as light as possible. It is a general holiday in camp, the men having things pretty much their own way. Our mess invested in a big turkey with the necessary accompaniments for a banquet on a small scale.

Yesterday I received by express a large box of apples and smaller one of cakes and other delicacies from home. In the small box were several jars of pickles from Mrs. S.C. Sherman and a fine pair of knit mittens from Miss Bromfoot. Ordinarily, I might not feel flattered at receiving "the mitten" from a lady, but all attending connecting circumstances in the present instance, however, tended to make Miss Bromfoot's very thoughtful present very acceptable.[42] Mrs. Davis was present when I opened the boxes, and seeing with what forethought and care everything had been prepared and packed exclaimed, "What a blessed thing it is to have a good mother." The preparation and packing of the many articles in my Christmas boxes had occupied her time and attention for many weeks, plainly showing how constant were her thoughts on her absent boy. God bless my dear mother.

Captain Delano, being absent on a flying visit to Springfield on some of his "outside business," it devolved on Lieutenant Catlin to preside over the festivities of the occasion, which he did with becoming dignity. Besides our regular mess, there were present by invitation Mrs. Davis, Dr. Kendall, and Private Dawson and wife; the latter, a very lively little lady, was invited for company for Mrs. Davis, as it was feared she would feel lonesome alone among so many "rude men," and in order to enjoy the society of Mrs. Dawson, it was necessary to endure that of her husband. We had a very good dinner and a very pleasant party, which combined, resulted in a very Merry Christmas to all.

In the evening, I took supper by invitation with Mess Number 1, of which Sergeant Burke is foreman. The boys were also in receipt of a large Christmas box from home. Obe Spence (Diah) did the honor of the occasion and presided over the feast with mingled dignity and nonsense. "Diah" is the drollest, most serio-comic fellow in the company. He can and does play the worst possible practical jokes on his comrades without the least scruple of conscience. He can both give and take the most unfeeling joke or trick with apparent indifference. He is, however, a good trusty soldier and well-liked by all his fellows.

The members of our headquarters mess, I think, enjoy themselves about as well as any small squad of troops in the service. The captain and company clerk Tom Woodruff wage a constant good-natured war of jokes and witticisms; both being pretty keen blades, there is much sharp cutting done. Lieutenant Catlin, Sergeant Turner, and myself occasionally pitch into them both or each other, as occasion may suggest or require, just to keep things lively.

Sunday, December 29th, Reverend William Locke, chaplain of our regiment, happened along and preached in our camp this morning. He is a very clever, blustering sort of a man and a pretty fair preacher. This is the first time we have enjoyed any of the privileges, blessings, or benefits supposed to be derived from the possession of a regimental chaplain. Our regiment is scattered at nearly as many different posts as there are companies. It is necessary, however, for someone to draw the chaplain's pay, and it looks well to have one on the regimental rolls and that's all.

One afternoon recently, while drilling on the beach, my new horse got so excited as to become unmanageable, and taking the bit in his teeth, ran away with me. After charging about madly for a while, he started straight towards Bird's Point on the opposite side of the Mississippi River, and but for the timely interference of some of the men, who stopped the mad brute just at the water's edge, he would doubtless have gone to Bird's Point or drowned himself and me in the attempt. He proved himself too many for me that time, and in order to have a majority on my side in the future, I have presented him with a new bridle, having a regulation jaw-breaking ring bit, which keeps him down to his level.

This afternoon, December 30th, we were honored by a visit from the "special war correspondent" of the *Cincinnati Gazette* and a "special artist on the spot," Simplot of *Harper's Weekly*, the former in search of sensation news, and asking many questions that were none of his business, the latter sketching scenes of camps and camp life.[43] He made several drawings, both interior and exterior, of our quarters; also a picture of Fort Holt. These "special correspondents" are getting to be a source of much trouble to our army. Not a movement, however trifling, can be made by our troops that is not the next day published in many of the Northern papers, which, before the ink is scarcely dry on them, are smuggled through our lines to the enemy.

Chapter Two

1862

Camp Crittenden—Fort Holt Abandoned—Charleston and Sikeston, Missouri—Siege of New Madrid—Wounding of Captain Delano—On the Mississippi—St. Louis—An Encounter on the Waters—Death of Captain Delano—Elected Captain—Hunting Guerillas—New Madrid, Missouri—Island Number 10—Visiting the Locals—Corruption at Cairo—A Skirmish with Guerillas—Administering the Oath of Allegiance—Reflections on War—Sickness in Camp—Chasing Faulkner's Guerillas—A Skirmish and Faulkner Captured —Winter Quarters at Paducah, Kentucky

The evening of Friday, January 10th, we received orders to prepare to march at a moment's notice with five days' rations. This afternoon, two ironclads went down the river about six miles to old Fort Jefferson. Troops from Cairo, Bird's Point, and Mound City have been going down all afternoon on transports and are now encamped at Fort Jefferson. The fog is so dense on the river that the boats experience much difficulty in moving; they are blowing and ringing all the time. The ferry boat has been nearly run down several times today.

Our men have now become so accustomed to alarms and sudden movements that they have about ceased to question or speculate concerning the object or policy of our order or expedition. They appear to have at last discerned that the first and most important duty of a soldier is to "obey and question not." However necessary such implicit and unquestioning obedience is to the observance of good military discipline, it is difficult to impress it on the minds of "fine and enlightened citizens" who all their lives have been in the habit of thinking and reasoning for themselves.[1]

So now (January 14th) we are in the "tented field" again. In accordance with orders received last night, we left our quarters at nine o'clock this morning and marched to Camp Crittenden, there relieving a company of the 4th Illinois Cavalry. We were accompanied by Company D of our regiment, the squadron being under the command of Captain Delano. At Fort Jefferson, we found five or six regiments of infantry, several companies of cavalry, and a field battery. The troops had struck camp and were beginning to move. A short distance below their camp they took the left-hand road, up the bluffs toward Blandville.

Arriving at Mayfield Creek, we found it running nearly bank-full at the ford, and at once set to work building a bridge, drawing on the old mill nearby (Elliott's Mill) for the necessary material, and by three o'clock, a large portion of the old mill had disappeared and in its stead a bridge had grown across the creek, and we proceeded to cross.

The opposite bank being much the highest, our bridge slanted up like the roof of a lean-to shed, and being wet and muddy, the mules could not obtain a foothold. Coaxing and flogging alike failing to have the desired effect, a long picket rope was tied to the wagon tongue and the mules tied by their heads to the rope. Just as our preparations were completed, the 28th Illinois Infantry came down. The rope was taken over the bridge and up the bank and, manned by several hundred men, was hauled taut. As soon as the mules comprehended the situation, they of course began to pull back and throw themselves down. At the word of command, with a loud shout and running pull, the entire team and wagon were jerked across the bridge, some of the mules sliding on their feet and some on their backs. The other teams were treated in like manner until all were safely across the creek.

Captain Delano with his squadron, accompanied by Colonel Johnson with six companies of infantry, made a reconnaissance in the direction of Columbus. The cavalry went within about three miles of the enemy's works on the east side of the town, where we could plainly hear the drums "beating off" for dress parade and the band playing "Carry Me Back to Virginia." Although we went so near the enemy's camps, we encountered no scouts, nor pickets. It is certainly very singular that while our scouts are on every road and path all over the country, and often close to the rebels' camps, we very seldom encounter their pickets or scouts. I am quite sure no rebel scouts could come anywhere near our camps without finding us "wide awake and full of fleas."

A few days ago, a rebel gunboat came poking up the river in the fog in search of adventure, which she discovered in the shape of one of our ironclads lying at anchor off Fort Jefferson. The ironclad heard her coming and was already cocked and primed, waiting for her to pass by, so as to cut off her retreat, but just a few minutes too soon, the fog lifted, and enabled the rebel boat to discover her position in time to save herself. After exchanging a few lively broadsides, the enemy steamed down the river closely followed by the ironclad to within a short distance of the Columbus batteries.

It is stated that the rebels have stretched a heavy chain cable across the river and also planted the river full of torpedoes just above Columbus, for the especial benefit of our gunboats and transports whenever we shall attempt to storm that stronghold, their "Gibraltar of the West." I think the battle of Columbus, when it does take place, will be a hard-fought one. Prisoners, deserters, refugees, and spies all agree in their reports of the strength of its works and great number of heavy guns. The land approaches, as well as the river, are protected by torpedoes.

Among the natives whose acquaintance I formed during our encampment here was a Mr. Turk, a professing Union man, but considered by us very unreliable. Although we never placed any confidence in him, nor believed anything he told us, we endeavored to keep up a show of friendly relations with him by calling at his house whenever occasion offered and partaking of his hospitalities.

Another was an old blind man living on the Blandville road; although very poor and perfectly blind, he was cheerful and happy, and his cabin was rendered inviting and attractive by the presence of his two very agreeable daughters. The girls were at first a little shy of Yankee soldiers, of whom they had heard many horrid stories, but frequent interviews had the effect of disarming their suspicions and rendering our visits tolerable, if not entirely agreeable. In fact, they required some excuse if we allowed more than two or three days to pass without visiting their cabin. One of the girls was a fat, dumpy, good-natured blonde. The other, rather slender with black hair and large black eyes, which latter Captain Delano described as "intellectual and owl like." Although there was much less of her, I considered her by far the prettiest and most intelligent of the two. The fat one had a peculiar and affectionate habit of hugging and shaking herself while engaged in conversation. It was perhaps, in her unenlightened mind, her interpretation of the Scriptural text, "as ye would that men should do unto you, do ye even so unto yourself." At any rate, it afforded her a considerable amount of exercise and apparent satisfaction. There certainly existed no necessity of her doing all of her own hugging. Their names as well as that of their very estimable old father, I regret being unable to recall, but their many little acts of kindness and hospitality extended to us are not forgotten.

Sunday, January 19th, we were ordered to march back to Fort Holt. We had much rain during our stay at Camp Crittenden, and our bridge over Mayfield Creek was washed away. The creek was now up again and running so strong as to be unfordable. An old flatboat was found a short distance down the creek and towed up, which with some more lumber from the old mill, made a pretty good pontoon bridge.

The entire force in that expedition consisted of nineteen regiments of infantry, three squadrons of cavalry, and several field batteries encamped at Fort Jefferson, Camp Crittenden, Blandville, and other points, all under command of General U. S. Grant. The object of the expedition, I afterwards learned, was not to attack Columbus as we first supposed, but to menace and attract the attention of that place and prevent reinforcement leaving there to join Buckner, who was then closely pressed by Buell near Bowling Green, Kentucky.[2]

The 52nd Illinois Infantry went into camp here yesterday, January 22nd. They have just come from northwest Missouri, where they have been at and near St. Joseph. They crossed the Mississippi River at Quincy on the ice. Both rivers here are running full of ice and rising at the rate of two feet a day. In view of their sudden and rapid rise, we are under orders to be ready to move at a moment's notice. Our quarters are yet ten or twelve feet, or about one week, above the water.

On Sunday, I went over to Cairo with Lieutenant Catlin, Dr. Kendall, and Tom Woodruff to attend church. Bishop Whitehouse preached in the morning in the Methodist church, in the afternoon in the theater, and at night in the Presbyterian church. Dr. Kendall and Tom Woodruff and two others were confirmed by the Bishop in the evening. This is the second Sunday I have attended church since leaving home; I went once in Springfield. We have Sunday services frequently in camp, either by Mr. Stokes or some wandering chaplain.

Troops, gunboats, and mortar flats continue to arrive from the north. So large a force as we have now in this vicinity certainly cannot remain long idle. Some great movement will doubtless be made soon. The general belief now is that it will be up the Ohio and Tennessee rivers or through Missouri into Arkansas and thus by the water route, flanking Columbus and Island Number 10. The battle of Columbus, which has been often threatened, and which a short time ago seemed imminent, now appears farther off than ever.

General Grant, our department commander, is a remarkably plain, unostentatious kind of man. Whenever he visits a camp he is generally dressed in a plain fatigue uniform and accompanied by only one orderly. Orders from his headquarters are always very brief and to the point. Every word and action from him plainly means work and business, as little "red tape" as possible, and no unnecessary flourish nor display. He is a great smoker, and is seldom seen without a cigar in his mouth. Other generals and commanders (and there are scores of them now here) of far lower rank put on all the style they possibly can, dashing around camp in their new uniforms accompanied by a staff of a dozen flashy officers, and issuing windy orders as long as the moral law. Colonel John Cook, our commander at Fort Holt, whose principal characteristics are a long black mustache, long hair, a red smoking cap, and unlimited bluster, and whose signature is as big as a turkey track, cannot order out a fatigue or guard detail without writing a long official letter and making extensive quotations from "army regulations," "articles of war" and previous general and special orders issued from his headquarters.

The river continues rising slowly, the water is now all around and under our cabins. Most of the troops have already left this post. There is a dry sand ridge just in front of our quarters in which the company musters for roll call. The swamp on the east of us is entirely overflowed. There are a few dry spots and sand ridges both above and below, on which our pickets are posted more for ornament than use, as it is as impossible for an enemy to march in now, as for us to march out. Our men have procured several skiffs and canoes, and with these and some small rafts, are rowing and paddling all about camp and through the timber. We are well-supplied with new Sibley tents and all hands are anxious to "go ashore."

Yesterday, February 8th, I went on board the ironclad *Louisville* commanded by Captain Dove of the Regular Navy. The captain said he had reason to believe some rebel gunboats were coming up that night and he was going down a short distance to wait for and interview them, and invited me if I wished to witness a naval engagement at night, to accompany him, which invitation I gladly accepted, as I had long wished to see a gunboat fight.

I took supper with the captain and after dark the boat steamed slowly down the river about three miles and came to anchor. No lights were shown nor bells struck all night. I laid down without undressing on a sofa in the captain's cabin, ready to jump up at the first shot. The night, however, passed quietly, no rebel fleet appearing, and early next morning the *Louisville* returned to her anchorage off Fort Holt, when I went ashore in the captain's gig.

Captain Dove I found to be a very pleasant, very fussy, and very particular old bachelor, as regular and systematic about everything as a well-regulated clock. He would occupy a certain number of minutes eating his meals and a certain number of seconds picking his teeth after each meal. His teeth must be picked just so long, whether there was anything between them to be picked out or not. He would promenade on deck at a certain minute, and after taking his regular number of steps, would return to his cabin where his steward would have his little glass of wine awaiting him. His every act and movement was so severely exact and systematic that I almost thought the old man was run by some concealed machinery and wound up every morning, and everything about his cabin was so severely nice and correct, that I felt in a strain all the time I was with him and was glad to get once more in my own quarters where I could spit on the floor and put my feet on the table and "enjoy life."

Grant has taken Fort Henry, the most of the enemy escaped to Fort Donelson. I recently saw the rebel flag captured at Fort Henry. It looked like quite a new flag, the colors being very bright, and was the regular "stars and bars" of the "Confederacy." It was flying under the Union flag on the jack staff of a steamer.

Troops keep leaving here as the water rises until our two companies of cavalry and the battery in the fort are all that are left. The fort is yet dry, but we are nearly drowned out. We stayed in our cabins until the water came up through the floor, when we evacuated and pitched our tents on a dry sand ridge two miles above the fort, where there are also a few companies of infantry and a battery of six pieces of the 2nd Illinois Artillery. Our present encampment is called "Camp Paine" after General Paine, at present commanding the District of Cairo, in which we are included.[3] Lieutenant Colonel W. L. Duff, 2nd Illinois Artillery, is commanding the camp. All are anxious to hear news from Fort Donelson. It was rumored here yesterday that Grant and the gun boats had been repulsed, but we don't believe it.

It is very stupid and dull here. The whole country is overflowed, so as to effectually prevent all scouting and raiding. We have no room to drill or parade, and it is difficult to find dry spots enough on which to post pickets. Yesterday, the water, if it did not fall, at least ceased to rise. It was also the coldest day we have had this winter. Snow fell to the depth of two inches, but with our new Sibley tents and stoves, we are very comfortable.

February 18, 1862, the battle of Fort Donelson has been fought and won.[4] Great numbers of rebel prisoners passed down the Ohio and up the Mississippi today. They are all very poorly clad. A few have coats or jackets, but none have overcoats, and to protect themselves from the weather, which is cold and stormy, they wear blankets of all colors, bed quilts, floor cloths, and pieces of carpet. Generals Pillow and Floyd, after striking their flag and surrendering, both escaped before our troops occupied. The rebel prisoners are much enraged at the conduct of their generals and say they would have shot them both, had they known they (the generals) intended to escape after surrendering them (the soldiers). It is said a number of shots were actually fired at the retreating generals by their own men.[5]

This morning, February 18th, we received official notice from General Paine that Governor Yates, ex-Governor Wood, Secretary of State Hatch, and other honorable gentlemen had arrived in Cairo, and all officers were required to call on them at the St. Charles Hotel. I went over with Captain Delano and Lieutenant Catlin, and together with some fifty or sixty officers of all ranks, was presented to the governor and other honorables, with a number of whom I was already acquainted. Messrs. Hatch and Dubois were old acquaintances of my father.[6] I also had the pleasure of meeting at the same time Jackson Grimshaw, Captain Virgil Ralston, Dr. Stahl, Colonel Tilson, and others of Quincy.

Very heavy firing has been heard today from the direction of Columbus. It is reported that the rebels are evacuating that fort, which is what I have anticipated. By the fall of Forts Donelson and Henry, their line has been broken and as we could now go around and occupy the river below Columbus, this boasted "Gibraltar" no longer possesses any military value. I don't know why they should be firing their heavy guns today unless to expend what ammunition they cannot take away with them.

Yesterday, February 22nd, we were ordered to report to General Paine at Cairo the serviceable force of our company, amount of ammunition on hand, condition of arms, etc. This sounds like business, and as if we had work laid out for us.

The river, which had fallen at least fifteen feet, commenced rising again last week and tonight is up to its former mark and still rising. A rise of about three feet more will drive or float us off the sacred sand of Kentucky, and it can't come any too soon for us. Although we have had rather an easy and comfortable time here, I am tired of scouting so often over the same country and seeing nothing but the same monotonous sand and swamp and canebrakes.

Troops and transports continue to arrive at Cairo, Mound City, Paducah, and other points. The war in northern Missouri being now virtually over, all movements have a southern tendency. As it is morally certain that we must sooner or later be borne down with the mighty army of the North, which after months of preparation, has now begun like an avalanche to sweep down and over the doomed South, we are anxious to be up and doing. Not that I am spoiling for a fight, but as we must go farther south, I wish to go before the hot summer weather begins. I dread the effects of a Southern summer on our men more than I do the fire of the enemy. If we go south in the spring, I think we can stand it better than if we should go in the mid-summer.

This morning, March 4th, we were awakened by the camp guard and read with pleasure an order from General Paine for us to proceed by steamboat to Bird's Point and thence to Charleston, Missouri, with camp equipage and two days' rations. The two days' rations clause looked as if only a short scout was intended, but we know we would never be ordered to take tents for a two days' scout, and we at once concluded that it meant goodbye to old Fort Holt, and in consequence, although there were a number on the sick list, not a man was found unable for duty.

Weaver the bugler was aroused and reveille sounded. As the shrill notes of the bugle sounded in the clear morning air at that unusual hour, the men hastily tumbled out without much regard to toilet, and in a very few minutes the line was formed. Roll was called and the order read when, with merry shouts, the boys began preparing breakfast and packing up. Tents and blankets were rolled, mess kits boxed or bagged, and by five o'clock the horses were saddled and all ready for the boat, which with the characteristic unreliability of steamboats generally, put in an appearance at about twelve o'clock. We embarked at once, but for some unknown cause did not get off until about four o'clock, when we bid a final—though by no means sorrowful—farewell to Fort Holt and all its surroundings.

We landed in Missouri about five miles above Bird's Point, where we encamped to wait for our baggage, which was to come over on another boat that night, but which of course did not arrive until ten o'clock the next morning. General Paine was doubtless familiar with the movements of these steamboat men and so, considerately, ordered us to start with two days' rations for a voyage across the Mississippi River.

We struck camp and started for Charleston about noon. For the first three or four miles, the road was very muddy, but the balance of the way, the road ran along the banks of a lake on a dry sand ridge, hard and smooth as a turnpike. Nearly all the houses on our line of march were deserted, but sometimes we saw women and children, but no men. The men had either joined the rebel army or run away, leaving their places to care for themselves or go uncared for. We passed through several large fields of old corn yet ungathered. We pitched our tents on a vacant lot in Charleston about two o'clock Wednesday afternoon, March 5th.

Charleston is situated in the middle of a level prairie about four miles across. It is a small, but very pretty village, and before the war was a flourishing business town. The streets are wide and straight and the houses well-built, many of them with neat and well-kept yards and gardens. There are two churches, one yet unfinished, a good courthouse, hotel, several large business houses, and a log jail. It is, or rather was, before the days of martial law, the county seat of Mississippi County. Our camp is directly opposite the banking house that was robbed by Jeff Thompson and his bushwhackers last summer about the time we were marching through Missouri from Ironton to Cape Girardeau. There are but two stores in town doing business; all the other stores, shops, and many of the best dwellings are empty or filled with U.S. soldiers or army supplies. A company of the 2nd Iowa Cavalry is quartered in the courthouse, and the largest of the two churches is used for a hospital. A railroad train runs to and from Bird's Point once a day.

A few miles out of town is the residence of one Swank, a lieutenant in Jeff Thompson's gang. Learning from an "intelligent contraband" one night that Swank was in the habit of occasionally visiting his family and was expected home that night, I went out with a small squad of our men, accompanied by Lieutenant Hollinger of the 26th Missouri Infantry, for the purpose of taking in Lieutenant Swank, should his love for his wife induce him to run the risk of visiting her that night. Swank enjoyed the reputation of being a lawless desperado, as ugly in nature as in name, and I instructed my men if they found him to take him, alive if possible, but any way, to take him. I aroused the family and searched the house, but found no Swank. His wife said she didn't know where he was, but supposed he was taking good care of himself somewhere. Anyhow, she knew he wasn't fool enough to come poking around home with the country full of Yankee soldiers. On being closely cross-questioned, the darkey from whom I had my information admitted that he didn't know anything about "Massa Swank" himself but got his information from "some of them other niggers." Some of the negroes bring in truthful and valuable information, but many more run to camp with every wild story they hear.

We stayed at Charleston, scouting and picketing, but without any event of interest until Tuesday morning, March 11th, when in obedience to orders from General Paine, we struck camp and marched to Sikeston.

I should have mentioned before that when our troops first took possession of Charleston, they found and took charge of the printing office, finding a good supply of type, ink, and paper, and there being plenty of printers among the soldiers, they at once established a daily paper. As there were plenty of contributors for its columns, and as everything offered was printed, it presented a very mixed and spicy assortment of reading matter. The paper, while it lasted, had a large gratuitous circulation and many copies were sent north by the soldiers. I found and captured in the printing office a small head cut of "Jefferson Davis, our first President."

The short road to Sikeston we were told was impassable, and the long one around the swamps nearly so, to the truth of which latter statement I could testify. We shipped all our freight and baggage by the railroad, and even then found the empty wagons heavy enough before we got through. For a few miles the road was good enough, but we soon came to the swamp, where we found the supply of mud and water abundant. Sometimes we would ride for two or three miles through water from six inches to three feet deep, then come to a corduroy road, much broken and worse than the mud.

The monotony of the ride was relieved by frequent beds of quicksand or "sink holes," into which a horse or team would plunge almost out of sight. My horse got into several of these holes, sometimes up to his shoulders, and floundered about in the mud until he looked like a clay model of an equestrian statute. We worried through, however, and finally reached Sikeston about four o'clock in the afternoon.

The village, if such it can justly be called, of Sikeston or Sikestown, is situated in a small flat prairie surrounded by heavily-timbered swamps, and consists of some seven or eight small houses and a name made notorious by having been for some time the headquarters of Jeff Thompson. Mr. Sikes, the father of the abortion that bears his name, still lives, or rather stays, here. We pitched our camp immediately in front of and near his house, and a short distance from the railroad station. In Mr. Sikes's front yard we found three one-pounder cannons that had been captured from Jeff Thompson in a skirmish a short time before, and thrown there by our troops after being spiked and dismantled.

General Pope, who passed through Sikeston a few days before we arrived with 20,000 men, has invested New Madrid, about twenty miles further south, and planted heavy batteries commanding Fort Thompson (rebel) and the river both above and below.[7] This will render the evacuation of Columbus inevitable (it was not evacuated as we supposed at the time of the fall of Donelson). The rebels have heavy works at Island Number 10, about ten miles above New Madrid, to which place they will probably move from Columbus for a last desperate struggle for control of the lower Mississippi.

It is reported by messengers from New Madrid that General Pope would open the siege today, March 12th, and we may expect to hear the thunder of his artillery at any moment. A large number of twenty-four-pounder guns went down from here last night, and this morning a long train, including our three company wagons, went down loaded with shot and shell, escorted by Captain Delano with about 100 cavalry. Four companies of the 16th Illinois Infantry arrived here this morning by railroad and immediately started for New Madrid.

General Pope, it is reported, has now more cavalry than he can use and no forage, Jeff Thompson having consumed or destroyed all the forage in the country, so I see no prospect of our being sent to New Madrid. At noon today we heard a few heavy guns from the south. The curtain has been rung up and the play commenced. One after another, as our troops assail them, do the rebels' strongholds fall. It is only a question of time with New Madrid, and all their other forts and strongholds, for sooner or later, fall they must.

It was reported this morning, March 13th, that both Columbus and Island Number 10 were evacuated. If the rebels leave the island, they must abandon their boats and go across the country, which I don't think they can do on account of the high water. The firing yesterday was only to get the range of our guns, which I suppose the gunners got all right, as heavy and incessant firing has been heard all day.

This morning, Friday, March 14th, an order came from Captain Delano, who had taken but a few of his own company with him, for the rest of the company to join him immediately at New Madrid. We gladly struck camp and started for the scene of action, the heavy firing growing plainer as we approached. We reached General Pope's camp three miles from New Madrid about 4pm, by which time, however, the firing had ceased. We found Captain Delano and were placed on the extreme left of the army under General Gordon Granger, commanding the cavalry.

This was the largest camp I had yet seen. The army consisted of about 30,000 men, of whom 2,000 were cavalry.[8] The camp, forming an arc of a circle, was about a half-mile wide by three miles long, almost a solid field of tents. Fort Thompson in New Madrid was in plain view. It was rumored that the rebels were then evacuating by way of the river, but I could learn nothing positive. I could not see any flag on the fort. Troops were continually marching to and from the trenches, a line of which nearly encircled the rebel works, and which were constantly growing closer, from which our sharpshooters could pick off the rebel gunners.

It soon turned out that Captain Delano's order for us to come to New Madrid was premature and issued on his own responsibility, for no sooner had we pitched our tents and begun to feel tolerably comfortable, congratulating ourselves on our escape from Sikeston, when an order was received from headquarters directing us to return to Sikeston. The nature of the order admitted of no delay, and in a few minutes the company was en route for Sikeston. The captain looked, and doubtless felt, not a little mortified and provoked. He is always very impatient of the inactivity and restraint of camp or garrison life. He wants to do, or at least to undertake, much more than properly belongs to an officer of no higher rank than captain.

This part of Missouri is called the "Spanish Grant," and the road between Sikeston and New Madrid called the "King's Road," it having been laid out many years ago by order of the king of Spain when this part of the country belonged to that government.[9] The road is perfectly straight the whole distance. It is piked, and where necessary, corduroyed. The corduroy is much worn and broken, making the road, in places, very rough. Almost 200 government teams pass daily over it, and it is in consequence much cut up.

Much of this country that is not too swampy is cultivated. Great quantities of corn, and nothing else, is raised. At nearly every house were large cribs filled with corn. The report that Jeff Thompson had destroyed all the forage certainly did not apply to the country between Sikeston and New Madrid. I have seldom, if ever, seen so much corn in the same extent of country elsewhere. No hay is raised and very little wheat or oats; the swamps and canebrakes furnish abundant pasturage at all seasons.

Columbus having been evacuated by the rebels, who have moved all their troops and much of their stores and heavy ordnance to Island Number 10, the Mississippi River is now open to the last-named place. Slowly but surely are we crowding them into their "last ditch" in which they say they are going to die. The sooner they find that celebrated "last ditch" and crawl into it and do their dying, the sooner will the war be over, for it will never be over so long as a single armed rebel lives. As Island

Number 10 is reported to be strongly fortified and well-defended on the Kentucky shore as well as on the island, and as there is now no road open for their escape, they will doubtless make a desperate stand there, or surrender.

I learned from a messenger who passed through here today, March 17th, from Cairo en route to New Madrid that a fleet of gunboats and mortar flats had started down the river to invest Island Number 10.

Business has evidently commenced at the island as heavy firing, sounding like mortars, was heard all last night and today, March 18th. Although we are between twenty-five and thirty miles from the scene of action, the firing of the heavy guns and mortars can be heard distinctly when the wind is favorable.

We are occupying as company headquarters at Sikeston a small frame house, lately used by the rebel general Jeff Thompson for his headquarters. This is just now a post of considerable importance, being the terminus of the railroad from Cairo, and all supplies for Pope's army are here transferred and hauled to New Madrid by wagons. The country about here is almost entirely deserted; although our men are scouting continually, we seldom see any traces of the rebels, nor of anybody else.

The country between here and Charleston and between here and New Madrid is well-settled, and I have become acquainted with many of the natives, with whom our men do a good deal of trading, exchanging their surplus rations of coffee, tea, rice, salt, etc., for milk, eggs, butter, and vegetables.[10] While visiting at houses in the country, I observed that the coffee served at the table was very deficient, both in color and taste, and the remark was frequently made by the old ladies that the coffee they obtained from the soldiers was not near so good as that they used to buy at the stores. I always insisted that all of our rations were of the very best quality and attributed the fault to their lack of knowledge of the culinary art. I soon ascertained that the old ladies had just grounds for complaint. The soldiers, always with an eye to business, had solved a knotty problem by the discovery that they could both use and sell the same coffee by boiling it without grinding, and after extracting all the strength, spreading the grains in the sun to dry, when it was traded to the unsuspecting natives for "No. 1. Rio" at one dollar per pound. In appearance it was as good as any coffee, but hardly strong enough to stand a second boiling. The other rations could not be "doctored" in this way and were sold in their original condition.

Amongst the stores received here en route to General Pope's army were large quantities of sutlers' stores. The soldiers, although they had at times to work very hard and at all hours of day or night, never complained nor objected to handling government stores, but when they were required to load and unload the private property of the sutlers, it went a good deal against the grain. Well knowing, however, that it would do no good to complain or refuse to work, they resolved to pay themselves for this extra labor, which they did by levying a special tax on all sutlers' goods handled at night. As the collection of taxes had necessarily to be done somewhat hurriedly, they were unable to make as careful a selection of articles as they would probably have done in daylight and under other circumstances. They managed, however, by strict economy and attention to business, to save many little articles that contributed in various ways to their comfort and convenience. Tobacco, cigars, canned fruit, cheese, boxes of crackers, baskets of wine (the latter "imported" expressly for the use of the staff), and many other little items found their way to the soldiers' quarters. Mistakes on the part of the collector, however, occasionally occurred. One night a barrel marked "claret" and a barrel marked "ginger cakes" were levied on and safely transferred to safe quarters. Having finished their work for the night, and desiring a lunch before turning in, the boys opened their treasures, when they made the mortifying discovery that their "wine" barrel contained a thousand (more or less) small bottles of ink, and the "ginger cake" barrel proved to be filled with matches; both very good articles in their way and place, but not at all appropriate to this particular occasion. The simple facts of the case I have recorded, but the few side remarks made upon the discovery of the mistake had better be forgotten.

The most distressing calamity that has befallen our company occurred at noon on the 25th of March when Captain Delano was mortally wounded by the accidental discharge of a pistol in his headquarters at Sikeston. I was sick and lying on a cot in the captain's quarters when Lieutenant Catlin entered, and seeing the captain's new pistol (a small Smith and Wesson revolver) hanging on the wall, he took it down and sat on the edge of my cot, holding the pistol between us.

We were examining and admiring the working of its different parts when he remarked, "It is easier on the trigger than mine, I do not like it so well on that account." The words had scarcely passed his lips when his thumb slipped off the hammer and it fell, exploding the cartridge. Captain Delano was sitting at his desk on the opposite side of the room, and not more than ten feet distant, with his back towards us, engaged in conversation with Judge Bennafield, a citizen living near Sikeston.

The pistol was so close to me that the flash of the powder burned my beard. The ball, a very small one no larger than a large buck shot, struck the captain just below the right shoulder blade, passing down and to the left and lodging in the spinal column. He threw up his hands and fell backward over his chair to the floor, exclaiming, "Oh! Oh! My God! I'm killed."

We immediately raised him to a reclining posture and held him in our arms until the arrival of Doctor Kendall, who came in a few minutes accompanied by

Major Thomas Smith, surgeon of the 11th Missouri Infantry (who chanced to be in our camp that day), when we laid him on the cot and removed his clothes. While the doctors were preparing to examine his wound he said, "Men, I am mortally wounded, I know it. Oh God have mercy on my soul." He continued to talk quietly and calmly but still appeared to think his wound was mortal.

The doctors were unable to extract the ball, and decided it would be best to send him to Cairo, for which place he started on the 3pm train, accompanied by Lieutenant Catlin, his brother Decatur Delano, Doctor Kendall, and Sergeant W. G. Gilpin, leaving me in command of the company. Lieutenant Catlin was almost beside himself with grief, but the captain told him not to reproach himself at all, saying, "I attach no blame to you, Lieutenant. It is hard to die thus, but I don't complain, God's will be done." At Cairo, it was decided to send the captain home to Quincy, and Doctor Kendall and Lieutenant Catlin returned to camp that night. I immediately went to Cairo and succeeded in obtaining a leave of absence for thirty days.

Having been up town to make some purchases, I was returning down the levee toward the boat when, just as I was passing a barroom, two men who were fighting inside rushed out into the sidewalk, still fighting. The largest of the two men caught his opponent around the neck from behind with his left arm, and with his right fist was pounding him (the smaller man) in the face and head. In an instant, the small man drew a large bowie knife, at least twelve inches long, and by a quick backward thrust stabbed the other to the heart. The wounded man fell with but one groan, and in less than a minute was dead, the black blood flowing in spurts from his heart.

Although the street was full of men, the whole affair was over before anyone could interfere. Seeing a squad of armed soldiers belonging to the provost guard, I called to them to arrest the murderer. Hearing me order the soldiers to arrest him, the fellow turned quickly and with an oath made a wicked thrust at me with the bloody knife. By quickly dodging aside, I evaded the blow, when he started to run up the street, closely followed by the soldiers.

I waited only long enough to see the fellow caught and on his way to the fort, when I hastened on board the boat and did not show myself on shore again for fear of being detained as a witness. As at least a half-dozen men and one woman (the murderer's wife) witnessed the deed, I knew that my evidence would not be indispensable, and I did not want to miss my trip home with the captain. The murdered man was lying where he fell when I left to go to the boat. I never heard anything more of the affair and know not what was done with the murderer.

Our party, consisting besides the captain of Decatur Delano, Sergeant Gilpin, Doctor Stahl, and myself, started up the river on March 26th, it having been decided that the captain could travel easier on a boat than by railroad. He was carried on board on his cot and laid in the after part of the ladies' cabin, which was kindly placed at our disposal by the captain of the boat. At St. Louis we were obliged to change boats. The captain was carried on his cot from one boat to the other and placed in the ladies' cabin. All the way up the river, from Cairo to Quincy, he was constantly watched and waited on by two of us at a time.

The news of the captain's accident having already reached Quincy, the moment the boat touched the wharf, she was boarded by a large number of his friends and acquaintances, all anxious to see him, and it was with difficulty that I kept them from crowding into the ladies' cabin where he was lying. A sufficient number to carry him were admitted, who took him up on his cot and carried him to the residence of Doctor Nichols on Vermont Street between Seventh and Eighth, followed by a large crowd. The news of the captain's arrival spread through the city, and the house was soon besieged by hundreds of people anxious to see him. So great indeed was the rush, that I was obliged to stop a soldier in the street (there being a good many invalids and recruits in the city at that time) and detail him to stand guard at the door with instructions to admit no one without the doctor's permission.

The captain was at once visited by many of the best physicians in the city, who all agreed that it would be useless to attempt to remove the ball, as an operation would only increase his suffering without at all benefiting him. The shock of the shot had paralyzed his whole body below the wound, and he was never able afterwards to move the lower part of his body or legs. His sufferings were at times very great, but I never heard him utter a word of complaint or regret.

When in fever, he would be delirious; his mind would at times be with his men in camp, calling many by name and giving orders and instructions. At other times, he would see a rebel soldier standing at the foot of his bed who he said was hurting his feet, and would order me to draw my saber and kill or drive him away, nor would he be quiet until I would take my saber and cut and thrust at the imaginary man and drive him out of the room.

He once expressed a desire to see the Stars and Stripes, and a large flag was brought and spread over the top of his bed and allowed to hang down so that he could reach it. After gazing at it a while, he exclaimed, "Oh that I might be spared to fight for you or to die on the field of battle." Then, pressing a fold of it to his face, he wept and kissed it, nor would he permit anyone to remove it, and until his death its bright folds hung a canopy over his bed.

He always appeared to think he must die in the night, he did not seem to think it possible that he could die in the daytime, and frequently on awakening in the early morning, after a restless feverish sleep, he would say, "What, is it morning again? Oh, I hoped and prayed I would die last night, now I must live and suffer through another day."

I was sick a short time with the mumps, but whenever able to do so, I assisted in nursing and watching him, day and night, until my leave of absence was nearly expired, so that I had very little time to spend at home or in visiting friends in the city. I visited the telegraph office nearly every day to learn news from the front. The operator was at first very reticent and would give me but little satisfaction, but when he learned who I was, and my real object in seeking information, he kept me well-posted concerning the movements of our troops.

A few days before I left Quincy, he told me that Pope's army was about moving, but could tell me nothing definite, this much he learned from dispatches passing through his office between the different commanders, and which, knowing that my company belonged to Pope's army, hastened my departure. Besides, in response to my application for an extension of my leave of absence, I was ordered to report to my company without delay.

When I told the captain that I was ordered to return to the company, and that the troops were in motion and I must now leave him, he said, "I am sorry to have you leave me, Lieutenant, for I well know I shall never see you again, but you must go where duty calls you." I expressed a hope that he would recover and return to the command of the company. "No," he replied, "I shall never leave this bed, I know I must die and I hope it will be soon. I suffer so much, kiss me, God bless you. Give my love to all the boys, goodbye." I kissed him goodbye, and never saw him again. A few days after my return to Sikeston, I received a dispatch from Doctor Nichols that he was dead.

I had previously bid my parents and friends a last goodbye, and postponed my parting with the captain until the last. All of my other friends, if I should be spared from the common dangers of war, I should probably see again, but the captain I well knew I should never see again. During the eight months we had served together a warm friendship had grown up between us. I had grown to look up to and love him, and it was with a heavy heart that I left him.

On the afternoon of Thursday, April 24th, accompanied by Sergeant Gilpin and Decatur Delano, I took passage on the steamer *Jeannie Deans* bound for St. Louis. The boat was advertised to leave at 3pm but, with customary steamboat punctuality, did not arrive until about seven o'clock. Having secured our staterooms, we ordered supper, to the great discomfort of the black waiters, who were just beginning to tune their fiddles and guitars for a dance, the regular meal having been cleared away. Being very tired and very hungry, we extended a cordial invitation to them to shut up their complaining and devote their time and attention to our present necessities, and in a few minutes we were refreshing our inner selves with liberal and frequent applications of hot rolls, coffee, and steak.

Supper over, I lit a cigar on strolling out on deck, and I watched the city, the home of my youth, gradually fade away in the dim twilight as the noble packet, walking the broad waters of the Mississippi like a thing of life, rapidly bore its cargo of human freight towards the sunny, war-distracted "land of Dixie." One by one, each well-remembered house was lost from view, then the tall spires of the churches towering towards the clouds and pointing with their iron fingers heavenward silently admonishing us to "look aloft," and as my eyes gazed upon their dim outlines, my heart did "look aloft" and my troubled mind found relief in the contemplation of a bright and happier world above, where friends shall meet to part no more.

On returning to the cabin, I heard sounds of music and found the ladies' cabin in possession of a gay party of dancers. My uniform (I was the only military officer on the boat) at once attracted attention, and I was soon waited upon by a servant with a message from the ladies, presenting their compliments and inviting me to join their party, which kind invitation, however, I declined with regrets and retired to my state room, where I lay for a long time pondering over the events of the past day.

To me it had been a most eventful day in several respects. During the past few hours, events had transpired the memory of which time cannot efface. Thus pondering, I fell asleep and did not awake until the gong rang for breakfast, when hastily dressing, I went out on the guards and found we were in sight of the city of St. Louis, where we landed at seven o'clock, being only eleven hours from Quincy.

The levee of St. Louis appeared almost deserted. The effects of war were here plainly seen. Instead of the huge piles of freight and merchandise and the thousands of busy draymen, laborers, and clerks with which this immense levee was thronged but a year ago, could now be seen but a few sorry-looking draymen lounging around on small piles of sacks or barrels, idly cracking their whips and looking in vain for a job. And instead of the hundreds of splendid steamers that lined the levee for miles a year ago, are now seen scarcely a dozen, and they mostly all small sternwheelers and ferry boats; all the larger boats have been chartered by the government and are engaged in transporting troops and government stores.

After breakfast, we went on shore in search of a down boat, but failing to find any, we went uptown to the office of the master of transportation, where I obtained passes for us all to Cairo on any government boat. After wandering about town a while, we returned to the river and found there one government boat, the captain of which said he expected to leave for Cairo in two or three days. This information, together with the general appearance of the boat, which was small and dirty, had not the effect of encouraging us to any alarming extent, so we concluded to look further in hopes of faring better, and finally secured passage on a neat, modest-looking little boat that had just come down, the *Emma Duncan* commanded by Captain Batchelor. It was twelve o'clock when we went on board, just in time for dinner.

As the captain said he should not start before five o'clock, we planned an extensive tour of observation up town. Among other places of interest, we visited Lafayette Park, where we spent an hour or two very pleasantly, returning to the boat in time for supper. The time for the departure of the boat was again postponed until early the next morning, so that night we all went to the varieties theater and witnessed the play of "Sinbad the Sailor." On going to my state room after supper for my revolver, I discovered that some light-fingered fellow had been there before me and captured it. I at once reported my loss to the captain and made diligent search and inquiry, but failed to hear anything of it.

I went to bed about twelve o'clock, expecting to awake next morning and find myself far down the river towards Cairo, but on looking out, found we had not yet left St. Louis. On going to the captain after breakfast, he informed me he would positively leave at noon, so Gilpin and I made another trip up town. While idly strolling through Washington Market, we most unexpectedly met Mr. E. S. Green and his daughter Fanny of Quincy.

We returned to the boat for dinner (having paid our fare to Cairo, we were careful not to miss a meal), and at half-past one, heard the welcome sound of the mate's voice as he ordered, "Launch in the stage, cast off the line," and the little *Emma* swung around and glided out upon the broad waters of the Mississippi.

It was announced that we were to have a "grand ball" on board that night, and as soon as the supper tables were cleared away, two darkies armed with violin and guitar made their appearance, and after an extravagant display of tuning up their instruments and adjusting themselves to their chairs, proceeded to open up. Before the dance, the darkies entertained the passengers with selections of plantation and war songs, which they sang very well. Dancing was continued until about ten o'clock, when the orchestra, having pocketed all the change they thought there was any chance of getting, disappeared in a sublime cloud of smirks and grimaces.

I spent the evening reading and writing until the dance was over, when quiet being restored, I retired to my state room and in a few minutes was sound asleep. I was awakened by the sound of the breakfast gong, and on going out on the guards looked down into the city of Cairo, at which place we had just arrived; the river being then very high, up to the top of the levee, at least twelve or fourteen feet above the level of the town.

Immediately after breakfast, I went up to headquarters and reported to General Strong, then commanding, who gave me passes to New Madrid on the steamer *Diligent,* which was to leave at noon exactly that day, Sunday, April 27th.[11] The *Diligent* arrived about ten o'clock, when we went on board. Knowing the regular irregularity of steamboats, we registered our names and promptly commenced boarding. As our passes were good for transportation only, we had to pay for our board, and as I always stipulated with the boats to board us to our destination and paid in advance, we did not care how long they kept us so that they fed us well. The departure of the *Diligent* was postponed from time to time until two o'clock the next afternoon (Monday) when we finally got away. As the railroad from Bird's Point to Sikeston was overflowed, our only way of reaching the lower place was by the way of New Madrid.

As we passed the place where once stood Fort Holt, I looked in vain for the long row of cabins our company built there last fall, and in which we lived all winter. Not a vestige of them remained. The bank of the river, which last summer was ten or twelve feet high, was now as many feet under water. Nothing remained to show that the place was ever inhabited, save here and there the bare ridge pole of some cabin that chanced to stand a little higher or to have been stronger-built than its fellows. The fort and everything else was entirely gone.

At Bird's Point, on the opposite side of the river, the scenery was much the same, except that a few more cabin ridge poles could be seen, as the water was not quite so deep as at Fort Holt. At one place on the point, where a sand ridge came nearly to the surface of the water, could be seen the tops of a few white boards marking the spots where some brave sons of the North had found their last resting places. Here unknown and almost uncared for, had they found graves in a strange land! With none to watch over and care for them and whisper kind words of comfort in their dying ears, none to minister to their wants but their rude, though perhaps kind, fellow soldiers, and even by them to be soon forgotten in the changes and excitement of war. There they died and were buried, a volley was fired over their graves, their names dropped from the company roll and entered on the long list of "Died at Bird's Point."

Those few white boards standing alone there in the water told a long silent tale of suffering and heartaches. I thought not so much of the body that lay there moldering in the mud, but of the hardships and sufferings that that body, ere it parted from the soul, once endured. The pains and aches, both of body and mind, the agonizing thoughts that filled his fevered brain, as on his death bed in some cheerless tent or hospital, he remembered his once happy home in the North, where, all unconscious of his sufferings, were those who to him were perhaps dearer than life and where he was perhaps a loved husband, father, or son. How they look in vain for some tidings from that brave young soldier, who a few months ago left them in the full strength and vigor of manhood, to fight the battles of his country in the cause of right and justice and against treason and rebellion. How long after his accustomed letters ceased to arrive did they anxiously read through the long list of killed and wounded that appear after every battle, hoping yet dreading thereby to learn some tidings of him? But his name is not there and they hope he still lives and will someday return to them. In the official monthly report of the hospital where he died, will they someday learn his fate. He has served his time out here and has reported at headquarters on high, where his name now stands recorded with the countless numbers on the rolls of the grand army of the past, awaiting the sounding of the reveille for the last grand muster.

After leaving Cairo and its surroundings, the next place of interest we came to is the well-remembered battlefield of Belmont, where on November 7th last, our little army of 2,700 fought for more than seven hours against more than four times their number of rebels, and held their own, and a good deal of the enemy's, until worn out with fatigue and overpowered by superior numbers, they were compelled to retreat and seek the protection of the gunboats.[12] The battlefield is now five or six feet under water.

Passing around a short bend in the river, we found ourselves opposite the celebrated fortifications and town of Columbus, Kentucky, now garrisoned by a small force of Union troops. From the top of a high bluff of hard white clay or chalk and brown sandstone known as the "Iron Banks," hangs the broken iron chain cable that the rebels had stretched across the river to catch "Yankee gunboats." Some of the guns still remain mounted in their batteries, but most of them were thrown down or rolled into the river by the rebels when they evacuated the place soon after the fall of Fort Donelson, February 16, 1862.

A few miles above Island Number 10, we passed a small, neat-looking brick house, entirely surrounded by water. On the porch in front of the house were collected some fifteen or more negroes of all ages and colors, from the huge field hand, black as midnight, to the little "white washed" pickaninny, not much larger than a toad. As we passed, they all began waving their hats and aprons. The captain of our boat, seeing they were surrounded by water, and supposing from their actions that they were in distress, sounded his whistle, rounded to, and in a few minutes was lying "on and off" a few hundred yards from the house, as near as he could get for the trees.

As soon as the boat stopped, a big negro put off in a skiff, which he propelled among the trees in a furious current with the care of an experienced whaler. When near enough, the captain hailed him, "What's the matter here?" "Oh dar ain't noffin der matter wid us Sar," shouted the darkey, resting on his oars. "What do you want then?" "Oh we don't want noffin Sar." "What did you hail the boat for then?" "Do what Sar?" shouted the darkey, evidently not comprehending the last question. "What did you wave your hats for when we passed?" shouted the captain, getting red in the face, and beginning to wax wrathy. "Oh Lord, Massa we gist did that cause we're all so mighty glad to see you'uns all." At this, all the passengers on the boat, who had been attentive listeners to this conversation, shouted and laughed heartily, which rather had the effect of increasing the captain's anger. The darkey, who had been drifting down stream all this time, now applied himself to his oars, and was soon again alongside the steamer, prepared to resume the interview. As soon as he could make himself heard above the laughter and side remarks of the passengers, the captain again shouted, as the boat began to swing around in the stream, "See here you black rascal, don't you try that again unless you want help." "Do what, Sar?" came faintly across the water as the darkey again rested on his oars. The boat having now swung completely around, we proceeded on our way down the river, the group of negroes on the porch of "Massa's" otherwise-deserted mansion waving us a fond farewell.

A few miles farther on, we came in sight of Island Number 10, one of the most celebrated places in the history of the war. From the hurricane deck of the steamer, I could overlook the entire scene. On the left, on the Tennessee shore, now completely overflowed, is a heavy "water battery," so called on account of its being situated (when built) nearly on a level with the river. Nothing could now be seen to show that it ever existed but the long black barrels of about a half-dozen heavy cannon, which at a distance looked as if they were floating on the water.

These are the guns that were spiked by a party of marines from the U.S. gunboats one stormy night during the celebrated siege of this post. It was a daring, dangerous undertaking, but was accomplished without loss on our side, and the death of but one rebel sentinel, and resulted in the silencing of one of the enemy's most formidable and troublesome batteries.[13]

Our little steamer now took the course traversed by the gunboat *Carondelet* the night she ran the rebel blockade. On each side of us, on the Tennessee shore and on the island, were long rows of heavy artillery, poking their grim black muzzles over the earthworks, and frowning upon us as if they only wanted the active assistance of a few rebels behind them to blow us out of the water. But as they could do no harm alone, and their late owners were not there to assist them, we passed safely and quietly through the once-strongest blockade on the western waters.

I counted on the Kentucky shore, six, and on the island, three batteries, some of which were quite extensive and all well made. There were also extensive works, heavily mounted, on the Tennessee shore. The many downed trees and broken earthworks on the island bore evidence to the warmth of the conflict lately witnessed here.

The natural advantage of the place, the short peculiar bend in the river, and the high island in the channel, improved by skillful engineering, combined to make this a most formidable and almost impregnable position. It was bravely defended, but in a wicked, unjust cause, and it fell, as others had fallen and all must fall, before the slow, steady march of the army of the Union, that like an immense avalanche is grinding and crushing all before it. The post of Island Number 10 is now garrisoned by a regiment of Wisconsin infantry. We did not stop here.

I found the town of New Madrid almost entirely inundated, we were obliged to wade knee-deep in water from the wharf boat to the camp of a battalion of the 1st Illinois Cavalry. I thought at first of starting out at once to walk to Sikeston, but as the day was already far spent, and there were indications of an approaching storm, I concluded to hunt a hole for the night. I hunted up Captain Burrell of Company H, 1st Illinois Cavalry, and offered him an opportunity of showing his hospitality by feeding and lodging a hungry, tired, and dirty fellow soldier, which he gladly and kindly did, my comrades finding accommodations with his men.

The next morning, April 29th, I borrowed a pony from Captain Burrell and rode to Sikeston with a young lieutenant going up with an escort of fifteen men for a load of ammunition. We left New Madrid about eight o'clock, arriving at Sikeston at noon. I found everything here about the same as when I left, except that it was much more quiet and lonesome. General Pope's army having left New Madrid, and the railroad from Cairo being abandoned on account of the high water, there is no freighting, nor travel of any kind. All our freight and mail now comes and goes by way of New Madrid.

On May 3rd, I received a telegram from Doctor Nichols stating that Captain Delano died Sunday, April 27th. Lieutenant Catlin was just preparing to go out to drill the company when I showed him the dispatch. He immediately wrote and pinned to the door of his tent: "The Captain is dead, there will be no drill today." He was very deeply affected, and for the remainder of the day kept close within his tent. Since my return to camp he had often spoken very feelingly of the sad event, taking it very much to heart and continuing to blame himself by his carelessness for being the cause of the captain's death; notwithstanding I repeatedly assured him that the captain attached no blame to him, but on the contrary, always spoke in the highest terms of him. But Catlin was a man of a very delicate and refined nature, and the mental suffering that he endured, I feel assured, far exceeded all the bodily pains and sufferings of the captain. He also feared that the men looked upon him unkindly, and it was long before he could be convinced to the contrary. He was for months very reticent and melancholy, spending much of his time in his tent or riding alone.

Lieutenant Catlin, having waived his right of promotion to the commission of captain, has decided to leave the choice to the men, and has ordered an election to be held on Tuesday, May 6th. Considerable log rolling and debating has been going on for some time among the men in a quiet way. Hearing my name mentioned in connection with the office, I plainly told the men I would rather serve as first lieutenant under Catlin, and wished to see him promoted to the command of the company, well knowing him to be the most competent man for that responsible position. But, my friends insisting upon the use of my name, I consented to become a candidate, although I honestly thought my chances of election were very few. Although myself a candidate, I urged the election of Catlin and finally voted for him. I knew he would make an excellent commander, and I would have been glad to serve under him.

At an election held in camp on May 6th, I was elected by a small majority over Lieutenant Catlin. Although Catlin, I think, desired and expected the office, he at once cheerfully gave me his hand and pledged me his earnest support and assistance in the discharge of my new and responsible duties. Sergeant John Cayton was at the same time elected to my late position as second lieutenant. Although Catlin and the men wished me to at once assume command, I decided not to do so until I should receive my commission from Governor Yates of Illinois.

As a sample of the intelligence(?) of the natives of this benighted portion of our boasted "free and enlightened country," I would mention an incident that recently occurred here. Lieutenant Catlin had occasion to hold a court of inquiry for the trial of a young man charged with the commission of a very delicate civil offense, and out of fourteen witnesses examined, both men and women, only seven could write their names, and the names when written could not be read. This is one of the evils of the accursed system of slavery. The rulers and leaders, who are the few intelligent and educated, find it much easier to lead and rule the masses if they are kept in ignorance. It is dangerous for the poor whites, as well as for the negroes, to know how to read, for a man who can read is very apt to think, and a man who thinks for himself cannot generally be easily beaten, cowed, and led like a bear by the nose. The education of these people would result in the downfall of the power of the masters. Education of the negroes is forbidden by law, and is denied or withheld from the poor whites, for the reason that it is dangerous.

Our duties now consisted almost entirely of picket and scouting, with an occasional trip to New Madrid for supplies. We see no enemy, except wood ticks and mosquitoes, with which we have frequent bloody skirmishes. The bushes appear to be alive with ticks, which fall off on us while riding through the woods, and which are very annoying both to us and our horses. The mosquitoes are truly awful, the largest and most ravenous I think I ever saw. They are so troublesome that calves, colts, and other young stock grazing in the swamps and canebrakes are nearly starved to death. I am told that young animals often die from annoyance, starvation, and the poison of the stings of the insects, and that deer are frequently forced by them to leave the cover of the swamps and seek the open fields.

About this time, a little incident occurred, which for a time seemed to break the monotony of camp life a little. I had been informed by one of our secret patrols that one of our neighbors, Joe Edwards, living some three or four miles from camp, was in the habit of carrying provisions into the west swamp two or three times a week at night. This confirmed me in the belief that a band of rebel deserters or guerillas were lurking in the swamp. Having ascertained what night the fellow would go out again, I started out about sundown for the swamp with ten men, dismounted. When near the place where I expected he would pass, I began posting my men within hailing distance of each other.

Having posted all, I was going to the corner of a field with Corporal Sexton, when we unexpectedly came upon two men sitting on the fence. The surprise was mutual, neither party seeing the other until we were within ten feet of each other. The men were sitting with their feet on opposite sides of the fence. The one with his feet towards us was the first to speak. Half turning towards us, he summoned up courage as soon as his first scare was over to say, "Good even.'" "Good evening, gentlemen," I replied, "are you out coon hunting tonight?" "Waal, yeas," he answered, hesitatingly, as if undecided whether he was hunting or hunted. "So are we, and I guess we've found our game." The words were scarcely out of my mouth when he slipped off the fence and darted off like a rocket. Disregarding my command to halt, Sexton fired at him with his carbine, and the next instant, was over the fence and in full chase, firing with his revolver at every jump. But the retreater was young and active as a rabbit, and ran so fast and crooked that the old corporal could neither catch nor shoot him, and he succeeded in making good his escape.

The other fence bird, a boy of about fifteen, proved to be a regular "swamp rat" of the most ignorant kind. He didn't know anything, never did, and never expected to. A little plain talk, however, with occasional allusions to shooting or hanging, had the happy effect of so far brightening his ideas that he was enabled to discover two sacks hidden in the bushes nearby, containing a lot of bacon, bread, a pail of lard, coffee, coffee pot, cup, griddle, a pack of meal, etc.—at least six days' rations. It had all been prepared with great care, and everything was as nice and clean as possible. The boy persisted in the assertion that he only came to help Joe bring the things, but did not know who they were for. A few minutes after our firing, I heard a gun far off in the swamp, and one of the soldiers saw a rocket go up in the same direction. Knowing that the enemy had become alarmed, and would not call for his rations that night, I returned to camp. There are doubtless passes through the swamp, which our scouts have failed to discover, leading to "islands" or ridges, where these fellows are probably encamped. They are believed to be stragglers or deserters from Jeff Thompson or the rebel army lately at New Madrid.

The next day, May 13th, while out scouting in the swamp, I found an old man, Mr. William Brown, with a rifle, who said he was out deer hunting. He had always passed amongst us for an honest, loyal man, and I did not doubt that he was then out on an honest deer hunt, but I was afraid some bushwhackers might find him and perhaps take his gun away from him, and so invited him to accompany me to camp and see the boys. Lieutenant Catlin put him through the regulation catechism, administered the oath, took away his rifle—for fear, we told him, some of the soldiers might steal it from him. He took it all in good part, and in return invited Catlin and me to dine at his house the next day, Sunday. He is a sharp old fox and may be loyal and may be not. He wants, however, to keep on the right side of the soldiers, but I guess we understand that game as well as he does. We dined with him the next day and had a very pleasant time. He has a nice place and is said to be a man of considerable means. Although possessing very little education, he is far superior in every respect to anyone I have yet seen in this land of Egyptian (mental) darkness. He is an everlasting talker, is always wound up, and it is only necessary to start him and he will run alone as long as there is anyone to listen. His favorite topic, and one in which he is perfectly at home, is the "Shakes" (the earthquakes) that have occurred here with more or less violence every year or two since the great quake of 1811, at which time New Madrid and the neighboring towns were nearly destroyed.[14]

The weather is becoming very hot and dry, and the ground—much of which was recently under water—is nearly baked. Having no thermometer, we don't know how hot the weather really is. The "Swamp Rats" say, "it's gist aginnin to git warm." We dare not seek the shelter of the timber on account of the ticks and mosquitoes, which wage a constant and bloody war against man and beast. Even the wild deer and turkeys have to leave their native haunts in the swamps and seek the open fields to escape the almost fatal attacks of these little blood suckers. The soldiers have built sheds of brush and canes over and in front of their tents, under the shelter of which they manage to enjoy life.

There are a few bears and panthers in the swamps, but they are very seldom seen. I have frequently seen where they have stood up on their hind feet and clawed the trees, the same as the domestic cat will claw a table leg. Wolves are quite plentiful and can be heard howling any night, but they do little harm beyond killing a few sheep, and occasionally a calf or pig. Although the days are so uncomfortably hot, the nights are quite cool and pleasant. The health of the company, notwithstanding the heat and overflow in the swamps, is excellent, not more than a half-dozen being on the sick list at any one time, and none of them so sick but that they can't take their rations.

Among the few acquaintances worth remembering that I made at Sikeston is Mr. Austin and his interesting family, the most interesting part of which was Miss Suzy. He had a very pretty place a few miles from camp, where I found it convenient to call frequently, and was always welcome and kindly entertained. I called thus one day and found the whole family in sore affliction occasioned by the swarming of the bees, which had lodged in an apple tree, and were preparing to migrate. All except Miss Suzy were afraid to go near the swarm of buzzing angry little insects, and she could do nothing alone. Having no fear of bees before my eyes, I volunteered my assistance. While Miss Suzy held the hive, I cut off the branch on which the bees were hanging, and shook them into it, and we soon had the satisfaction of seeing them all safely hived and going about their accustomed occupation of "gathering honey all the day, etc." Soldiers are proverbially fond of honey and our messes are seldom without a supply. In saving Mr. Austin's swarm, I perhaps acted a little selfishly, for I felt that the country could not afford to lose that swarm and its prospective supply of honey.

With Mr. Sikes I had very little acquaintance, notwithstanding he lived but a few rods from camp, in fact a little too near for his own profit or conscience, as some of the men contracted the habit of milking his cows and visiting his hen house at most unreasonable hours of the night. He was a cross, quaint sort of a man, not at all kindly disposed towards Yankee soldiers, who, he appears to think, should be required to subsist on a less luxurious diet than milk and eggs. I never was in his house, but he had frequent occasions to visit company headquarters on official business, in the transaction of which our soldiers and his cows, hens, and garden were prominent features. The old gentleman became quite annoying and disagreeable by reason of his many complaints and much fault-finding. I was finally obliged to tell the boys it was naughty of them to annoy the old gentleman so and they must behave better, which latter they promised to try to do. To oblige Mr. Sikes they would try to drink their coffee without milk. I don't think, however, that any of them choked themselves with trying.

On Saturday, May 17th, we received orders to report immediately with camp and garrison equipage to Colonel Ryan, commanding at New Madrid. This was a most welcome order, as we had become heartily sick and tired of Sikeston. We struck camp and marched out at 1pm, and about six o'clock pitched our camp near the walls of Fort Thompson, about a mile south of the town of New Madrid. The fort is quite large and well-built of earth and sand. Many of its guns have been dismounted, its present armament consisting of only six guns, twenty-four and thirty-two pounders. It was named after the rebel General M. Jeff Thompson.

Nearby are the trenches, dug by the 10th and 16th Illinois Infantry, and from which they operated on the rebel gunners during the siege. I picked up a piece of shell near the trenches that had been sent there with the compliments of Fort Thompson.

On the 24th of May, the paymaster made us a most welcome visit, leaving as mementoes of his visit sundry "green backs" to the amount of about $9,000, being four months pay due our company to the 1st of May. The most of the money was sent home by express, the men retaining only sufficient to supply themselves with certain little conveniences as tobacco, stationery, postage, seven-up, etc., articles not included in the supplies furnished by the quartermaster or commissary.

The river is now open to Memphis, Tennessee. Boats are continually passing up and down, occasionally touching here to land stores or mail, but we can learn nothing from them. Our gunboat fleet is somewhere down the river. As the river falls, we find great quantities of balls, shells, muskets, etc. that were thrown into the river by the rebels.

The swamps becoming dryer and more passable as the water falls enables us to do a good deal of scouting. A few miles west of this post is an extensive and very ugly swamp known by the very appropriate name of "Nigger Wool Swamp," so called on account of the great masses of black, tangled moss that cover the tops of stumps and cypress trees, giving them somewhat the appearance of immense nigger heads. The swamp is crossed by many streams, all flowing towards the south, the largest of which is the St. Francis. They are all deep and mirey, with steep banks. Crossing the swamp from west to east is a corduroy road, which we found in a very bad condition, the poles in many places being washed out, and nearly all the bridges either washed away or destroyed by the rebels. The bridge over the St. Francis, which is here quite wide, was burned, so that in our scouting expeditions we were never able to get beyond that river.

One day, while out with about twenty men, I suddenly came upon a small band of bushwhackers, who after firing a few shots, retreated down the corduroy road. They had a few hundred yards the start of us, but I followed in pursuit as fast as I could. The road was in a very bad condition and difficult to travel, but I rode a very powerful and sure-footed horse, my black "Ned." Some of the horses of my squad fell, and others could not be forced to make the dangerous leaps over broken bridges. My horse never flinched, but appearing to enter into the spirit of the chase, leaped every broken bridge, and never once missed his foothold over the worst part of the road.

I followed as fast as I could, occasionally firing a shot from my revolver whenever I could catch a glimpse of the fleeing graybacks, but they being quite familiar with all the passes, knew just when it was safe to leave the corduroy, and by dropping out singly or in small squads, slipped off into the swamp, where it was impossible for us to follow.

By the time I reached the St. Francis River, not a rebel was in sight, but in the mud were tracks where a number of them had taken water and swam across. It was probably very fortunate that I did not overtake them at the river, for on halting, I found I had only two men with me. They were, I think, Corporal Paris and Charley Wilcox. All the rest had fallen far in the rear in the wild race. Our three horses were panting dreadfully, and dismounting, we unsaddled and waited for the rest of my men to come up.

Many refugees are daily arriving at New Madrid from Memphis and vicinity, from which places they are fleeing to escape conscription into the rebel army. A small squad of our men having gone to a house a short distance from town to arrest a couple of tramps, one of the soldiers picked up what appeared to be a roll of manuscript stitched together in the form of a book, and which on examination proved to be the diary of a young lady, running back to the time our troops first made their appearance before New Madrid, and continued down to the date of the book's discovery. She described in a very peculiar gushing style the events of each day, and in the wildest, most passionate and extravagant manner portrays the hopes, fears, and many conflicting emotions that filled her little rebel heart during that short but eventful season of "hard trials and great tribulations."

One day, while standing on the riverbank below camp, I saw floating by the body of a man. Some of the soldiers with a skiff caught the fellow and drew it to the shore, when it was found to be much decomposed, so much in fact, that it would not bear handling. He was a stout, heavily-built man about five feet six inches high, dressed in a flannel shirt, army pants, and boots, but without coat or vest. His head and face were badly broken and mashed, so that it would be quite impossible to identify him. The pockets of his pants were both cut and empty. It was quite evident that he had been murdered and robbed and thrown into the river, where he had evidently been a long time. I had an old tent brought from camp in which we wrapped the body, and tying a rope around under the arms, dragged it to the top of the bank and buried it in the sand.

We remained at New Madrid from May 17th to 29th, when we received orders to report with camp and garrison equipage to Colonel Heg, commanding at Island Number 10.[15] Although the soldiers persisted in calling me captain, I had never yet assumed command of the company, except during the temporary absence of Lieutenant Catlin. On this occasion, Catlin and Cayton having both gone to Cairo for a few days, the command necessarily devolved on me for the first time, and for a few hours I had my head and hands full of business.

Although our company was composed mostly of good, substantial men, there were a few who were either always behindhand or in trouble of some sort, fellows who ought to have stayed at home or else have brought a guardian with them, who have to be looked after and taken care of like school children. No sooner is it announced that we are to strike camp, than they become perfectly bewildered; notwithstanding the training and discipline of nine months, there are always some who are never ready at the right moment. One man's horse has a lame back, which might have been cured, but wasn't. Another's horse has cast a shoe, which could have been repaired, but wasn't. One has no rations, and another, no ammunition. One has just discovered that he has had no haversack for a week. One asks if he shall load his arms, and another if he had not better discharge his. After the ordnance is all packed and loaded, someone discovers that his saddle girth is broken, or that he has no cartridges. There are always a few "lame ducks" who appear never to think for themselves and must run to the commander with every trifle, and who think they are abused and their officers cross and "stuck up" if they are reprimanded for neglect and inattention to their duties.

I received the order to move at noon, and at eight o'clock that night I reported at Colonel Heg's headquarters. We crossed the river about three miles below New Madrid and marched across the bend, a distance of some eight or nine miles, guided by a native who I impressed soon after landing. The poor fellow and his wife were scared nearly to death, and thought I wanted to arrest and perhaps execute him, but the gift of a silver half dollar and the assurance that I only wanted him to guide me to the island calmed his fears, and mounting a mule, he led us through all right.

The night being clear and warm, we did not pitch our tents, but each man coiled down to sleep wherever he could find a soft spot. With my saddle for a pillow, I slept soundly until nearly dawn, when I was discovered by a flock of mosquitoes, who claiming me as their meat, at once proceeded to devour me. The mosquitoes here are fully as numerous and hungry as their Sikeston brethren. The night guards tell of seeing them walking around and examining the horses to find the best blooded stock, or sitting on the picket rope sharpening their bills while waiting for some favorite horse to come in from duty.

We found this post garrisoned by one regiment of infantry, the 15th Wisconsin, and a battery of light artillery. They are all on the Tennessee shore, except two companies of infantry, who man the batteries on the island. We pitched our camp in an open space on the riverbank. Rebel tents were lying about in every direction, which our men gathered up to make kitchens and stables.

The weather is very hot, but we have become in a measure accustomed to the climate, and from being so much exposed to the weather, have become case-hardened and fare quite as well, if not better, than the "natives" who are nearly always grunting and shaking with the ague.

On leaving New Madrid, we became separated from Company D, with which we have been connected since the first of September last. Since the death of Captain

Delano, Captain Frank Moore of Company D has commanded the detachment. On the 3rd of July, I received from Governor Yates of Illinois my commission as captain with rank to date from May 6th, the date of my election, and the next morning at roll call, I formally assumed command of the company. Lieutenant Cayton's commission as Second Lieutenant was also received at the same time.

Our duties here are light and easy compared with what other companies of our regiment are doing in the interior of this state, where they are engaged in guarding railroads, building and repairing bridges, etc.[16] Having spent so much of our time at posts on the river, I would now be loath to leave it. There is always something new and interesting about the river. The boats and gunboats passing up and down, rowing, fishing, and bathing afford change and amusement that cannot be had at inland posts.

The river here makes several long, sharp bends. The loop thus enclosed by the river is called "Madrid Bend" and is a part of Obion County, Tennessee. There are a good many well-improved farms in the bend. That is, well-improved for this country. They would hardly be entitled to that name in the North. I have made a number of very pleasant acquaintances here, chief among which I would mention "Uncle Tommy" Merriweather and his very estimable wife "Aunt Dolly" and niece Miss Cassie Merriweather. Willis Jones, an old bachelor and a man of considerable intelligence and consequence, has a very neat and well-improved place about halfway to Tiptonville, a village consisting of one little warehouse and a steamboat landing on the opposite side of the neck, or narrow part of the bend. Near this landing is the residence of Widow Merriweather, whose family consists of two or three other widows and a young lady, Miss Polly Thompson, a niece of the rebel general Jeff Thompson.

Colonel Heg with all but two companies of his regiment was ordered away from here soon after our arrival, and Major Quincy McNeil of our regiment sent to take command of the post.[17] The two companies of the 15th Wisconsin Infantry remaining here are under the command of Captain John A. Gordon. My old friend Tom Woodruff, our company clerk, has been detailed as clerk in General Quinby's headquarters, and has gone to Columbus, Kentucky.[18] Tom and I have been together ever since we entered the service, and I was very sorry to have him leave us, although I knew his position in the general's headquarters would be far pleasanter for him than in camp or knocking about with us over the country.

It is just one year today, July 15th, since we first rendezvoused at Camp Flagg in Quincy. We were mustered at Springfield on the 12th of August 1861, one hundred strong. Many changes have occurred on our roll since that date. We have lost: by death, three; by discharge for disability, twenty-one; and have recruited at different times and places, nine; making our total number at present eighty-five.

We have been engaged for some time picking up loose stock and other property left by the rebels, and which has been allowed to run at large or unmolested until this late day. A few days ago our scouts made a good haul, bringing in about thirty horses and mules and twenty asses once belonging to the rebel army. Some had been caught and used by the citizens, but the greater part were running at large in the canebrakes. Horses and mules are quite necessary, and are used to good advantage in an army, but what use could be made of jackasses, and some of them quite young, is beyond my comprehension.

One little donkey, about as big as a Newfoundland dog, and about half of him being composed of head and ears, afforded the soldiers much amusement during the few days we kept them in camp. They would dress the little fellow in a rebel uniform and parade him about camp, he meanwhile keeping up an incessant "he-haw-ing" when separated from his mother. He didn't appear to care much for his father, who he had either forgotten or ceased to love. The soldiers would sometimes swim out in the river with him just to see him swim ashore and shake the water out of his long ears. His comical appearance alone was enough to make an owl laugh.

There being some very good animals in the captured herd, I improved the opportunity to do a little horse and mule trading. Having a number of invalid or exhausted animals in my company, and doing the trading entirely on my own terms, I made some very satisfactory exchanges, after which the whole herd was shipped to Cairo, ostensibly for the use of the U.S. government, but in all probability for the individual benefit of some thieving quartermaster in Cairo, that sinkhole of military iniquity. It being the base of supplies for our army in the south and southwest, the amount of business transacted there is immense, and the opportunities for stealing (that's the plain English for it) are proportionately great. It has become a common saying in the army, which time and experience has proven a true one: "if you would spoil an honest man, make a quartermaster of him." I do believe that next to Washington, there is more iniquity planned and executed in that mud-hole of a town, than anywhere else in the United States.

An order has recently been issued by General Pope, directing that when on the march, cavalry shall carry no baggage whatever, neither forage, tents, nor provisions, but shall subsist off the country through which they pass.[19] This arrangement suits us exactly. It might be supposed, perhaps, that a sudden change of diet from hardtack and bacon to fresh eggs, milk, chickens, and vegetables would be detrimental to the health of the soldiers, but that is an old fogy "regulation" idea that is fast losing its popularity. Experience has proven that the change is not only beneficial, but extremely agreeable to the soldiers, if not the country.

I noticed about this time in the Quincy and other northern papers, that recruiting by volunteering was getting to be slow, and there is some talk of the probability of a draft being enforced in order to fill up the broken ranks of the regiments now in the field. My company having become reduced in number by reason of transfers, discharges for disability, and other causes, I have advertised in the Quincy papers for recruits. From numerous visitors from Adams County, I have the gratifying information that "Delano's Dragoons" enjoy an agreeable reputation at home, and rank "A no. 1" and that many young men are preparing to join us rather than take their chances of being drafted and sent to some other company. Not only at home, but in the South wherever we have been thus far, our boys have made friends. The citizens and non-combatants we treat kindly and as leniently as circumstances will permit, and our enemies we fight bravely, in both cases commanding and securing their respect.

By letter received from father and my brother Chan, I apprehend that the latter is beginning to get uneasy at the prospect of being drafted, and he and his particular friend Jule Sherman are talking of joining us.[20] John Bywater, a recruit from Quincy, joined us today, August 17th. In the absence of a regular mustering officer, I accepted and mustered him myself.

Lieutenant Catlin, with twenty men, went up the river on the Missouri side this morning in search of guerillas who fired on a boat coming down, ten miles from here, at three o'clock this morning. The practice of firing on boats all along the river by small bands of guerillas is becoming, to say the least, very annoying. It is seldom anyone is hurt, but the situation is sometimes very embarrassing to the pilots and intensely interesting and exciting to passengers. Occasionally, when the guerillas catch a boat at a wood yard without troops on board, they will overpower the officers and crew and "go through it" and the passengers for whatever valuables they can carry off.

We have at different times picked up a good many guerillas and bushwhackers and sent them to Cairo, but nearly all have been released on taking the oath of allegiance, and return to their former occupation of intercepting and robbing steamboats. If Catlin comes upon the gang he is now in pursuit of, I hope he will not encumber himself with a lot of useless prisoners. Catching the same man at the same devilry two or three times becomes rather stale sport.

John Whitbread and wife, who have been visiting friends in our company, started on their return to Quincy yesterday, August 16th. By him I sent a cage of parakeets to Miss Mary Skinner. These beautiful little birds are quite plentiful in this part of the country, and when caught, make very tame and interesting pets. Hearing me express a desire to possess some of them, an old negro living near camp offered to bring me all I wanted for a dollar. He soon discovered the roosting place of a flock in a hollow tree, and cutting the tree down at night, secured about a dozen birds, of which I took nine, about as many as I thought I had use for, and clipping their wings, I turned them loose in my cabin, where they soon made themselves perfectly at home. They are very noisy and quarrelsome, continually screaming and fighting among themselves. Their chief delight is to get on my desk, upset the inkstand, and tear to pieces all papers or books they can get hold of. They will eat almost anything offered them, holding their food in one claw like a parrot. About this time a young rebel lady made me a present of a mockingbird. If I get many more pets, I shall be obliged to obtain other quarters, either for them or myself.

Lieutenant Catlin and party returned this morning, August 21st, covered with glory and Missouri mud. We have been in so many "wild goose" chases after guerillas, seldom catching more than a few stragglers, that our boys began to despair of ever finding enough at once to make a good fight, but this time they were agreeably disappointed. They not only found, but fought and completely routed, a gang of more than double their own number.

Lieutenant Catlin came upon their trail soon after leaving New Madrid, and after chasing them closely all day, came upon them in the evening. The rebels, doubtless thinking our men had abandoned the pursuit, and feeling safe on their swampy retreat, had bivouacked without taking the precaution of posting pickets or even camp guards. Some were feeding their horses, some engaged in preparing supper, and the rest idly loitering about, all in blissful ignorance of the close proximity of their enemies. They were not to be blamed for getting whipped, they couldn't help that, but any captain who will neglect to protect his camp and guard against surprise deserved to be whipped.

Catlin, on seeing their superiority in numbers, knew he had not a moment to lose. To give them time to rally would be to throw away his opportunity and give them every advantage. So, opening a lively fire with pistols and carbines, he charged upon them. This was more than the rebels expected or desired; having neither pistols, nor sabers, their favorite mode of fighting is at long range from behind logs and trees. They were not up to this dashing "neck or nothing" style of fighting. They were completely demoralized and, after firing a few rounds with their long rifles and shotguns, scattered in all directions into the brush.

This was the first good chance our boys had had at the bushwhackers, and they made the most of it. The fight lasted about five minutes and resulted in a loss to the enemy of one killed, one wounded, and twenty prisoners, together with their arms and horses. Among the prisoners were two captains, or rather chiefs. Although called "captains" by their men, they have no commissions, nor receive pay, from the rebel government, but are mere freebooters. While it gives them no commissions or pay, the rebel government recognizes all these guerillas sufficiently to accept them in exchange for prisoners. Lieutenant Catlin himself took one of the captains, who had a fine Colt's revolving rifle. One of our men,

John D. Patton, was slightly wounded with small shot in the face, breast, and arms. Another had his saber straps cut by a ball and a horse belonging to an artillerist, who went from New Madrid, was killed.

While Catlin was having this skirmish in Missouri, I had, if not an adventure, at least a nice little escape, in another direction. I had been appointed acting provost marshal and was sent by Major McNeil with twelve men to a schoolhouse in Horn Ridge Precinct, about twenty-five miles south of Island Number 10, for the purpose of administering the oath to the would-be loyal citizens of that part of the country. Notice of my coming had been sent down the week before by some citizens, and I found a much larger audience than I expected assembled about the old schoolhouse; all men, women, and children were anxiously and wonderingly awaiting the arrival of the first Yankee soldiers many of them had ever had the pleasure(?) of seeing. All were willing and anxious to take the oath, and I found a much more loyal sentiment existing there than in the immediate vicinity of our camp at the island. We were well fed and treated with much kindness and respect.

I worked until dark, and that night slept, or rather stayed, in the old schoolhouse, which, like many houses in that swampy country, was built upon posts about a foot or eighteen inches high, thus in dry times affording a safe and convenient refuge for all the vagabond hogs in the neighborhood. A change of diet from pork to soldier was evidently agreeable to the fleas, and we were nearly eaten out of our clothes before morning. I can never forget those Horn Ridge fleas.

The next morning, the people came so thick and fast that by ten o'clock, I ran out of blanks, it being necessary to give each person a copy of the oath subscribed to. Although very few could read, it was expected that the possession of a copy would be a constant reminder to them that they were true and loyal citizens of the United States. A fact, however, which some of the young men doubtless forgot, as we afterwards frequently captured bushwhackers with their oaths taken somewhere else in their pockets. Sometimes we would catch a fellow with two oaths, federal and rebel, and passes from commanders in both armies, a very convenient arrangement when he wishes to visit either one or the other camp, and can read enough to know the proper papers to show, but when caught in arms by either party, the consequences are sometimes unpleasant, if not fatal.

My supply of blanks being exhausted, I was preparing to shut up shop and return to camp, when my movements were somewhat hastened by the arrival of a loyal old man from over the lake, who reported to me privately that a force of sixty guerillas, that had been whipped a few days before by a company of our regiment from Trenton, Tennessee, were aware of my presence at the schoolhouse with only twelve men, and were coming that afternoon to wipe me out. My guards had seen two of their spies or scouts the night before, and their scouts, the old man said, had just got to their camp and reported when he left to warn me.

My men at first wanted to stand and fight at the schoolhouse, or go to meet the rebels, but when informed that the odds were sixty to twelve, agreed that we had better make tracks, and make them far apart, too. Our newly made friends(?), expressing a wish to have me come again and "finish up this swearing business," I appointed another day to meet them at the same place, at which time, I promised them I would come prepared to stay. In a few hours we were safe in camp at Island Number 10. I afterwards returned with a larger force and a piece of artillery. I then learned that, on the occasion of my first visit, I had been gone but about an hour when the rebels dashed up and surrounded the schoolhouse, expecting to find me there, but just in time to be too late. Having ridden hard through the swamp all the morning, they were in no condition to pressure us on our fresh horses. My informant, an old native, said "it was a merciful Providence" that I lit out just when I did, for "that secesh captain had just been licked by some of you uns and was as mad as hell." I think many of the people in some parts of Tennessee really wish to be loyal to the old flag, but being situated, as it were, "between two fires" they are obliged to pray "Good Lord and good devil," not knowing into whose hands they will eventually fall. They have friends and relatives in both armies, and the interior parts of the country not being permanently occupied by either, but overrun by scouting parties of both, their situation is truly an unenviable one.

Grant is pushing the enemy at every point, and from the amount of fighting being done, and to be done, I do not think we shall be kept at this now unimportant post much longer. We are by no means idle here. We do a great deal of riding, scouting, and picket, but it all seems to amount to little or nothing. The government is altogether too careful of rebels and rebel property. Nothing must be molested. The worst rebel in the country, if he comes in and takes the oath (for which he cares nothing at all), is all right and can go on raising grain and other supplies for the use of the enemy, unmolested. The rebel farmers in this vicinity are much more afraid of the irregular guerilla bands of their own men than they are of us. There are men living almost within gun shot of this post who have never tried to conceal their hatred for the U.S. government, and who have done all in their power to aid and assist the rebellion, but they and their property are safe and protected, merely because to save themselves and property, they have taken the oath, to which they attach no importance and which they do not keep nor observe in any particular.

The soldiers who are fighting to suppress the rebellion are tired of seeing rebels and traitors treated thus kindly. War means death and destruction, and a war cannot be successfully conducted on humane principles, and I believe that by destroying the enemy's homes and resources, we can bring him to terms sooner than by fighting him. So long as the rebel soldiers feel that their families and homes are safe, even though in our hands, and the crops and supplies undisturbed, they have heart and courage to fight. But let them understand and feel that the safety of their families and home depends upon their return and good behavior, and I believe they would return by thousands. I would see all property of every rebel destroyed or confiscated.

I do not like war. It is cruel and distressing in its mildest form. But if we must have war, and it has been forced upon us, the hotter we make it and the harder we push and punish the enemy, the sooner will it be over. I know it sounds hard and cruel to destroy the homes of women and children, and nothing pains me so much as to feel obliged to distress them in any way, but these same women who cry to us for protection are the "power behind the throne" that is filling the ranks of the rebel army with men and conducting business and raising crops at home for their support. I cannot but admire their patriotism and zeal, and the earnestness with which they work for their cause. I honor and admire them and respect their sentiment because they are earnest and sincere, however much I hate their cause and principles. There are no lukewarm ones amongst the women. They are all "red hot and still a-firing."

While I fully realize that it is a soldier's duty to "obey and question not," and that it is not for me to question the conduct, nor orders, of my superior officers, I cannot quite ignore the fact that I am no common hireling, nor are my men common regular troops. We did not join the army for want of an occupation, nor for the few dollars we receive, but for a principle to save our country and the flag of our fathers from rebels and traitors, and our homes from the power of a slave aristocracy. We took up arms to put down rebellion, and we want to see it put down, and not only put down, but crushed and buried root and branch out of sight and so deep that even the smell of it shall never come to the surface. I know that the early termination of the war would throw a good many shoulder straps and shoddy contractors out of a job, and blight the aspirations of many office-seeking patriots, but it's little we care for them. Of course, it would "spoil their little game."

Captain Frank Moore of Company D came up from New Madrid, where he is stationed, about four o'clock this morning, September 6th, for reinforcements, reporting that the enemy was advancing in considerable force on that place. One company of infantry, a section of artillery, and forty men of my company at once embarked on the steamer *Tecumseh* for the scene of action, which we reached at daybreak, just as a solitary bugler standing on the riverbank commenced sounding reveille. The soldiers soon came tumbling out of their quarters, yawning and rubbing their eyes, and looking very unlike soldiers in a besieged or alarmed camp, and were not a little surprised to learn that they were in danger and that a boatload of troops had come to their assistance. I expected, of course, to find the troops all under arms and the rebels advancing, if not already before the town.

An old woman had come into camp last evening with a long and dreadful story, which grew longer and more dreadful as she told it, and on the strength of her report, Captain Moore was at once sent for reinforcements, but what seemed a little strange, in the face of supposed danger, the camps were not aroused nor alarmed. After the old lady had recovered from her fright and the importance of being a bearer of dispatches sufficiently to speak calmly and with discretion, we managed to make out that she had seen about one hundred guerillas come out of the swamp and pass southward about three miles from town. As there was no prospect of them attacking us, it was decided to pressure, and if possible, overtake them.

When breakfast was over, we started out about seven o'clock, our force consisting of one hundred cavalry and one section (two guns) of artillery under the command of Captain Moore of Company D. We made a rapid march to Weaverville, twenty miles distant, in the extreme southwest corner of New Madrid County, where there is a long bridge over Little River, and where we thought Jeffries, commanding the rebel squad, would perhaps make a stand. But Captain Jeffries didn't want to fight, and so instead of waiting for us, had passed on through the town the night before, and was by this time far out in the swamp, where it was impossible to follow him. So we went into camp, threw out pickets, and blockaded the roads and bridge.

From Weaverville to Clarkston, twelve miles, is the remains of a plank road, which had been well-made and was once much traveled, but is now torn up in many places and many of the bridges burned or washed away. On leaving New Madrid, we were ordered to cross the plank road, as it was feared the rebels who had been for some time concentrating on Hawkins' Island in the St. Francis River might be too strong for us. They were reported to be 500 or 600 strong, all mounted, but poorly armed with squirrel rifles and shotguns. If we could get near enough to the island with our artillery, we could soon shell them out, but it would be impossible to haul the guns through the swamp, and nearly if not quite as difficult to operate cavalry, as the rebels, being quite familiar with every pass and trail of which we are ignorant, would have every advantage of ambushing or escaping from us.

The next morning, Sunday, September 7th, Captain Degolzer of the artillery, while out scouting with a small party, came upon the fresh trail of four horsemen, which he followed to the house of a guerilla chief, Captain Davis. Davis had come in from his camp in the swamp to spend a quiet Sunday with his family and get a square Sunday dinner, and feeling annoyed on being disturbed by the approach of a squad of Yankee soldiers, stepped out of the door and very impudently fired his pistol at Captain Degolzer, who promptly returned the compliment, and Davis fell with a ball through his body and died in a few minutes. He was killed by the revolving rifle captured by Lieutenant Catlin recently from a guerilla captain in Missouri. The three men with Davis were captured.

The plank road, before mentioned, is the only way of crossing the swamp in that direction, and as we had that guarded and allowed no one to pass going out, the rebels were yet ignorant of our presence. Amongst others arrested and brought in by our pickets was Mr. Hawkins, who reported that the rebel pickets at the other end of the road knew nothing of us being so near. I had never heard any good of any of the Hawkins family, who are rather numerous hereabouts, nor did I like the looks or actions of this particular one, nor believe a word of all he was telling us. And then the island on which the rebels were encamping was called Hawkins, though perhaps this latter fact could not be given in evidence against this man's loyalty, but taken all together, I was very suspicious that he was after no good. He said he was afraid of being pressed into the rebel service and was running away to Kentucky, having taken the oath last spring. He had been to New Madrid quite often and was well-acquainted with Captain Frank Moore. Captain Moore thought he was all right and would have passed him through without further question. He was in a very great hurry to be gone, was afraid the rebels would conscript him, and if they should catch him with that oath in his pocket, he didn't dare to think what the consequences might be. I insisted on searching the fellow before letting him pass, assured him that he was in good company, and that the rebels could not conscript him so long as he stayed with us, and that he need not be in any rush to go to Kentucky, as there were more rebel soldiers there than in Missouri, and that the conscription was being vigorously enforced there. He was very prompt and proud to show the copy of the oath, which he carried in his pocketbook, the possession of which he thought ought to permit him to pass unchallenged all over the United States. That was well enough as far as it went, but on further investigation, I found neatly concealed in the lining of his hat a transfer from an "independent" (guerilla) company to a company in Price's army in Tennessee. The transfer was dated September 3, 1862 and signed "Benj. Moore Lieut. Comdg. Co." and approved by Colonel V. W. Hall and Major Taylor. Hawkins had no doubt been for a long time acting the part of a spy, and when I told him so, and that that "transfer" was proof that he had been in the rebel service since taking the U.S. oath, and was evidence enough to hang him, he was scared nearly to death. We took him with us to New Madrid and turned him over to the provost marshal, and I heard no more of him.

Seven steamboats loaded with rebel prisoners passed down the river today, September 11th, escorted by a gunboat. The prisoners are to be exchanged (and taken again?).

Lieutenant Catlin has been detailed as adjutant of our regiment and ordered to report to Colonel Noble immediately. I regret very much to have him leave us, as he is an excellent officer and a man I esteem most highly, and in whom I have the utmost confidence. He has been of so much assistance to me that I scarcely know how I shall get along without him. My other lieutenant, John Cayton, is post quartermaster.

I have been quite sick for some time (September 27th), confined to my quarters and part of the time delirious with fever. Doctor Kendall said he feared for some days I would not possibly pull through. Being very weak and unable to write, I had to ask Mr. Stokes to write to father for me.

Monday, September 29th, was a sad, dark day in the history of our little company. Early this morning, word was brought to me that Corporal William G. Gilpin was dying, and had asked to see me. I got up and attempted to walk, but was too weak to stand, having been in a fever all night. Doctor Kendall then said I must not attempt to leave my quarters, that all that could be done had been done for Gilpin, and that I would endanger my own life by going out of my quarters at that time. So I was obliged to send word to Gilpin that I could not come to see him. He died about sunrise.

Towards evening, it was reported to me that Quartermaster Sergeant John N. Wilks was dying and wished to see me. I was feeling a little stronger by that time, and the doctor consented to have me carried to Wilks's tent, which was but a few steps from my quarters. The poor fellow was nearly gone, and too weak to talk, but he recognized me and shook hands with me and bade me goodbye. At five o'clock, about an hour after I saw him, he died. On account of my own severe illness, I had not been informed of the illness of either of these men, and did not know they were sick until it was reported to me that they were dying. The next day, the bodies of Gilpin and Wilks were sent with a detail to Cairo, where metallic cases were procured and they were forwarded to Illinois—Gilpin to Quincy, and Wilks to Camp Point.

The late hot weather was very hard on the men, and a good many were at different times down with malarial fever, but the weather has now turned so much like winter, in fact, that the men are putting up stoves in their tents. With the change of weather, the health of the men is improving and the "sick list" rapidly decreasing. Jeff Kemp, one of my soldiers, who has been sick in my quarters for some time, is so much better that he says he wants to trade his daily allowance of quinine for regular rations of pork and hard tack. Jeff's spirits are very much like a thermometer: when he is well they are away up boiling in the shade, and he is the happiest boy in camp, always designing and full of fun; but when sick, they are correspondingly low, and he is then one of the most despondent, gloomy, and unhappy fellows I ever saw.

The appetite of the men is the most serious thing Doctor Kendall has now to contend with. As soon as the fever leaves them and they begin to convalesce, they become as hungry as wolves and are too apt to over-eat, or eat improper food, and so cause a relapse. The doctor has had several such cases, and a relapse is often worse than the original sickness, very much like the south end of a cold north wind, and so to guard against future troubles of the kind he has adopted the original and somewhat novel expedient of giving his convalescing patients something in their medicine to make their mouths and tongues so sore that it hurts them more to eat than to go hungry, and they must per force content themselves with soups and "spoon victuals," which is just the object of the intention, and the doctor saves his patient, his credit, and his medicine.

Being now (October 10th) greatly improved in health and able to ride a little, I go occasionally out to Uncle Tommy and Aunt Dolly Merriweather's, a mile or two from camp, where I am always most kindly received and entertained by that estimable old couple. I called today at Aunt Dolly's, taking a late northern paper containing an account of our late victory at Corinth. Miss Cassie, who has a sweetheart in Price's army, was much interested in the details of the battle. The ladies were, as usual, all very agreeable, Mrs. Dick Donaldson "The Rampant" of course excepted. She never misses an opportunity of giving me a red-hot dose of rebellious hatred.

About this time, exact date not remembered, I returned one afternoon from a little scout down the river towards New Madrid, and on riding up to my quarters, was greatly surprised and delighted to find my father there. Having heard nothing from me since the letter written by Mr. Stokes during my late illness, my letter since then not having reached him, he had hastened down expecting to find me very ill, if not dead. He brought messages and packages from home for many of the men.

It was his first visit to any of the camps in the field and everything was, of course, new and of interest to him. He had not seen a camp of soldiers in the field since he was himself a soldier in the War of 1812 on Long Island, New York. He stayed with me two or three days, taking several short rides in the country, I taking him out to see my old friends Uncle Tommy and Aunt Dolly Merriweather. When he returned, I sent home by him the horses of Gilpin and Wilks, and numerous interesting trophies of the war that I had collected from time to time. My black cook "Gilly Blackburn," who had been working for me for several months, went north with him.[21]

Thursday night, October 16th, Colonel Faulkner, the somewhat notorious guerilla chief, crossed the Obion River from the east with two hundred mounted men, and advanced to attack this post.[22] The effective force of our cavalry being so small on account of the number on the sick list, we had not been keeping out cavalry pickets lately at night, but scouting the country pretty thoroughly during the day and depending on the infantry pickets and guards at night. This evening, my scouts came in and reported all quiet in the bend. It appeared afterwards that Faulkner was aware of the fact that we kept out no cavalry pickets at night, and doubtless watched, or was informed of, the return of our scouts that day.

In a lane opposite Donaldson's house, between one and two miles from camp, Faulkner dismounted the greater part of his men and advanced on foot from the west, while the mounted portion were to go around and attack us on the east. But by some mistake, his cavalry missed the road, the night being very dark, and about five hundred yards from camp, came upon his dismounted men. The latter, supposing them to be a squad of our cavalry, opened fire on them. The cavalry, thinking they had come upon our infantry, promptly returned fire, when both parties turned and fled in opposite directions. The ground and leaves being wet with dew, and the night very dark, our infantry guards could neither see nor hear the approach of the rebels, and this firing was the first notice we had of their near presence. But in less time than it takes me to write this, we were all out and in line of battle, ready and expecting every moment to be attacked. The firing we supposed, of course, was between our outer guards and the enemy.

Sergeant Obe Spence and his gun squad ran up the six-pounder near headquarters "loaded for bear" with short-range canister. I sent out to the infantry guards, but could learn nothing from them. They had heard the firing, but had seen no enemy. I happened to be lying awake when the firing commenced, and with my pistol in my hand, and no uniform on to speak of, was the first one out, before the camp guard even had given the alarm, expecting to find the camp full of rebels and a hand-to-hand fight. This was at half-past three o'clock Friday morning.

As soon as it was daylight, I ordered the "breakfast call," then "boots and saddles," and just as the sun was rising, I started out with fifty men to reconnoiter and learn the occasion of this untimely disturbance. I soon struck the enemy's trail, and learned from some negroes that the "Confeds" were about an hour ahead of me and riding hard towards Reelfoot Lake, but could learn nothing of who nor how many they were. One old darkey assured me, "dars an almight sight ob men. A heap more den you uns."

I knew from the appearance of the trail that the enemy outnumbered me. My men were, however, elated with the prospect of a fight with the guerillas, regardless of the odds in numbers. As our horses were fresh, I pushed on as rapidly as possible. My advance guard, commanded by Sergeant Murdock, soon captured four rebel soldiers returning from their main column, each leading an extra horse saddled to pick up more stragglers or wounded, which rather singular movement would indicate that their commander did not anticipate a pursuit, and which I did not accept as a compliment to us. From these men, who did not hesitate to give any information, I learned that I was pursuing three hundred men commanded by Colonel Faulkner.

While I was questioning these prisoners, a courier arrived from camp with this dispatch: "Capt. Moore, cautiously—there are 300 Faulkner's cavalry. We have a prisoner. Quincy McNeil, Maj." I strengthened the advance guard and continued the chase rapidly, hoping to come on the rebels unawares, as I was now assured they did not expect pursuit. Hearing a few shots ahead, I galloped up and found the advance guard had surprised a party of six rebels who were feeding their horses in a barn yard. These were a pretty good draft to begin with, as the captured squad consisted of Colonel Faulkner, Captain Robert Merriweather, Lieutenant Donaldson, and another captain and lieutenant whose names I have forgotten.

Sergeant Murdock captured Faulkner as he was running on foot for the woods. I dashed up just in time to save Captain Merriweather, who with one foot in the stirrup, was trying to mount his frightened horse. We had been riding hard now for nearly two hours, and I knew we must be getting pretty close to the enemy, and I wished to overtake him before he could learn of our presence, so I halted only long enough to breathe my horses and learn the names and ranks of my prisoners. I sent the prisoners to the rear with orders to the guards to keep them, dead or alive, and to shoot any who attempted to escape.

After a sharp gallop of five or six miles, the advance guard came upon two men in the road, who they supposed were stragglers, but who were really the enemy's pickets. As the two men fled, Murdock and his squad gave chase, and before they knew it, had dashed right into the midst of the rebels, who had halted to rest and wait for their commander, and were sitting and lying about in the canes and fallen timber. The advance guard fired and wheeled, but only three of the six escaped. Sergeant Murdock, Corporal Garrett, and Private W. A. Wilcox fell at the first fire. I immediately formed my little force in line of battle and opened a brisk fire on the rebels, which was promptly returned.

Being in a somewhat exposed position, I pushed my line forward until I gained the cover of some trees, the opposing lines being now not over one hundred yards apart. Being unable to charge on account of the thick timber and brush, I was obliged to dismount my men to fight on foot, directing Lieutenant Cayton to take charge of the right of the line, while I remained near the left.

The rebels were armed chiefly with double-barrel shotguns loaded with buck and ball cartridges, and as their guns were of different calibers, their cartridges did not fit, thus rendering their aim at any great distance very uncertain. From my position, I could plainly see the lines and fighting on both sides. The rebels at first fired very wild and rapidly; many of them, I learned afterward, were raw recruits and conscripts never before under fire. I have never been able to learn who commanded them in the fight. They had some old soldiers in their ranks, and these, doubtless, led and directed the others. They seemed to fight without much, if any, command or order, but had they been well commanded, they might have had the fight all their own way very soon, as they outnumbered us more than six to one.

My men, throughout the chase and fight, behaved most nobly, responding promptly to every order with the coolness and precision of a parade. They had been drilled to fight on foot, but had not before had occasion to practice it. All of their fighting had been dashed through on the charge, and if I could only have charged here, I do believe I could have routed the rebels in a few minutes in spite of their greatly superior numbers.

I soon became so much interested in watching the fight, that I thought not of the danger to myself, and would sometimes step out from the shelter of my tree to obtain a better view, when a rebel bullet or charge of buckshot whistling about my ears would direct my formal attention to my tree again. I had never before witnessed a cool stand-up fight. I soon discovered that I was not, at first, fighting the enemy's whole force, a part having gone farther on, but started to return when the firing commenced, so that the force opposing me was constantly increasing, and as their numbers increased, their fire became heavier.

After fighting against these odds for fifteen or twenty minutes, I discovered a movement on the part of the rebels to get around my left flank, and at the same time, a soldier came from Cayton reporting that the rebels were endeavoring to flank him. Some officer who understood his business was evidently in command of them now, having doubtless returned from the advance, and was handling his men more like soldiers than a mob. I at once saw that further fighting on that line was useless and must result in our destruction or capture, and if I would save any of my men, I must get them out of there, and quickly, too. Mounting my horse, I ordered my men to "fall back and rally." I was the only man mounted, and my voice and gestures appeared to attract the especial attention of all the rebels in my immediate vicinity, and a perfect storm of bullets and shot whistled by me on all sides, my horse receiving a charge of small shot in his hip.

The moment my men ceased firing and commenced falling back, the rebels sprang from their ambush and charged, most of them on foot, yelling and firing as they came. So closely did they press us, that two of my men whose horses were wounded and unmanageable, were unable to mount and escaped on foot. Another horse near me was shot and fell just as his rider was mounting. We fell back a few hundred yards, where the canes were not so high or thick, and where we could operate better mounted, and there formed a line, where I waited for Cayton to join me.

Before he could do so, the rebels came out of the woods, and for the first time saw the smallness of the force they had been fighting. They advanced, mounted, yelling and firing. The woods seemed full of them. I saw at once that an orderly retreat was out of the question, that we must fight or run away, and without a moment's hesitation, I chose the former. It was a desperate choice with such odds against me, but I well knew my men would stand by me, and as I looked down my little line and saw how cool and steady they were, I felt that it was an honor to command and serve with such men.

I wanted to get the rebs all out of the timber into the open ground where I could charge, but I did not want to charge without Cayton, and as he had not yet come up, I feared he might be killed or captured, so I directed my bugler to sound the "rally." Never did Weaver blow so loudly, or so well, or to so good a purpose. Every tree echoed the sound until it seemed as if the swamp was full of buglers. The moment the rebs heard the bugle and its many echoes, they ceased firing and fled back into the woods. They thought, as I afterwards learned, they heard a dozen bugles and that reinforcements had reached me.

Taking advantage of the enemy's confusion (I knew not then the cause of it), and fearing he might get through the swamp in my right and cut me off from camp, I fell back rapidly, though in good order, about two miles to an open field, where I halted to ascertain my loss and rest my horses. The men who had lost their horses managed to remount themselves on something. Some had doubled up and were riding two on one horse. One young man, Joe Chase, came dashing up on an unbroken colt without saddle or bridle, and only a rope around the colt's head.

I sent a courier on in advance and marched slowly back to camp, which I reached about half-past two, having been out about ten hours. Our loss was three killed and three slightly wounded, and six horses killed or disabled. The killed were Sergeant Arthur T. Murdock, Corporal Richard Garrett, and Private William A. Wilcox. The wounded were Corporal William Green, struck in the stomach with small shot, Private James T. Berrian, struck in the left breast by a spent ball, and Private Steven Allen, thrown from his horse and right elbow dislocated. One man had one of his saber straps shot off, and another had a ball through his cap. Private Decatur Delano received a bullet on the muzzle of his carbine.

We captured thirteen prisoners, seventeen horses, and about thirty shotguns and squirrel rifles. The most of the guns we destroyed, taking only a few of the best ones. Towards evening, I took Captain Bob Merriweather on his parole out to see his wife, who lived but a short distance from camp. I wanted to take Colonel Faulkner and Captain Merriweather, on their paroles, to my quarters and felt, under the circumstances, that my wishes in the matter were entitled to consideration, but Major McNeil, with much bluster and display of authority, ordered them put in the guardhouse with the other prisoners. I sent them supper from my mess and spent the evening in conversation with them in the guardhouse.

Faulkner, in appearance, was about six feet and one or two inches high and quite slender, features rather sharp, with keen grey eyes. He was neatly dressed in a uniform of "Confederate gray," but without any marks or insignia of rank. In conversation he was entertaining and agreeable, and a man of good education. He was rather quiet and did not seek conversation, but when addressed was quick to reply. Very proud and erect in his bearing, he was a man that from his very appearance would anywhere command respect. He is said to be a good commander, reckless and daring.

He had a perfect plan of our camp and the roads and approaches. He knew where all the officers' quarters were, and knew the officers themselves by description. The moment I rode up to him when he was captured, he asked if I was not Captain Moore of the Illinois cavalry? He said, "I knew you at once, Captain, although I never saw you before." Major McNeil he described as a "big-bellied, bald-headed old duffer." He showed me his map of our camp and names and descriptions of officers, but would not tell me how he obtained his information. Speaking of the fight, he said, "I never saw such a spunky little crowd of men as you have. I was told your men were good fighters, but I did not think you would follow me so far." The fight occurred about eighteen miles from camp. I saw that his blunder, and failure to surprise us, and his own capture away from his command, was a rough thorn in his side, but he was too proud to complain. He carried, when captured, a splendid gold-mounted revolver, a present from a lady of Charleston, South Carolina, and valued at five hundred dollars. I gave it, for safe keeping, to Wilcox and it was lost when Wilcox was killed.

I wrote no account of the fight for publication, nor do I think any of my men did, but in a few days, a very imperfect account appeared in the northern papers, giving all the credit to Major McNeil, not even mentioning my name, nor the letter of my company. It was doubtless written by the major himself. The major had nothing to do with the fight. He did not even go out of camp. In fact, I do not think he could ride ten miles. But three days afterward, when we expected every moment to be attacked, he made an excuse to leave his post and go up to Cairo where he remained several days on a drunken spree.[23]

The loss of Sergeant Murdock was a severe one to my company. He was a dear and valued friend to me, and one of the noblest young men I ever knew. He was a general favorite. I can never forget his last words and the last time I saw him alive. He was riding a short distance ahead of me, and seeing some signs of the enemy, he left his guard for a moment and rode up to me saying cheerfully, a little excited, "we'll have them now Captain, they are down in the canes," and away he dashed to his death.

When I enlisted as a private, I belonged to a mess of which Sergeant Murdock was chief. One night while sitting around our campfire at Fredericktown, Missouri, talking of the dangers and chances of a soldier's life, we pledged ourselves together not to leave a messmate's body in rebel soil if by any means we could possibly recover it and send it home. The surviving members of that old mess redeemed their pledge, and the remains of our fallen comrade at last found a resting place in Rushville, Illinois.

At the time of his enlistment, Sergeant Murdock was engaged to marry a young lady, Miss Anne Hicks, then residing in Emerson, a little town in Missouri a few miles from Quincy, Illinois. Often when on picket at night or riding together, he would talk of his sweetheart, telling me of the threats and insults of her brothers, who were rebels, and the difficulties he often encountered in meeting her, and then he would draw bright pictures and lay happy plans for the future, when after the war should be over, he would return to claim his waiting bride. Poor girl, she has seen her brave and faithful lover for the last time, and has his last letter. Their next meeting will be in the great hereafter. He had often requested me, if he should fall first, to write to Miss Hicks and return all of her letters, which I would find amongst his effects. This I did, and sent her also a lock of his hair.

The news of our fight having reached New Madrid, a company of cavalry and a section of light artillery came up early the next morning to renew the pursuit of the enemy. I said it would be quite useless, as the rebels being in full retreat, afraid of pursuit, and with more than eighteen hours the start of us, we could never overtake them. But go they must, although they had orders to return to New Madrid that night. We followed the enemy's trail across the ford of Reelfoot Lake, where we gave up the chase.

On our way back, I stopped at the battlefield, where I found the graves of Murdock and his companions, who had been buried by some kindly disposed neighbor. I pressed a wagon and team and brought their remains to camp, and a sergeant was at once sent to Cairo for metallic cases. I also recovered Murdock's horse and Garrett's horse and saddle. Murdock's horse was shot in six places, two balls passing through his neck (more than ten years afterwards, I saw the same horse in Quincy, Illinois, the property of Mr. Van Dorn; he was then a good, serviceable horse). The watches, purses, etc. of the killed were taken by the rebels. Garrett and Wilcox, I think, were killed instantly. Murdock may have lived a few minutes; he had two balls through his body.

Wooden coffins were procured, and that night we buried them by torch light. It was a strange, weird sight that dark night in those thick woods. The soldiers, unarmed, standing silently around while the fitful, flickering light of our few torches served to make the surrounding darkness more dark. Slowly, sadly, and silently we laid them in one shallow grave. As I read the Episcopal form of burial service over those three boys that night, I felt perhaps more keenly than ever before the awful truth: "in the midst of life we are in death." I had often before seen death sudden and in many forms, but this seemed to be so suddenly sudden and so near home. I had been for so long a time so intimately associated with these men that they seemed a part of my family. Three braver, truer soldiers never fought and died for their country. Brave and fearless almost to a fault, they rather sought than shunned danger. Where Sergeant Murdock dared to lead, his comrades dared to follow.

There was nothing remarkable nor unusual about the deaths of these men. They fell as soldiers fall, and as any of us may fall at any time, in the discharge of their duty. Thousands have fallen like them, and thousands more will fall. But, as I said before, this loss seemed to come nearer home to all of us than any we had yet sustained. None who witnessed that sad and singular burial scene that night can ever forget it. The next morning, Sunday, October 19th, the company was paraded under arms, and the customary volley, the last tribute of respect, was fired over the graves of our dead comrades. May they rest in peace.

During Sunday and Monday we received several reports, chiefly from negroes, to the effect that a large force, doubtless fugitives from Fort Donelson, Corinth, and other places, was concentrating at some point on the Obion River. Knowing that the rebels would feel a little sore over their numerous late defeats, we had every reason to believe they would make another attempt to take this place. The pickets were therefore strengthened and the men slept on their arms.

About twelve o'clock Tuesday night, just as I had laid down, I was aroused by a shot from the pickets, which proved to be a false alarm. I went back to my quarters, and soon Captain Gordon came in (Captain Gordon was commanding the post in the absence of Major McNeil, who had gone to Cairo). We sat talking a few minutes, when Captain Gordon said it would be useless to go to bed, as he believed we would be turned out again before morning. Scarcely were the words out of his lips, when five shots were fired by the infantry pickets on the west side of camp. The men turned out on the "double quick," and Sergeant Spence quickly got the gun in position. The sergeant of the guard could give no satisfactory explanation of the firing. He said the men thought they saw or heard something. Scouts were sent out a short distance, but could discover nothing. There seemed, however, to be a warning in the air, and in the sighing of the tree tops. Everybody seemed reluctant to lie down again, so the men loitered around camp under arms until daylight.

Numerous rumors and reports came in the next day, October 22nd, that the force on the Obion River was about to march against this place. I had no doubt there was a camp of rebels somewhere on the Obion, but I did not believe the commander would publish to citizens and negroes several days in advance just where he was going and what he was going to do, and while I never paid much attention to such rumors, I never entirely ignored them. If there was a camp of rebels on the river, they were lying mighty low, for our scouts, as far as they went—and I was out nearly every day myself—could discover no camp, nor saw any rebel scouts. This doubling of guards, and being up all night and every night, and the cavalry riding all day, was beginning to tell on our little force, and the men were about tired out. As the major had not returned, Captain Gordon not wishing to assume all responsibility, called a council of war consisting of all the officers at the post, at which it was decided to remove all the commissary and ordnance stores to the island and evacuate the post on the main shore.

A gang of negroes, about twenty-five, who had been brought in from the country for the purpose, were set to work moving stores to the landing about 5pm. The steamer *Platte Valley*, coming up, landed for the mail, when I went on board and pressed her into our service. She made two trips, and a little sternwheeler we caught coming down, one trip, to the island. Before midnight all the troops and every article of value were safe on the island. We well knew that our little garrison, situated as it was without fortifications and only one piece of light artillery, could not successfully resist an attack of any considerable force. But here on the island, although we cannot do much outside work, we feel pretty confident of our ability to hold the post anyhow. I did not try to make any camp that night, but completely tired-out, found a soft dry place in the grass under the bushes and, wrapping my overcoat about me, was soon sound asleep, and slept without fear of intending rebels.

Soldiers who went over to the main shore today, October 23rd, learned that the rebels have a camp on Reelfoot Lake, and some had been to Tiptonville. They are said to be commanded by General Lovell, who escaped when the rebels were beaten at Corinth recently.[24]

Some families in the bend have gone to Fort Thompson at New Madrid for protection. The men who cannot leave their homes are hiding out in the swamps to escape rebel conscription. We have a little steam ferryboat so that we can go and come and send out scouts as often as may be necessary. We expect to return to our old camp as soon as we can construct breastworks and mount a few guns.

Just before leaving our old camp, Lieutenant Russell of the 15th Wisconsin Infantry shot himself twice in the body with a small revolver in a fit of temporary insanity. He is perfectly sane now, and in a fair way to recover. He declines to give any reason for his act, merely saying in answer to my inquiries: "I was very foolish." I was the first one to reach him after he shot himself and found one of the bullets in the back of his shirt, it having gone clear through his body.

On the 24th of October, Tom Woodruff was detached from the company and ordered to report to Captain J. C. Cox, commissary of subsistence at Columbus, Kentucky. I was selfishly sorry to have Tom leave; we had been messmates and companions so long. He was company clerk and had made all rolls and reports, and was of great assistance to me, but I know that a clerkship in Captain Cox's office would be more to his liking, and more pleasant to him, than life in camp.

Mr. Peter Garrett arrived from Camp Point, Illinois on the morning of October 25th and started to return the evening of the same day with the bodies of his son and Wilcox. I learned today that troops have been sent from some point east of us to dislodge the rebels on the Obion River, but could learn no particulars.

Considerable change has taken place on the island since the evacuation of it by the rebels. Nearly all the heavy earthworks on the upper end of the island have been washed away, and a large sand bar is forming at the lower end. The island is slowly but surely moving downstream. The large rebel cannon "Lady Polk" that exploded during the bombardment is lying quite near the bank of the river and must soon fall in. In a short time, nothing will remain to show that this historical island ever contained a soldier, or was the scene of a long and hotly contested bombardment.

Captain Gordon had, of course, reported promptly to the district commander at Cairo our removal from the mainland to the island, and reasons for so doing, and the little ferryboat sent for our use. But when Major McNeil returned from his Cairo frolic, he was very wroth because we had moved without his orders, and in moving had omitted to move or in any way take care of his personal effects, but had left his bed and baggage to the mercy of the enemy, negroes, woodrats, or anybody or anything that might come along.

On October 28th, we moved back to our old quarters on the mainland, where we have fifty negroes at work on fortifications, our commissary and other stores remaining on the island for greater safety. The gunboat *Tyler* is anchored opposite our camp, where she will probably remain until our works are completed and we are better able to take care of ourselves. The fortification on which we are at work is from original designs by Major McNeil, and in which all military architecture is set at defiance. It is about 100 feet square, with walls four feet high, surrounded by a ditch four feet deep and six feet wide. It is more like a corral than a fort. Our boys call it "Mc's Bull Pen," and it has been proposed, in the event of an attack, to put the major in the pen and take up the bridge. In one corner was mounted a small howitzer on a revolving trail, that could be fired in any direction. While practicing with it one day, I loaded it with canister and trained it so as to fire across the fort to see how it would affect an enemy approaching from that direction. The result was not entirely satisfactory. The "little" gun was loaded pretty heavily, and the recoil threw it off its carriage and over the wall into the ditch. Thinking that a gun that could not be kept within its own lines could not be relied on for defensive purposes, I let it stay where it fell and where it will probably remain until the Mississippi may some day wash it out to plant it deeper in the mud. I am afraid the major's little fort will never be of much service to its country. The infantry officers say they will never fight in it while there are so many good trees outside, and I am quite sure the cavalry will have no use for it. If I get whipped outside, I would rather scatter and run than be corralled, so we all think if worst came to worst, the major will have to occupy it himself.

October 30th. The rebel camp on the Obion having been dispersed, all is again quiet in the bend. The infantry hold the camp while the cavalry ride about the country collecting little etceteras not included in regular rations, and visiting the neighbors.

On November 17th, I was ordered by Brigadier General Davies to report with my company to Major Smith, commanding at Columbus, Kentucky, to which place I proceeded at once by steamboat.[25] We had been at this little post since the 29th of May, five and a half months, and had become pretty well acquainted with nearly every man, woman, child, negro, crossroad, and trail within twenty or thirty miles of camp. In fact, we had been there so long that some of my men seemed to think they had acquired a right or title to a good deal of the property, and that the "Bend" and all therein belonged to them. But when the time came to go, we braced up for the occasion and bid goodbye to Island Number 10 and Madrid Bend with all their associations without a regret. During my stay here I had made several very pleasant acquaintances, who will always be kindly remembered.

We camped at Columbus one night, and the next morning I was ordered to march to Paducah and report to Colonel Noble of our regiment, commanding that post. The weather was dry and warm and the roads in good condition, and our march to Paducah, about fifty miles, was a very pleasant one, not marked by any event of special interest. We camped one night on the way, reporting at Paducah about noon the next day. I pitched my tents on a little common on Broadway, about a mile from the Tennessee River.

Many of my men were here detailed on provost guard duty, some as orderlies at headquarters, and some as clerks in the hospitals and quartermaster's office, so that I was left with but little more than half of my company.

The weather soon turned cold and wet, and as I should doubtless remain here some months, I obtained permission to erect barracks on the opposite side of the street from my camp, and convenient to a large shed, which could be used for stables. All necessary material and tools being furnished by the post quartermaster, my men soon had a row of neat and very comfortable quarters, each room being furnished with a stove, bunks, and benches. In the rear, extending the whole length of the barracks, were the kitchens and mess rooms. My quarters were on the right of the line.

As my duties here were very light, consisting chiefly of drilling a little so that the men should not get rusty, and an occasional scout in the country, more for exercise and pleasure than duty, I had considerable spare time on my hands, which I improved by making quite a number of very pleasant acquaintances, amongst whom I remember Mr. Norton of Norton Brothers Bankers; Mr. Lyon, a school teacher, and family; Mr. Bronson, postmaster, and family; and several others. The Bronsons and Lyons were truly loyal people, and I found them very good friends. During my stay in Paducah, I was a frequent and welcome visitor at their houses.

Snow fell several times during the winter, and my men improvised a number of sleighs and jumpers to which they harnessed their horses with ropes, surcingles, and saddle straps, and had many jolly rides. One outfit I especially remember: it was what the boys termed a "grass hopper jumper." It was a log about twelve feet long with legs, the lower ends of the legs being set into long poles, which bending up in front, served for both runners and shafts. To this was hitched four horses in tandem, with a rider on each horse, and eight or ten men sitting astride on the log. It was a novel turnout and attracted no little attention as it circulated through the streets with its noisy load.

Our barracks were built close to the sidewalk so that the guidon which hung at my headquarters projected out over the walk and hung so low that a person passing under it could touch it, and it afforded me no little amusement to watch from my window the treatment my little guidon received from the many passers-by. Many would pass without noticing it at all. Others, with a sour look at it, would pass near the curbstone so as not to pass under it. Some (women), with a sneer and a disdainful toss of the head, would turn clear out into the street so as not to come near the "hateful thing." A few, with a smile as if recognizing an old friend, would pass directly under and often reach up and touch it. The women, especially the young women and girls, were far more conspicuous in their behavior than the men. The soldiers soon noticed this, and on seeing one or more ladies approaching, would lay little wagers as to how they would act on reaching the flag. Broadway was a favorite promenade for the ladies, and as there was no sidewalk on the opposite side of the street, they were obliged to pass in front of our quarters.

One day the sentinel at my quarters reported that while I was out, a young lady while passing under the guidon, reached up on tiptoes, and pulling it down to her lips, kissed it. I had seen many manifestations of regard and affection for the flag, but was unprepared for anything quite so demonstrative as that, and my interest in that loyal young lady was only exceeded by my curiosity to find out who she was. Some weeks afterwards, the soldier saw the same lady on the street downtown and pointed her out to me. On inquiry, I learned that she was Miss Fanny A. Bronson, the daughter of our loyal postmaster. I, of course, sought and soon found an opportunity of making her acquaintance, which proved a very agreeable one during my stay in Paducah.

While quartered here, a number of my men formed a band and procured instruments, and in a short time, under the instructions of Bugler Weaver, became very fair performers, and every evening, when the weather permitted, would play on the common opposite the barracks. The band soon became popular and one of the attractions of the city, and every fair evening, quite a large crowd would collect on the common to hear the band play. Another attraction was our Sunday morning dress parade and inspection, which never failed to attract a crowd of spectators.

My men made so many acquaintances and were so popular among the young people of the city that they came to feel almost like citizens themselves, and I sometimes had some little difficulty in preserving strict discipline. Their breaches of discipline were, however, generally light and trifling, such as overstaying their passes, or absent from roll call, etc. No drunkenness, quarreling, nor serious offenses occurred while in the city. Our duties being very light, and there being little or no danger of an alarm, I readily granted the men all the privileges I could, and so great was the demand for night passes to attend parties and social entertainments, that sometimes I would have only the guard detail in camp in the evening.

The post quartermaster, Captain Pierce, having been ordered to report to General Grant, I was ordered by Colonel Noble to take charge of the post quartermaster department. I did not want the position, preferring to remain with my company, and remonstrated with the colonel against taking me from my company, as I was then the only officer present, Lieutenant Cayton having remained at Island Number 10. I finally consented to take it until he could get another officer. Captain Pierce was anxious to transfer his invoices to me and take my receipts, which would have been a very simple transaction, but a very one-sided way of doing business, which I declined doing, and insisted on an inventory of stock on hand, the inventory to be made by one of his men and one of mine. Before the inventory was completed, another officer arrived to take charge, which relieved me. The inventories, as far as they were taken, were anything but complimentary to the late quartermaster's mode of doing business, showing a shortage against him of several thousand dollars. How he settled with the new officer, I never cared to inquire, as my interest in the business ceased when I was relieved.

I was much pleased to find here an Episcopal church and a clergyman, and had the pleasure of attending services for the first time since leaving home. I also met here my old friend Reverend Dr. McMasters, who was chaplain at the hospital.

Sergeant Stokes is very sick in the general hospital, and I fear his chances of recovery are very doubtful. But being of strictly temperate habits, and possessing a strong, robust constitution, he may pull through. Several of my men are or have been sick in the hospital, and I visit there every few days. It is in a large building (courthouse, I think) and is well-conducted, and the sick seem well and kindly cared for. On one occasion, I visited the "dead room," where bodies were laid out previous to burial, or to await orders from friends in the north.

Paducah being so near the dividing line between North and South, a good many Northern families reside here, and there is a pretty strong Union element prevailing in society. There are but few slaves now in the city, many having joined the Union camps, but the greater part have been run farther south into the interior. The city is well laid out, the streets being mostly wide and straight and crossing at right angles, but there are very few large or fine buildings, either public or private. Many of the residences are surrounded by extensive grounds and gardens filled with fine shade trees, but everything has the appearance of being old. The stores are small and old-fashioned and make little or no attempt at display. In the southern part of the city is a large rolling mill, or ironworks of some kind, but which is now idle.

I spent the last hours of the dying year at a little social party at Mr. Bronson's, where we had music, singing, cards, etc. The old year, laden with great events, passed into history, and the new one, coming in, found us still struggling with rebellion.

1863

Winter Quarters at Paducah—Smuggling Contraband Goods—Reflections on Black Soldiers—To Columbus, Kentucky—General Asboth—Experimental Military Riverboats—Reflections on Copperheads—Application to Raise a Black Cavalry Regiment—Sick in Hospital—Fort Pillow—Memphis—Battle of Coldwater (Hernando), Mississippi—Wartime Conditions in Memphis—Administering the Oath of Allegiance in Tennessee—Chasing Guerillas in Tennessee—Reflections on the Cost of War—Faulkner's Guerillas Again—Arrested—Winter Quarters at Union City, Tennessee—Further Reflections on the Cost of War

I observed the time-honored custom of New Year's Day by calling on my numerous acquaintances in Paducah. The custom is here quite generally observed, and the ladies all expected and were prepared to receive callers. In the evening I attended a little dance at Lyon's. Frank Weaver and Charley Craine, my company buglers, furnished the music for the occasion. The ladies favored us with several songs, assisted by the military voices of Cox and Ralph.

My soldiers think, and not without reason, that garrison life in Paducah is a pretty nice and easy kind of soldiering. A small daily detail for scouting, a fatigue squad to haul wood, and the regular camp guard constitute their chief duties. The boys are entitled to a little rest and recreation, and I am glad they have it. They have had some pretty rough times, and will probably have much more before the war is over. They are always ready for any emergency, and will respond just as promptly and cheerfully to an order to turn out in the middle of a stormy night to support the pickets as to an invitation to supper or dance.

Notwithstanding the many privileges granted the men, and the many temptations by which they are surrounded, I have very little occasion to find fault. Sometimes a soldier will overstay his pass at night, but he thinks the "game is worth the candle," and cheerfully submits to the light punishment imposed. During our three months' stay in Paducah, I do not remember having a single case of drunkenness or other serious breach of discipline to deal with.

On January 10th, I rode out with Sergeant McMurray to witness a drill of a battalion of the 15th Kentucky Cavalry, by invitation of the commander, Major Waller. I put the battalion through fair maneuvers, but it was hard and very unsatisfactory work, as the day was cold and the wind blowing almost a gale.

I rode out the afternoon of January 12th with Lieutenant Alexander to his father's farm and mill, five miles, where we took supper, returning to camp about dark. Old Mr. Alexander and his estimable wife are Scotch and most excellent people. I have visited them frequently this winter, and have always been most kindly received and treated. Mr. Alexander is a miller and has a large stone mill near his house.

I called several times on January 13th to see Sergeant Hill, who has been sick for some time in Central Hospital. He has been failing rapidly of late. The surgeon in charge wished me to tell Hill that he could not live much longer, a few hours at the most. This was a tack I did not like and wanted the doctor to do it, but he said he thought Hill would rather receive the message through me. When I told Hill what the doctor said, he said he was neither surprised nor alarmed, that he realized his condition and felt that his time was nearly come. At his request I read to him from the Bible, and sitting with my ear close to his pillow—for he could only speak very faintly and slowly—I wrote to his wife as he dictated. He asked me to write to his wife again after he was dead and to send his body home; also to sell his horse and other effects and send the money to his wife. Then, growing more feeble and knowing the end was near, he bade me goodbye and fell into a doze, from which he never awakened in this life. When I called to see him the next morning, he was still unconscious. I stayed with him until he died at half-past ten. I bought a metallic case and had his body placed in the dead house until arrangements could be made for sending it home.

Rain has fallen nearly every day for the past week, and the roads and streets are in a dreadful condition. The town is so flat that the water all soaks into the ground or flows off very slowly. The sidewalks are mostly of planks that flop up at one end as a person steps on the other, and considerable skill is required by pedestrians to dodge the shower of mud that flies up when least expected. I find it safer and some more agreeable to expect flops all the time during wet weather, and then I am never taken by surprise. But however diligently one may expect, he is never just prepared to receive a squirt of liquid mud in his eye or under his chin.

Troops all around us are being paid off, but we can hear of no payments coming this way. My men have not been paid for six months and are beginning to complain and do not perform their duties as promptly and cheerfully as they used to do. They say if the government had no money they would not complain, but would serve willingly without it. But they know their money is ready and they think it is the neglect and fault of the paymasters that they do not get it. The pay department seems to be the most inefficient and poorly conducted branch of the army. In all other departments business is conducted with promptness and dispatch. If a commanding officer wants arms, ammunition, clothing, horses, tents, or anything else for the better equipment and service of his men, he can get them with little or no delay. If there are not officers enough in any particular department for the prompt transaction of business, more are ordered into it, and if a department officer is too slow or negligent in the discharge of his duties, he is very quickly removed. The big machine must not only work smoothly, but quickly in all its parts, and our vast army must be promptly supplied with all the necessaries of war. Uncle Sam doesn't expect his fighting boys to wait six months for cartridges, shoes, or hard tack, but see that they get what they want and when they want it. Then why not get their pay as promptly? Is it because the paymasters get no commission from the soldiers? Shoddy contractors somehow manage to get <u>their</u> pay promptly. There is certainly something very rotten in the pay department, and I would like to see the mess stirred up and ventilated.

Many of the wounded rebels from the Fort Donelson fight were brought here, and so great was the rush of rebel ladies to the hospitals to minister to the wants of their friends, as to very materially interfere with the doctors and the routine business of the hospitals. Colonel Dougherty ordered that all citizens visiting the hospitals be required to subscribe to the oath. This for a time somewhat checked the tide of lady visitors, but so great was their desire to see and talk with the rebel soldiers, and to supply them with little delicacies not found on the hospital bill of fare, that a great many ladies finally signed the oath. Many were the devices used in order to gain admission without subscribing to the objectionable "terms and conditions." Young ladies who had been to school in the northern states, and others who had ever crossed the Ohio River, would declare that they "came from the north," and it was therefore quite unnecessary that <u>they</u> should take the oath. But the Provost Marshal was equal to the occasion. An exchange of signatures were his only terms, and he would sign no passes until the applicants first signed to the oath.

Notwithstanding the vigilance of our officers and soldiers, we have reason to believe a great deal of smuggling is carried on at this place, chiefly in whiskey, ammunition, and quinine. A popular, and until it was discovered, a successful trick, was to conceal a lot of contraband goods in a load of manure and haul it outside the lines, where the garbage would be overhauled at night by interested parties. Another was to load the carcass of a dead beast and drag it boldly through the street and into the country, where it would be disemboweled and its precious paunch sent southward to gladden the hearts and "break the chills" of rebel soldiers, and put dollars in the pockets of the successful "contractor."

The "Nigger Bill," as the soldiers term the bill now before Congress for the enlistment of negro troops, is causing some little excitement and discussion amongst the soldiers.[1] The Southern federal soldiers, and some few prejudiced ones from the North, are the only ones in any way opposed to it. All others are strongly in favor of raising negro troops. I hope it will be done. The negro in the South is a strong element of war, and I have always been in favor of making use of him. If we cannot make soldiers of the negroes, they can at least work in trenches and elsewhere, thus relieving our soldiers of much labor and giving us just so many more effective fighting men, besides depriving the enemy of their help, which is by no means inconsiderable, as the negroes who are not working in the rebel army are working <u>for</u> it on the farm and plantations. The "contrabands" may do well enough to work, but I have little faith in their fighting qualities. I may be mistaken. At any rate I am willing to "give the boys a chance," and shall be glad to see the experiment tried. Freedom, the realization of their lifelong dreams, will of course be a great incentive to them. But it is hardly reasonable to expect that the poor wretches, ignorant and superstitious, and for generations past down-trodden and oppressed and living in continual fear of their masters, without homes or names of their own, should stand up and fight like men, and that too against men who have always been their masters, and who they have always both loved and feared, for like well-trained dogs, they lick the hand that strikes them. Years of slavery have made them craven. They have the muscles and sinews of oxen, but I fear they have not the hearts and nerves of men. That they are <u>loyal</u> there is no question. They look upon our soldiers as their friends, and are always glad to give us information against their masters. They are always obedient, respectful, and industrious, three good soldierly qualities, and it is possible, under good discipline and instruction, that they will fight. It is said, and truly too, that "a coward in a corner will fight like the devil." I think a corner can readily be found for them.

Private William C. Wilks, brother of the late Corporal Wilks, who died recently at Island Number 10, died on January 16th in Central Hospital. He had not been sick long, nor was he considered in any dangerous condition, and his death was quite unexpected. I had seen him every few days and thought he was getting along all right. He was not a strong nor very healthy boy, nor capable of much endurance, but was a good, honest man and soldier, much liked by all of his comrades. His body was placed in the dead house, and his father telegraphed to.

On January 22nd, Mr. D. Wilks and Dr. Lewis of Camp Point, Illinois, arrived in the morning and left in the evening with the bodies of Hill and Wilks.

A case of smallpox was reported the morning of January 26th in a cabin occupied by Mrs. Hogan and daughter, near my company stables. I immediately placed a guard over the house, and as soon as I could procure a tent, had both women removed outside the lines, where I had them provided with food and fuel. Old Mrs. Hogan didn't want to be moved and swore she wouldn't go and that I could not make her go, but she did go. She was a terror when her Irish was up, and she gave me the hardest and hottest cursing I ever had. I employed a city teamster with a big spring wagon, and saw that the daughter, the sick one, was carefully moved on a cot and well cared for. It was a cold, wet day, and the old lady said she would never forgive me for putting her and her sick daughter out of their house in such weather, and I guess she meant it. They were a bad outfit, and I was glad to get them away from near my quarters. I at once procured a quantity of vaccine virus from the surgeon at St. Mark's Hospital, and vaccinated myself and most of my men.

I took a gallop down to Metropolis Landing the morning of January 31st, accompanied by Sergeant McMurray and Corporal Cramer, in hopes of finding a lot of whiskey reported to be there. If there was any whiskey there it must have been a very small quantity and so well cared for that I could not find it.

The recent "January thaw" and consequent damp weather laid me up with rheumatism, and for several days I was confined to my quarters, but am so far recovered that I was able to take a long sleigh ride this morning with Miss Bronson, and this afternoon had a lively snowball encounter in the street with Mr. Bill Travis, one of *Harper's Weekly*'s special artists.

The weather being again clear and pleasant, and the roads in good condition, I have ridden several times lately with Miss Bronson, who is an excellent rider. She said one day that she was tired of riding her father's old family horse, he was too big and slow, that when she rode she wanted a horse with more life, one that could keep up with her, and asked me if I would not lend her one of my fastest and wildest horses. I told her I had in my company some fast and wild horses, but I did not consider them safe for her to ride. But she must have one, so the next time I went to ride with her, I took the untamedest steed in the company, and she not only rode him, but rode him well, although he had never been ridden by a lady before.

I wrote recently to the recruiting officer in Adams County, complaining that I thought I was not getting my share of recruits, and informing him that in consequence of the "backbone of the rebellion" not being broken, I could give steady employment to about twenty-five good bone breakers who could come well recommended, no jailbirds nor official wire pullers wanted.

On Wednesday, February 18th, I received orders to report with my company to Brigadier General Asboth, commanding at Columbus.[2] Of course, we are always ready to go wherever duty calls, but the boys seem to think we have been so long in Paducah that we have acquired a kind of citizenship or possessory right here, and it is not just right and not at all agreeable to be obliged to give up our nice quarters, and all the girls and parties and other comforts and conveniences of Paducah, for the "tented field" and the cold and mud of Columbus. To all of which I heartily subscribe, but I tell the men we have had our rest and good time, and our time has come to take the field again and give place to some other tired and worn-out company. I have applied to have all of my men now on detached service here ordered back to the company. The next day was occupied in getting camp and garrison equipage together, horses and mules shod, and everything ready to move, and I spent the evening making a few parting calls.

Friday morning, February 20th, at half-past nine, we marched out of our old quarters. I marched my company down to post headquarters, where we gave three goodbye cheers for Colonel Dougherty and Adjutant Bartling, then turning southward, marched out of town. On account of the muddy condition of the roads, I sent my wagons and mules down by river. I stopped at my old friends Alexander, where I took dinner. The good old lady made me promise to write to her and was moved even to tears when she bade me goodbye, and insisted on filling my haversack and pockets with nice luncheon. The day was warm, bright, and pleasant, but the roads were very muddy. Having no teams, we did not confine ourselves to the roads, but rode across lots and fields, avoiding much of the mud. Although the men had rations in their haversacks, I permitted them to scatter out about noon in small squads to dine with the farmers. We marched only twenty-five miles and encamped in an old tobacco barn near Blandville, where we found plenty of corn and hay for our horses and comfortable quarters for ourselves.

Early the next morning, we left our comfortable old barn and continued our march. The scanty supply of fair weather had become exhausted during the night, and the morning opened cold and wet, and during the remainder of the ride we experienced cold, fog, drizzle, sprinkle, rain, sleet, snow, and other changes incidental to the season and climate.

Arriving at Columbus soon after noon, I left the company on the bluff near Fort Halleck and rode downtown to report to Colonel Martin commanding the post. To say that the streets of Columbus were "awfully muddy" would be too mild an expression, and would convey little or no idea of their real condition. The mud was black, soft, and sticky, ranging in depth from six inches to two feet, and covered with a thin sheet of ice, and when stirred up emitted an odor that would make an old sewer feel weak.

I was ordered to camp on the bluff near the fort and was fortunate in securing good new tents for my men. I stayed that night with my company at the Soldier's Home, where we had comfortable quarters. After breakfast the next morning, I pitched my camp on the best and driest place I could find on the bluff.

My quartermaster sergeant was unable to get a new wall tent for me and was obliged to take one that had been used. On opening it, I was surprised to find painted on the front: "Maj. 10th Ill." By a singular coincidence I had drawn the tent lately used by my brother-in-law, Major J. G. Rowland. I had a good little stove in my tent and was soon comfortably at home. My mess chest with the baggage not having yet arrived, I had rather a light dinner, but before night our baggage was hauled up from the river, and I had a supper equal to my appetite.

While down at headquarters in the afternoon, I was introduced to General Asboth. He is in appearance quite an elderly man, a Hungarian, tall, thin, and very straight, and has the reputation of being a rigid old-school disciplinarian, and is said to be one of the hardest riders in the service and has but one officer on his staff who can keep up with him when he says "now we sall go shentlemans." He must be a wild rider if he can keep away from some riders in my company.

A little incident occurred on February 25th, which served to prejudice me against General Asboth and his old country style of treating volunteer soldiers who enlisted to serve <u>this country</u>. I was invited to dine with him, and while at dinner he informed me that there was to be a ball tonight at Clinton, ten miles distant, at which certain rebel officers were expected and would probably be present. He wished me to go with my company to Clinton and surround the hotel about midnight and arrest every man in rebel uniform and all that I might suspect belonged to the rebel army, and as though he thought I was a savage or a guerilla, he charged me with particular emphasis that under no circumstances must the least discourtesy be shown the ladies, and this he repeated several times. In conclusion, he said he would accompany me "as a <u>guest</u>, just for the fun of the trip," but that I must command the expedition. He would meet me at the picket line at nine o'clock.

I thought the whole affair, from my point of observation, looked rather singular and very unreasonable. I did not believe there was an officer in the regular rebel army who was fool enough to come to a public ball within ten miles of Columbus, where he would be almost sure of meeting federal soldiers, and as the day had been very stormy, and the night promised to be even worse, I thought the old general must be rather short on amusements to want to go out such a night on a scout "just for fun." Young man as I was then, and fond of balls and dancing, and always ready to take any chances for a little fun, I don't think I would have gone to Clinton that night "for fun." But I had my orders and "questioned not."

I was at the lines with my whole company promptly at nine o'clock, and in a few minutes the old general dashed up at the head of his staff and a company of regular cavalry. Here was a dilemma, one horn of which was that I was ordered to command the scout, and the other was the presence of another captain, my senior. Before I could decide which horn to grasp, to follow out my instructions, or recognize the other officer's seniority, the general relieved me of further embarrassment by promptly assuming command, and with his customary warning, "Now we sall go," ordered "gallop march," and away we went as though we had been sent for and couldn't get there on time. In a few minutes, every man and horse was so covered with mud that we looked like an animated squadron of clay statuary. Before reaching Clinton I was fully convinced that he was entitled to be called "a hard rider."

Arriving at Clinton, instead of surrounding the hotel where the dance was going on, I was ordered to dismount my men in the street and await further orders. I now saw how badly I had been sold. The general had no more idea of finding a rebel officer there than he had of finding one in his headquarters. The truth was, he had been invited to this ball, but not wishing to order out two captains with their companies to escort him to a dance, had made up the "rebel officer" story. The general took with him a complete change of clothing and appeared in the ballroom as neat as a dandy. He went in for a good time and had it, dancing and flirting with the girls. He soon sent out an invitation for the other captain (I regret that I cannot recall his name) and me to come in and join the dance, but as we had on our heavy riding boots, were wet through, and covered from head to heel with mud, and as mad as we knew how to be, we declined his invitation, and stayed outside and growled and said hard words together until nearly daylight. We returned in much the same manner as we went out, the general dismissing me at the lines, and I reached my camp just as the morning gun in Fort Halleck was fired. My cook had breakfast ready, which I ate and went to bed and slept until noon.

While downtown the morning of March 2nd, I met Mr. Will Wells, an old Quincy acquaintance who came to camp and took a ride in the country with me, after which we dined at the "Shakespeare" restaurant.

Wednesday, March 4th being the first anniversary of the occupation of Columbus by the Union troops, all the officers called by invitation on General Asboth and Colonel Martin at ten o'clock in the morning, when we were invited to a banquet to be given by the general at two o'clock on board the steamboat *Diadem*. Dinner commenced promptly at two, the general occupying the head of the table, and was the stiffest and most uncomfortable affair of the kind I ever participated in. The day was very hot and we were all in full uniform, buttoned up to the chin and wearing side arms, and the sternness and rigid precision with which every course was served and every toast offered was tiresome to men long accustomed to "catch as catch can" meals in camp and field.

I was, to my great joy, on duty that day as "grand field officer of the day," and at three o'clock I rose, and stating to the general that I was most unfortunately(?) on duty, asked to be excused. A little French captain of the 24th Wisconsin Infantry, who was "officer of the guard," also asked to be excused. The captain, mounted on a little, unruly pony, rode the grand rounds with me. He had already "toasted" a little too much during his one hour at the banquet, and experienced some little inconvenience in managing his pony, which ran away with him twice and threw him off once. It was more fun than a whole row of banquets.

Having obtained a short leave of absence, I started for Paducah at 4:30pm on Monday, March 9th, accompanied by Private Maurice Bywater, reaching Blandville (twenty-five miles) at eight o'clock, when I put up for the night at the tavern, and the next day rode to Paducah, stopping at Mr. Alexander's for dinner and spending the evening at Mr. Bronson's. I went the next morning to see my sick men: Peabody, Triplett, Berrian, and Cramer in the hospital and found them all doing well.

As I was not in any rush of a hurry, I made several calls during the afternoon and stayed all night with Lieutenant Key at the provost marshal's office. I did not intend to return until Saturday, but learning Friday morning at the telegraph office at headquarters that General Asboth was preparing to move up the river with troops, I decided to return at once, though I was obliged to leave much important business with the post quartermaster unfinished. I told Bywater to meet me at the picket line at four o'clock, or at Alexander's at five. I dined at Mr. Bronson's and left town at four o'clock, reaching Alexander's at five, where I took supper and waited for Bywater until seven, when, as he had not reported, I started alone. The good old lady tried to dissuade me from undertaking such a dangerous journey alone and in the night, but I felt it was my duty to go, and assured her I felt safer traveling at night than in the day, for alone I did not expect to fight, and if waylaid, my chances to escape were better in the night.

The first part of the night was very dark, for which I was glad, as I always feel safer in the dark than in moonlight. If it is difficult for me to see an enemy in the dark, it is equally difficult for him to see me, and I know from experience it is almost if not quite impossible to shoot or catch a man in the dark. I jogged along and made good time for several miles, but being very tired and less watchful than usual, I fell asleep on my horse, and just before reaching Blandville, where the road forked, my horse took the wrong road and had gone four or five miles before I awoke. Failing to recognize the landmarks, I knew I was off the right road, but did not know where I was, so stopping at a saloon, I awoke a man and enquired if

I was on the right road to Mayfield. "Yes, straight ahead, but what in the world are you traveling this time of night alone for, stranger?" "Thank you, I am attending to my own business. Good night." I had all the information I wanted. I wanted to go away from instead of towards Mayfield, but to satisfy my inquisitous friend, who stood in the door watching me, I rode straight ahead a few rods, then turned and rode quietly back. I preferred being alone that night, or with company of my own choosing, and thought if that fellow or his companions in the cabin should try to overtake or intercept me to ascertain my business, they would have a good time following me towards Mayfield or waiting for me at some crossroad.

I soon reached the main road again and passed through Blandville just as the moon rose. I slept no more that night, but kept eyes and ears open, and every stump and shadow along the road was viewed with suspicion. The owls were out in force and very social, calling to me or to each other from all sides. I do not know of anything that can break the stillness of night more abruptly or more disagreeably than the hooting of an owl. You are expecting it all the time, and when it comes you know just what it is, but it will startle you all the same and make a cold streak run up and down your back. You feel ashamed of yourself and place on record a resolution to the effect that you will never again be scared at the hooting of an owl, and you keep your resolve most religiously until the next one "hoot, toot, toots" over your head, and another arctic wave flows over you, and however dark the night or distant the owl, and you know just what the noise is, you will always look in the direction from which it comes. Perhaps the above has not been your nor everybody's experience, but it has been mine.

I reached camp safely at sunrise to find all quiet and no one expecting to march anywhere. I did not return any too soon, however, as during my absence some of my men had been on a spree in town, and I found one sergeant under arrest and one soldier in the guardhouse. I soon straightened matters by obtaining the release of both men, giving my personal parole that they should appear when wanted for trial.

I went to see the man in the guardhouse, against whom charges had been preferred for drunkenness and resisting the provost guard. He said, "I ain't afraid of the sentence of a court martial, though I expect it will be severe, I can stand that, but," with a sigh and tears in his eyes, "they will hear of this at home." I feel truly sorry for the boy, for I knew his family, his widowed mother and a sister in Quincy, and they were most worthy and estimable people. I had talked and reasoned with him time and again, but all to no purpose. He would promise most faithfully to behave himself and then get drunk and disorderly again in the first opportunity. So it is. A soldier, surrounded by temptations and without the sustaining influences of home and home surroundings, seems to forget all amid the temptations and evil influences that constantly beset a soldier, and he becomes at last so hardened and reckless as to ignore even the dreaded severity of the sentence of a court martial, but considers and regrets when too late the hurts and heartaches his misconduct will bring to loving ones at home.

I rode out in the country the morning of March 15th with Adjutant Stiles and Lieutenant Martin of the 111th Illinois Infantry and took dinner at Mr. Jennings', and this afternoon was honored by a call at my quarters by two ladies, whose names I regret I have forgotten, wives of a surgeon and steward at the hospital. I had just returned from a long ride and had laid down on my cot for a nap with my toilet in a somewhat disordered condition, not expecting and quite unprepared to receive lady callers. But they made all due allowances for me, and apologies for themselves for calling uninvited and unannounced. They were out strolling and sightseeing, had been to the fort, and having never seen a cavalry camp, thought they would call and inspect mine and would begin at the captain's tent. I showed them through camp, which seemed to interest them. Their visit was as pleasant as it was unexpected, and on leaving they invited me to call on them at the hospital.

A few days ago I met an old acquaintance, Colonel W. L. Duff of the 2nd Illinois Artillery. He had been home and was returning to his command in front of Vicksburg. He said he was "superintending" the digging of the big canal, through which our gunboats were to pass below Vicksburg. I believe I have not seen a general staff or field officer, who had at any time been to Vicksburg, who was not "superintending" some part or something about that canal. If there are workmen in proportion to the number of superintendents, that canal should soon be done and bigger than the main river, which just now is very high out of its banks and all over the bottoms. The lower part of the town and many of the streets are under water, which has driven thousands of rats into the homes and under the plank sidewalks. They come out in swarms at night and are so <u>tame</u> with hunger that it is difficult to walk without stepping on them, which distracts very much from the pleasure of a moonlight or dark night stroll, for if there is anything more uncomfortable to walk on than a live snake, I think it is a live rat; a rat with a broken back or his bowels crushed out is just as apt, on being released, to run one way as another, and in his frantic efforts to escape, not infrequently attempts to climb up one's trousers. They are exceedingly annoying to ladies.

Nearly all the steamboats on the western waters are being ordered to Vicksburg. Twenty-eight passed down yesterday, which must mean a movement of Grant's large army now operating against Vicksburg. A fleet of fine large boats of the "Marine Brigade" passed down recently, loaded chiefly with cavalry and flying artillery. These boats are enclosed all around and so constructed that their sides can be let down by means of hinges at the bottom, thus forming a stage the entire length of the boat. The sides of the cabin deck are bullet proof and pierced with loopholes for musketry. When a company of guerillas appear on the shore, or if for any reason it may be necessary to land troops rapidly, the boat can be run up to the shore, where the bank is suitable, the sides thrown down, and whole squadrons or batteries disembarked at a single rush under cover of the musketry above. They are a novel experiment in warfare, the efficacy of which I think has not yet been proven.[3]

The guerilla chief Cushman, who escaped recently from prison here, has been recaptured near Fort Pillow. If he can't be kept in prison and in irons, he should be tied with a short rope to a high branch of a tree. He will not be liable to run far with his feet off the ground.[4]

I learn by the northern papers and private information that the "Copperheads" in Illinois contemplate "armed resistance to the draft." My men are half wild with the desire to be detailed on provost duty to enforce the draft in Adams County. I certainly should like nothing better than such duty myself for about six months, and have written to the provost marshal in Quincy, asking him if he cannot get my company detailed. The feelings of the soldiers against these home traitors and anti-war men, the "Copperheads," is more bitter than against the guerillas. The guerillas, although belonging to no regular army or organization, are rebel soldiers and are recognized by the rebel government. Their duties are to do pretty much as they please and harass and annoy us as much as possible, and collect conscripts and supplies for their army, thus compelling us to keep every little port and town quartered by troops that would otherwise be in the large armies at the front, and prisoners captured from these roving bands are accepted in exchange, the same as prisoners from the regular rebel army. But these Northern Copperheads belong to neither side, to no party. They pretend to sympathize with the South, but have not courage to fight for it, and while denouncing us and our cause, they continue to live under our protection. They are outlawed by both sides, hated by the Union soldiers, and damned by the rebels. Among the old troops, all political and party feeling is about played out, and we all stand shoulder to shoulder on one grand platform: "Our country and our country's cause; and our country, right or wrong."

I witnessed, unobserved, a little scene in my camp recently that was not only very amusing, but served to illustrate the popular sentiments of the men. A peddler selling little odds and ends in the camps, thinking probably to gain favor with the soldiers, expressed himself rather mildly against certain measures adopted by the government. I do not remember the subject they were discussing, only the circumstances attending it. Scarcely had the poor peddler expressed his views than a sergeant took out his watch and, mentioning the time, told the peddler he had just three minutes in which to get himself out of camp. The serious manner of the sergeant, and the rough edges of a rail that suddenly appeared on the scene, had the effect of hastening the departure of the Copperhead peddler. I thought if this poor man, ignorant and without influence, who could do very little of either good or harm, would not be tolerated in his disloyal expressions, how would certain rich and influential Copperheads that I could name in the North, who publicly in speeches and through the press denounce the government and its soldiers, fare at the hands of these men! If certain well-known men in Adams County should happen to get into my camp, I am strongly of the opinion they would go out of it on both sides of a fence rail, and volunteers to carry the rail would not be wanting.

On Saturday, March 28th, I rode out to Clinton, this time "just for fun," accompanied by Orderly Sergeant Fred Turner, and took dinner at the Clinton Hotel. I here unexpectedly met an old acquaintance, Joe Best of Quincy, a captain in the 21st Missouri Infantry, whose regiment was then stationed at Clinton. We rode back, ten miles, in a little over one hour.

Sunday morning I called at Goodall's printing office. Goodall is printer by appointment to General Asboth, and has a very snug little office where he does all the work alone. He is also proprietor and publisher of the *War Eagle*, a very sharp and spicy little weekly.

On the occasion of my last visit to Clinton, I discovered and seized a quantity of conscripting rolls and rebel official blanks. Their system of conscription appears to be very complete. Every man in the rebel states capable of doing any kind of military duty is considered a soldier, and failing to report when ordered, is considered a deserter and is arrested and forced into the army.

I also picked up a boy on the road who had a letter from a lady in Columbus to "Maj. Bremen C.S.A.," in which the major is informed (or would have been had I not got his letter) that "the Yankee Cavalry are shoeing their horses and preparing for some kind of a movement." The letter was highly interesting, aside from the above information conveyed in it, and of a decidedly inflammatory nature, and meant to be read by no one but the major himself. I was sorry to deprive the major of his letter, and had the lady confined herself to sentiment, and said nothing about the doings of the "Yankee Cavalry," I would have let the letter pass, but I felt obliged to confiscate it, and out of regard for the writer, destroyed it. If the girls will write tender, gushing letters to their rebel lovers and entrust them to the care of boys, they must expect them to miscarry sometimes, and by giving contraband information, they are liable to compromise themselves.

On Thursday, April 1st, General L. Thomas, Adjutant General, U.S. Army, reviewed the troops at this post.[5] He made a short speech to the soldiers explaining the object of the government in raising negro troops, a subject that has always been of interest to me and one that I always favored, and the more I have thought of it, the more it has grown upon me. After hearing General Thomas' speech, and at the solicitation of a number of my men who were anxious to go in with me, I decided to apply for a commission to raise and organize a regiment of negro cavalry, the regiment to be officered by men from my company. I fully realized that there would be much hard and disagreeable labor attending such an undertaking, but I had counted the cost. I did this not with any sentimental love for the negroes, but because I believed I could thus better serve my country, and I thought if they could not be made to fight, of which I was still in doubt, they could at least do for us what they are obliged to do for the rebels—work—and I believed I could raise a regiment of 1,000 within sixty days.

When I presented my application to General Asboth to be forwarded with his endorsement to the adjutant general of the army, I fortunately found him in one of his occasional spells of good humor. After reading it over, he asked me how I proposed raising my men. "By volunteer enlistment in the rebel states," I replied. "Ah! But my tear sir, to do zat you vill have to induce ze slaves to leave zair owners. I do not like zat ver mooch," he said looking at me sharply. I said we took their horses, cattle, forage, and everything we could find that was wanted, why not take their negroes? Besides, those negroes were now free men and were held in slavery in violation of the president's proclamation, and that I believed in taking every possible advantage of the enemy and making every edge cut, and if we can make use of the negroes in any way, if only to deprive the enemy of their services, I thought we ought to do so. He finally approved my application and promised to use his influence in my behalf, and there the matter rested until the return of my paper from Washington, "disapproved, as no colored cavalry would at present be received." As far as I like war at all, I like the cavalry service, and would not under any circumstances accept a commission in a regiment of infantry or heavy artillery, and these were the only branches in which negroes were being enlisted.

Information was received Friday night, April 3rd, that a force of rebels were in the vicinity of Hickman, ten miles down the river. The 27th Wisconsin Infantry and Captain McNulty's cavalry company were at once sent down by boat, and the next morning I was ordered with my company to Clinton to report to Colonel D. Moore of the 21st Missouri Infantry, commanding at Clinton. I stopped at Clinton with Captain Larrison, Company B of our regiment, who was then stationed there, and sent Orderly Sergeant Turner with ten men to Jacksonville. I took dinner with Colonel Moore and spent the greater part of the afternoon with him awaiting Sergeant Turner's return. The colonel had but one leg, having lost the other in a battle, I think in Missouri. A prisoner was brought in from the pickets, who was questioned, abused, and scared nearly to death by the colonel, who I thought liked to be considered "rough." Sergeant Turner returned in the evening without having seen anything of the rebels.

I remained at Clinton over Sunday and returned to my camp Monday morning.

Tuesday, April 7th, was my 25th birthday.

Wednesday evening, I was ordered out to Clinton again, where I stayed all night, returning to camp the next evening, and took supper with Lieutenant Ewart of our regiment at his quarters, where I had the pleasure of meeting Mrs. Ewart and Miss Dement. I had an invitation to attend a military ball that night at Masonic Hall, but being very tired and not feeling very well, declined.

We have had a long season of "masterly inactivity" at this post, little or nothing doing, and many of my men are yet absent on detached service at Paducah. Not having such pleasant acquaintances here as I had at Paducah last winter, time hangs heavily on my hands. I have a number of good correspondents in the North, but letter writing, when there is nothing interesting to write about, ceases to be interesting. This is a bad town in which to keep soldiers. Many of my soldiers appear to have served out their term of probation and have relapsed. Men who were exemplary in conduct last winter are here continuously getting themselves and me into trouble. A low variety theater of the lowest order is run here, and the town is full of barrooms, sports, and disreputable characters, and no effort seems to be made by either the commanding general, the post commander, or provost marshal to improve matters. Why such troublesome places and characters are permitted to remain in towns occupied by troops I cannot understand, when it would be just as easy to keep them out of town as out of camp.

The 4th Missouri Cavalry, Colonel Waring commanding, and Company M of our regiment, arrived here recently. As there is at present nothing for such a force of cavalry to do here, I hope this means a movement soon. Commanding officers have all been ordered to report to the adjutant general at Washington the number of men required to fill up their commands that they may be filled by <u>draft</u>. Good. Now with good live provost marshals, and guards in the North to make "good music," I hope "the ball will go on."

On Sunday, April 19th, I visited with Sergeant Cox the battlefield of Belmont, opposite Columbus, but found the ground so muddy from the recent overflow that we could ride over only a small part of the field. I recognized several familiar places and landmarks.

I received notice on April 21st that Charley Crain, my second bugler, died in hospital at Paducah on Saturday night, 18th instant. Charley was one of the best, good-natured boys in the company, and he with his violin will be sadly missed by his comrades.

On Monday, April 27th, I was taken sick with chills and fever and confined to my quarters. My fever increasing the next day, I sent to the hospital for Dr. Castalina, who visited me and sent an ambulance the next morning and took me to the hospital. Lieutenant Cayton and Sergeants Spence and Turner called to see me the next day, Thursday. There being but few patients at present in the hospital, I can have a room to myself where I am very comfortable. Dr. Snyder, surgeon in charge of the ward I am in, is very kind and attentive. My nurse Claus Peters, a private of the 1st Kansas Infantry ("Jennison's Jayhawkers"), is a Dutchman and a first-rate fellow. I pay him one dollar a day, and as he has only two or three other patients to take care of, he devotes much of his time to me.

I have been very sick during the past week, and I have hardly left my room, but feeling better and stronger today, May 10th, and very weary of confinement, I sent for my horse and rode to camp, where I rested a while and returned to the hospital. I enjoyed the ride and visit to my camp, but it proved too much for me and brought a return of my fever, and for a week I did not again leave my room.

On May 16th, I applied for a short leave of absence to go home. My application was approved by Dr. Snyder, but disapproved and returned by Dr. Derby, the medical director, which I thought, and always shall think, was very hard. It was the first leave I had asked for since I went home with Captain Delano a year ago. I was very sick and wanted and needed a change, and Dr. Derby, who had never seen me, of course knew nothing of my condition. Although he visited the hospital, he never came to see me while I was there.

On May 21st, while eating supper in my room, sitting on my bed with a small stand before me, the house was shaken by an earthquake, the hardest I ever felt. My dishes rattled together and a bottle of medicine on my table was tipped over. Claus was badly scared and thought the end of all time had come with four months' pay due him from the government.

Private A. H. Bates of my company, who has been sick in the hospital since the 21st instant, died about ten o'clock the morning of May 27th. I had been to his ward several times to see him and was with him when he died. He was delirious for several hours before he died. He was buried in the afternoon on a hill back of the hospital.

Becoming thoroughly tired of the dull, monotonous routine of hospital, I decided to return to my camp on May 29th, against which Dr. Snyder strongly protested, assuring me that I was yet quite unfit for duty and would endanger my life by going to camp in such cold, wet weather. But I felt that I should die of the blues, if nothing else, if I stayed there much longer, so I told him if I found I could not stand it in camp, I would come back to him. So I settled for my board at the hospital and, bidding Dr. Snyder and Claus goodbye, sent to the livery stable for a buggy to take me to camp. The doctor said he had not discharged me, that according to his morning report I was not in a condition to be discharged, and he would not then give me an official discharge. So I told him he would have to report me "dead or deserted" the next morning—that I was deserting them, and might be dead before morning. But as he had to dispose of me somehow in his morning report, he sent me my discharge the next day.

I was in the hospital just one month, and although I had a very comfortable room, the most of the time to myself, and received every possible care and attention, and made a number of very pleasant acquaintances, it was a long, dreary month to me. I had been so long accustomed to camp life and active exercise that it came very hard for me to be sick and shut up in a house. I shall ever bear in grateful remembrance the kindness and consideration of Dr. Snyder and the nurturing attention of my nurse Claus.

I did not return to camp any too soon, for that very night at eleven o'clock, my company received orders to be ready to march at any moment to Fort Pillow, and the next day the order came to march. Being too weak to ride, I sent the company under command of Lieutenant Cayton, who started at 6pm, while I remained to go down by boat with the baggage. I was glad indeed to get away from the red tape, Dutch style, and general cussedness of Columbus. I was sick and perhaps a little irritable, and was reported twice that day to General Asboth because I would not quietly submit to the intolerable insolence of some of his young lieutenant "aides," and the old general gave me a good scolding in Dutch, which did me no harm and may have pleased him.

On Monday, June 1st, my baggage was inspected and reduced, and I was obliged to leave all my tents and other heavy baggage, such as stoves, mess chests, cots, etc. and was given thirty-four little shelter tents. I was permitted to keep my private mess chest and a hand valise, but not my tent nor cot. A little shelter tent and two blankets, weighing all together not over ten pounds, comprised my headquarters.

It was amusing to those who, like myself, had before had their baggage "reduced" and had long been accustomed to the little inconveniences of field service, to witness the trials and tribulations of certain young officers lately from the North, when the inspecting officer ordered their tents, spring mattresses, and buffalo robes to be piled up in the warehouse. One young lieutenant of infantry wanted to quit the service immediately and go home to Chicago and let the country go to the dogs because he was not permitted to take three large trunks, a big bundle of bedding, a spring cot, and wall tent with him to Vicksburg. They all start out that way, I remember doing something of the kind myself, but they soon get weaned and learn to take things rough and tumble as they come, and are glad sometimes to have even a shoddy blanket made of hemp and cow hair, about as wide as a thin man and half as long, to sandwich between their tired bodies and the cold ground.

After much delay, which to me in my weak condition was very tiresome and vexatious, I finally got off at 9pm on the steamer *O'Brien*, commanded by Captain Bradley. We reached Island Number 10 at ten o'clock in the morning, where the boat tied up. I went on shore early the next morning and called on Captains Gordon and Montgomery, who were still stationed at that post. We left Island Number 10 at 6:30am and reached Fort Pillow at 7pm, when I at once reported to Colonel Wolfe of the 52nd Indiana Infantry, commanding the post, and stayed that night with Captain Frank Moore of Company D of our regiment.

Lieutenant Cayton arrived about 4pm the next day with the company, all under the command of Captain Felter of the 4th Illinois Cavalry. My men report having a good time generally; being the most of the time in the advance, they had their choice of stopping places and lived on the best the country afforded, and the boys of Company L, always ready to make any sacrifice for their county, were willing to subsist for a few days on chickens, eggs, butter, and other country produce in order to reduce the expense of the government. I have known some of our men to subsist on such country fare for a week so as to save a few commissary rations.

My health continues to improve so that on Thursday, June 4th, I rode a few miles out in the country with Colonel Wolfe. In the evening, all the cavalry officers assembled in Captain Frank Moore's quarters for a sort of reunion and general good time.

Fort Pillow, so named after the rebel General Gideon Pillow, is on the east bank of the Mississippi River 150 miles below Columbus, and is the first point below Hickman where the river touches the bluffs. The bluffs or hills here are high and very rough and much broken and with steep sides. The tops of the hills in all directions are covered with earthworks. It is more properly a fortified post than a fort. All the interior works are enclosed by a line of breastworks about seven miles long in the form of a half circle, the two ends of which rest on the bluffs overlooking the river. Outside this line is an extensive abatis. It is a strong point and much labor has been done to improve the natural advantages of the position. But after all their work here, and their talk about this being "the last ditch" in which they were all going to die, the rebels evacuated it after the fall of Fort Donelson and Corinth without firing a gun, and moved their forces to Vicksburg. So great was their haste in leaving that they abandoned many of their heavy guns, some of which they threw off the top of the high bluff into the river. Inside the lines of earthworks is a good spring of clear, cold water. The surrounding country is well settled and cultivated, and in the bottomlands are many good farms.

Returning from a ride in the country about noon on Sunday, June 7th, I found marching orders for Memphis. I struck camp and loaded the wagons that night and marched about nine o'clock the next morning, the battalion consisting of six companies of the 2nd Illinois, being under the command of Captain Frank Moore of Company D.

We reached Covington about noon, where we took dinner and four rebel soldiers, one of the latter being Captain Churchill, on the staff of General Looney.[6] Soon after leaving Covington, we met an officer with a small scouting party from Fort Pillow to whom we turned over our prisoners. We camped that night in the village of Portersville. It is reported that Faulkner, with his army of guerillas, is somewhere in our vicinity. When I captured him last fall, he said it would be his turn next, and that he would take me in the next time we met. If Faulkner wants to fight us he can easily find us, for we are leaving a broad trail and making our marks all along the road, and if we can hear of him within striking distance, we will go out of our way to make him fight, or run away. If he once found our company of Illinois cavalry too much for him, I don't know what he would do with six companies.

Leaving Portersville early the next morning, Thursday, June 9th, we reached Memphis, thirty miles, at 2pm. We found deep water in the Loose Hatchie River; and the bridge destroyed, and the stream being very rapid and full of floating debris, we experienced considerable difficulty in crossing. Two or three old leaky boats and canoes were found, and the men made some rafts of logs, but the most of the men swam the river on their horses or behind them, holding the horse by the tail. I crossed with two or three of my men in a leaky dugout canoe, which we managed to keep afloat by industriously bailing with our hats. Ropes were tied to the boats and rafts so they could be pulled back across the river. My negro hostler "Wash" attempted to swim the river on one of my horses, but in the crowd and rush of horses in the water, Wash's horse became unmanageable and threw him off and he was struck and knocked under water by the horses following. As he came to the surface, a soldier caught and pulled him ashore, where he was laid on the bank out of the way, head downward so the water could drain out of him. We were all too busy to pay much attention to Wash, and he laid there until he was well drained, when he got up and hunted up his horse. It was a pretty close call for Wash.

At 2pm, we pitched our little shelters, or "dog tents," about a mile from the city of Memphis. A camp of these little tents, after having been so long accustomed to the large regulation tents, presented a very curious spectacle. It looked like a toy camp. A shelter tent is made in two pieces of rather light and poor canvas buttoned together, and when pitched stands about two and a half feet high and accommodates(?) two men, and being open at both ends, it affords about as much shelter as a large umbrella. General Veatch, commanding at Memphis, ordered us to make a permanent camp, so I at once procured good tents and other camp equipage.[7]

Just before reaching Covington on our march from Fort Pillow, one of my men, John F. Brooks, was shot through the right foot by the accidental discharge of his carbine hanging from the pommel of his saddle. At Covington, I pressed a mule and buggy and negro driver and had Brooks brought to Memphis and placed in the hospital.

While making the grand rounds as brigade field officer of the day on June 11th, I saw for the first time a squad of negro ("contraband") soldiers. Dressed in new uniforms, and with bright muskets on their shoulders, they looked as wild and brave as oxen. How they manage to "order arms" without serious inconvenience I don't know, for as they stood in line, no ground could be seen between their feet. Their feet seemed to occupy as much space as their shoulders. They are known here as "the web footed brigade." Accustomed all their lives to the severe discipline of slavery, they make willing and obedient soldiers, and with proper training and assurance of protection and freedom, they may yet prove themselves to be men.

There is a large camp of fugitive slaves, old men unfit for military duty and women and children, the latter largely in the majority, just below the city and also on an island. They are furnished government rations, but at both camps they cultivate the ground, raising small crops of corn and potatoes, so that they are to a small extent self-sustaining. The question that has for so long vexed our military and civil authorities: what to do with the "contrabands"? may yet answer itself.

Guerillas are the same here as elsewhere, wherever we have been. Numerous bands in the country are constantly firing on our pickets and scouts, and committing depredations in the country. They are not strong enough, all combined, to attack the post, but they serve the purpose of obliging us to keep quite a large force here that would otherwise be with Grant or Burnside.

On Sunday, June 14th, I was sent out with a small scout party. I crossed the state line and went about ten miles into Mississippi. I was out all day and saw no rebels, but captured a rebel conscripting officer, Captain Elkins, and a couple of smugglers near Horn Lake. One of the latter had concealed about his person twenty ounces of quinine worth at this time in the "Confederacy" $100 per ounce. One bottle (1 oz.) I kept for my own use, and the balance I turned over to our surgeon.

While the large part of our battalion was out on a scout in Mississippi, orders were received late at night for the balance to march at 2am, June 17th, to pursue and attack the rebel General Marmaduke, who recently fired on the steamer *Platte Valley* with artillery, fifteen miles up the river, and who was supposed to be now in Mississippi, somewhere in the vicinity of Hernando.[8] We marched out at three o'clock next morning, our force of 300 consisting of detachments of 1st Missouri, 5th Ohio, and 2nd Illinois under the command of Major Henry of the 5th Ohio. I commanded the 2nd Illinois detachment, eighty men. We marched through the town of Hernando to Cold Water River, where I was left to hold the ford while Major Henry went a few miles farther. We camped that night between Hernando and the river. We had seen no large force of rebels, but had encountered several scouting parties, who were intently watching our movements. That night, our pickets were fired on several times.

Once during the night, about 2am, a sergeant of my company, who had charge of one of the picket posts, came in and reported to me that the rebels appeared to be in considerable force in front of his post, that he could plainly hear them moving about and their officers giving commands, though on account of the fog, he could see nothing. He also thought he could hear the movements of artillery. I at once reported these facts to Major Henry, and ventured to suggest that we either change our position under cover of the fog, or march out and attack the rebels before they should be in position to receive us, or perhaps surround us. As they were doubtless fully informed of our strength and position, and were taking advantage of the fog and darkness in getting into position to fight us in the morning, I was in favor of either getting out of their way or forcing the fight. Other officers who were present agreed with me, but the major was disposed to make light of it, and thought we were needlessly alarmed. He said he had reliable information that there was only a small force, about two hundred, with one little cannon.

We left our bivouac at four o'clock the next morning (Friday) in a dense fog. I was in advance with the 2nd Illinois detachment. We had not marched more than a half-mile, when we were fired on with two small cannons, or howitzers, throwing canister, which passed over our heads. The rebels could not see us, but fired at random. Nor could we see them, nor even the flash of their guns. Being then in a lane, we threw down the fence on our left, and formed a line of battle in a cornfield with my command on the right. I was ordered by Major Henry to, "hold this line but don't fire." In a few moments, a small squad of rebels appeared on my front, coming out of the timber about 100 yards distant, who, from the long guns they carried, I took to be mounted infantry. They did not at first see us, but as soon as they did, they fell back under cover of the trees and fired a few shots at us, killing one man of my command, but a few feet from me.

We were now marched by the left flank and formed on three sides of a hollow square, which I thought was rather a novel formation for cavalry. The 5th Ohio was posted at right angles to my line on my right. I was ordered by Major Henry to hold my position as long as possible, and if obliged to fall back, I would find a supporting line a short distance in my rear.

In front of my line was a small open ravine or valley. I could not see across this ravine on account of the fog, but could occasionally see the tops of the trees beyond and could plainly hear the rebel cavalry moving and the voices of their officers, on the opposite side of the ravine. I threw out a line of skirmishers, covering the whole front of my line, who dismounted and engaged the rebel skirmishers at short range.

Major Henry was continuously moving his forces about here and there until, in the fog, we could not tell friend from foe. At one time, a column of rebels appeared so near the Ohio battalion that questions and answers were exchanged before either party knew who the other was. Sharp firing was kept up for some time, my men coming up to the work coolly and bravely, but the fire on my front became so heavy that I was on the point of falling back to the support I supposed was behind me, when the rebels charged with a heavy column, breaking my line and throwing it for a few minutes into confusion. I soon rallied my men, but my support, if any had been there, was gone, and I could by this time see the enemy endeavoring to close in on both sides of me, firing heavily. I followed the Ohio battalion through an open space in the timber, closely followed by the rebels, our men firing as well as they could in retreat, and for about a half-mile it was a wild running fight.

Having been over the same ground the day before, I knew there was an open field a short distance ahead, and I made a dash for it, knowing that unless I could soon rally and reform my command, it would be cut to pieces. A young rebel officer, riding at the head of his company, doubtless saw the object of my movement, and knowing of the same field himself, endeavored to head me off. Riding side by side, less than 100 yards apart, at full gallop, we emptied our revolvers at each other without either being hurt. At least I was not. As he was on my right, I had the advantage of him in firing, but do not know that I touched him. I reached the field first and, crossing it, rallied my men and formed a line just as the rebels appeared, coming out of the timber. This was the opportunity I wanted: an open field and fair fight and no favors. Infantry can fight as well, perhaps better, in the woods, but it is no place to operate cavalry. I had now about 100 or 150 men in line, half with drawn sabers and half with revolvers, and although the rebels came charging across the field with more than double my number, yelling and brandishing their long guns, for they had no sabers, I felt master of the situation. It was not my purpose to receive, but to meet the charge, so when the rebels had charged about halfway across the field, and were within about 500 or 600 yards of us, I gave the word and we charged in a solid line.

During all my service thus far, more than two years, this was the first fair open-field cavalry charge I had participated in, or even seen. My line charged at full speed with the precision of a parade until the two lines met with a shock. The rapid firing of our revolvers and the flashing of our bright blades, for the sun was now shining, seemed to make "confusion worse confounded." The confusion, however, was all on the side of the rebels. In the swamps and timber, shooting from behind trees and logs with their long rifles and shotguns, they were at home, but neither men nor horses could withstand our saber charge, and in a few minutes they were flying disordered back to the shelter of the timber. I saw a good many riderless horses, but how many, nor how many of their men fell in the charge, I know not, as I had no time to hunt them up to count them, but taking advantage of the rebels' momentary confusion, I rallied my men and continued the retreat in good order, until a bridge over a branch of Cold Water River was reached. The greater part of our little army passed over safely, but as the rebels pressed our rear, the rush on the bridge became so great as to break it down. I had crossed a moment before, and was on the bank watching the troops cross and reforming my battalion, when the bridge fell. It was here that we suffered our greatest loss, as nearly all who failed to cross on the bridge were captured, the stream being deep and full of cypress knees, was not fordable, and on account of the density of the timber, those who had crossed could give little or no protection to their less fortunate comrades.

I saw Major Henry on the field when I charged. He seemed to be endeavoring to rally a portion of his command, but I did not see him again. He was captured at the broken bridge. Lieutenant Crawford of Company M, 2nd Illinois, was captured about the same time.

As soon as I was assured of the loss of Major Henry, I assumed command, and having no fears that the rebels would press us beyond the river, and the men and horses being well nigh worn out, having eaten nothing since the night before, and it was now late in the afternoon, I marched leisurely towards Memphis.

At Normandy Creek, about five miles beyond the broken bridge, I met Colonel Moore at the head of his brigade coming to our assistance. We turned back with him in hopes of again meeting the rebels, and this time with sufficient force to redeem the morning's defeat. But for my part, I did not think the rebel cavalry would allow themselves to be overtaken by a brigade of infantry, nor did they. After marching five or six miles, we bivouacked soon after dark. That night a rebel picket stood within a few hundred yards of our picket, but retired early in the morning. I slept soundly that night between two rows of cotton with only my overcoat for a bed. The next morning we turned back towards Memphis, reaching camp about noon.

Although I soon discovered on the morning of the fight that the rebels greatly outnumbered us, I did not know who, nor how many they were. I afterwards learned there were about 2,000 cavalry and mounted infantry, with six pieces of light artillery, commanded by General Chalmers, instead of by Marmaduke, as was at first supposed.[9] I also learned that my old antagonist Faulkner was in the fight. Owing to the fog and our frequent changes of position, the rebels did not use their artillery after the first fire in the morning, and then only two or three rounds. Had the morning been clear, the rebels were strong enough to have captured or destroyed all of our little force.

During the entire day, all the men in my battalion, consisting of parts of Companies B, D, L, and M, behaved most nobly. In the absence of their commissioned officers, who were all out on the other scout, Sergeant Blessing commanded Company B, Sergeant Bucks, Company D, and Sergeant Anglemeir, after the loss of Lieutenant Crawford, Company M. Our total loss was about seventy men. My battalion lost in killed and missing one lieutenant and twenty-one men and thirty-one horses. Two men of my company, Ben Bimson and George Floyd, were captured on the skirmish line early in the fight.[10]

At one time during the fight in the fog, I saw indistinctly a squadron of cavalry approaching me from the left front, behind and close to a high rail fence. Supposing it, of course, to be a company of the enemy coming into position, I ordered my men to fire. Seeing the company halt and the color bearer ride out of the ranks and come galloping alone towards me, I ceased firing, I was surprised at such a singular maneuver, and still more surprised to see that the soldier bore the guidon of a company of the 1st Missouri Cavalry. Fortunately, no men were hurt and only a few horses wounded, but the officer in command said my boys wore that fence out with their bullets.

Sunday evening, June 21st, Captain Frank Moore and Sergeant Fred Turner of my company, with a small party, went out with a flag of truce to ascertain, if possible, the condition of our wounded and missing men. Two wounded and paroled men of Company D came in today. They report the rebels have gone south with the prisoners. They saw nothing of Bimson and Floyd. Captain Frank Moore returned on June 25th. He was met at Hernando by a flag of truce and kept waiting for a reply from Chalmers, who finally sent him word that our dead were buried, the wounded paroled, or well cared for, and that he had better return at once.

On Sunday morning, June 28th, I attended services at Dr. White's church, and Monday evening went to the "New Memphis Theater" with Major Larrison and Dr. Troyer.[11]

On the 1st of July, I went on a little scout near Horn Lake, Mississippi, and picked up a couple of rebel soldiers who claimed to be deserters from Colonel Bly, who was encamped beyond Cold Water River.

On Friday, July 3rd, Colonel Faulkner came to our lines with a flag of truce, but I could not learn the object of his visit. If I had known he was at our lines, I should certainly have gone out to see him.

There are doubtless a good many rebel troops scattered about in the vicinity of Memphis, and reports come in almost daily of a contemplated attack. I think when the rebs get ready to attack us, they will come without the courtesy of sending us notice a week or two in advance. In fact, such politeness would be as unnecessary as unusual, for they will find us always ready to receive them; that's one thing we are here for.

The people of Memphis are very fearful of an attack, and well they may be, for whichever way the tide of battle might turn, it would result in great injury to, if not destruction of, their beautiful city. The people are largely rebels or rebel sympathizers and would, of course, like to see their cause prevail and their friends victorious, but for prudential reasons, they wish us to remain and do not want to see a fight in the city.

Business of all kinds is in a fairly prosperous condition. The stores, markets, hotels, theaters, etc. are liberally patronized by the Union troops, who spend a good deal of good money in the city. Should the rebels again possess the city, business would be nearly if not quite suspended, for what goods and supplies their troops would not take forcibly, they would pay for with Confederate government vouchers or equally worthless scrip. In the event of an actual attack, the city would be between two fires, the rebel guns on one side and our gunboats and Fort Pickering on the other.

On July 4th, the customary national salute fired from Fort Pickering was the only public demonstration here. I was ordered out with a small force to reconnoiter as far as Normandy Creek, but found nothing. Brooks, the soldier who was accidentally shot in the foot on our march from Fort Pillow, had his foot amputated today.

I was ordered out again on July 5th at midnight to hunt for a rebel picket reported eight miles out, but finding nothing, returned about daylight.

All the camps illuminated tonight, July 6th, and great rejoicing over the news of the surrender of Vicksburg to General Grant. Candles were procured in the city, and all the tents and trees in all the camps were a blaze of light, making a truly beautiful spectacle. Not content with illuminating their camps only, the men of Companies D and L distributed more than 100 candles in the front yard of Mr. Pearson, a rebel citizen living near my company camp. Pearson and his family took the joke good-naturedly, but of course could not be expected to feel very happy over the occasion. The soldiers everywhere are cheering and singing, and the camps, usually so quiet, seem like bedlam let loose. A salute is ordered to be fired at all the forts and posts tomorrow at noon in honor of our Vicksburg and Helena victories.[12]

In the fall of Vicksburg, and the unconditional surrender of Pemberton's large army, the rebellion has received a very serious, if not a mortal blow. Rosecrans is pushing Bragg almost to death in Tennessee. Meade is fighting hard and winning victories in the east, and Grant will not stop long. He is not the man to loiter and waste time rejoicing over his own victories, but is probably already on his way to Port Hudson farther down the river. Now that the rebels' large armies are scattered in the west, many of their soldiers may, regardless of their paroles, join the guerilla bands. But with gunboats on the river, and plenty of cavalry in the country, we can take care of them.

My unfortunate soldier Brooks died in Overton Hospital on July 10th, and in him my company lost another truly good man and soldier. He was a quiet, earnest young man, always willing and ready for any duty, and was a general favorite with his comrades. We can ill afford to lose such men by accident.

On July 14th, I was out scouting all day but could hear of no guerillas. I brought in a few mules and horses, and found plenty of very fine wild blackberries, which grow all about here in great abundance. My cook keeps my mess well supplied with berries prepared in every way.

Contrary to general expectation, we have had very little to do since the fall of Vicksburg. It is possible that the guerilla troops have been called in to reinforce the large armies of the South. We have heard of very few in our vicinity lately.

Sunday, July 21st, I was field officer of the day, and while mounting the brigade guard, I was taken very suddenly sick and faint. I asked the adjutant, who was standing behind me, to assist me into Dr. Stanley's tent nearby, and to excuse me from duty. In a few minutes, I had a regulation chill, a perfect personal earthquake, which with the fever following, lasted nearly all day. Towards evening I was able to walk and went to my own quarters.

I skipped one day, but had another chill and fever on the 23rd. As I am always very flighty and quite out of my head when in fever, I did not like to be left alone, so I relieved Sergeant McMurray from other duty and asked him to stay with and watch me. He stayed with me all day and said I was very wild in my fever and fighting over again the battle of last month.

I missed my chill on the 25th and felt well enough to ride downtown.

Port Hudson has fallen, and several steamboats loaded with rebel prisoners passed up the river today. The order of General Butler forbidding the paroling of prisoners in his department has never been countermanded, so the Port Hudson rebels must go north to prison to await exchange. I may perhaps underestimate the strength and resources of the rebels, but I really can't see how they can hold out much longer. They seem to be approaching that "last ditch" in which Jeff Davis says they "will all die fighting." Such bravery and endurance as the rebels display are worthy of a better cause. Confederate scrip is badly depreciated and the rebel brokers in town are not as anxious to buy at any price as they were a month or two ago.

A part of Colonel Ed Prince's regiment, the 7th Illinois Cavalry, passed through here today en route for La Grange. This is one of the regiments that raided from

La Grange to Baton Rouge last winter with Grierson. They are just up from Port Hudson. The boys of the 7th think they are invincible and can go anywhere and do anything now, and Ben Grierson is their patron saint. The 7th is a good regiment and has made for itself a good record.[13]

"Contrabands" (fugitive slaves) are daily coming into our lines by hundreds, and all able-bodied ones are "listing" in the negro regiments. They are enlisted for five years.

On July 29th, our battalion was ordered back to Fort Pillow, and the next morning, Thursday, we struck camp and marched out, reaching Fort Pillow Friday afternoon in advance of our baggage, which had gone up by boat. We found the Hatchie River very high and had to swim our horses over, but all crossed without delay or accident. The day was hot and the roads dusty, and the ride far from pleasant. We all wanted to march southward, and did not like to return to Fort Pillow.

The next morning, our battalion was ordered out on a scout accompanied by three companies of mounted infantry, in all about 225 men, it being reported that Richardson with a few hundred men was somewhere in this vicinity conscripting.[14] We passed through Durhamville and camped a few miles beyond, where Sergeant Beard of Company D caught two rebel soldiers. At two o'clock in the morning, our pickets were fired on and camp alarmed, but no attack. I took breakfast next morning with Mr. Graves, a reported good loyal man in the little town of Brownsville. We marched all the next day without incident to Denmark, where we got supper and camped a few miles beyond in the woods. Two or three stragglers of the mounted infantry were captured in Denmark by guerillas after we left.

Returning to Denmark early next morning, we found the town full of guerillas. We gave chase and made things hot and lively for four or five miles. They were better mounted than armed, and could run faster than they could fight. We scattered them in all directions, but succeeded in capturing only a few. In the skirmish, Lieutenant Dement's horse was shot under him. We spread out over the town, and after a heavy breakfast with the Denmarkers, started on our return to Fort Pillow, where we arrived about sundown the next day. My baggage had arrived in our absence, and I found my tent pitched and my cook ready with a good supper. We were out on the scout five days, and two days marching from Memphis, making seven days in the saddle. The weather being fine, I slept every night on the ground with only my overcoat for bed and shelter.

August 21st. For nearly two weeks I have been laid up and unable to do duty on account of a film on my right hand.[15] It is the first I ever had, and has been so painful as to keep me awake nearly every night and make me quite sick. Dr. Kendall lanced it some days ago, and I am getting to be of some use again.

We have here a very pleasant and comfortable camp in the hills. My tent is under a large cottonwood tree near the spring. The days are very hot and the high hills shut off the breezes, but the nights are quite cool, sometimes almost cold enough for frost, and the dews are almost as heavy as rain, so that the night guards are obliged to wear their overcoats or ponchos.

Orders have been issued from department headquarters in Memphis requiring <u>all</u> citizens, men and women, to take the oath. All refusing to do so before the 31st instant shall be put south beyond our lines, and as our lines are being extended about as fast as our troops can travel, it may inconvenience "refugees" somewhat to find a resting place. All who can come to any post occupied by our troops must do so to take the oath. To accommodate those who cannot come in, our battalion is ordered out to visit the neighboring towns.

On Saturday, August 22nd, we marched with 200 men for Dyersburg. Captain Frank Moore commanding, and Captain Sam Whitaker, deputy provost marshal. We marched all the next day, stopping to feed at "Double Bridge," where the ambulance carrying Captain Frank Moore, who was sick with ague, broke down. Leaving a guard to repair and come on with the ambulance, we continued our march, reaching Dyersburg at seven o'clock that evening, and camped in the courthouse yard.

Early Monday morning, the natives began coming in from all directions and continued coming all day: young and old, men, women, children, and babies, in wagons, buggies, and on horseback. Captain Whitaker soon found he had more business than he could attend to, and called on me for assistance. I opened another office the next morning in the courthouse and worked until twelve o'clock that night, during which time I administered the oath to over 600 persons. None were accepted except women and old or infirm men. All who could ride were required to go to the fort. There were not many young men qualified to take the oath, nearly all being paroled prisoners. I had no idea there were so many women and children in Dyer County as came to town on Monday and Tuesday. It was a regular jubilee for the old women to swap gossip, the old men to talk about the war, and the young folks to flirt. The majority appeared willing to take the oath, but for some, especially the young women who had husbands or sweethearts in the rebel army, it was a bitter pill to swallow and I was the recipient of much abuse, all of which I took for what it was worth.

At first we required all to sign their names to the oath, but I soon found there were so few who could, and they wrote so poorly and slowly, that we could not spare the time, so I would take down a long list of names, stand them up in a row with their right hands up, and swear them in squads. Such ignorance is a shame and disgrace to any people claiming to be "free and enlightened." Such are the bitter fruits of the tree of slavery and slave aristocracy, and yet these poor ignorant beings cry out loudly against "abolitionism and negro equality." Although they may not believe nor realize it, it is nonetheless a fact that they are just about as ignorant and superstitious, and as much in bondage, as the black slaves. And not until negro slavery, which is the real cause of the war, is forever abolished in every state in our country and the poor people permitted and encouraged to be educated, can the South lay any just claim to rank amongst the "civilized and enlightened" peoples of the United States, and sooner or later, and the sooner the better, abolition must come. Slavery was the cause of all this trouble and is the bone of contention, and until the bone is taken away and buried or thrown over the fence, the dogs will fight.

Leaving Dyersburg Wednesday morning, August 26th, we marched to Ripley, where we encamped about 5pm. I took supper by invitation at Dr. Francis's, who is a very loud Union man; in fact, a little too loud. I am always suspicious of these very loud, demonstrative Union men, who manage to live in peace with their rebel neighbors and escape conscription.

On Thursday morning, Captain Frank Moore was so sick that he was obliged to return to the fort in the ambulance, and I took command of the expedition, and seeing no occasion for keeping so many men (200) I sent back all but Companies B and L. We remained at Ripley all of Thursday and Friday morning, then went to Durhamville, six miles distant, where I was hospitably entertained by the Widow Green. At Durhamville I had a little verbal encounter with Miss Gaus of Double Bridges, a 200-pounder, and as savage as she was big. She said she would a heap rather fight me than take the oath, and she knew if she took that Yankee oath, her fellow, who was paroled at Vicksburg, would go back on her, but finally said if I could whip her in a fair stand-up fight, and no favors, she would "take the d——— oath and keep it." Not being pressed for time, business in my line being a little dull just then, and the young lady being very earnest and somewhat entertaining—in her way—I was disposed to be amused and entertained by her. I declined fighting her and told her it was contrary to my principles to fight with any lady who had a fist as big as my head, and assured her that it was a matter of indifference to me whether she took the oath or went beyond our lines, but as our lines were constantly and rapidly moving southward, she might have to travel farther and faster than would be agreeable to one of her size and weight in such hot weather. And as to her fellow, I suggested that she bring him in and I would not only administer the oath to both of them, but would strain a point and marry them, and she would then have a man of her own to fight, and as often as she pleased. If she was not a better fighter than scholar, she would not count for much, for when she signed the oath she did it with an "X," and I had to write her name for her.

At Dyersburg I found a little printing office issuing a little weekly secession paper. Seeing here a chance to save much time and labor in writing copies of the oath, I gave the proprietor a copy and ordered him to print a few thousand oaths, which he flatly refused to do without pay in advance. I told him he should be paid when his work was satisfactorily done, and when he still refused, I placed a guard over him with orders to put him in irons if he stopped work without orders. This brought him to terms and he worked like a little hero until midnight, when I paid him about twenty dollars and discharged him. After my contract with the publishing company, I exacted a fee of twenty-five cents from each of my clients until I had collected enough to pay the printer. He was the most pleased man and the best friend I had in town when I paid him, for he did not believe I would pay him anything.

Leaving Durhamville on Saturday morning, August 29th, we marched to Fort Pillow, reaching camp about 2pm, and thus ended one of the gayest little trips of the season. Notice of our coming had been sent to all the towns and settlements, and the people were prepared to entertain us. Over 2,000 persons took the oath. During the trip, I conversed with a good many paroled Vicksburg prisoners, many of whom say they will never go back into the army. Rebellion with them is "played out." They said it was a fact that they were so short of provisions they were obliged to eat mules and rats for some time previous to the surrender. Two dollars fifty cents (Confederate scrip) apiece was the regular price for good merchantable rats, and the demand exceeded the supply.

September 15th. Having had little or nothing to do besides routine camp duties since our peaceful Dyer County raid, I have improved the time, or endeavored to kill time, by an occasional duck hunt in the bottoms and a more thorough inspection of the works of Fort Pillow, and picking up items of its construction and history. It is situated on the east side of the Mississippi River about seventy miles above Memphis, and is the first point below Hickman, Kentucky, where the bluffs come to the river. The bluffs, which are very high and much broken by deep ravines, come to the river in the form of a great wedge. On the north side is Cole Creek with its wide swamps and canebrakes, and in the south flows the deep and rapid Hatchie with its wide and often overflowed bottoms of cypress swamps and canebrakes.

The outer wall of the fort, where many angles command every possible approach by land, is not less than four miles in length, and although named in honor of the celebrated fort builder of the Mexican War, the ditch, a deep and wide one, is <u>outside</u> the wall. Beyond the ditch for a distance of more than 1,000 yards, every tree and bush has been felled and the branches cut off and sharpened, forming an abatis that, with the exceeding roughness of the ground, is as nearly impassable as anything of the kind can be made. Inside the wall is an excellent road with good bridges, over which troops and artillery could be moved rapidly to any part of the works.

The summits of the many high and steep hills are covered with earthworks commanding every ravine and road in the fort as well as the river. At the foot of the bluff, on the riverbanks, is an extensive and well-constructed water battery. It was once a splendid piece of work, but is now in ruins, having been much injured by the landslide caused by an earthquake last fall. All the works, walls, batteries, abatis, etc. were constructed in the most substantial manner and exhibit engineering skill of a high order. They were constructed, I think, under the direction of General Beauregard. The labor was done by slaves, more than 2,000 being employed, having been brought here from as far as the Gulf states.

During the winter and spring of 1862, Forts Donelson and Henry, Bowling Green, Columbus, Pittsburg Landing, New Madrid, and Island Number 10 had fallen in rapid succession, and refugees from all these places were collected at Fort Pillow, forming a large and badly scared and beaten army. This was to be their last stand. Here they had dug their "last ditch" and, made desperate by frequent defeats, they resolved to go no farther, but would here conquer or die in that "last ditch." All of which comprised a very attractive program and would have looked well played to slow music. The ditches are all here and will remain for many years to come, but the rebel soldiers found it desirable to omit the conquering and dying parts of the show, and most ingloriously fled when no one pursued.

Soon after the fall of Island Number 10, one of our large ironclads, while lazily floating down the river in search of adventures, in making a short turn in the stream, suddenly came upon a little rebel steamer on the lookout to see what was going on up stream. A single glance at the huge "mud turtle" by the rebel officers on the deck of the steamer was sufficient. They had had experiences with gunboats and knew them to be dangerous, so putting their little craft about, they paddled for home, closely followed almost under the guns of the fort, by the ironclad. At the alarm, "the Yankee gunboats are coming," the whole camp was in an uproar of confusion. The garrison at that time, as before stated, was composed largely of detachments of troops who had been whipped from one place to another until the fire in their Southern hearts was well nigh quenched. In every instance where they had encountered those dread engines of destruction, had they been beaten and they had no spirit to meet them again. The officers tried in vain to rally their men to meet the anticipated attack. Expostulations, entreaties, and threats, availed not. The retreat once started, like a boy's snowball, increased as it rolled, until in a few hours it attained the importance of a stampede of the first quality. Cannons were spiked or dismounted, storehouses containing large quantities of quartermaster and commissary stores were burned, and everything that could not be easily and quickly removed was destroyed. The gunboat, after waiting some time and seeing no hostile demonstrations, sent a boat ashore and took peaceable possession of the deserted post.

The story of the alarm and evacuation I had from a rather "intelligent contraband," who was compelled by force of circumstances to take an active part in the hasty movement. My dusky informant illustrated his narrative with many grimaces and facial contortions that I cannot here reproduce, and doubtless indulged to some extent in exaggeration, so I have thought it safe to reduce his story at least by half. From other information I have received, I have reason to believe the account as I have given it is about correct.

Reports have been coming in for several days that Faulkner, Newsom, Bell, and others were conscripting, arresting deserters, and plundering generally in this and adjoining counties.[16] On the strength of these reports, our battalion was ordered out early on Saturday morning, September 19th, to investigate matters and render a verdict in accordance with the facts. Our force consisted of five companies of cavalry, two companies of mounted infantry, and a squad of Tennessee "home guards," or as our boys call them, "Yankee guerillas"; in all about 200 men.

The receipt of the order had the happy effect of reducing the "sick list" quicker and better than all the doctors in camp could, and men who had been grunting around camp for a week or two reported at once for duty. Our men are pretty well acquainted in the country, and every one had his particular boarding house selected in every town and settlement within 100 miles of camp.

Leaving camp about 7am, we marched fifty-five miles and camped on the plantation of Mr. Trias. The next day being very hot and the roads very dusty, we marched only thirty miles, passing through the towns of Brownsville and Denmark, and camped at Mr. Alstine's, six miles from Jackson. At Denmark, we picked up a straggling guerilla belonging to Captain Dodd's company. All along the road the natives greeted us with "mighty glad to see you uns all," and "hope you uns will catch that villain Newsom," etc. But although Newsom had passed over the same road only a day or two before, no one could give us the least information of his movements or whereabouts, but all "allowed he was somewhere in the neighborhood." They really wished him caught, but did not want to be informers against him, for if we should follow and attack him on their information and fail to catch him, they knew he would return and make it hot for them.

We expected to find Newsom in Jackson, and so made an early march on that place, the next morning, September 21st, but he was not there. Our advance guard found a few rebel soldiers in the town, but failed to catch any of them. Stopping only long enough in Jackson to eat up what the people had left over from breakfast, we marched towards Trenton. At a mill about halfway between Jackson and Trenton, the command was divided into three columns, one to go by the way of Humboldt to the northward, another to cross Forked Deer River farther south, while the third, mine, marched direct to Trenton, and was the first to reach the town, which we entered at a gallop, but found nothing there. I waited until the others came in when we all moved out of town and camped.

We had now lost the track of Newsom, but were on that of Faulkner and Bell, who were said to be together and not far from Trenton. Faulkner had been in Trenton on the morning of the 21st. Although a diligent search all that day failed to find him, I have no doubt Faulkner was within a few hours' ride of us in the swamps of Forked Deer River and did not mean we should find him. From a woman in Trenton, I learned that Captain Blackmore and Bob Merriweather, who I captured last fall at Island Number 10, were again with Faulkner.

On leaving Trenton the next morning, September 23rd, the command was again divided to march by different roads and meet at Dyersburg. My command (Companies B and L) marched northwest through Yorkville to Newbern, where I stayed all night. Near Yorkville, my advance guard discovered a small squad of guerillas, with whom they exchanged a few shots and gave chase, but the rebs escaped in the bushes.

Arriving at Dyersburg the next morning, I found the command all in and waiting for me. We here again divided into three divisions. I crossed Forked Deer River at Fortner's ferry and camped that night at Ferguson's, three miles south from Ripley. Leaving Ferguson's early the next morning, I stopped for breakfast in Ripley and, pushing on in advance of the main column, reached Fort Pillow at 3pm. Had we been allowed more time, I think we could have found Faulkner or Bell. They were reported to have had 200 or 300 men each, mostly conscripts and poorly armed. Trenton was the farthest we went, as we had orders to return within eight days. I was far from feeling well when we started, having had a chill the morning we left the fort, but returned feeling quite well and hearty. I slept on the ground in the open air every night we were out.

Our friends in the north read the laudatory letters of "correspondents" attached to some general headquarters and the brief official reports of battles, and may think they are kept well informed of all that is going on at the front. The sensational account of a battle, or the glowing description of a cavalry raid, can convey to them no real idea of the dreadful destruction and desolation war brings upon a country. The most they can see are the sick and wounded soldiers and rebel prisoners sent north to be kindly cared for. They are spared the scenes of suffering and destruction that are constantly before us. Wherever we go, the villages are all quiet and almost deserted. No taverns, no stores, nor shops. No business of any kind. At every town, heaps of ruins and blackened walls, and lone chimneys show where houses once stood and families lived, while the people loaf around as if they had no object in life, dreading alike the approach of federals or rebels. In the country the prospect is no better. Many large plantations are lying idle and going to ruin, the master has gone to the rebel army, the negroes have all run away, and the horses and cattle have been taken by soldiers of both armies, and the once comfortable and beautiful homes now look like haunted houses.

Between "Yanks" and "Rebs" the resources of the country are about exhausted. I don't believe there are enough really good horses or mules between here and the Tennessee River to make a dozen good wagon teams. The smokehouses are empty and the beefs and hogs are all killed or driven off. The barns are empty and what little forage is raised is consumed by the cavalry of both armies. We have sometimes fed 200 horses from the same barn or stack where as many rebel cavalry horses were fed a day or two before. A rebel planter recently put on a long face and complained of such hard treatment. I asked him: "did you not vote for secession and contribute of your means to furnish and equip an army to enforce secession?" "Well, yes, I was obliged to go with my state, but I never wanted nor thought there would be such a war." "Oh! I see, you wanted secession without war, and yet you called out troops. Well, we have received your decision and have given you war without secession. We are not here from choice. We would much rather be at home attending to our business, but your people wanted war and we are here to give it to you." They wanted war without knowing just what war meant. It is a hard lesson they are learning, but it will be a lasting one.

I ate supper recently with a once rich old planter, Mr. Haswell, who said he had fed over 2,000 men and horses in the last two years, and now he had not an ear of corn, nor a blade of fodder on his plantation. There was not an able-bodied servant on the place, and his horses and cattle were all gone. Two years of war have reduced him, and thousands of others, from wealth to want. The old gentleman wanted war, but he didn't want so much of it nor so near home. I comforted him as well as I could by saying I had seen worse cases than his, where families had been burned out and lost everything, but my medicine did not seem to make him feel much better.

Owing doubtless to our elevation here above the river and overflowed swamps, we have been troubled very little by mosquitoes, while at Island Number 10 last summer they nearly ate us up. Our worst plagues here are fleas; they are everywhere and infest everything. It is scratch, hunt, and scratch all the time. We can neither eat nor sleep in peace. My clothing and blankets are always full of them, although I strip and shake my clothes a dozen times a day, and my blankets are hung in the sun and beaten nearly to pieces. Snakes, scorpions, and lizards also abound in abundance, but they are only offensive to sight, nobody has been bitten by them. Some of my men recently killed a rattlesnake twelve feet long and which had seventeen rattles, and it was not considered a very good day for snakes, either.

On Sunday, September 27th, four companies of our battalion were ordered to march to Union City. My transportation has lately been reduced from three wagons and fourteen mules to one wagon and six mules, and my company baggage reduced to the least possible weight.

We left Fort Pillow Monday morning at eight o'clock, marched twenty-five miles, and camped at Mr. Chipman's, two miles north from Ripley. Notwithstanding Mr. Chipman's secession views and rebel sympathies, he contributed somewhat liberally to the Union cause that night in turkeys, chickens, and honey for the troops, and forage for about 200 horses and mules.

The next day we crossed Forked Deer River at Yellow Bluffs, took supper with our numerous acquaintances in Dyersburg, and camped three miles beyond the Foulkes plantation, where turkeys, chickens, and honey again comprised a part of our diet. A little rough on Mr. Foulkes, but good for the soldiers.

The next day we passed through the town of Newbern without stopping, to the great joy of the Newberners, and crossing the Obion River about noon, camped that night at Parson Jackson's, six miles from Troy. Just before reaching the Obion River, we passed a little distillery where, in spite of the guard placed over it, some of the soldiers managed to fill their canteens with fluid lightning. As I had command of the rear guard and wagon train that day, all the "drunks and disorderlies" fell to my care, and I soon had a bad lot of goods on hand. One teamster got just drunk enough to run his wagon against a tree and break a tongue, which delayed us about an hour.

The next day, Thursday, October 1st, we passed through Troy, the county seat of Obion County, reaching Union City at 3pm. Near Troy one of the wagons broke through a small bridge over a creek, but doing no greater damage than dumping the load into the mud. At Union City, we reported to Colonel Mills, commanding the post, and camped in the woods about a half-mile from town.

Union City, Tennessee, twenty miles from Columbus, is a poor, scattered little town built without any regularity of streets and is nearly deserted. There are no stores and no business is done except by the camp sutlers. There is a daily train to Columbus, and also between Paducah and Mink Station, the latter being five miles from Union City. We seem to be quite near home again, as we get Chicago and St. Louis daily papers only two or three days old. There are wells in all the camps from which the horses have to be watered, as there is no stream near here. We found here the 4th Missouri Cavalry, composed almost entirely of St. Louis Dutchmen.

On Monday, October 5th, our battalion under command of Captain Frank Moore started out at 2am on a scout towards Madrid Bend, it having been reported that Farris, a guerilla captain, was encamped near Reelfoot Lake and was enlisting and conscripting recruits in that part of the country. Soon after passing through Troy, our force was divided, Captain Frank Moore with part going to Stone's Ferry on Reelfoot Lake, while I with forty men went down the Obion River and crossed the lake at Harris' Ford. I camped that night at Horn Ridge schoolhouse and took supper at Mr. Donahower's, having marched about fifty miles. Our plans were for Captain Frank Moore, who crossed the lake above and in advance of me, to find and attack the rebel camp, all the rebs who might fail to be killed or captured by him were to attempt to escape by the lower ford, where I was to take them in. Our plans were well laid and we all performed our parts, but the rebels failed to respond. We found their camp all right, but the swamp rangers, either through accident or design, had quite recently moved out. So great was their haste in departing that they left a lot of blankets, quilts, and other camp equipage, all of which we destroyed. We also picked up a few stragglers and horses.

That night I took supper at Donaldson's, and after breakfast next morning at Mr. Ward's, we ranged up towards our old camp at Island Number 10 and camped that night at Willis Jones's. I took supper with my old friend Aunt Dolly Merriweather, where I learned with much regret of the death of Mr. Merriweather, or as all called him, "Uncle Tommy," a most worthy and estimable old gentleman. His sons and many of his relatives were in the rebel army, and his sympathies were, of course, to a great extent with them, but he was not himself much of a rebel. I do not think he voted for secession, nor did he ever seem to think the rebel cause would succeed. His worthy old wife was an out-and-out rebel, but was one of those good motherly souls who could not be otherwise than good and kind to all, whether friends or foes. Her niece, Miss Cassie, a young lady of about twenty years, was much like her: a free, outspoken young rebel, but at all times a lady and very considerate of the feelings and opinions of others. Having been suffering for some days with a cold in my head, which made me almost sick, Aunt Dolly prescribed for me a hot whiskey punch, which Miss Cassie very kindly and skillfully prepared, making it hot and strong and of very liberal proportions. After spending a very pleasant evening, I retired with Captain Sam Whittaker to sleep on the porch.

During the past summer, the planters in "the Bend" had been quite successful and had raised good field and garden crops. Their chickens and bees had also been attending to business, and all were well prepared to entertain a squadron of cavalry. The soldiers improved the opportunity and left "the Bend" in good spirits and with some better horses than they rode the day before.

After a good breakfast next morning at good old Aunt Dolly's, I marched over to our old camp on the riverbank. Everything there was about as when I left it, and the old camp seemed almost like a home. Leaving Island Number 10 at nine o'clock, we continued our march up the river. On the way, I made a short call on an old acquaintance, Mr. Craig, and that night we camped at Mr. Lauderdale's, two miles from Hickman. We passed through Hickman the next morning, and before night were again in camp at Union City.

Having had little or nothing to do since our return from our recent trip to Madrid Bend, and becoming tired of inactivity, I thought to vary the monotony of routine camp life by a flying visit to Paducah, so on Wednesday, October 14th, I rode to Mink Station, six miles, where I took the train for Paducah, sending my horse back to camp by Corporal Joe Chase, with directions to send him to the station again in two days. After supper at the St. Francis Hotel in Paducah, I called at Mr. Bronson's, where I spent the evening.

The next day I was busy attending to business at the quartermaster's office and buying many little things for my soldiers. I called on Colonel Martin, commanding the post, and found my old friend Adjutant Bartling still at headquarters.[17] I dined at Lyon's, took tea at Bronson's, and made a number of social calls during the afternoon and evening, and left the next morning on the railroad and found Barr and Welsh with my horse at Mink Station. I took supper at Dr. Allen's near the station, and reached camp at ten o'clock to find my company just gone out on a scout.

I found the loyal people of Paducah much displeased with the conduct of their present post commanders, and the rebel element correspondingly jubilant. It is a matter of no little surprise to me that a man holding his political views should ever join the Union army, and that he should be permitted to occupy such a responsible position: although wearing the uniform of a Union soldier and holding a responsible position in the Union army, his sympathies are evidently with the rebels. I was informed that charges of a serious nature had been preferred against him and sent to Washington. Amongst other offenses of commissions and omission, he is charged with forcibly returning fugitive slaves to their rebel masters.[18]

The result of the recent state election in Ohio is received with joy by the troops. The Ohio soldiers, so far as I can learn, voted to a man for the patriot Morton and against the traitor Vallandigham.[19] They voted as they fight, and their ballots like bullets were fired for the Union.

My company returned from scout today, October 20th. The men report having had a good time. They had a little running skirmish and brought in five or six straggling guerillas picked up along the road. Captain Frank Moore brought in a fine large bloodhound that had been trained to trail runaway slaves. The captain says he is going to educate him now to trail guerillas. He is an ill-favored, fierce-looking brute, devoid of either political or conscientious scruples, and I don't suppose it will make any difference to him on which side he fights, nor who he trails.

One of our spies came in Saturday, October 24th, reporting that he had seen 860 rebels under Faulkner, the day previous, marching towards Mayfield. They were then about fifty miles from Mayfield, and about the same distance from Union City. Our battalion and one battalion of the 4th Missouri were ordered out immediately, and left at 4pm, camping that night at Dukedom on the state line and arriving at Mayfield at noon the next day. Learning here that the rebs were at or near Boydsville, we pushed on to that place, but did not find them there, nor could we learn anything definite of them more than that they were then supposed to be somewhere in the neighborhood of Como, twelve miles distant. It being too late to go farther that day, we camped at Boydsville, and early next morning marched to Como, but like a Jack-o-Lantern, the rebs were still beyond. Between Como and Caledonia we met a man in a hack returning from Faulkner's camp, where he had been pressed to take a rebel officer who had been wounded recently. He said Faulkner had 800 men in camp at McLemoresville, about eighteen miles southwest from where we met him.

This was the first information we had received that we considered reliable. Captain Frank Moore, who was in command, called a council of the officers, and we agreed that it would not be prudent to attack with only 200 men, so a courier was sent back to Union City, thirty-five miles, for reinforcements. We continued to move on cautiously and soon came to where the rebs had camped Saturday night and where they had heard of us and turned back. We followed their trail to Caledonia, where we learned that they had left McLemoresville and were retreating rapidly southward. Faulkner evidently did not want to fight. He was not out on a fighting expedition. His work was to collect men and horses for the rebel army and get away with them. Another object in coming this far north was to supply his men with blankets and clothing at Mayfield, the nearest town he could get at where there were stores and goods. He had told his men a few days before that he would get them blankets and clothing in Mayfield if he had to go through hell to get there, and in thus turning back and retreating before the approach of only 200, we felt that he was paying us a rather flattering compliment.

In turning back Faulkner and his 800 cold and hungry men, we saved the town of Mayfield from plunder and placed the merchants and inhabitants under obligation to us. Had he reached Mayfield, he would have taken all the blankets, clothing, and provisions he could have found, and the only pay the people would have received would have been "vouchers payable at the Treasury of the Confederate States." Being well assured that Faulkner was beyond our reach, we turned back, and next morning met our reinforcements (200) near Dresden. We reached camp at Union City about nine o'clock that night.

On October 27th, we learned that Captain Hayes, commanding a company of Tennessee (Union) cavalry, was captured about a week ago by a company of guerillas said to belong to Faulkner's command, and murdered, and his body thrown into Forked Deer River.[20] One of our companies at Fort Pillow has since captured two officers of the company that killed Captain Hayes, and the commanding officer at Fort Pillow has reported the case to Washington and placed the captured guerillas in irons. Our men are highly and justly incensed at such unsoldierly and barbarous conduct, and say if the rebels in West Tennessee want to fight a war of extermination under the "black flag," they will accept the terms. Such a strife would, of course, be savage and brutal and I hope never to see it, but it would be short and decisive, and would hasten the destined doom of the "Confederacy." When the enlisting of negroes into our army was commenced, the rebels in the southwest threatened to raise the black flag. If their object in uttering such a threat was to intimidate the northern troops, they greatly misunderstood the character of their enemies. Instead of being alarmed or afraid to accept the services of the negroes, our soldiers sought commissions in the black regiments, and said they could stand such terms if the rebels could. At one time while we were at Fort Pillow, it was reported that a squad of guerillas had displayed a black flag in their camp, and when one of our companies was sent out some of the men actually prepared a black flag and said if they found the guerillas with one, they would fly theirs and fight on the terms indicated. Happily, however, no black flag was found.

The town of Caledonia, where we stayed Monday night, October 26th, was a new one to us and had not before been visited by any of our cavalry, and as the town was well supplied with poultry, smokehouses, beehives, and other "contraband" supplies, our tired and hungry troopers gave themselves a banquet and fared as well as circumstances would permit.

Captain Frank Moore was today (October 31st) sent out with 100 men to look after a company of guerillas, and Monday night, November 2nd, all the remaining cavalry in camp was ordered out. While forming on the parade ground at ten o'clock, Major Hendricks of the 4th Missouri, who was going out in command, was thrown or fell from his horse and hurt, being too drunk to ride. Colonel Waring, commanding the post, then sent for me and placed me in command.[21] After informing me that Faulkner was then in Mayfield, he said, "You must follow him wherever he may go and fight him." I replied, "I will do the best I can, Colonel." This was the first intimation I had of the object of the expedition. My command (300) consisted of detachments of 2nd Illinois and 4th Missouri. I left camp at

11pm, marching towards Boydsville. The night was so dark and stormy that my guide lost the road and my command became separated. I marched steadily until six o'clock the next morning, Tuesday, when I succeeded in getting my command together again. Owing to the darkness, the storm, and the bad condition of the roads, at six o'clock I was only fifteen miles from camp. I halted only long enough to feed the horses and allow the men to make some hot coffee. Learning of a squad of guerillas at Feliciana a few miles north of me, I sent a lieutenant of the 4th Missouri with one company to rout them and rejoin me at Dukedom.

At Dukedom, I learned that Faulkner had passed through that town sometime during Sunday night, November 1st, but could learn nothing more of him. Believing he would cross the state line farther eastward, I pushed on towards Boydsville. Halting to feed and rest that evening about six miles west from Boydsville, I sent one of my guides (a citizen) with orders to go to Boydsville, learn what he could of the enemy, and report back to me before midnight, intending, if I could learn anything positive of the enemy's whereabouts, to continue the pursuit that night. The guide reported back that he could learn nothing.

At Boydsville the next morning I learned that Faulkner with about 1,000 men well-mounted and leading nearly as many extra horses, had passed through that town going southward about noon the day before, November 3rd. I at once concluded that my spy was afraid to go to Boydsville as ordered and had not left camp at all.

At Boydsville, I struck the enemy's trail and followed it as rapidly as possible to Como, twenty-five miles, reaching Como at 4pm, where I learned that Faulkner had passed through that town about nine o'clock that morning. The reports of his strength and condition corresponded with the reports received at Boydsville that he had about 1,000 men and nearly twice as many horses, and that he was marching rapidly and in good order toward Caledonia. During the day, I picked up a number of stragglers who had stopped at houses along the road, who reported that Faulkner had been collecting recruits and horses and was then on his way southward. That night I camped at the Widow Irvine's, ten miles east from Dresden, where I took supper and was kindly entertained by Mrs. Irvine and her ward Miss Mary Moore, good Union people. A nephew of Mrs. Irvine's was in the Tennessee (Union) cavalry.

I here decided to abandon the pursuit, believing that further pursuit was not only useless, but imprudent. The enemy was at least seven hours ahead of me, 1,000 strong, under a commander who did not mean to fight if he could avoid it, and marching directly for an exceedingly rough part of the country, where if forced to fight, every possible advantage would be on his side. I had, all told, only 300 men, and they chiefly of the 4th Missouri, in whom I had very little confidence.

Unless Faulkner should stand to fight, I knew I could never overtake him; if he should make a stand, it would be on ground of his own choosing among the hills. With my little command of "Flying Dutchmen," I did not care to force a fight on Faulkner's terms, so calling for all the officers, I told them I should abandon the pursuit and return to camp, to which they assented, agreeing that it was the best thing to do.

Leaving Mrs. Irvine's after an early breakfast the next morning, Thursday, I passed through Dresden at 10am, and at 7:30pm that night was back in camp and reported to Colonel Waring, who did not seem well pleased with the result of the expedition.

On Friday morning, November 6th, I received a note from Colonel Waring placing me under arrest, which was to me entirely unexpected, and for which I could assign no reason. To say that I was surprised and indignant would be stating the case very mildly. Lieutenant Cayton, who had for some time been detailed as battalion quartermaster, was at my request relieved from that duty and ordered to take command of my company.

After waiting three days and receiving no charges, I wrote to Colonel Waring asking for a copy of the charges on which I was arrested. The following is an extract: "Charge 1st: Misbehavior in pursuit of the enemy. Specification: Unsoldierly conduct in losing his way and halting to feed and rest without occasion. Charge 2nd: Cowardice in pursuit of the enemy. Specification: Camping when he had information and reason to believe the enemy was but a short distance ahead of him, poorly armed and mounted on jaded horses and demoralized by retreat. Continuing the pursuit slowly and in an unsoldierly manner. Abandoning the pursuit with a large force of well armed and mounted troops to the humiliation of his comrades in arms when the enemy, broken down, demoralized, and fleeing from him was but a few miles ahead. Charge 3rd: Disobedience of orders. Specification: Having received imperative orders to find, follow, and fight the enemy, he abandoned the pursuit without giving the enemy battle."

Such were the alleged reasons for placing me in arrest and depriving me of the command of my company, and so plainly absurd were they that I thought at first I would make no defense, but finally concluded to submit a brief statement of facts, supported by the testimony of my comrades and copies of official papers in Colonel Waring's office, which were obtained through the assistance of a trusty friend W. W. Temple, a private of my company, who was at the time a clerk in Colonel Waring's headquarters.

Answers: To Charge One: It was the fault of the guide assigned and recommended to me by Colonel Waring that I was lost and led off the road in the storm. To Charge Two: My past record with other, better, and braver commanders will disprove the charge of cowardice. To Charge 3: His orders were absurd and unreasonable. No officer can fight an enemy he cannot catch.

Now for what I know to be the real reason for arresting me. A disgrace seldom witnessed had fallen on our arms in permitting the enemy to plunder a town at his leisure, within our lines, and escape with all his recruits and plunder. Somebody was to blame and somebody must suffer, and that somebody, as I could show, was Colonel George E. Waring, and that he endeavored to make me the scapegoat, to suffer for his "disobedience and unsoldierly conduct."

When Faulkner was balked in his first attempt to get to Mayfield some two weeks before, it was generally believed that he would make another attempt at the first favorable opportunity. General A. J. Smith, commanding at Columbus, was evidently of that opinion, and ordered Colonel Waring to keep his cavalry well in hand and be prepared to intercept Faulkner at any moment.[22] On October 29th, General Smith telegraphed to Colonel Waring, "Keep your cavalry together and scouts in the direction of Boydsville to give you early information, etc." On the 31st, in direct violation of the above order, Colonel Waring sent over 100 men under Captain Frank Moore to Trenton, forty miles distant, after a squad of guerillas. At ten o'clock Monday morning, November 2nd, Colonel Waring was informed that Faulkner with 1,000 men had passed through Dresden the night before on his way to Mayfield, which placed him in a very awkward dilemma. In violation of General Smith's orders, he had so divided his cavalry as to render him powerless to oppose Faulkner, who he knew was then marching quietly and safely past him. The little squad of guerillas raising Cain at Trenton were sent there by Faulkner for the very purpose of attracting attention in that direction, and Colonel Waring now realized that he was outgeneraled and the victim of a feint.

Fearing to send out the small force of cavalry he had in camp, Colonel Waring waited all of Monday in hopes that Captain Frank Moore would come in. Couriers were dispatched with orders for him to return immediately, but he could not be found. In the meantime, Faulkner continued his march unmolested and before the next morning was in Mayfield. At ten o'clock Monday night, Waring received a telegram from General Smith ordering him to send out all of his cavalry, except two companies, immediately to intercept Faulkner, who was then in Kentucky. But for this last order I do not believe Colonel Waring would have sent out my expedition at all.

For the escape of Faulkner, Colonel Waring was alone to blame. First, because he allowed himself to be so badly outgeneraled; second, because he disobeyed orders in dividing his cavalry; third, because he was aware of the presence of Faulkner thirteen hours before he attempted to intercept him, and then only in obedience to an imperative order from the general, and in order to shield himself, he was willing to sacrifice that little force of 300, as evidenced in his orders to me to "find, follow, and fight" no matter what the odds or circumstances might be. As I had copies of all the orders and telegrams from General Smith to Colonel Waring, I felt very secure, and instead of fearing the result of a trial, I used every effort to bring my case before a court martial.

November 13th. The country seems to be again full of small bands of guerillas, conscripting and collecting horses. Richardson with a considerable force has slipped in between Memphis and Corinth, and is operating in West Tennessee. Our position here I consider a very exposed one. Our present force consisting only of two regiments of infantry, two battalions of cavalry and one section of light artillery, we have no works, nor defenses of any kind except a very imperfect abatis that a man can ride through almost anywhere.

On Monday, November 16th, a flag of truce came to our lines from Faulkner asking an exchange of prisoners. Amongst some hostages taken recently by us to hold for the return of some citizens taken by Faulkner, was Mrs. Faulkner's father. The lady, it was said, raised such a domestic disturbance when her father was arrested and lodged in the Columbus guardhouse, that Faulkner was obliged to release certain of his conscripts and ask for the release of his father-in-law. The next day the hostages were sent out under a flag of truce.

One hundred guerillas were reported at Hickman on November 18th, and Captain Frank Moore was sent in pursuit with seventy-five men. He overtook the rebs under Major Street early the next morning at Merriweather's ferry on the Obion River and routed them after a sharp little fight, killing ten and taking a number of prisoners. While charging down a rather steep hill, the horse ridden by Sergeant Cox of my company fell, breaking his neck. The sergeant was thrown violently to the ground, but was not injured. None of our men were hurt in the fight.[23]

I have been waiting most impatiently for summons to appear before a court martial, but none has yet come as of December 1st. Being thus deprived of my command when there is so much to do is most provoking. I do not, nor do any of my comrades, think nor feel that I have done anything to merit such treatment, nor that I am in any way disgraced, as the reason for Colonel Waring's action is pretty well understood. No limits being prescribed in my order of arrest, I go pretty much where I please, and in my rides outside the camp lines have made a number of very pleasant acquaintances.

During the past week or two I have busied myself building a little cabin and fireplace, so that if we remain here all winter I shall be pretty comfortably fixed. All the troops have been erecting cabins and shanties, and our camp presents quite a city-like appearance. On a frosty morning the smoke from several hundred low mud chimneys, many of which are finished off with an old barrel, gives our camp the appearance of a city of bake ovens. Our city is divided into three grand divisions or wards, known as "Illinois Town," "Indianaville," and "Holland"—the latter being the camp of the "Flying Dutchmen."

The construction of a stick and mud chimney may appear to a disinterested observer a very simple piece of architecture, and so thought I when I commenced mine, but I soon found it to be a very serious and responsible undertaking, and one not to be entered on thoughtlessly nor unadvisedly. It was the first job of the kind I ever attempted, and I don't care if I never attempt another. The mud would freeze faster than I could work it, and my contraband servant, benumbed and stupefied with cold, would persist in mixing up chips, sticks, and bits of ice with the mud. However, in spite of many conflicting circumstances and emotions, I finally finished my cabin and chimney. My cabin, although a very rude and small affair, being only thirteen feet square, was far more complete and comfortable than many of the homes of the "poor whites" I have seen, in which generations have been born, grown old, and died.

General Sherman's recent "conscript order" requiring all able-bodied men within our lines to report for military duty, in connection with the news of our late victory at Chattanooga, is causing a terrible rattling of dry bones in West Tennessee.[24] It is remarkable what a combination of diseases and disabilities have suddenly appeared to afflict the butternut populace within the last few days. "Rhumatiz" that for long years has lain dormant, and "mule kicks" long since healed up and haired over, have all at once reappeared in most aggravating forms. Men who for years have spent all their time and spare change at the country grocery have just awakened from their Rip Van Winkle slumber and become conscious that they are the sole supporters and protectors of sickly wives and numerous little "butternuts." There is nothing like a draft or conscription to develop a man's bodily infirmities. When Faulkner or Sol Street are conscripting for the rebel army they don't waste any time listening to complaints and excuses.[25] If a man can't ride or bear arms, they elect him to cook or drive a team.

On December 4th, General Roddey (rebel) was reported to be in West Tennessee with 4,000 men and ten pieces of artillery.[26] A picket from this post, stationed at the little Obion River, was driven in last night, and at four o'clock this morning, the 2nd Illinois was ordered out under Captain Frank Moore. I did not learn his orders, probably to "find, follow, and fight."

On December 7th, the 19th Pennsylvania Cavalry reported here, direct from the Army of the Potomac. It is a hard-looking regiment, both men and horses appear to be starved and worked down. They are a poor advertisement of the country fare of Virginia.

On Tuesday, December 8th, I went to Columbus and saw Captain Hough, assistant adjutant-general, whom I showed a copy of the charges against me and asked that I be granted a trial, as I wanted this business settled one way or another. He said no court was then sitting and none would probably be convened for some time. After reading the charges, he said the whole thing was absurd and wanted me to return to duty, offering me an honorable and unconditional release from arrest. I declined accepting a release without a hearing. I said, "If those charges are true, I am certainly unfit to command a squad of home guards. If they are not true, then Colonel Waring is a coward and a liar and I want the case thoroughly investigated." I told him further that however much I wished to return to duty with my company, I would rather never return than to return with any suspicions attached to my name. If I should accept a release without a trial, Colonel Waring, and any other enemies I might have, might think and say I had taken some undue advantage to obtain it, and that I feared an investigation. It would be his and everybody's privilege to say I got out of a bad scrape to avoid the consequences. But the adjutant could do nothing for me more than to again offer me an honorable release, which I again declined.

The next day, I called on Major Smith, 40th Iowa, president of the late court martial, but of course he could do nothing, as his court had been dissolved. I took supper at the hospital where I was sick last spring, and spent a very pleasant evening with Dr. Snyder and my old nurse Claus Peters, and returned to camp the next morning.

The battalion came in December 11th from a scout to Madrid Bend. It had a skirmish with Sol Street's guerillas at Moran's, killing one and capturing eighteen. Amongst the captured is Bud Donaldson. Bud is a good deal in or out of luck, as he manages to spend about half of his time in Northern prison camps.

December 13th. The rebel General Forrest is at Jackson with, reports say, 10,000 men and seventeen pieces of artillery. Besides the natural advantages of that place, Jackson is well protected with earthworks, and if Forrest makes a stand there, he may make an ugly fight. Troops have been collecting here for several days, and a movement is looked for at an early day in connection with like movements from Memphis and other points below.

Two large scouting parties, in all about 1,200 men, are out tonight, December 15th, with three days' rations.

On the 16th, General A. J. Smith came down from Columbus. It has been raining hard all day and last night, and the weather is cold and windy.

The scouts sent out two days ago returned this evening, December 17th. They went as far as Boydsville, but saw no rebels, but heard of Forrest at Jackson. With all of Colonel Waring's bluster and office bravery, I have not yet seen him go out himself to find, follow, and fight. On Tuesday 22nd, three regiments of infantry (17th New York and 24th and 25th Missouri) and two batteries (3rd and 9th

Indiana) marched out at 2pm, destination supposed to be Jackson, and the next day General Smith went out with the cavalry, Lieutenant Cayton in command of my company. I wished very much to go out, but as I could not march in my accustomed and rightful place at the head of my company, and as Colonel Waring went in command of the cavalry brigade, I would not go.

Forrest may possibly stand to fight at Jackson, but I do not think he will. He will have nothing to gain and all to lose by fighting. Even if he should repulse General Smith, he cannot long hold his position. I think he is there only for the purpose of collecting men, horses, and supplies and will get away without fighting if he can.

On Christmas Day, I dined with Lieutenant Lebold, Company D, at his quarters, and after dinner rode out to call on Miss Harelson, where I arrived just in time for another good big dinner. I expected to make one or two more calls that afternoon, but as I did not feel like doing much riding after so many dinners, and finding myself in very agreeable company, I spent the balance of the afternoon and evening resting at Harelson's.

All the darkey cooks, having nothing else to do now that the troops were all out, had a grand hoedown and fight in camp tonight, and as it amused them and hurt no one else, no one interfered and they danced and fought nearly all night.

Sergeant Jim Burke of Company D came in from Smith's expedition on December 26th. He reports Forrest at Forked Deer River, and Smith within sixteen miles of him, the 2nd Illinois in advance when he left. He remained in camp one day waiting for mail, and on the 28th started to return, with letters and dispatches.

Calling at Harelson's while out riding on December 29th, I found the house full of girls, all anxious for a frolic of some kind, so we arranged to have a dance at Naylor's on New Year's Eve. They promised to get all the girls within reach in the country, and I agreed to find enough "sick and disabled" soldiers in camp to supply them with partners.

The old year is dying hard. The morning of December 31st opened cold and stormy, and all day the storm has raged furiously. Snow, rain, and wind have combined to make the last day the worst of the year. I am sorry for the men in the field, they are having a rough hard time today. I spent the most of the day in my quarters writing letters and in the afternoon rode out to Harelson's. On account of the storm, we agreed to postpone the dance, and so ended, for me, the year 1863.

Smith's brigade has left a broad trail. The weather has been cold and stormy, and the roads very muddy ever since it left, so that the infantry are obliged to march slowly and halt frequently. At every halt, great fires are made of rails, so that the country through which they have marched looks as though a hurricane of fire had passed over it. Between one army and the other, this country is having a hard experience. Farther south, where there have been larger armies and more fighting, it is worse. Although to all appearances ruined and bankrupt, the South will yet come out of her baptism of fire all the better for the scorching, slavery once and forever abolished, root and branch; and the eyes of the masses once opened to the fact that their leaders and masters are not really gods, and that industry and intelligence and not wealth alone are the nerves and sinews of a nation, and slave aristocracy will give way to northern thrift, education, and enterprise and the country will begin to grow.

I have never seen a better agricultural country than parts of western Tennessee, but it is away behind the times. The only labor saving farm machines I have seen here are one threshing machine and a corn sheller, dropped here by some wandering Yankee years ago. The thresher had broken down in a field, and no native being found with ingenuity enough to put it in repair, it was left there to rot. There having been no Yankee clock tinkers through the country since the war commenced, nearly all the clocks are out of repair, and their expressionless faces and motionless hands no longer note the flight of time. But time, waiting for no man, goes on all the same. Their masters having joined and become part of the Union army, and their almanacs grown out of date, the natives have no means of computing, nor regulating time except by the last earthquake, the birth of a baby, or some raid of the Union cavalry.

An old man living near camp told me today that he had nothing in his house to eat except a little meal and three hogs, two of them in salt and one alive, and that would probably be eaten by the next cavalry scout that stopped at his house, and he would then be compelled to draw government rations, if he could get them. This old man was once well-off, was rich, with plenty of slaves, good crops, and plenty of everything, but not content with leaving well enough alone, he wanted secession and war. He can't get secession, but he is getting more war than he has use for.

Chapter Four

1864

Furloughs—Released with No Charges—Rendezvous at Memphis—The Smith-Grierson Raid—Destroying Railroads—Skirmishing with Forrest—Disappearance of Lieutenant Catlin—Contraband Camp Followers—Reflections on the Raid—Life in Memphis—Leasing Abandoned Cotton Plantations—Baton Rouge—The Creoles of Louisiana—War Profiteering—Arrested Again—Company L Mustered Out—Battle for Clinton, Louisiana—Cotton Speculation and Corruption Among Officers—The "Regulation Mess"—A Dandy Adjutant—A Midnight Adventure—Commanding Highland Stockade—A Christmas Tragedy

January 10, 1864. The weather for the past ten days has been truly horrible: cold, rain, snow, and mud. Our camp and the country about us are low and flat so that the water cannot run off, but soaks in where it falls. It is mud everywhere and mud of the blackest and stickiest kind. The Mississippi River is full of floating ice, and the northern railroads are so blocked with snow that our mails are much delayed and very irregular. St. Louis and Chicago papers reach us five or six days old. Besides an occasional call on some of the nearest neighbors I have been able to ride but very little outside the lines.

General Smith's expedition has returned, the men and horses frozen, dirty, and half-starved. Besides a half-dozen guerillas captured and a few arms and legs broken by horses falling on the icy roads, the men have nothing to report. There was altogether too much "Army of the Potomac" style about the whole affair to catch Forrest. Even General A. J. Smith with all of his staff and 1,000 men it seems could not do it. It would be in order now for somebody to arrest somebody for failure to "find, follow, and fight." When Forrest or Faulkner want to fight they can be found and heard from. We discovered that at Hernando.

I have tried time and again to bring my case to trial but can get no satisfaction. I wish not only to vindicate myself, but to show how Colonel Waring is making a scapegoat of me to cover his own incompetency and disobedience. Such is the annoying "insolence of office." After nearly two and a half years of constant service, during which time no word of complaint has ever been brought against me, to be accused of "cowardice and unsoldierly conduct" by such an ape "clothed with a little brief authority" is an insult that is hard for me to bear.

The soldiers have had a heavy and hotly contested snowball battle in which over 100 were engaged. They fought so long and hard that I was afraid some would be seriously hurt. Their treatment of prisoners was unprecedented in civilized warfare. Instead of sending them to the rear, to be held for exchange or paroled, all who were so unfortunate as to be captured were at once overpowered and rolled over and over or completely buried in the snow in view of their comrades. Very few inducements were offered either side to surrender. Fortunately, no one was seriously hurt and no one got mad and the fight finally ended pleasantly by all parties becoming tired-out.

Our New Year party, which was postponed on account of the weather, came off a few nights ago at Percly's and was in every respect a brilliant success. The night was dark and somewhat stormy, and some little difficulty was experienced in getting outside the lines without the countersign, but by a little strategy in which I took some chances of being shot by the pickets, I finally got there with a little squad of soldiers, good brave fellows who would, if necessary, cut their way through anything to get to a dance. The party had been well worked up and girls, lots of them, were there from all around and away off. Knowing I could not get back through the lines without the countersign, and not caring to "hurry off" anyhow, we concluded to make a night of it, so with an abundance of good eating, drinking, and flirting we kept the dance going until five o'clock in the morning, when mustering my little squad, I marched bravely through the lines into camp. The young officer on duty at the outpost took in the situation and omitted any mention in his report of a scout passing his post that morning (the countersign is required and can be used only between sunset and sunrise).

The ground is covered with four or five inches of snow, under which is mud varying in depth from "shoe deep" to "no bottom." I have been so long comfortably housed here and have had such an enforced idle time of late, that I fear I may have become a little too delicate and fine-blooded for a return to the shelter-tented field. While I always prefer the field to the routine duty of camp, I do not anticipate with feelings of delight an active field campaign just now, when the ground is covered with snow and mud, and the rivers all running full of ice. It is all very fine in the summer when the nights are warm and spring chickens are ripe enough to pick, and eggs, milk, and honey are in season. But in such weather as we are now having, I am weak enough to prefer serving my country in a little cabin with a tight roof and warm fire and a mess chest full of commissary supplies, to a bed in the mud and snow on the warm side of a fence or beside a huge fire of rails that only serves to melt the snow and make the mud more muddy, and snaps sparks into a fellow's eyes or on his shoddy blanket, and with rations limited to a few hardtacks and a slice of very old and very lean bacon. But such is life in the cavalry; 'tis either a feast or a famine. When not feasting and flirting we are foraging or fighting. But we take comfort in the hope that the rebellion can't possibly last much longer, and we take things as they come and improve opportunities as they present.

Our men feel that they have not been fairly treated in the matter of furloughs. Furloughs have been freely granted to other commands, but applications from our battalion are nearly all refused at district or departmental headquarters for the reason that "the service cannot spare any of your men." Our men have served faithfully and cheerfully and are willing to do so to the end of the war. They like to be appreciated, but they like also to be rewarded. If no furloughs were granted to anyone, they would not complain, but they don't like to see others who have done less than they have going home for twenty or thirty days and they denied that pleasure.

On Saturday, January 23rd, I went to Columbus to see General Reid, our present district commander, but found he has recently removed his headquarters to Cairo.[1] At Columbus I went to the hospital to see Henry Goulty, one of my men who was sick there. I found him very feeble, but well cared for. At his request, I wrote a letter to his father. I remained in Columbus over Sunday and the next day went to Cairo. I found General Reid very busy and he asked me to call again the next day.

The next day, Tuesday, I again reported to General Reid and asked that I be granted a trial or at least that the charges against me be investigated. The general was much surprised that I reported under arrest and said no charges against me were on file in his office, and I now learned for the first time that no charges against me had ever been filed at district headquarters, but that Colonel Waring had kept me in arrest and off duty all this time maliciously and at his own will and pleasure on trumped-up charges that he dared not prefer against me at headquarters, which he did only to cover his own offenses at the time and never meant to bring me to trial.

The forty days prescribed by Army regulations having expired since I was arrested, I was at liberty to return to my command and post of duty, which, however, I did not wish to do without an investigation. My only reason now would be to prefer charges against Colonel Waring for false accusation and malicious persecution, and which I was strongly tempted to do. General Reid advised me to let the matter drop and return to duty and gave me a special order honorably relieving me from arrest and directing me to report to my company for duty. I took the order, but would not report to Colonel Waring for duty and was not fully decided to let the matter drop there.

I went down to Columbus that evening and the next day returned to Union City, which I found nearly deserted, being garrisoned by only the wagon guards and a few sick soldiers, the troops having marched for Memphis. I packed up and took all the sick men, extra horses, and baggage by rail to Columbus for transportation by river to Memphis. Knowing it would take the troops some days to reach Memphis, and having nothing else to do, I decided to make a last flying visit to Paducah. So taking one man, J. S. Homan, I left Columbus early Saturday morning, January 30th.

The road enters the town of Blandville from the south up a steep hill and around a short curve so that the town cannot be seen from the road, nor can one be seen approaching from that direction. As I reached the top of the hill, a little in advance of Homan, who had stopped to water his horse in the creek, I found myself almost in the midst of some fifteen or twenty "shotgun rangers" in the village, to whom my sudden appearance was a matter of no little surprise and interest, and they at once began mounting their horses in view of possible emergencies. I thought I was in for a scrape this time surely, and I thought very rapidly for a few moments. Of course, we could not fight the whole crowd with only our pistols, and escape by flight seemed out of the question, as we were within short range of their shotguns. It was a desperate case and demanded quick and desperate action. I quickly decided on a little strategy, and if that failed, to make a dash and take the chance of being killed or captured, for surrender quietly we never would. So, partly turning in my saddle, I called to Homan, who had just reached the top of the hill, and loud enough for the rebs to hear, "How far are we ahead of the regiment?" He took in the situation at a glance, and replied loudly, more for the benefit of the rebs than for my information, "It is right here at the creek." The rebs took the hint and were quickly out of town and making long jumps for the nearest timber. Taking advantage of their momentary surprise, and fearing they might soon discover their mistake and give us chase, we put our horses down to their level best for the next five or six miles, and saw no more of them. We reached Alexander's at five o'clock, where we stayed that night. I here learned with regret of the death of my friend Mrs. Gould, eldest daughter of my old friend Mr. Bronson, who died soon after last Christmas.

Leaving Alexander's early next morning, I reached Paducah in time to attend church and hear a sermon by Reverend Doctor Hendricks. After service I dined with Major Gibson, provost marshal, and spent the evening and night at Mr. Bronson's.

I expected to return on Monday, but my horse, a new one I had recently purchased, was taken sick and unable to travel, so I left him with Mr. Bronson, intending to go down on a steamboat expected that day, and all day I waited impatiently for it. The boat came at last, but I was at the theater and missed it. I caught one the next morning, and that night slept on the parlor floor in the McKay House in Columbus. The trip down the Ohio was a very rough and stormy one, and the long narrow steamboat warped and squirmed like a giant serpent until I thought sometimes she would break her back.

Wednesday morning, February 3rd, I left Columbus, I hoped for the last time, with my horses and baggage on the steamer *Hope,* arriving at Memphis at noon the next day. I at once called on Lieutenant Catlin at General Grierson's headquarters and learned that our battalion had not yet arrived. Catlin, who I found well and busy, was aide-de-camp on the staff of General Grierson. I also met Captain Woodward of Paducah, with whose family I was well acquainted. Being a little short of money, I did not feel able to stand the pressure of $5.00 at the "Gayoso" and so put up at a less pretentious hotel, the "Whitemore House," where I had very good accommodations, and that night went to the theater with a party of officers from headquarters.

Finding there was no court martial sitting in Memphis before which I could bring my case, by the advice of Catlin and other friends, and at the request of General Grierson, who said he had work all ready for me, I consented to return to duty under General Reid's order. I called in the afternoon on our rebel friends the Piersons, and in the evening went again to the theater in company with Ewart, Catlin, and Dement and that night stayed at the "Gayoso."

The next morning I was ordered by General Grierson to take command of all stragglers, details, and baggage of the 2nd Illinois. The boys had been in Memphis several days without any special command and were getting into all kinds of trouble and scrapes. After considerable trouble and delay, I finally collected my much-scattered forces, finding some of them in charge of the provost guard, and moved them out to the camp of Colonel Kitchen, 2nd New Jersey Cavalry. Having no tent nor mess of my own, I engaged board for a few days at Pierson's.

Monday morning I was ordered to take my "Gideon's Band" out to Collierville, where I went by rail and found our battalion just in from Union City, when I resumed command of my company. About 8,000 cavalry were encamped here. The next day, all the troops were reviewed by General Sooy Smith, chief of cavalry.[2] The afternoon was very hot and the review and inspection long and tiresome. General Smith was very particular and critical and had many orders and suggestions for every officer.

The following day our baggage and transportation were again subjected to a reduction and were cut down to almost nothing. All extra and surplus horses and wagons were turned over to the quartermaster and a firing squad detailed to shoot all condemned horses and mules; about fifty animals were killed. Shelter tents were issued to the men, and five pack mules to each company. I was allowed a whole little mule for myself and Cayton, on which we packed our blankets and what little mess kit was allowed us. Packing a mule was a new experience for me, and I don't think my little mule entertained a very high opinion of me as a packer, but I soon learned the ropes and ties and in a few days could lash on a pack that a mule could not buck off.

All the preparations must mean business and we look for lively times soon. General Ben Grierson is considered one of the best cavalry officers in the army, and is very popular with the troops. We are all ready and in light marching order tonight. We have, as nearly as I can get the figures, about 7,500 effective men, 250 to 300 pack mules, two or three ammunition wagons and a few ambulances. It's the largest cavalry force I have seen together.

The mules of the pioneer corps are packed with axes, spades, drills, and other tools and blasting powder. Of course, we know nothing of the object nor destination of the expedition, but it is generally believed to be a march of destruction from Memphis to the Gulf. About a year ago, General Grierson made a successful raid from Memphis to Baton Rouge.[3] The division, consisting of three brigades, is under the command of General W. S. Smith, Grierson commanding one of the brigades. We all hoped and expected Grierson was to command the expedition.

On February 11th, the several brigades left Collierville by different routes. Ours (the first) left at 4:30pm, marching eastward about ten miles and camped at ten o'clock. We found the roads muddy and were delayed by the ammunition wagons sticking in the mud and breaking down. We were off again at three o'clock the next morning, marched all day, and reached Hudsonville about one o'clock that night, where we halted for a short rest. Our route was so crooked and our march so slow that I cannot estimate the distance travelled.

At Hudsonville I got about half an hour's sleep. The men were too tired to cook, or even make coffee, and laid down for a little rest, holding their horses by the bridles. I had only just fallen asleep when I was aroused by the bugle sounding "to horse," and at half-past three we were again en route, passing through the town of Holly Springs just as the sun was rising, where we halted about an hour to wait for the wagons and pack train.

Holly Springs is, or rather was, a very pretty little city, situated in a fine prairie and surrounded by a rich farming country. Much of the town is now in ruins and is almost deserted. A battle occurred here about a year ago in which Colonel Hogg of our regiment was killed.[4] Beyond Holly Springs, we found the roads very hilly and muddy, and so slow was our march that when we camped at 1pm at Walker's Mill we were only seven miles from Holly Springs. During the day and last night a number of horses of the 19th Pennsylvania and 2nd New Jersey stuck in the mud or fell dead on the road. This morning, a soldier of the 19th Pennsylvania straggled from the column and was shot by rebel scouts. From Walker's Mill foraging parties were sent out who soon returned with good supplies of corn fodder and provisions.

We remained at Walker's Mill all day Sunday, February 14th, for a much-needed rest. The foraging parties sent out in the morning brought in a number of horses and mules. Sunday night it rained hard, but I fixed up a little shelter with rails and my rubber blanket and had the first good night's sleep since leaving Collierville.

Leaving Walker's Mill at seven o'clock Monday morning, we marched two hours to the Tippah River, a deep and rapid stream, where we worked the balance of the day building a bridge. At 7pm the brigade commenced crossing, but the night was so dark and stormy, and the roads so muddy, that the crossing was attended with much labor and delay, and it was four o'clock in the morning before the rear guard crossed. Our battalion crossed about one o'clock and marched two or three miles, when we halted until 6am. Owing to the rain, the river rose rapidly in the night, and the bridge was continually breaking and in danger of floating away, and it was only by keeping it constantly loaded with horses that it was kept down.

When we halted after crossing, I was very tired and hungry, but could find neither my servant nor mule and had nothing to eat. While hunting a dry spot to lie down, I came across Captain Reader of the 19th Pennsylvania boiling a little pot of coffee, who kindly shared his coffee with me, although he had only about half enough for one man, and was himself as hungry as I was. That little cup of hot coffee was worth more to me than a banquet, and I shall ever kindly remember Captain Reader for his self-sacrificing generosity. I slept about an hour, marching again at eight o'clock in the morning.

Beyond the Tippah River, the country is rough and hilly and covered with pine forests, the first pine timber I had seen in the South. We crossed the Tallahatchie River at New Albany, where we found General Smith in camp with one regiment, the 4th U.S. Cavalry. Our battalion being in advance, we marched about four miles beyond New Albany and camped at midnight.

Wednesday morning we were up and off again at four o'clock and marched until ten o'clock, when we halted to feed and where the three brigades came together and the division marched under the command of General Smith.

Up to this time, we had met no enemy, save a few squads of scouts that continually hung on our flanks and near our camps watching our movements, but this morning it was reported that Forrest with a strong force was at Okolona waiting to give us battle. When Forrest is ready and wants to fight, we will find him fast enough, and not before. We passed through Pontotoc and camped at 8pm. General Smith had sent ahead and ordered all the inhabitants of Pontotoc into their houses and the doors and windows closed, so that when we passed through the town not a living soul was to be seen. I never saw a town in the daytime so completely deserted and dead; not even a negro was to be seen. I could never understand the object of Smith's order. A light snow fell this night, but the weather continued warm and mild.

The next morning, Thursday, February 18th, we were aroused at four o'clock, but as our battalion was to march in the rear today, we did not start until eight o'clock. The command that marches in advance one day goes to the rear the next day and so works up to the front again.

At Redland, a little village of some half dozen homes, our advance guard was fired on. After some little skirmishing, the guard burned the town. We passed through Okolona, where the advance guard met and drove off a small scout or picket about dark and camped a few miles beyond at ten o'clock. I got a few hours sleep and was up again at four o'clock next morning, but did not march until about eight o'clock. That morning I had a royal good breakfast of hot corn cakes, molasses, and chicken, the fruits of my cook Scott's little foraging enterprise of yesterday.

Up to this time, no property except Redland had been destroyed, but now we commenced our work of destruction, and our trail was marked by fire and ashes. Soon after leaving Okolona, we struck the Mobile and Ohio Railroad at Egypt Station. There was no town here, nothing but the station and sidetracks. On both sides of the main track and switches were long lines of rail cribs, about half a mile long and eight or ten feet high, filled with corn. A train of boxcars stood on the switch, which a squad of rebel soldiers and laborers were loading with corn. As our advance guard charged down on the station, the engineer of the train tried to pull out, but finding he could not start his train, the brakes being all set, and as our men were rapidly closing in on him, he drew the draw pin and escaped with his engine. The train station and section houses and corn cribs were fired. The train and cribs must have contained not less than 100,000 bushels of dry corn and made a big and very hot blaze. Leaving Egypt as soon as the fire was well started, we followed down the railroad a few miles, burning bridges and tearing up and destroying the track.

It takes a long time to build a railroad, but it can be unbuilt very quickly. On level ground we would draw the spikes and pile up the ties with the rails laid across the top, then fire the pile and the heat of the burning ties would warp and bend the rails. On embankments, 200 to 500 men standing on one side of the track would, at the word of command, lift their side of the track and turn it all over down the bank. This was merely a temporary injury as the same ties and rails could be used again. We also cut the telegraph poles and wires.

Leaving the railroad, we turned eastward, when our advance guard was fired on by a considerable force of the enemy. Colonel Waring, believing Forrest's army was in front of him, wished to communicate with General Grierson, who was at that time at Aberdeen, eight miles distant. As usual, when any specially important or dangerous work was to be done, the 2nd Illinois battalion was called on to carry this dispatch. The battalion was drawn up and the object and probable danger of the trip explained to the men. They were told that in order to get to General Grierson, they might and probably would have to cut their way through a rebel column, supposed to be between us and Grierson, and that none who wished to remain would be required to go. At the command "volunteers for forlorn hope, forward," only three men in the line of 300 stood fast; one of them was sick, one had a lame horse, and the other I guess was tired. Then, taking blankets and overcoats off our saddles, which were left with a guard, we cinched our saddles tighter, and with carbines "advanced"—carried in a position for immediate use—wheeled into "column of fours" and started on a gallop.

The road through the timber and lanes was in splendid condition, and our horses, although already overworked and tired, seemed to take new life as though they understood the importance of the duty required of them and came down to their work in fine style. We saw no enemy, but crossed a large and very fresh trail over which a large force of enemy had just passed. We reached Aberdeen, where we found General Grierson, having made the eight miles in just forty minutes. We stopped at Aberdeen only long enough to rest our horses and get dinner for ourselves. I dined by invitation at Dr. Ward's.

Aberdeen is situated on a branch of the Tombigbee River and is one of the prettiest little cities I have seen. In a little park in the center of the town is a sulphur spring that bubbles up clear and cold from an artesian well 900 feet deep. We were the first Yankee troops ever in the town and of course attracted no little attention, especially from the ladies who were at first a little shy of us, but who, on discovering that we were kindly inclined towards them and were neither barbarians nor monsters, and that the most we wanted just then was something to eat, became quite sociable and hospitable, and as the men were not permitted to leave their horses, the ladies brought them lunches.

I halted with my company opposite a young ladies' seminary, where we sat on the sidewalk holding our horses. At first not a soul was to be seen about the house, and I thought it was deserted, or maybe it was the courthouse. But very soon faces appeared at the windows. Then some girl, reckless with bravery or curiosity, would look out of the half-opened door, and growing bolder and more reckless would step out on the porch. Her companions, seeing she still lived, ventured out one by one until the porch was full. They continued drawing their lines closer and closer until there was a long line of pretty girls leaning over the fence, shaking hands and chatting with the soldiers, and begging buttons until some of the soldiers had not a button left on their coats, and every girl asked more questions in ten minutes than could be answered in a day. None of those girls will probably ever forget their first sight of the Yankee cavalry.

Leaving Aberdeen with General Grierson, we marched to Prairie Station, where after feeding our horses, we burned the station, corn cribs, and a freight train on the siding loaded with corn and flour. All that day we burned cotton and tobacco barns, corn cribs, and stacks of hay and fodder, and took all the horses and mules we could find. It was a beautiful and rich farming country called "Grand Prairie" and had supplied the rebel armies in the southwest with great quantities of flour and grain, and the cotton, of which we burned thousands of bales, was, I believe, bonded to the British government or English capitalists. Cotton was at that time worth one dollar a pound in Memphis or anywhere within our lines. Late that night I counted from the top of a little hill thirteen large fires. My bed that night was a $200 bale of cotton, which I ripped open. I was pretty tired, but it was as good a bed as I wanted.

Saturday morning, February 20th, the three brigades came together again at Prairie Station, or rather where Prairie Station once was, and marched southward, tearing up the railroad and burning bridges, barns, and cribs. About noon our advance was checked by the enemy a few miles from West Point, where a brisk skirmish occurred, in which the 2nd Iowa Cavalry lost one lieutenant and four men. The enemy gave way and fell back towards West Point.

We advanced to within a half-mile of the town, where we formed in order of battle with our battalion on the right, and that night slept in line of battle without unsaddling our horses. I was near the extreme right of our line. I could sleep but little, as our pickets kept up a scattering fire all night, and I could plainly hear the enemy in motion crossing a bridge with cavalry and artillery, and I felt sure there would be a battle in the morning. I have always thought that if Grierson had been in command, he would have forced the fight that afternoon or night and not have given the rebels all night to maneuver and get into position.

Wearied at last with watching and listening, I fell into a short but sound sleep before morning and dreamed of home and friends I might perhaps never see again. There is a point beyond which tired nature cannot go without rest in sleep, and many a soldier enjoys his sweetest and often last sleep the "night before the battle." I cannot here record my dream of that night, but I can never forget it.

Forrest was at last ready to fight. We had "followed" and "found" him and now he meant that we should "fight" him. Nor did he wait for us to commence hostilities, but opened the ball by engaging our right with light artillery. Our battalion advanced into a large open field, where we engaged the rebel skirmishers at long range. Beyond their line of skirmishers, I could plainly see about 2,000 cavalry quietly sitting on their horses in line of battle. There was soon pretty sharp skirmishing all along our line, but no general engagement. Instead of advancing on the enemy as we all expected to do, or even standing on the defensive, to the surprise of all, our march was directed northward over the same road we had traveled the day before. It looked to me very much like a retreat.

As soon as the march was commenced, the enemy made a furious attack on the rear (Grierson's) brigade. In the line of march, our brigade came in the center. From every hilltop I could plainly see the fight going on behind. Our artillery took advantage of every hill and favorable opportunity and position and played sad havoc with the rebels, many times preventing them from charging and breaking our column.

About the middle of the afternoon, our brigade was halted to allow Grierson to come up. We were then in the timber. I was here sent to a ridge or hill about a half-mile distant in an open field or prairie to reconnoiter. We could distinctly hear the artillery and musketry in the rear where Grierson was fighting, and supposed the enemy's force was all there, but on reaching the top of the ridge I was not a little surprised to see beyond it in a valley and not over a half-mile distant, a solid column of not less than 2,500 or 3,000 rebels with several pieces of artillery marching rapidly in a direction parallel with our column, evidently endeavoring to get around our right. Indeed, a few shots far ahead just then assured us that the rebels' advance was already engaging our advance flankers.

A messenger was sent back to report to Colonel Waring and ask him to send up a battery at once to engage the rebels and check their advance. Seeing that the battery could not reach us in time to do any good, a few of us rode part way down the hill towards the rebs and sent a few shots after their rear guard, just to let them know what we thought of them. They promptly returned the compliment, and a few spent balls fell amongst us, but without doing any harm. The occupant of a buggy in the rebel ranks seemed somewhat disturbed and whipped his horse into a run when the firing commenced. An officer on a white horse, after viewing us a few moments through his field glass, galloped up toward the head of his column. They soon passed and we returned to our brigade, which was again in motion.

We continued our march in pretty good order, with occasional fighting in the rear, that night until about 2 o'clock Monday morning, February 22nd, when we halted to rest and cook breakfast near Okolona. About sunrise, a large force of rebels was discovered on our right front about a half-mile distant in the edge of the timber. As the firing in the rear had nearly ceased towards morning, I thought the enemy had marched past us during the night and now meant to cut off our retreat and give us battle in front.

Our battalion was ordered out to engage the enemy's attention while the brigade was getting started. We threw out a line of skirmishers, who were soon briskly engaged with the rebel skirmishers in plain view of both armies. With a field glass I plainly saw the rebel officers viewing us with their glasses. As soon as we were ordered to leave the field and rejoin the main column, then marching, the rebels also withdrew.

Our brigade passed through Okolona without molestation, but had only just left the town when Colonel McCrillis's brigade was attacked with great fury, the rebels charging with such force and violence that his brigade was soon broken and demoralized.[5] His soldiers, many of whom were Tennesseans, seemed completely panic-stricken and came rushing like a stampede of cattle through our ranks. Our battalion, which was at that time in the rear of our brigade, was ordered to form a line across the road and check the stampede. The line was easily and quickly formed, but the wild rush of panic-stricken soldiers could not be stopped. Those behind pushed on those in front and broke through our line. I did not fear for our little battalion of the 2nd Illinois, but I did fear at one time that the soldiers of our brigade, seeing the rush through and past their ranks, might also become panic-stricken. Some little confusion did once or twice occur, but it was soon quieted.

Wherever the nature of the ground would permit, the different regiments and batteries of Grierson's and our brigade would wheel into line and meet and check the fierce charges of the rebels, then quietly and orderly retire to be relieved by others already in line of battle. In this way we fought retreating until nearly noon, when the panic in the Second Brigade, which had somewhat subsided, broke out again, this time affecting portions of the other brigades. The rebels now attacked not only the rear, but both flanks. Frequently would they charge in column of squadrons down one hill and up another, for our road ran much of the way on ridges, in the face of a deadly fire of canister and carbines, and were every time repulsed. They seemed determined to cut off our train of pack mules and the host of negroes that had fallen into our line, and which were kept near the center of our column.

Soon after the fight commenced after leaving Okolona, I was sent with my company to act as flankers on our left, to guard against surprise or ambuscades. The country was in some places very hilly and difficult to travel so that sometimes I was obliged to make long detours, which would sometimes take me a mile or more from the line of march. At one time, I think about noon, I was on top of a ridge watching the movements of a regiment of rebel cavalry and wondering where it was going to strike, when Lieutenant Catlin galloped up to me saying, "I have been looking for you and feared you were lost. The 7th Indiana Regiment is ordered to charge that rebel regiment there in the valley, and I am going with it." He appeared nervous and much excited. His lips were compressed and there was a wild and unnatural light in his eyes. I tried to dissuade him from his purpose and asked him to stay with me. I said to him, "Please stay with me, Catlin, I need you more than that regiment does, and I expect to have hot work before this day is done." "No, Moore, I'll make the charge and you must do the best you can. God bless you, goodbye," and giving me a long last handshake, he was off. I saw the charge and the rebels driven before it, but I never saw Catlin again.[6]

We continued fighting in retreat until towards evening, when the firing ceased and the rebels withdrew. Why they did so, I know not. They certainly had no occasion to. About ten o'clock, the head of the division halted near Pontotoc, and the balance of the night was spent in collecting and reorganizing the scattered commands. It was a beautiful moonlit night, clear and calm, and almost as warm as summer. I formed the few men I had with me in an open place in the timber by the roadside, and as the brigade marched past I called for the 2nd Illinois, and all stragglers of our battalion as they came up fell into my line until I soon had a mixed, but very creditable, command. Soon a negro sergeant with a few men of the Pioneer Corps rode up and asked permission to report to me, saying his officers were all lost. I told him to form on my left and he at once began shouting with a voice like a siege gun: "First African Pioneers, fall in here," accompanying his commands with many profane exhortations. He succeeded in collecting quite a large squad of his company and stayed with me the balance of the night.

Having collected perhaps 100 men, I moved on with the still-disorganized column. Seeing Generals Smith and Grierson standing together at the corner of a fence, and without any of their staffs with them, I rode up and reported for orders. Grierson looked discouraged and disgusted. He acknowledged my salute, but said nothing. Smith seemed very nervous and much excited. He said, "I have no special orders for you, Captain. If your command is in good order, get it as far to the front as you can and do the best you can," which somewhat indifferent orders I proceeded to obey. I galloped forward as rapidly as I could through the moving mass of soldiers until I came to where the head of the division was halted, when I dismounted my men for a short rest, which I thought was about the "best I could do" just then.

Having seen nothing of either my servant nor mule since the fight commenced, I had neither blankets nor rations. I found Lieutenant Dement of Company B, who had a little fire, but who like myself had lost his "supply train." So congratulating ourselves that things were no worse, and comforting each other as best we could, we laid down hungry and tired for a little rest. I had been asleep perhaps an hour when I was awakened by my saddle blanket on which I was lying being on fire. As we were already dressed, it did not take us long to get out of bed. As my blanket was too much burned to be of further use, I threw it in the fire. Besides a few holes burned in my uniform and one side of my beard scorched, no damage was done.

My cook came up with his mule during the night, so I had a good square breakfast of coffee, crackers, and beans.

At three o'clock Tuesday morning, we were off again with our battalion at the head of the division. As we approached the Tallahatchie River, I was ordered to gallop ahead about five miles to the bridge to guard against it being destroyed by the rebels. Just as I came in sight of the bridge, going up the river, and about a half-mile from it, I saw coming out of the timber above the bridge about twenty rebel soldiers. A race for the bridge commenced, but the rebs being nearer to it than I was, reached it first and dashed over (it was a large covered wooden bridge). They must have been well prepared for their work, for when I reached the bridge, only two or three minutes behind them, it was on fire. We soon whipped out the fire with our blankets and waited unmolested for the division.

Having been in advance all morning, and having saved the bridge, I thought we should have been allowed to cross first and keep our position in the advance, but instead our battalion was sent to the top of a hill nearby to guard against surprise until the entire division had crossed, which was after noon, when we brought up the rear. As we left our position, a small force of about 100 rebels appeared on a neighboring hill and quietly watched us as we rode down the hill and over the bridge. They did not offer to molest us and we were in no mood just then to court a fight unless something to eat was to be gained by it.

The most undesirable position in a column is that of rear guard. The officer in command of it is a sort of deputy provost marshal and must take charge of all soldiers in arrest and punishment, lame horses, and stragglers. The rear guard gets all the discomforts, inconveniences, and annoyances of the march without any of its pleasures and benefits. The advance guard has first choice and pick of everything, and while it is the post of danger, it is also the post of honor.

After leaving the Tallahatchie, our brigades separated, our brigade being ordered to push on in advance with the negroes and pack mules. We camped that night about ten o'clock and were off again at four the next morning, February 24th. We crossed the Tippah River about noon, where much confusion was occasioned amongst the stragglers and negroes by a few shots fired in the rear and the report that Forrest was crossing the river below us. We continued our march that night until six o'clock. We passed through the little town of Mount Pleasant about noon, where I was fortunate enough to get a good meal of corn bread and bacon. As I had eaten nothing since early Tuesday morning and had been riding hard all the time, I was as empty as a gourd and correspondingly hungry.

We reached Collierville that evening about sundown, and here ended the great Smith-Grierson Raid. I cannot estimate the amount of cotton, corn, and tobacco we destroyed. It was very great, and we so completely destroyed all railroad communications that the enemy could not get out what supplies we did not destroy. Grand Prairie was without exception the richest farming country I ever saw. On nearly every farm or plantation were large fine residences, good negro quarters, and large barns and cribs for the storage of cotton, tobacco, and corn. From the plantations in Grand Prairie not less than 2,000 able-bodied negro men and perhaps half as many women and children followed our troops to Collierville.

We struck the rebels a hard blow and gave them a bad back set, but we did not do enough. We should have gone through and formed a junction with Sherman, who was marching northward to meet us, and I do and always shall believe that if Grierson had been alone in command of the expedition we would have gone through.[7] From what I saw of Forrest's army, I think it was very little if any stronger than ours, and we could certainly have fought better advancing than retreating. Nothing so demoralizes troops as a retreat. An "orderly retreat" is a maneuver much oftener heard of than witnessed. However good troops may be, it is impossible to preserve good order amongst soldiers who feel that they are beaten and are flying before the enemy. Every shot terrifies them, and when once panic-stricken, they are beyond all control; they are deaf to commands, entreaties, and threats. I cannot understand how nor why men who have fearlessly braved a thousand dangers will, without any good cause or occasion, become so terrified as to lose all control over themselves and rush like a flock of frightened sheep, climbing over and trampling each other in their frantic endeavors to get away from they know not what. It is not fear of death nor injury, for these same men, perhaps an hour before and on many former occasions, have bravely charged right up to the enemy's guns, or received without flinching a charge of cavalry or bayonets, and without a thought of personal dangers. In a rushing, panic-stricken mob of soldiers, there is not a man but who well knows that by making a firm, determined stand, all together, they could check if not repulse the enemy, and that there is far less danger in fighting in good order than in fleeing in disorder. I know that stampedes do occur, and that the best and truest soldiers will sometimes become panic-stricken, but why, no one can tell.

The mob of negroes that followed us to Collierville was a very mixed and interesting outfit. The majority were young farm hands but there were also a good many old men and women and children, and they came in every possible way: in carriages, buggies, wagons and carts, on horses, mules, and on foot, and it was astonishing to see how they could travel and keep up with us day and night. I saw many old white-headed "uncles," crooked and deformed with "rheumatiz" and long years of toil, limping along on their canes and crutches, happy in the thought that they had lived to see the day of <u>freedom</u>. And women, too; I saw both old and young trudging along with heavy packs of clothing, bedding, or provisions on their heads or shoulders, and often with a baby in their arms, careless of fatigue or danger, and all happy in the one thought that they were at last free. What that freedom might be to which they were all flying, they knew not. In exchange for their comfortable quarters, surrounded by plenty, and where for generations they had lived and been cared for, they accepted privation and dangers to be <u>free</u>. This love of freedom is born with every creature. Even the meanest and most inanimate bug or reptile that crawls will struggle and fight to be free, and the slaves had heard of freedom, though they knew not what it was. It had been whispered to the baby at its mother's breast and been talked of clandestinely as they worked in the fields. It was to them a forbidden fruit, and for that reason the thought of it was sweet. That dusky crowd of beings, toiling along after our army, cared not for the past, nor thought of the future. They only felt that their "day of jubilee" had come and that the Yankee soldiers were their deliverers

During the fifteen days we were out, I did not have one whole night's sleep, and had only two or three chances to wash my face. It was a hard and unsatisfactory trip, but we lived well most of the time, though I was sometimes as hungry as a hawk, and the roads and weather were as good as could be desired. We had but little rain and the roads were muddy for only a few days.

At one time during the hardest fighting, I was out on the left advance flank and came to a little cabin occupied by two women and a lot of little children. Being very hungry, I asked the women if they could give me something to eat. They offered me a gourd containing about two quarts of hominy, which they said was "all the food they had," and as it corresponded with the extreme poverty of everything else about the place, I believed them. The firing could be distinctly heard coming nearer and nearer, and the poor women and children were terribly frightened. As the cabin was very nearly in our line of march, and there would probably be fighting all around it soon, I told the women to take their children and the gourd of hominy and go towards a distant creek, away from the line of march, and to keep going as long as they could travel, and the last I saw of them, they were going as fast as the children could trot towards the timber on the creek, hurried, if not encouraged, in their flight by the firing in the rear. Here was a helpless family of "poor whites" on the verge of starvation, and only the day before and a few miles distant, we had destroyed thousands of bushels of corn. I have never since seen a mess of "whole hominy" without thinking of those destitute, frightened women and children and their little gourd of hominy.

On reaching Collierville, we found the rebels had been there during our absence and burned the railroad depot, which was about all they could do in retaliation for the loss and destruction we had inflicted on them.

No sooner had we reached Collierville than the weather turned cold and stormy, and as we were without tents, except our little shelters, which we now pitched for the first time since we drew them, and with a very limited supply of camp equipage, and there being no fuel except a few board fences that the men had to carry a long distance, both we and our horses suffered more that one night after our return to Collierville than we did all the time we were out. Seventeen horses and mules belonging to our battalion died that night from cold, hunger, and fatigue. I know not how many animals died in the other camps. The next morning, Friday, February 26th, our whole brigade was sent out in the country to find and bring in forage for the horses.

On Saturday, we left Collierville and, crossing Wolf River, camped at the fairgrounds, three miles east from Memphis. I procured a supply of new tents and cooking utensils, and for the next two days was busy making out reports and getting camp in order besides doing field officer of the day duty.

On Tuesday, March 1st, having got things in good running order once more, I embraced the first opportunity to go to the city, accompanied by Sergeant Obe Spence. My horses being pretty well worn down, I spared them, and for the first time in my life, rode a mule. My little "government mule" that had carried my pack all through the late raid, came in about as fresh as she went out. She was lazy, good-natured, and at all times perfectly oblivious of all surroundings. Nothing seemed to disturb or interest her. If I spurred her hard enough, she would run as fast as she could for two or three miles without an apparent effort, and if I dismounted and left her an hour or two she would not, of her own accord, move ten feet in ten hours.

The first thing I did after reaching town was to take a hot bath and change of underwear, and the next thing, dinner at the Gayoso for which latter I paid $2.00. Notwithstanding the high price, the dinner was so good and I was so hungry that I don't think the house made any money out of the speculation.

After calling on General Grierson at his headquarters, I went to Fort Pickering to see some of my men who were sick there in hospital and convalescent camp. During the day I most unexpectedly met an old Quincy acquaintance, Joe Van Dorn, in the streets. In the evening, I went to the theater and stayed all night at the Washam House, my little mule being well cared for at the government corral.

During the month of March, our duties at Memphis were very light, consisting chiefly of furnishing a few pickets and posts and an occasional little scout into the country. I came on duty as officer of the day, either camp or field, about once a week. The line of outposts around the city was about fifteen miles long, and as the field officer of the day must make the grand rounds three times in twenty-four hours, he is kept on the jump and pretty busy while on duty. The first round is made soon after the guards are posted, which is usually about nine o'clock in the morning, the next after noon, and the third after midnight, and he reports off duty at the next morning's guard mount.

I have ridden about the city a good deal and have visited all the places of amusement and of interest, but have made no acquaintances. I called several times on Reverend Dr. White, who always received me very kindly and friendly. The city rebels don't take kindly to Union soldiers. It is in our country camps and amongst the country folks that we have our fun.

Besides the two theaters there is a hippodrome, a large temporary building for the production of "horse opera." I have been there several times to see "Mazeppa," "Dick Turpin," and other circus plays. I admired the performance of Miss Kate Vance's horse more than I did Miss Katie herself.

The veteran movement, which was started about the time we started out on our late raid, has been revived, and a good many soldiers are reenlisting as veterans. The inducements offered by the government to all who will reenlist for a longer term of service are $100 bounty, thirty days furlough, and an increase of pay.[8] Our battalion is not responding very heartily to the call for vets, only seventy-six having reenlisted thus far, six of whom are from my company. If our men had been granted more furloughs last summer, I am quite sure many more would now be willing to reenlist.

On Friday, April 1st, our battalion was ordered to move into the city and pitch camp on the riverbank near the Gayoso House and be ready to take boat for New Orleans. Being under marching orders we were, of course, relieved from all duty and had nothing at all to do but to <u>wait</u>, which after all is about the hardest duty a cavalry soldier can do.

A house near my tent was ordered to be torn down, being in the range of some guns in Fort Pickering, and a squad of negro soldiers were ordered to the work. Hearing a great outcry and commotion, I went over to see what was the matter and found two ladies, Mrs. and Miss Odlam, the only occupants of the house, in a deal of trouble. The negroes had no white officer with them, but were in charge of a colored sergeant, and were behaving in a very insolent manner towards the ladies, and without giving them time to move anything out, began tearing the house down. I made the sergeant stop his work until the ladies could get men and a team and move everything safely out of the house. The negro soldiers are often insolent and overbearing in their behavior towards citizens, but are always respectful to and recognize the authority of white officers.

On Thursday, April 7th, the city was in a turmoil of excitement. A flag of truce came to our lines from Forrest, who was at Bolivar, and it was reported that he had asked that all women, children, and militia be sent out of the city at once, as he proposed to attack in a few hours. What the message really was I knew not, but there must have been something serious in it, as all the camps around the city were struck in a hurry and the troops moved into the fort. The militia were ordered out, not out of the city, but under arms, the stores closed, and the streets barricaded with wagons, drays, and lumber of all kinds. The men looked very uneasy while the women flew about as nervous and fussy as a flock of hens on the approach of a hawk, all hoping yet dreading that Forrest would really attack.

The Paducah affair was yet fresh in their minds, and they well knew that should a battle occur, no matter which side might be the victor, they would be the victims, and the final result would be the destruction of their beautiful city.[9] They knew that if the rebels entered the city, it would be to plunder, and that we would open on them from the fort and gunboats. They were never in such a dilemma. They wanted Forrest to come and whip us, and were afraid he would. They knew they would find no mercy at his hands, he would rob alike friend and foe, and they didn't like to fly to the fort with their valuables for safety, even if they could gain admittance, for they knew the artillery was manned by negroes, their former slaves, whose backs yet smarted from the effects of their last flogging, so mercy and protection there were at a discount.

While they would like to see us whipped, they didn't want to pay for the fun by being robbed and shelled out of town. A few scattering shots from the pickets, and aides and orderlies galloping to and from headquarters, confirmed their hopes and fears. But Forrest did not come, the militia returned to their homes and businesses, the barricades were removed from the streets, the few cotton speculators resumed their accustomed smiles, and soon the streets were again thronged by "fair women and brave(?) men." An occasional troop of cavalry dashing through the streets or the heavy tread of the provost guard were the only indications of the presence of foes whose "brutal outrages are only equaled by their contemptible cowardice," as the Richmond papers have it.

My venerable friend Reverend Dr. White, who at the time of my first visit to Memphis was a strong rebel and an advocate of secession, and who at that time would not use the prescribed prayer in the church service for the President of the United States, has experienced a radical change of view since the occupation of the city and his more intimate acquaintance with our troops and the opportunities he has had of comparing them with the rebel soldiers. I think he is fully satisfied of the hopelessness of the secession cause and disgusted with the vain boasts of the Southern leaders and their manner of conducting the war. In a recent conversation with him on this ever-interesting subject, he said: "Previous to the occupation of the city by the federals, and while the 'chivalry' were preparing for its defense, they made loud and frequent boasts of how they would fight and die in the 'last ditch' before they would see their beautiful city fall into the hands of an enemy notorious for his deeds of wanton outrage. Murder, rapine, and fire were what we were taught to expect in case of defeat, and the women believing all the wild stories they had read and heard of the atrocities committed by the Yankee soldiery, used every effort in their power to encourage and cheer their friends, husbands, brothers, and lovers on to the struggle that was inevitable, and to them of such vital importance, and to save them from the power of a merciless foe. And yet no sooner did your gunboats effect a landing after a very brief fight, than the exodus commenced. Promises on one side and entreaties on the other were alike unheeded, and like frightened sheep these chivalrous fire eaters turned their backs on their doomed homes and families to seek that 'last ditch' elsewhere." The old man's eyes flashed with righteous indignation. He has foresworn all allegiance to the "Confederacy" and again uses the church prayer for the President of the U.S. and says he recognizes no president but Lincoln.

Every one here admits that the city was never before so quiet, clean, and free from disreputable characters as at present, under martial rule. And just how the deserted and unprotected women suffer at the hands of the invaders can be seen by reference to the marriage notices in the daily city paper recording the fact that scores of the proudest belles of "La Belle Memphis" are being led captive to the hymeneal altar by our gallant invaders. Dr. White said that during the past week he had married five federal officers, all to Memphis ladies. If the social and other accomplishments of the Memphis ladies correspond with their personal attractions, I cannot wonder that so many of our young officers form what our old company doctor calls "entangling alliances." Having had few or no opportunities of making acquaintances in the city, I can only judge from appearances, and appearances are certainly in their favor, for in no other city have I seen so many beautiful women as can be seen any fair afternoon riding or promenading in the streets and in the evenings at the theater. What proportion of their charms of face and form are the work of nature, or the result of art, a young bachelor is not supposed to be a competent judge. I can only say if they are not natural, they reflect great credit on the tastes and skills of the ladies, and they look well too in the prevailing costume, black, for more than half of the ladies I saw were attired in mourning for some relative fallen in the rebel army.

On Sunday, April 10th, I attended services at Dr. White's church (Calvary). Many of our officers and soldiers are frequent attendants at his church, and the old gentleman is much liked by all. I observed that the responsive "Amens" to the prayer for the President of the U.S. came almost entirely from the military part of the congregation. In his sermons he studiously avoids any allusion to the war.

On Monday, April 11th, Companies B and C of our battalion embarked on the steamer *Watson* for down the river. The boat, being small and already heavily laden, could take only two companies. The next day, Companies D, L, and M got on board the large steamer *Superior* commanded by Captain Dexter about noon, but we did not leave Memphis until nearly night. While waiting for the boat to get sailing orders, I made a brief call on the Odlams. They had become pretty well reconciled to the military necessity of tearing down their house, but still felt hurt at the rude treatment they received from the negro soldiers. Miss Odlam was very emphatic and pronounced in her opinions and denunciations of the "niggers."

Leaving Memphis about dark, we steamed down the river all night, passing Helena at four o'clock the next morning and the mouth of White River at ten o'clock. At the latter place is a large settlement of negroes. Reaching Vicksburg soon after breakfast the next morning, we remained there all day, where I went on shore and found quite a number of old Quincy acquaintances: Captain Joe Gilpin, Captain Jonathan Field, George Burns, Ed White, and Tom W. Moore. I did not visit any of the fortifications, nor walk much about the town, as the main part of the town is situated back from the river on very high and rough hills, and the fortifications were all on the hills back of the town.

While loitering on one of the lower streets, my attention was directed to a young lady who was one of five banished from the town by order of the post commander for disrespectful conduct in the Episcopal Church some months ago. She had just been permitted to return, it is to be hoped, a wiser girl and that she has learned to behave herself and keep her little rebel mouth shut.

At Milliken's Bend, as we passed, I saw thousands of shanties where Grant's great army was so long encamped during the siege of Vicksburg. I also saw the mouth of the canal made by Grant, and through which he expected to pass his gunboats below Vicksburg.

The many large plantations along the river were abandoned or worked by contrabands hired by lessees. The plantations, having been confiscated, were leased by the government for a very low rental, say about one cent per pound on all cotton raised. An average crop of cotton was from 400 to 500 pounds per acre, and negroes could be hired for $10 per month. Many Northern men, tempted by the prospects of large profits, had leased and attempted to cultivate these plantations, but through ignorance of the business and the management of negroes, have in nearly every instance failed or been driven off and their property destroyed by guerillas. George Burns, when I saw him, had just lost all of his mules, plows, and crops, and his negroes been driven off by a raid of guerillas, and he said he was going out of the cotton business. I thought he was already pretty badly out. Only a few days before, a man was taken off a leased plantation by guerillas, compelled to dig his own grave, then get into it, and was shot dead. A negro who was pressed to fill the grave came into Vicksburg and reported the case. The murdered man, whose name I did not learn, was a partner of Charles Howland of Quincy.

Leaving Vicksburg during the night, we stopped at Natchez early the next morning, where we remained a few hours. While the boat was lying here, one of my company horses, Guy Lonnsbury's, getting tired of the confinement on the boat, and thinking to go off on a little scout of his own, jumped overboard and swam ashore. He was soon recaptured and returned to the boat. Continuing down the river, we reached Baton Rouge at 5pm on April 15th, where we found our Colonel Mudd with the greater part of our regiment, just arrived from New Orleans. We were here ordered to go ashore and into camp near Fort Williams just outside the town.

When we left Memphis winter was hardly gone. Here we are almost in the midst of summer, and many flowers, including many kinds of roses, are in full bloom. Much of the vegetation here is strange and interesting to me. Palm leaves, similar to those from which Chinese fans are made, grow in great abundance in the swamps, and the canes grow much larger and taller than I ever saw elsewhere. Another very peculiar vegetable growth is the Spanish moss, hanging in heavy festoons from the branches of the trees.

The town of Baton Rouge is smaller and different from what I expected to find. It is a very old town, but there is not that display of wealth I expected to see. The houses are mostly small, with neat and well-kept yards in front, but there are no large, nor handsome houses. The streets are wide, straight, and shaded by many old trees. The state house and state prison are here. The former had been a fine building but is now in ruins; nothing but the blackened and cracked stone walls remain. It was burned by the rebels about the time the town was occupied by General Banks. The state prison, a large and very complete building, is open and unoccupied.

We were not permitted to remain idle long, for about ten o'clock the next morning, Saturday, April 16th, I was ordered out with forty men on a scout under Colonel Boardman, 4th Wisconsin Cavalry. We went about twenty miles north, seeing several squads of guerillas and having several interesting and exciting chases, and capturing a lieutenant of the 7th Confederate Cavalry.

The country, as far as we went, was a level, swampy forest, through which it was difficult, and in many places impossible, to travel except on the roads. The roads are wide, straight, and hard, with many bridges over the numerous little bayous: deep, sluggish streams with mirey banks and bottoms.

On our way back, I stopped for a few minutes with Colonel Boardman at "Major" Dunn's, where I made the acquaintance of Miss Lou Alley and her sister. I don't know why Mr. Dunn was called "Major," but suppose because it was customary and the correct thing for every man of any prominence in the South to sport a military title, or he may in his younger days have been in the state militia. He and all of his household were rebels.

Ever since Banks' repulse on the Red River last week, an attack on this place has been anticipated, and we hear all manner of contradictory rumors and reports. One citizen or negro comes in and swears straight up and down that he has just seen 1,000 or 10,000 rebels at a certain place; another soon follows from the same place or direction, and as positively swears it is no such thing. Our scouts, which are out in all directions, see nothing but small scouting parties and guerillas.

We are now in the 19th Army Corps, Department of the Gulf. Brigadier General Philip St. George Cooke, commanding this district, has his headquarters here.[10]

On Tuesday, April 19th, I was sent out on scout with thirty men by order of General Cooke, whose adjutant gave me special instructions. I went southward, stopping at the house of Mr. L. Caldwell, who with his wife, profess to be strong Union people. They may have been all right, but like some other Union people I have met in the South, they talked altogether too much and are too loud in their protestations. Mrs. Caldwell was a regular lightning talker against time. Being quite unfamiliar with the roads, trails, bridges, etc., Caldwell volunteered to ride with me as guide. Returning, I stopped at Highland Stockade, a strong little outpost twelve miles south from Baton Rouge, where I made the acquaintance of Captain Gregg, 4th Wisconsin Cavalry, in command there. It was quite late when I reached town, and sending my men to camp, I went at once to General Cooke's office to report. The general had gone home, but had left orders for me to report at his house. When he heard me give my name to the servant at the door, he called me into the parlor, where he introduced me to his two daughters, and received my report. He was an old-time West Pointer, very polite and courteous, but without the official red tape and ostentation affected by many regular officers, especially in their intercourse with volunteers. He was the author of *Cooke's Tactics,* used by all the cavalry in the army.

On Monday, April 25th, I crossed the Mississippi River with twenty-five men to escort a telegraph working party putting up a line on the west side of the river, where I was joined by Lieutenant Mower of the 4th Wisconsin Cavalry with twenty-five men. I kept the men some distance back from the river to guard against surprise, and our little steamer the *Landis*, with our rations and forage on board, moved slowly upstream as the working party advanced.

Sometime during the night, I was awakened by the sergeant of the guard bringing in a young man who said his name was Philip St. John, that he owned a plantation a few miles distant and was on his way home when he came to my guards, and asked permission to continue on his way home. He spoke in broken English and said he was a French Creole. Of course, I could not permit him to leave our camp, and without taking more notice of him, I told him to lie down by the fire—which, by the way, was all burned out—and go to sleep and he would feel more like traveling in the morning. After a while, I was again awakened by hearing him moaning and shivering, for the night was quite chilly and the ground damp, and he was probably not accustomed to lying around loose. He said, in answer to my question if he was hungry or had the colic, that he "Vas most froze to dead." I believed him and, without looking up, told him to crawl under my blanket, which he gladly did and cuddled up to me like a kitten.

On awakening early in the morning, and looking at my guest and bedfellow, who was still sleeping, I was not a little surprised and indignant to find him as black as a boot. Not liking the idea of having a negro in my bed, I ordered him off and asked him, perhaps rather roughly, why he presumed to take such liberties, when I was again and more surprised to discover that he was my unwilling guest, the "French Creole."

He was a fine looking, slender, and delicate young man, handsomely dressed, with diamonds and jewels on his fingers and shirtfront. He said his father and he owned a large plantation and before the war owned two hundred slaves. I told Sergeant Spence to give him some breakfast and take care of him until we should move. The sergeant thought the best use he could make of him was to put him on the fatigue squad and made him help carry oats and hay off the boat for the horses. The poor fellow, who said he had never done any work in his life, thought that pretty rough treatment and was paying dearly for his last evening's sparking. Nor did he seem to relish his breakfast of coffee, hard tack, and bacon, seasoned with the rough jests of the soldiers, but he had to grin and bear it like many another slave aristocrat had done before him. And such was my first acquaintance and experience with the "French Creoles" of Louisiana.

We continued moving slowly up the river and that night, Tuesday, April 26th, I camped in the garden of a deserted plantation mansion. It was a beautiful garden, large and well arranged, with gravel walks, rustic arbors, and beds of choice flowers. As I walked through that garden the next morning, I recognized many old acquaintances amongst the flowers that reminded me of my dear old mother's garden at home, but it was going to ruin and growing up with weeds and grass. During the day, we had passed several large sugar and cotton plantations, all deserted. The houses, barns, and other improvements were costly and substantial, but all empty, and the fields and gardens uncultivated and going to waste, showed the desolation of war. These people wanted war and they are getting it.

The next day we crossed the river at Port Hudson, where I saw the telegraph cable, 3,500 yards long, laid across the river. I did not go on shore at Port Hudson, but having finished our duty, returned to Baton Rouge on the boat, reaching camp about 8pm.

Monday afternoon, May 2nd, I was sent out with a small scout accompanied by Lieutenant Mower. We went sixteen miles on the Clinton road to White's Bayou. Having orders not to go beyond that point, we turned west to return by the Port Hudson road. It was reported to us at different places along the road that the rebels were having a barbecue at Clinton and that there was a rebel picket at Red Wood Bayou, three miles beyond White's Bayou. On reaching camp, I found that nearly all the troops, including my company under Sergeant Spence, had marched for Clinton, and that by returning on the Port Hudson road I had missed them.

The force that went out found the rebels near Clinton, thirty miles distant, and in the fight that ensued, Colonel Boardman was killed. Boardman was as reckless as he was brave, possessing far more bravery than discretion, seldom taking the precaution of sending an advance guard when marching, but always dashing ahead of everything himself. At last he paid the penalty of his recklessness with his life; galloping at the head of his regiment without an advance guard, he dashed into an ambuscade and was killed at the first fire. He was the only man killed in the fight.

We have news today, May 6th, of the capture and burning of the steamer *City Belle* by the rebels on Red River. From what I can learn, it was a most cowardly and horrible affair. The boat was fired on with artillery, a ball passing through her boilers, scalding many of the soldiers on board. After surrendering, the boat with the dead and wounded on board was fired and set adrift. Nine soldiers who escaped reached here this evening and report that Colonel Mudd of our regiment, who was a passenger on the boat, was killed.[11]

On May 19th, it was rumored that Banks's great Red River expedition, about which so much has been said, and of which so much was expected, is about to come to an inglorious termination. His whole army is reported now on its way down the river, or rather trying to get down. The flood on which he went up the river having subsided, there is not enough water in the river to float his gunboats and heavy transports.[12]

Every mail brings better and more glorious news from Grant on the Potomac. Our western soldiers have unbounded confidence in Grant and believe that under his command, even the ditch-digging, winter-quartered Army of the Potomac may be productive of much good, and the boasted quiet of the valley of the Potomac will soon be broken by the glad shouts of our victorious army, and may it never know "quiet" again, but the quiet of war-brought peace. If Grant can but keep reporters and politicians out of his lines, and is not hampered nor interfered with by department red tape, the days of the Confederacy are numbered, and that too in small figures. But I fear for him, he is doing too much good. Shoddy contract and political pressure will doubtless be brought to bear against him. If he is let alone to fight his own way, the rebels will soon be glad to give up the contest, but if he is removed or in any way molested, it will not only discourage our men, but will give new life and hope to the now almost broken spirits of the enemy.

The weather is already about as hot as midsummer at home; what it will be when the southern summer fairly sets in, I don't like to contemplate. We generally have during the heat of the day a breeze from the south, but which dies away towards evening. The nights are generally cool, sometimes uncomfortably so, with heavy dews and foggy mornings.

The abatis outside the line of works is overgrown with blackberry vines, which are now full of ripe fruit, and which constitute an important item of our diet. Our soldiers gather many bushels of them daily. Living here is pretty high, but the most expensive luxuries are the Northern papers, which sell for twenty cents and are seldom less than six days old when we get them.

Never anywhere have I seen such a mixed population, as regards complexions, as in Baton Rouge. All the possible shades from tar black to pale white can here be seen, and everything that is not pure black or pure white is "Creole." Real black negroes are scarce in the city. The popular city shades are from a dark tan up to pale pink with blue eyes and sandy hair. A sad commentary on the morals of Southern society, and this too in the proud aristocratic state of Louisiana, whose lordly planters pretend to look with disgust and contempt on the free institutions and sentiments of the North, and whose proud ladies, although bound by ties of consanguinity to they know not how many liver-colored mulattos, turn up their pretty noses with virtuous indignation at the mere mention of "Yankee abolitionists." This curse of slavery I find much worse here than in the more northern slave states. Truly no greater curse could be inflicted on any country than that of slavery.

There are five companies of our regiment now here, but only about 200 men are mounted. We have lost a good many horses, and many are sick and disabled, and horses are so scarce now in this department that we cannot get others.

Opportunities for trading off sick and lame horses are not nearly so numerous here as they were in Kentucky and Tennessee. I have managed thus far to keep my company pretty well mounted. Our dismounted men are doing infantry duty.

There has been for some time a feeling of general dissatisfaction amongst our line officers at the manner in which our regiment is managed and commanded, which of course seriously impairs the effectiveness of the regiment; neither officers nor men work as cheerfully and heartily as they used to do. I have endeavored to put up with the reign of misrule without openly complaining, but it has at last become so distasteful to me that I recently tendered my resignation, intending either to leave the army or seek some other service, but my paper got no farther than department headquarters, from which it was promptly returned "disapproved."

I entered the service to serve my country and fight against rebellion, and not for personal advancement nor to advance others, and to serve my country I have ever been and am ready and willing to endure all dangers and hardships incidental to a soldier's life, and obey unquestioning all right and lawful commands of my superiors as implicitly as I require obedience from those under me, but I am not willing to tamely and quietly submit to ignorance and insults. I have observed that many officers from generals down seem to think that the war was commenced and armies organized for their especial benefit and in order to promote them and give them opportunities to display their uniforms and stupidity, and they do not seem to realize the fact that accidental promotion in rank is not necessarily accompanied by advancement in intellect. A man that is a fool in a cook's apron will be a fool in a commander's uniform, and he that has not sense enough to command the respect due his position is unfit to occupy that position or to command volunteer soldiers.

On returning from picket and reporting at regimental headquarters on May 2nd, I was placed in arrest by Colonel Bush, on charges preferred by Captain Frank Moore of Company D. In the charges I am accused of using disrespectful language to my superior officer and disobedience of his orders, all of which can be easily proven. He is my "superior officer" by reason of his commission antedating mine a few months, and I did disobey an unreasonable order given in an insolent manner, and my language to him might perhaps be very easily construed disrespectful. I was provoked into saying what I did, and I said it with a good deal of emphasis. I accepted the order of arrest and asked for as early a trial as possible, as I was anxious to bring the matter to an issue. I had not long to wait, as a court martial was sitting at the post, and on Wednesday 8th I was summoned to appear before it. To the charge of disobedience I pleaded "not guilty," stating in my defense that, as the order was irregular and uncalled for and given insolently, I was guilty of no breach of discipline in disregarding it. To the charge of "disrespectful language" I pleaded "guilty," stating in my defense that I was provoked to say what I did by the insolent behavior and language of Captain Frank Moore. As I presented no witnesses and had no counsel, my case was soon disposed of. The president of the court said he recognized the aggravating circumstances under which I was placed, and thought he would have done the same had he been in my place, but that the court could not do less than impose some light penalty on me.

On Thursday, June 16th, Major General Sickles arrived here and reviewed the troops. General Sickles has been quite a prominent officer in the east and commanded a brigade in the battle of Gettysburg, where he lost a leg. I don't know what he is doing in the west.[13]

In some of the Northern papers is an account of the evacuation of Baton Rouge by the federals and its occupation by the rebels—a rare bit of news to us. Instead of evacuating, new troops from Banks's army are constantly arriving, and our position has lately been strengthened by the construction of new earthworks.

By late letters from home, I learn that old Governor John Wood of Quincy has taken the field at the head of a 100-days regiment.[14] His most noble example should put to shame many young men I know who have for three years been hanging back on the most trivial excuses. How I would like to see a rigid and vigorous prosecution of the draft in the North. Such an act would do more to encourage our troops and advance the reenlistment of veterans than all the bounties the government can offer. The rebel conscription spares no man, all must go when wanted if they can be found and caught, and if a man can't do one service, he must do another. If our government would enforce the draft with the same rigor, the now broken ranks of our regiment would soon be filled.[15]

The sentence of the court martial in my case was published June 27th. For resenting the insolence of my superior(?) officer, I am gently reprimanded in writing by General Benton and forfeit forty dollars of my pay, cheap enough, and I will take some more at the same price. As commercial commodities, the satisfaction I had and the precedent I established were well worth much more than they cost me.

Company B moved to Highland Stockade today to relieve the 4th Wisconsin Cavalry, ordered to Morganza. Troops have been moving about in this department pretty lively of late, and we are under orders to be ready to march at any moment. All the horses in the town and country are being seized for cavalry and artillery use, and our men are kept busy, and many amusing incidents occur in the prosecution of their search for horses. One of our lieutenants, while out in the country, found a young lady mounted on a very good looking horse, which he told her he must have, and to which of course she objected. In her inventory of her horse's afflictions and infirmities, he was represented as "old, lame, give-down, and no account for you uns." She was informed that if the board of inspection rejected him, he would be returned to her, and if accepted, she would be paid his appraised value. But she wanted her horse, not his value, and finding she could not prevail by a direct attack, she resorted to a little strategy, saying: "If you don't believe my horse is lame, let me move him and you can see how he travels," to which reasonable request the gallant young officer assented. Seeing her way clear, she gave her old horse the whip, and he did travel, and at such a lively gait that she gave a soldier well-mounted a race of over a mile before she was caught and brought back. Finding herself baffled and obliged to give up her horse, she resolved to die game and gave the lieutenant a volley of red hot abuse, front, flank, and rear, that made him feel old and tired.

As fast as horses are accepted and appraised they are branded "U.S." and vouchers made out in blank before the owners are known, so that all shall be treated fairly and alike. A span of very fine horses was seized in town today, appraised, branded U.S., and turned into the corral before it was discovered that they belonged to the French consul. I did not learn how the matter was finally settled, but probably by condemning and returning the horses.

The soldiers have begun already to talk about the November presidential election. I hope the troops will be allowed to vote, which will ensure Lincoln's reelection and the success of our cause. If they are not permitted to vote, and the Democrats in power will doubtless use every effort to prevent them, I shall await the result of the November elections with fear and misgivings. I have read with surprise and disgust the proceedings of the Democrats' state convention in Springfield. The resolution to sustain the traitor Vallandigham is a direct insult to every Union soldier and every loyal man and woman in the country.[16] With such men and influence working against us at home, and the corruption and misrule in the army, it is no wonder we meet with difficulties and reverses. It is rather a matter of wonder that we succeed at all in anything. With the army and resources we have, we should have wiped out the rebellion, root and branch, and conquered peace long ago. We have altogether too many speculating generals in the field who don't want the war to end too soon. It is worth money to them to prolong the struggle as long as possible.

The term of service of all the old soldiers of my company who were mustered August 12, 1861, will expire on the 11th of next month, and the boys are all looking forward to that day with happy anticipation. I have been in correspondence with the adjutant general of the Army, the adjutant general of Illinois, and the chief mustering officer of this department, and am satisfied that I cannot be mustered out with my men, but will be held to serve three years from the date of my commission as captain. The feeling of dissatisfaction amongst the line officers continues and increases, and there is much "log rolling" and "wire-pulling" going on in anticipation of some being mustered out and others promoted.

The nights, which heretofore have been cool, are now becoming uncomfortably hot, and the mosquitoes are dreadful, fully as bad as they were in "Nigger Wool Swamp" and Island Number 10 two years ago. The soldiers are supplied with good nets, without which it would be quite impossible to sleep at all. When going on picket or scout, the men will take their nets if nothing else. But as great a nuisance are the "jiggers," a very small insect, a cross between a flea and a tick, which get into the feet and under the skin, causing very painful and troublesome little sores.

On Sunday evening, July 3rd, I called by invitation on Colonel Dudley commanding our brigade, who desired to know all the facts relating to my recent difficulty with Captain Frank Moore, an account of which I submitted to him in writing.

A national salute fired at Fort Williams is the only demonstration here for July 4th. A "military parade" would be neither novel nor interesting here just now.

The excitement concerning the anticipated raid or movement some time ago is rapidly subsiding. There seems to be very little doing in the southwest just now. Troops are quietly concentrating at different points along the river. There is yet a strong force of the enemy in the vicinity of Mobile, and that may be our next objective point.

Our duties for the past few weeks have been constant, but light and somewhat monotonous. I am officer of the day, on picket, or other regular duty about three times a week and fill up the intervening days by scouting in the country, occasionally seeing small squads of guerillas. I have become quite familiar with all the roads and country for ten or twelve miles around, but have made very few acquaintances.

On Sunday, July 31st, my fine black horse "Ned" was missing, as was also Lieutenant Cayton's horse. Thinking they might have been "strayed or stolen" I offered a reward of $25 for the recovery of Ned, which set all the idle soldiers in camp to horse hunting. Failing to find or hear anything of either of them, I increased my offer of reward the next day to $50. My black hostler "Wash" was scared nearly white and told the cook he was afraid Cayton and I would kill him for turning our horses loose against orders. After three days of fruitless search through all the country for miles around, one of my men, John Elwood, found the missing horses not over 200 yards from my tent in an old well, dead. The mouth of the well was so covered with brush and weeds that I never saw it before. Wash had tied the two horses together and they had both fallen into the well. He was so scared and repentant that I let him off that time with one day's hard work filling up the old well.

The cavalry pickets of the 4th Wisconsin on the Clinton road were attacked and driven in about noon on August 4th. The bugles and drums sounded "to arms," and three companies of cavalry and four guns of the 13th Wisconsin Artillery were at once sent to reinforce Highland Stockade, as it was possible the attack on our pickets on the Clinton road might be only a feint to cover an attack on the stockade in the opposite direction. The troops remained on the qui vive until three o'clock in the morning, but without any further alarm.

Some of our general officers, tempted by the great profit, take advantage of their positions to speculate in cotton, in direct violation of orders from the War Department. Being on picket a good deal, I am enabled to see and know much that is going on. While on infantry picket today on the Greenville Spring road, Mrs. Blakeman came to my post with several loads of cotton, and a pass signed by General Benton, our present post commander, and she did not hesitate to tell me she was selling cotton to General Benton.[17]

About daylight on August 6th, the mounted videttes in advance of my tent were attacked by a small squad of rebels. I turned out my guard in readiness to support the advance, but the boys did not fall back nor need any support, and after a few shots, drove off the rebels without alarming the camps.

On Monday, August 8th, all of our horses were appraised and branded "U.S." in compliance with orders from the War Department. All the soldiers in our regiment had theretofore owned their horses and have been entitled to pay for their use. All horses in the service, except those owned by officers, now belong to the government. Our horses all went in at fair price. Sam Goff, a soldier of Company B, had a fine large racehorse, "Yellow Tom," which I bought for my own use for $125.

The eventful, long-anticipated day has come at last, and all of my old soldiers with whom I entered the service, three years ago, all mustered out on August 11th. I have long looked forward to this day myself, believing that having faithfully served out my original term of enlistment, I should be entitled to an honorable discharge, but there is yet nearly another year of service for me. It makes me feel lonely and homesick to see all of my old comrades preparing to leave. There are amongst them many as brave and true men as ever lived, and to many I had become strongly attached, and to part now is like the breaking up of a family. For three years we have shared together the dangers, hardships, and privations of war. They have been to me more than soldiers, they have been friends and comrades, and some of them are as good and true friends as I ever had or want.

We have, of course, had our ins and outs, our ups and downs, I have more than once said and done things that I have been sorry for afterwards, and the boys, even the best of them, have been sometimes unruly and disobedient, and without thinking of the responsibilities of my position, have committed breaches of discipline for which I have been held responsible. I have always prided myself on having one of the best-disciplined companies in the service. My men have been well drilled and at all times ready for any emergency. In my official capacity it has been my duty to maintain and enforce discipline, and in that capacity it has sometimes been my painful duty to inflict punishment. But I believe in every case where I have been obliged to impose punishment on a soldier comrade, it has hurt me far more than it did them.

I have always felt that I am one of the boys, I went in with them as a private with no thought of, nor aspiration to, promotion, except that at the organization of the company I did want to be a sergeant, but was left out, and to my promotion I have ever recognized the fact that I am indebted to them and not for any superior qualification. I have had many a struggle and trial they know not of, and considering my youth, for with the exception of some few recruits, I am one of the youngest men in my company, and previous inexperience, I am only surprised that I have done as well as I have. For their long, honest, and faithful service to their country, may the boys enjoy at home the blessings of peace. By my friend and messmate W. F. McMurray, I sent home to my mother a cage of young mockingbirds.

I am not tired of the service, nor have I ever entertained a doubt as to the final result of the war, and if my associations in the regiment were more agreeable, I would gladly stay until the war is over, but my company will now be so small, only the veterans and recruits, and there are so many disagreeable surroundings and associations in the regiment, that I would leave at once if I could. But, it is well said, "needs must when the devil drives," and I think he is driving the old 2nd now. In fact, he seems to be largely interested in much that is transpiring at this post.

Amongst the few acquaintances I have made here is the Bernard family, living at Magnolia Grove, about a mile out of town. We have a reserve picket post in the grove near their house, and by being promptly on hand at guard mount, I can usually get my detail into the proper place in the line to get this post, which insures a very social and pleasant time for me for the next twenty-four hours. The family, consisting of the mother and three daughters, are all rebels, but nonetheless hospitable and entertaining. The old gentleman being an officer in the rebel army, I think with General Dick Taylor, is necessarily absent on business connected with his profession, as is also the husband of one of the daughters.[18] I have spent many pleasant evenings at their house when "Officer of the Guard, Post No. 3." As the officer of the guard must not sleep during his tour of duty, I would often, after seeing the guards posted all right, spend the evening until twelve o'clock with the ladies, being much more comfortable and pleasantly entertained in their parlor than sitting by a smoky little guard fire, fighting mosquitoes and trying hard to keep awake. The grove, composed entirely of large magnolia trees, is a beautiful place, and just now when the trees are in full bloom, the fragrance of the flowers, increased by the falling dew, is almost too strong to be agreeable. I shall long and pleasantly remember Magnolia Grove "Post No. 3" and the hospitable Bernard Mansion.

On August 19th, my company was detailed as escort and bodyguard to General A. L. Lee, commanding the cavalry division, and I moved into town and camped on a vacant lot adjoining the foundation for a large building that had been commenced for a hotel or theater, and only two or three blocks from General Lee's headquarters. It is a very pretty and convenient place for a small camp. I am very glad to get this detail, although it was quite unexpected, if for no other reason than it takes me away from the regiment. I have had very little acquaintance with General Lee, but he is said to be a good cavalry officer and a live fighting man.[19]

On Monday, August 22nd, General Lee with his whole cavalry division marched out at 5pm with three days' rations in the direction of Clinton. When about five miles out, we met Colonel Landrew returning from an exchange of prisoners, who had agreed with Colonel Scott (rebel), commanding at Clinton, to an armistice until Tuesday noon August 23rd, so all we could do was to return to camp, which we reached about nine o'clock.[20]

For a long time, in fact ever since the occupation of this state by our troops, the rebels had held the town of Clinton, thirty-five miles northeast from Baton Rouge, as a kind of reserve or rallying post from which they sent out raiding parties to fire on steamboats, pickets, etc. It was commanded by Colonel Scott, who made Clinton his headquarters, although he was himself most of the time in the field, scouting around the country collecting conscripts, horses, and supplies. His entire force consisted of about 3,000 cavalry and eleven pieces of light artillery.

About a year ago, General Grierson made an attack on Clinton, but was repulsed and obliged to fall back to Baton Rouge. Last spring, General Birge attempted to take the place, but was also repulsed at the Comite River.[21] These several failures to reach Clinton and dislodge the rebels only served to render them more daring and troublesome, and to subject our army to insult and ridicule from the rebel citizens. "Why don't you go to Clinton and see for yourselves," would be the taunting reply of the country folks, especially of the women coming to our lines, when asked anything about Clinton or Colonel Scott.

General Lee seemed determined to see what he could do with Colonel Scott and Clinton, for on Wednesday, August 24th, the termination of the armistice agreed on by Colonel Landrew, he marched out again at 4pm with two brigades of cavalry and four pieces of light artillery. Our men seemed to have great confidence in General Lee, and although we felt sure of meeting with strong resistance, all felt confident of final success. We felt that we were going out this time to take Clinton.

We marched to Red Wood Bayou, thirteen miles, where we halted to wait for the moon to rise, the night being too dark to march. At half-past twelve, the march was resumed. The rebels were on the lookout for us, for no sooner had we crossed Red Wood Bayou than we encountered their pickets, who ambushed our advance guard, wounding several men, and killing two horses. The guard charged and captured several of the pickets, but the reserve fell back slowly, skirmishing all the way to the Comite River, which we reached about daybreak. At the river we found, as we expected, the enemy in force, guarding the ford, the bridge having been destroyed.

General Lee here dismounted about half of his command, and leaving the horses at a safe distance, advanced his line and flankers on foot. The rebels were concealed in the bushes on the opposite side of the river, and gave our men a warm reception, and the fight continued about an hour without an apparent advantage on either side. During the entire battle I was with General Lee on a little open hill where we could see all the fighting on both sides. The rebels had as yet used no artillery, though we were quite sure they had some in position, and in order to draw their fire, the general ordered one gun brought to the front, which threw a few shells at random into the timber. This had the desired effect of drawing their fire and disclosing the position of their guns. Another gun was now brought to the front, and shot and shell were exchanged pretty lively for perhaps half an hour or more, when the general said: "This is too quiet, we are not making noise enough," although I thought for the number of men engaged we were making a pretty lively disturbance. An aide was sent to bring up a battalion armed with "Henry repeating carbines," a magazine arm recently introduced and not in very general use, the greater part of the cavalry in the army being armed with Sharpe's breech-loading carbines. The battalion came down the hill towards the river on the "double quick," and the next minute opened up with their magazine carbines, and I am sure I never before heard so few men make so much noise.

The rebels were so occupied with affairs on their immediate front that a strong force of our flankers succeeded in crossing the river a short distance below on a jam of drift, unobserved. As soon as the rebels found they were flanked and in danger of being surrounded, they fell back towards Clinton and we crossed the river. About a mile from town, we found the rebels in line of battle. Our artillery was posted on a hill commanding the town, and the "charge" sounded and we swept down on them like a tornado. The rebels, not looking for what General Lee called a "smash," but probably supposing we would work our passage by skirmishing the balance of the day, were taken completely by surprise, and before we reached their line, broke and fled in disorder. In the rout many were captured and a few killed. We entered Clinton on the charge, only to find it one of the most quiet and peaceable towns in the country. Not a rebel soldier, not even a straggler, was to be seen; Scott had skipped out with his entire force.

Every door and window framed a tableau of terrified women and children, whose fear of the dreaded Yankee soldiers was exceeded only by their curiosity to see them. When the head of our column halted in the street, a citizen stepped up to General Lee and handed him a note, which the general read and passed to me. It was as follows: "Genl. Lee. I permit you to take peaceable possession of the town to prevent the effusion of innocent blood, but shall be happy to meet you on an honorably contested field. Scott Col. Comdg. C.S.A." The note being without date, and judging from the short time that elapsed between our charge on his line and our entrance into the town, it looked a little as though "Scott Col. Comdg. C.S.A." had prepared and kept this note on hand in anticipation of just such an event, for he certainly had no time to write it after he found he could not hold the town.

Lee, supposing Scott had selected his "field" somewhere in the vicinity, but far enough from town to prevent innocent blood being effused, sent out scouts in all directions to find him. The scouts encountered a few scattering bushwhackers, but Scott was not to be found within fifteen miles. It was then supposed he had retreated to Liberty, thirty-five miles distant.

A column of infantry moved from Port Hudson to cooperate with us and was to have reached Clinton first and from the north, thus bringing the rebels between our two fires, but the infantry were detained several hours by encountering a small force of rebels at Jackson, by the breaking down of an ammunition wagon, and by having to rebuild a bridge. They turned back on learning that we were in possession of the town.

We remained in Clinton until Saturday morning, August 27th. I camped with my company in the Methodist Church yard, where we were very comfortably fixed and living well and were willing to extend our visitation a month or two, and the citizens were just as willing to have us leave at once. Clinton had been a very pretty and busy little inland town, but war with its attendant evils had despoiled it of much of its former beauty. The public buildings, courthouse, seminary, Masonic Hall, and several churches were large and substantial structures. The private dwellings were mostly small, neat, and surrounded by tastefully arranged gardens and shade trees. The populace was at that time composed entirely of women, children, and old or disabled men. I do not think I saw one able-bodied young man in the town. The women were at first very insulting and abusive to our soldiers before any occasion had been given. Soldiers on duty or passing quietly along the street were subjected to taunts and insults the most provoking. But we stayed long enough to make them sing another tune. Finding at last that their sex would not protect them in their insolence from rudeness, they became frightened and demeaned themselves to publicly beg our officers for that protection they so lately scorned. Had they behaved with proper and ladylike respect towards our soldiers, there would have been no occasion for them to seek protection. They learned a lesson that may be of use to them in the future. I think if the citizens of Clinton consult their own interests, they will insist on Colonel Scott establishing his headquarters elsewhere. If we go there again soon and are treated in like manner, I fear their little town will cease to exist.

We captured thirty prisoners and killed six that we knew of. The enemy's loss in killed and wounded was much greater, as citizens and negroes reported seeing a good many carried away in ambulances and wagons. All the killed and captured rebels I saw were ragged and dirty and had in their haversacks for rations nothing but corn meal. Men who have the heart to fight clothed, fed, and armed as they were, and fight well too, are enemies entitled to respect, and such courage and fortitude are worthy of a better cause. Refugees and deserters tell the most dismal tales imaginable, but I never yet saw a captured rebel soldier, however dirty, ragged, or hungry he was, admit that their cause was hopeless or that they would ever be conquered.

Several hundred contrabands followed our command in from Clinton and the neighboring country. Many negro women with babies in their arms walked all the way, some of them even reaching Baton Rouge in advance of our column, and the day so hot and the roads so dusty that several horses gave out and had to be led.

General Lee rode back in a buggy and drove so fast that it was all I could do to keep up with him with my company. When about eight miles from town, he dismissed his escort and went ahead, telling me to follow slowly. Leaving my company to rest and wait for the column, I galloped ahead with Lieutenant Mower a mile or two to old Major Dunn's to see the girls and rest until my company should come up. But the column turned off before reaching Dunn's and went in by the Port Hudson road. We were kindly entertained at Dunn's and refreshed with a bountiful supply of cake and wine while telling of the late battle and our visit to Clinton. While we were talking, Miss Lou Alley suddenly left the hall, where we all were, and went out on the back porch, where I saw her take off her white sun bonnet and wave it over her head. Stepping quickly up behind her, I seized her arm and held it down, asking her why she was making such signals. She denied making signals and said she was only fanning herself. I knew at once by her confused manner that something was wrong, so calling to Mower to get away from there quickly, we mounted our horses and started for the road. Mower, who was having a jolly good time, was at first a little loath to leave and asked me what I had seen to make me in such a hurry. I said I had seen nothing serious yet, but we probably would see something, and perhaps smell powder very soon. At the gate, we meet a soldier coming in, and I asked him if he was well armed. He said his carbine was broken by a shot, and showed me where he was shot in the hand. Lieutenant Mower had lost his revolver in the fight, so I was the only one of the three armed, and I had only one revolver besides my saber. Telling the soldier to keep with us and ride for his life, we put spurs to our horses and dashed down the road toward Baton Rouge. We had gone but a short distance when a squad of rebel cavalry came out of the timber back of Dunn's house and gave us chase. They followed, firing at us for a mile or two, when they gave up the chase, as we were then approaching our advance pickets.

That was about the closest call and hardest run I ever had. I knew the girls at Dunn's were little rebels, but I never suspected them of such treachery, but the moment I saw Miss Lou's singular actions on the porch and confused behavior when detected, I knew she meant mischief. I learned afterwards that a young rebel officer, Miss Lou's lover, was in the house when we entered the gate and had only time to escape before we entered the house. As soon as Miss Lou learned from something we said that the troops had taken the other road and would not pass the house, she gave the signal which came so near resulting in our death or capture.

Lee was one of the coolest men under fire I ever saw. At one time during the hottest of the firing at the Comite River, several shells passed close over our heads and one finally passed between us (we were not over twenty or thirty feet apart) and struck the ground just beyond us. He had just asked me for a match and was lighting a cigar. Taking two or three puffs and looking at the end of his cigar to see that it was well lighted, he blew out the match and, turning to me, said slowly, "Those fellows seem to be getting their range down pretty fine, I guess we'll move out of their way a little," and to my great relief, for I was getting very uneasy, we took another position. He was at all times cool and brave, never excited nor reckless. A young officer was being carried to the rear by three or four soldiers, and as they passed near us, I recognized him as a captain of the 4th Wisconsin and asked the soldiers if he was dead, to which one of them replied, "we don't know, he seems to be." Lee, who was intently watching some movement in the fight, attracted by our remarks, turned and said, "Why that's little Captain —— (calling him by name), handle him carefully boys, he may not be dead." I liked Lee from my first acquaintance with him for his quiet, courteous manners and cool, dashing bravery, and often called on him at his headquarters.

But I was soon to lose my good opinion of General Lee. In a few days, I was ordered to report at his headquarters with my company for escort duty and had the honor(?) of escorting him and Madam Foley, who rode together in a buggy to Granville Pierce's, five miles, where they dined while I and my soldiers waited for them. This was not the kind of service nor treatment I and my men had been accustomed to, nor did we submit very gracefully. We felt that we were soldiers in the service of our country, not servants to wait on generals and their mistresses. I had no fault to find with Lee for liking a little frolic and taking a good country dinner when he could get it, for he was a gallant officer as ready for fight as for fun, but he had no right to take a company of soldiers in the service and pay of the country to escort and guard him and a disreputable woman.

The next night, General Lee and Madam Foley, again escorted by 300 men of the 2nd Illinois and 4th Wisconsin, under command of our Lieutenant Colonel B. F. Marsh, attended a negro wedding and dance at Pierce's. I was very glad I was not detailed to go. The proceedings of the day previous were bad enough, but this was much worse. When the men saw for what purpose they had been called out for all night, they became unruly and refused to stand guard to protect a negro wedding dance, and they not only invaded the kitchen and took everything prepared for the banquet, but cut the general's harness to pieces and smashed his buggy, and were very loud and pointed in their remarks and observations in his hearing, which were anything but complimentary to him and the madam. The officers were perhaps not quite so demonstrative as the soldiers, but they made no effort to enforce discipline.

To such base uses have we come. Volunteer soldiers, men who are <u>men</u> in all that the name implies, who left all they had in the world and <u>enlisted</u> to fight against rebellion, to serve and save their country, obliged to do such menial service for petty officers who are a disgrace to the uniform they wear, and who use their position more for their personal pleasure and profit than for the advancement of the cause they are sworn to "protect and defend." I thought it was bad enough in the Department of the Tennessee under such officers as Smith, Asboth, Martin, Waring, and others of like caliber, but here in the Department of the Gulf it is much worse. Red tape and speculation are here the ruling spirits. I believe all or nearly all the general officers I have seen here are engaged to some extent in cotton speculation, and from the fact that they are far too careful of rebels and rebel property, and that notorious rebels have passes through our lines, entitles them to the suspicion of disloyalty. It really looks now and here as though we were kept for the pleasure and profit of our commanding officers, and I see little encouragement for a subordinate officer or soldier to do his duty. But, as complaining and fault-finding avail nothing, I try to keep quiet and do the best I can. General Lee is by no means the worst officer in this department, he only "follows suit." In spite of so many disloyal, incompetent general officers, I still believe we have enough good and true ones to wear the war out, but it will take longer time and a greater expenditure of life and treasure than if all worked together for one common cause.

The interest in the approaching presidential election increases as the eventful time approaches. The soldiers, of course, all want to vote, and I hope they will be permitted to do so. If the question "peace on any terms," or conquered peace, is the great one to be decided, we who have thus far "borne the heat and burden" of the war, and who have staked all on the result, should have a voice in the discussion. To permit noncombatants alone to vote and forever decide the fate of our cause and country would be an act of great and foul injustice to the soldiers. If the soldiers vote, "Uncle Abe" will be reelected by a majority never before heard of.

I went out the morning of September 6th with Lieutenant Charley Painter to meet a flag of truce at the advance picket post on the Clinton road, where we found Lieutenant Walter of Colonel Scott's staff and five soldiers. I did not learn the nature of the communication, as it was sealed and directed to General Lee, so it was sent in by a soldier, and I stayed and talked with the rebel soldiers about an hour. They had just heard of the fall of Atlanta and were a little blue, but tried to appear brave and put the best face possible on the matter. They said the fall of Atlanta did not at all affect their cause, that the position was of little importance to them. The rebel soldiers looked rusty enough in their suits of grey and butternut beside our well-uniformed men, and this little squad was perhaps detailed on account of their good clothes. After about an hour of friendly conversation, a reply was received to their message, and they were dismissed with a courteous salute and "goodbye" on both sides, Lieutenant Walter remarking, "when we meet again, Captain, it may be under less pleasant circumstances."

Notwithstanding my camp is near the center of the town and I keep no regular camp guard, and the men are allowed every possible freedom, I have very little trouble in maintaining good order and discipline. They are on their honor for good behavior. I only require that every man shall be at roll call, morning and evening, and to report at my tent on going out and returning to camp, so that I may know where all can be found when wanted.

One morning my cook found in my mess chest a large roast of fresh beef, and thinking I had been to the market very early, as I sometimes did to see the pretty French girls and get a cup of their fine coffee, he fried some for my breakfast. The meat was very good, and when I complimented Scott on his purchase, he denied all knowledge of how it came to be in the chest. Soon after breakfast, my camp was visited by the provost guard, the sergeant of which said he was looking for a young beef steer that had been stolen from a butcher's corral during the night. I gave him permission to search my camp, which he did, but failed to find any sign of the missing beef, although he said the animal was tracked from the corral in the direction of my camp, and from the numerous men's tracks with it, it was believed to have been taken by soldiers. The missing steer and the piece of beef in my chest seemed to fit together somehow, but I did not feel called on to investigate matters. But the joke was too good to keep long, and some of my men had to tell on themselves. A squad of them had taken the steer out of the corral and into camp, where they killed it and divided the meat, and so quietly and neatly was the job done that not a particle of noise was made, nor a hair nor drop of blood left to testify against them. The blood was all scraped up and the ground strewn with dust and ashes and the hide and offal carefully deposited in an old cistern. I was in my tent writing at the time, but heard no unusual noise in camp. I did hear someone open and close my mess chest, but thinking it was my cook, took no notice of it.

On September 12th, the "Regulation Mess," composed of a few officers of General Lee's staff, was organized, and of which I was elected treasurer, the only officer we had any use for. The mess consisted of Lieutenant George Moore, Aide-de-Camp, Captain H. B. Baker, 4th Wisconsin Cavalry, Picket Officer, Captain Herbert H. Rottaker, 6th Missouri Cavalry, A.A.I., Lieutenant C. P. Painter, 118th Illinois Mounted Infantry, Aide-de-Camp, and Captain F. T. Moore, 2nd Illinois, commanding escort.

I engaged a widow, Mrs. Bacon, living opposite my camp to cook and furnish dining room for the mess. We were a jolly, congenial set of young fellows and had a good time and many a good meal together. Our hostess was a good cook and housekeeper, and a very good foster mother to her little family of big boys. We found we could live much better and more economically in this manner than by boarding or messing in camp.

As our pay is constantly being decreased, and the cost of living on the increase, we are obliged to cut our shirts to fit the cloth. I do the purchasing and marketing for the mess, and it takes from $5 to $10 per day to run it in good shape. The stalls in the market place are kept mostly by French and Creole women and girls, many of whom are pretty and all polite and pleasant, so that it is a pleasure to deal with them even at their way-up war prices. I have to pay for cabbages $1.00 per head, pumpkins and squashes $1.00 each, eggs $1.00 per dozen, new potatoes, onions, and other roots 10 cents each, butter $1.00 per pound, milk 10 cents per pint, fruit and berries in proportion. Quartermaster and commissary supplies are nearly twice as high in price as they were two years ago, and the merchants and trades people here charge us war prices for everything. As an example, I recently bought a pair of pants from the quartermaster's for $3.10 (for which I used to pay about $1.75 to $2.00), and as they were too large for me, I had to pay a tailor $4.00 for altering them.

Some time after the Clinton fight, I happened to be at the picket post on the Clinton road, as officer of the day, when Miss Lou Alley came in a buggy to pass in. I detained her and, sitting by her in her buggy, had a long talk with her about the affair at Dunn's after the battle. At first, she positively denied any evil intentions towards us, but finally admitted that my suspicions were correct, and that she was in the act of giving a pre-concerted signal with her sunbonnet when I caught her hand. I asked her if she had ever thought of what the consequences might have been if we had been attacked in her house. No, she hadn't thought much about it. She didn't think the consequences would have been very serious, but thought if I had been caught there, I would have been taken a prisoner of war, and she would have been justified for her part of the affair. But when I explained to her that there would have been a bloody little fight in her presence, and someone perhaps killed, and that if I had been killed or captured through her means, my soldiers would undoubtedly have burned the house, the situation seemed more serious to her, and she showed a good deal of true womanly feeling. She said she couldn't help being a rebel and hoped I would not blame her for holding views different from mine, but that she would never again act treacherously, nor knowingly be the means of getting anyone into trouble. She admitted that in her zeal, she had acted thoughtlessly and wrongly, and promised me she would never again be guilty of such conduct, and said if I would come to her house again she would be glad to see me and that I should be free from harm or danger, so far as she was concerned. I told her I would accept her repentance and promises in good faith and believed they were sincere, but as I had her then in my power, I was disposed to balance accounts by imposing a penalty on her, and as punishment for her offense, I should not permit her to pass the lines that day, but should send her back home. She accepted the sentence in good humor and, giving me her hand, pleasantly bade me goodbye.

I met her again a few weeks later riding horseback, when she told me she was going to be married soon to a rebel lieutenant of cavalry and invited me to the wedding. I told her I could not come alone, and the presence of a company of federal cavalry might not be agreeable, but I would promise to try and if possible catch that young officer and indefinitely postpone the wedding, but she said she thought I had punished her sufficiently and that we were even now and should play quits.

Quite an exciting and interesting event in the way of a fire occurred about three o'clock Wednesday morning, September 21st, in the northern part of the city near Fort Williams. Nearly an entire block of buildings were burned. The fire department of the city being somewhat out of running order, having neither men nor engines, nothing could be done but let the fire burn itself out. The soldiers turned out to look on, but did not molest anything, nor did they make any effort to check or put out the fire. They no doubt could easily have put it out with buckets, there being nearly if not quite 2,000 soldiers present, and would have done so had their treatment from the citizens been a little more courteous and considerate. That was one of the times when the rebs didn't want to be so much let alone.

I have been getting into trouble again, and was today, September 29th, tried by court martial on charges preferred by Lieutenant W. B. Moore, regimental adjutant. As I was his superior officer, he could not place me in arrest, but could only prefer charges, which he did a week or two ago because I resented some of his insolence and discourtesy. The findings of the court justified me and censured the adjutant. Colonel Landram of the 19th Kentucky Infantry was president, and Captain Stevens, aide-de-camp to General Herron, judge advocate of the court. There seems to be a lack of family love existing between the several Moores in our regiment. I have had no open, serious troubles with any other officers.[22]

On October 5th, General Lee marched out with his division on the Clinton road, object and destination unknown. Being sick, I could not go, and sent the escort under command of Sergeant Paris.

Lieutenant Cayton, who had gone to Illinois in charge of the discharged soldiers on August 11th, returned Sunday, October 9th and brought encouraging reports of the progress of the draft in the north. Many young Copperheads were being drafted, notwithstanding their threatened "armed resistance," but very few get to the front. The north was full of fugitive negroes, who for a few dollars could be hired as substitutes. The Copperhead bugbear cry of "nigger equality" was quite forgotten when "niggers" were wanted to take their places in the army and stand between them and their Southern rebel friends. The presence of a few troops in Chicago and elsewhere had the happy effect of enforcing compliance with the "insane policy of the administration." Cayton went as far as Springfield with the men, where they were paid off and disbanded.

General Herron at one time had for his adjutant an egotistical young lieutenant who delighted to find fault with and put on airs over officers older than he and who had seen more hard service than he would ever live to see. He was the butt and ridicule of all the troops at the post, but hadn't sense enough to see it. One day he came to brigade guard mount near the old state prison, attired like a show window soldier in white pants, patent leather shoes, white gloves, and a plume in his hat. He at once took exception to the manner in which the brigade adjutant was mounting the guard, and said he would show us how a guard should be mounted. Taking his position at the right of the line, he commanded, "troupe beat off" (our troupe was an infantry drum corps of 16 pieces). The moment the troupe sounded the customary roll, the dandy little adjutant's horse, unaccustomed to such rude war noises, dismissed himself and started for somewhere else down the front of the line, which was rather a long one, containing about 200 mounted guards. The dandy's little feet slipped out of his stirrups, his white pants slipped up to his knees, his plumed hat fell off, and holding on to his saddle with both hands, he came down the line on a charge. The first company on the right were regulars, who stood as grim as so many wooden men, too well disciplined, or too stupid, to see any fun in the circus performance, but as soon as the adjutant reached the center of the line, where I stood with the 2nd Illinois detail, he heard from the boys such encouraging remarks and suggestions as: "grab a root," "come ashore," "jump off," "pull down your pants," etc. Having passed the entire length of the line under such a running fire, his horse turned to the right, and the last we saw of him he was making good time towards the pickets on the Greenville Spring road. I know the pickets didn't shoot him, for I had another experience with him later, but he never again attempted to mount guard, but continued to exercise his talents in giving instruction in "special orders" from his office.

Our regimental and brigade commanders had been in the habit of giving passes to their men to go into the country to buy vegetables, eggs, etc. In a special order from post headquarters, this was forbidden and it was ordered that "no person be allowed to pass the lines without a written pass from post headquarters and the pass must be written on official blanks." Shortly after the promulgation of this last order, I was on picket and the little adjutant came to my post with a lady in a buggy. The sentinel, having been instructed by me, refused to recognize him and called for the officer of the guard. Addressing me very pompously, for the entertainment of his fair companion, he said, "Captain, how is this, sir? Your sentinel refuses to recognize me and I want to pass out." "The sentinel is obeying orders, sir, you can pass out if you have a proper pass." "But I don't need a pass, sir, I am the adjutant of the post, and you will please instruct your sentinel to let me pass." I told him he had himself written the orders under which I was acting, and for aught I knew he might be attempting to pass and then report me for disobedience of orders. Taking out his memorandum book and pencil, he said he would write a pass. "No," I said, "your pass must be written at headquarters and on official paper." He stormed and fretted a while to show his importance before his lady, but when he began to be insolent to me, I ordered him off and threatened to send him back under guard. Although an adjutant, he did not seem to have sense enough to know that no one is permitted to be in any way disrespectful to an officer or soldier on duty. He was going out to dine in the country, and as it was then about dinnertime, he was getting anxious and hungry. As it was near the middle of the afternoon when he returned with a proper official pass, I guess he had to take his soup and gravy cold, or eat warmed-over leavings. These ornamental soldiers don't like to bear the red-tape yoke, yet they delight to impose it on others.

On Tuesday, November 15th, Lieutenant Cayton, in command of the company, started out on a raid with General Lee. I wished very much to go, but having been detailed a member of a general court martial a week or two before, which was still in session, I could not. As the court sits only six hours a day, I have considerable leisure time, and nearly every afternoon and night I ride with Captain Baker, division picket officer. Baker has charge of all the pickets and outposts, and to him the officers of the day report for instructions.

On November 18th, Baker and I becoming tired of the monotony of our respective duties, and the mess room being lonely and deserted, all the others being out with General Lee, we decided to go out in search of adventure of some kind. So we each made up a disguise of rebel uniforms, over which we put our blue overcoats. We knew a scout was going out that night, and we took advantage of it to get through the line. We could, of course, have passed out with the countersign, but we did not care to be recognized by the guards and pickets, and the night, being very dark and stormy, was favorable to our undertaking.

Riding out to near the line on the Greenville Spring road, we concealed ourselves in the bushes until the scouting party came along, when we fell into the rear of it. The sergeant at the rear, hearing us behind him, stopped and ordered us to keep up in our places. We wanted to get away from the party as soon as possible after passing through lines, but the watchful sergeant behind us gave us no opportunity of giving him the slip. But get away we must, for it would never do for us to go back to camp with that company of regulars, nor to be found in its ranks after daylight. It was about midnight when we joined it, and we had a long ride mapped out for ourselves. In a very dark place in the woods, I dropped my rubber poncho, which striking my horse's legs, frightened him so badly(?) that my companion had to stop to hold him while I dismounted to pick it up. The sergeant, impatient at our delay, called back authoritatively and profanely to, "hurry up, there." Fearing he would come back for us, we did "hurry up" through the bushes and were soon safe beyond his reach and hearing.

Both of us being quite familiar with the country, we avoided the roads and rode through the timber and across fields to the house of Mr. Pratt, an old rebel, whose house we approached from the rear, by the negro quarters. By this time the clouds had all cleared away, and the moon was shining out bright and clear. Our approach was announced by the barking of a pack of hounds, and we heard a negro's voice calling off the dogs. We had taken off our blue overcoats and were as mean-looking a couple of butternuts as Captain Brown could muster in his company of bushwhackers.

Just as we turned around the corner of a negro's cabin, I, who was next to the cabin, was halted by a big darkey stepping out into the moonlight and presenting the muzzle of a double barrel shotgun not more than three feet from my breast. Having my pistol in my hand, quick as a thought, I leveled it on him and commanded him to "drop that gun." The brave fellow never flinched, but lowering his gun slowly, he held out his hand to me saying, "Lor bless you boss, I made sure you was some of dem Yankee sogers from de fort. If it wasn't for dat grey coat ob yourn, you'd a been a ded man by dis time sure." "O pshaw," I said, "you need not try to fool me, you are just as bad a Yank as the rest of the niggers." "No I ain't boss, dem Yankee niggers all done run off to de fort, I'se just as good a rebel as Massa Pratt hisself." Seeing the fellow eyeing me very closely, and fearing he might discover my disguise or that my speech might betray me, I asked him to let me see his gun, which he rather reluctantly handed to me. I then asked him if Captain Brown was not in the house. He did not know, as he had been at work in the field all day and came home late in the evening, but said, "Like as not boss, de Captain comes here right often." I told him to go to the house and call his master.

Mr. Pratt and his daughter soon appeared at the door, and seeing our grey coats, kindly invited us to "dismount and come in." We said we were looking for Captain Brown, that we belonged to his company and had just come from Clinton and had a message for him. We thought if Captain Brown was in the house, that would bring him out unarmed and we would easily capture him. The old gentleman said Captain Brown had been there to supper and spent the evening, but went away about ten o'clock, and again invited us to come in and have something to eat. We would not dismount, but the young lady at my request brought me a glass of water. As we were leaving, the negro asked for his gun, but I told him I would have to borrow it for a while, as our men were a little short of guns. "Well den take good care of de ole gun boss. Dars a mighty big load ob buckshot in it for de Yankees."

Leaving Pratt's, we followed the rebels' trail, which was very distinct in the mud, for a mile or two when it turned off towards the east. Disguised as we were, and out without orders or leave, we were as much afraid of meeting that company of regulars as we were of Captain Brown's company, and we kept a double lookout on all sides. Seeing a lot of ripe turkeys in a tree by the roadside in a barn yard, we picked two or three apiece, which we concealed under our overcoats and ponchos. As it was daylight when we reached the pickets on the Magnolia Grove road, we passed in without challenge. We were both known to the officer on guard to belong to General Lee's staff.

On Sunday, November 20th, I rode out to Mr. Dougherty's on the Port Hudson road, where I dined in company with Lieutenant Greeley of the 14th New York Cavalry, and after dinner made the grand rounds with Captain Baker, closing the exercise of the day by calling on the Bernard ladies, where I spent a very pleasant social evening.

On Monday, November 21st, General Lee and his command returned from one of the most successful raids of the campaign. He went as far as Brookhaven, Mississippi, and was out just one week. With a loss of only one man killed and two or three wounded, he captured 260 prisoners, twenty-four of whom were officers ranking from second lieutenant to major, and about 800 head of horses and mules. He also recaptured three pieces of light artillery taken by the rebels last summer near Port Hudson, and destroyed a large quantity of quartermaster and commissary stores belonging to the enemy. Following his little victorious army came a nation of contrabands with their miscellaneous outfits, baggage, and plunder.

General Lee's triumphant entrance into Baton Rouge was the occasion of the public exhibition of many conflicting sentiments and emotions. On one side of the street, as the column passed, a crowd of soldiers would cheer loudly for Lincoln and General Lee, while directly opposite would stand a crowd of citizens and ladies with faces longer than the moral law, "mute spectators of the scene," occasionally silently bowing like sun flowers in a breeze as some familiar face was recognized amongst the "grey back" prisoners, while all along the street, the negroes crowded close to the moving column to see if "Old Massa" was there, and I heard not a few such exclamations as "How is yer ole man?," "Is yer come to look for yer niggers?" accompanied by such snorts and laughter as only negroes can give utterance to as they recognized their former masters or drivers, while their welcoming yells, gestures, and exclamations to their former slave companions were indiscernible: they screamed, snorted, laughed, and rolled on the ground, cried, laughed, swore, and prayed in their ecstasies of delight.

The prison where the rebs were confined was soon besieged by hundreds of ladies desiring to see and minister to the wants of their unfortunate friends, but the officer in charge, a gruff old major who had but recently returned from a rebel stockade prison in Texas, gave them very little satisfaction.

As a soldier and commander, General Lee is as brave and competent as the best, but I much fear his loyalty will not stand a critical examination. Personally, I have always found General Lee brave and courteous, but on account of his excessive vanity, abuse of the powers of his position, and evident disloyalty, I cannot feel for him the respect his position and abilities should command.

The old state prison here occupied by the post quartermaster as a wagon yard, corral, and stable was destroyed by fire on the night of November 22nd. About 100 mules and a lot of harnesses and wagons were also burned. The cells and dwelling part of the prison, which were filled with refugees and contrabands, were not injured, only the sheds and wooden buildings.

Several regiments of infantry have arrived here lately, and all the cavalry have orders to be ready to march. A pontoon train has also arrived from New Orleans. I am unable to learn what movement is contemplated. Last night we had an old-fashioned white frost, a very rare occurrence I believe here. Owing to the late rains, the roads are very muddy and the streams and bayous all full.

On Thursday, November 24th, General Davidson, chief of cavalry, arrived at Baton Rouge, and all the cavalry received orders to be ready for another raid.[23] The court martial of which I was a member, and which had been sitting several weeks, was adjourned *sine die* and all the members ordered to rejoin their respective commands. Which, by the way, was about the most fortunate thing that could have happened for a certain surgeon who was being tried under numerous serious charges and whose case would have been disposed of in a few days more. The evidence, which was about all in, was very uncomplimentary to the doctor and reflected on his morality and professional abilities. As the court was never reconvened, I know not what became of the doctor or his case.

General Davidson with his command left Monday morning, November 28th. My company was divided, part going with General Davidson and part with General Bailey, who had relieved General Lee. Cayton went with General Bailey.[24] Being quite unwell and unable to ride, I did not go out. The "Regulation Mess" was entirely broken up, I being the sole survivor (Note: I met Captain Baker in 1870 on a train on the Union Pacific railroad in Nebraska).

From November 28th to December 15th, I did little or nothing, being sick and having no command except a few sick men who could not go out on the raid. The city and camps were deserted and lonely, there being only just enough troops left to do necessary guard duty. I continued to board with Mrs. Bacon, who was my only messmate.

By December 15th I was well enough for light duty and was wishing for something to turn up, when I was ordered by General Benton to take command of Highland Stockade. This stockade was a small but strong outpost twelve miles south from Baton Rouge and three miles from the Mississippi River.

Amongst my few citizen acquaintances in Baton Rouge was Mr. R. W. Knickerbocker, a young lawyer, a professedly Union man, and a very pleasant acquaintance. I first met him while serving on the court martial, before which he was conducting a case. Having more horses (3) than I expected to have use for at the stockade, I lent one of them, "Alick," to Knickerbocker to use for his keeping until I might need him.

On Friday, December 16th, we heard from General Davidson, who had reached Pascagoula, Mississippi, but had no particulars. I wrote to Cayton and sent mail to my company.

On Saturday morning, December 17th, I sent my tents and baggage down to the stockade, and after dinner with Knickerbocker at Mrs. Rodd's, I rode to the stockade and took command. The force I found there consisted of forty-five cavalry (2nd and 12th Illinois) under command of Lieutenant George Prentiss of the 2nd Illinois, and 100 infantry (2nd Louisiana) under command of Lieutenant

Weise, and a six-pounder cannon. The stockade was built of logs set endwise in the ground about 10 feet high, pierced with loopholes for musketry. Extending all around inside was a platform about five feet high on which men could stand to shoot over the wall. Surrounding it was a ditch crossed by a drawbridge. The fort was about 200 x 300 feet in extent. The men were quartered in comfortable little cabins and tents, the horses being kept outside the walls. In the lower or western end of the fort was a spring. The fort was located at the junction of the main road running south from Baton Rouge and a road leading to a landing on the river. I established my headquarters near the entrance.

The next afternoon I was called on by Major Clybourne and Captain Smith of the 11th New York Cavalry, Captain Elliott of the 2nd Louisiana Infantry, and Lieutenant Wood, who were out riding from town.

Thursday night, December 22nd, about twelve o'clock, my advance pickets on the Highland road south of the stockade were attacked and driven back on the reserve, which rallied, and after a sharp little skirmish, repulsed the guerillas. Although I do not anticipate an attack in any force, my little garrison is well prepared to defend itself against considerable odds, until assistance can be had from Baton Rouge. With plenty of ammunition, provisions, and water, we have no fears except from artillery, which of course could knock our little stockade into splinters in a few minutes. But we are not expected to do much fighting here; this is merely an outpost protecting the southern approach to Baton Rouge. Our duties here are scouting and picket, the cavalry doing all the scouting and advance picket, and the infantry doing all camp and guard duties.

On Christmas I was honored with two invitations to dinner, at Alfred Duplantia's and Mr. Berden's, but the weather being very cold and raining all the morning, I did not go out until after noon. The officers had a little jollification dinner in camp, after which, the weather clearing up, I rode out with a little squad of eighteen men to Mr. Berden's, three miles east from camp. Just before reaching Berden's house, a negro started to run across a field towards the timber. His movements were so suspicious that I ordered Andy Steele of Company D, who was riding near me, to stop him. Andy called to him to halt, but the darkey only ran the faster until brought down by a bullet in his leg from Andy's carbine. He proved to be one of Berden's hired field hands, and when asked why he ran away from the soldiers, and would not stop when ordered to, could give no reason. I was very sorry the affair occurred just when and where it did, as Berden, who was an Englishman, was considered by all to be a good Union man, and I was calling by special invitation.

I was right royally entertained by Mr. and Mrs. Berden, who had a splendid luncheon prepared, including a bountiful supply of eggnog. A generous lunch and whiskey were sent out to the soldiers.

As I started to return, my sergeant remarked with some surprise, "Why, Captain, that's the road we came out. Can't we go back the other way?" (I would here explain that it is a custom, almost a rule, with cavalry scouts to never return to camp by the same road they go out if possible to avoid it. With some it amounted almost to superstition.) I told him the bridge over the bayou on the other road was gone, washed away, and we would have to return the way we came out. "Well, if we must we must, but I don't like it," he said. "Neither do I, but this time we can't help it. We must keep our eyes peeled," I replied.

From Berden's to near the bayou, the road was in lanes through open fields where we could see long distances on all sides. Near the bayou and on both sides of it was a thick growth of timber and bushes. Sergeant Jack Hays of Company D, with two or three men, were riding a short distance, about fifty yards, ahead of me, and just as they reached the bridge, a small squad of rebels concealed in the bushes shouted, "Here's a Merry Christmas to you, Yanks," and fired a volley into them. Sergeant Hays and Private McKeene fell, seriously wounded. I charged instantly over the bridge and down the bank, but the rebs being dismounted, escaped in the brush, which was too dense for us to ride though.

I at once sent to Duplantia's for a carriage and team and had the wounded men conveyed to camp. It was rather a serious ending for our little Christmas frolic. McKeene was shortly afterwards sent to the hospital in Baton Rouge, where he died. Hays would not go to the hospital, but remained in camp where he was cared for by his comrades and recovered, but was never again fit for hard duty.

This was my fourth Christmas spent in the army, and one that I shall not soon forget. The first was spent at Fort Holt, the second at Paducah, the third at Union City, and this fourth, and I trust last, in the swamps of Louisiana. The first three I remember with pleasure, having on each occasion enjoyed a good Christmas dinner, the first with our company officers and the other two with ladies.

Ever since the departure of General Davidson's expedition, the country here has been overrun by small squads of guerillas, who commit their depredations with impunity, well knowing the weakness of our cavalry force and our inability to hunt them on all sides at the same time.

About this time I called one evening on the ladies at Alfred Duplantia's, less than a mile from camp, where I stayed until after nine o'clock. About eleven o'clock, the house was visited by a squad of guerilla scouts, and this within a few hundred yards of one of our picket posts. The society of the young rebel ladies is sometimes very agreeable, but the enjoyment of it is often attended with danger. I have taken a good many such chances and have not been caught yet.

On Tuesday, December 27th, a flag of truce came to our picket post near Duplantia's, and on going out to see what it was, I found Lieutenant Colonel Watts, rebel commissioner of exchange of prisoners, Captain Gillman, Lieutenant Boyd, and a small guard at Duplantia's. Colonel Watts had twenty-one Union prisoners to exchange. I took the prisoners on their parole to the stockade and sent Colonel Watts' communication to headquarters at Baton Rouge.[25]

On December 29th, I called at Madam Daigre's on the "coast" (river), where I met several lady visitors, amongst them Mrs. Von Phul and Miss Lou Rodie of New Orleans. Madame Daigre, an elderly lady and a widow, has one of the finest plantations in that vicinity, and a large and finely furnished residence, and before the war had been very wealthy. I found the ladies very pleasing and was entertained with music and singing.

Friday, December 30th, I visited Baton Rouge and had an interview with Generals Benton and Andrews concerning the visit of Colonel Watts, and other business at the stockade.[26] They had no authority to negotiate for the exchange of prisoners, and the men would have to stay, for the present, at the stockade.

Chapter Five

1865

Relieved at Highland Stockade—Colonel Watts—Mexican Soldiers—Back to Baton Rouge—Cotton Speculation—New Orleans—The French Market—Carrolton—Mardi Gras—A New Orleans Dance—Military Storekeepers—Discharge of Lieutenant Cayton—Guarding the Levees—Hickox's Landing & Pensacola—Fort Barrancas & Fort Pickens—A Surf Bath—General Asboth Again—A Phantom Cavalry Company—More Reflections on Black Soldiers—End of the War—News of Lincoln's Assassination—A Final Scout & Holiday—Explosion at Mobile—Mustered Out—Homeward Bound—A Steamboat Race —Arrival at Quincy

On New Year's Day, I arrived by invitation at Madam Daigre's, where I met Colonel Gooding of the 31st Massachusetts Mounted Infantry, and Captain Keene, commanding Gunboat Number 53 of the Mississippi Squadron, which was lying at anchor in the river opposite Madam Daigre's plantation. I had also the pleasure of meeting Mrs. Batchelor, Miss Lucy Daigre, and Miss Lou Rodie. We spent a very pleasant afternoon being entertained by the ladies after dinner with music, singing, and flirting. All the male members of the Daigre family were in the rebel army, but the widow and the ladies of her household make themselves very agreeable to Union soldiers and sailors, and we are always welcome at her house. The next day, Monday, I called on Captain Keene and dined with him on board his vessel.

On Tuesday, I called by direction of General Benton at William Walker's to examine the papers and passes of his brother, Judge Walker, who was banished from

New Orleans by General Butler in 1862. Judge Walker was formerly editor of the *New Orleans True Delta,* and was one of the signers of the ordinance of secession. The judge showed me his order of banishment and pass from General Butler, and said he should in no wise violate the conditions of the order, nor go beyond the limits of his pass. I found him very courteous, but he declined to speak or express an opinion of the war.

On January 10th, I was relieved of the command of Highland Stockade by Major Craige of the 4th Wisconsin Cavalry. I sent my different detachments of cavalry to their respective regiments and moved into town and stayed that night with Mr. Knickerbocker. Up to the time I left the stockade no terms of exchange of prisoners had been agreed on, and I left them in charge of Major Craige.

Immediately after the arrival of Colonel Watts, I had moved my picket post farther out a little beyond Duplantia's house, so as to bring it inside my lines. Although the little flag of truce emblem of "peace and good will" hung over the gate, I deemed it prudent to take this precaution. By thus taking Colonel Watts and his company under my protection(?), they could not leave the house, nor could visitors enter, without my permission. I plainly saw that the young officer in command of the colonel's escort did not like being so completely "taken in," but he was too much of a soldier to say anything about it.

Colonel Watts was quite an elderly man, I should think between fifty and sixty years old, quite fleshy, and perfectly bald headed. His manners, when quite sober, were courteous, dignified, and ostentatious, but when a little under the softening influence of eggnog or hot toddy, which occurred at brief intervals, he was inclined to be very familiar and patronizing. On such occasions, he always called me his "son," and several times wanted to hug and kiss me. I had no objections to his calling me all the pet names he pleased, but I did very seriously object to being pawed and slobbered over by a tipsy old rebel.

On the occasion of one of my visits to Baton Rouge, he asked me to bring him a jug of whiskey, a dozen packs of playing cards, and some little toilet articles, which he paid me for in fresh new green backs, with which he seemed to be well supplied. When I asked him how he came to have so much new federal money, he replied, smilingly, "Oh I've been attending to business. I saved a little cotton."

From the facts that no negotiations were pending for the exchange of prisoners, that there was no officer at Baton Rouge with authority to make exchanges, and that the commanding officer there was unprepared for and surprised at Colonel Watts' visit, I had grave doubts in my mind as to the honesty of his visit. Although he came under a flag of truce and with apparent good intentions, I did not know what might be behind it all. The rebel cause was fast failing and I knew they were desperate, but I did not know to what means they might be tempted to resort to gain some object or some advantage over us, and I was resolved that I should not be caught unawares, nor taken by surprise.

In order to test the old gentleman's honesty and oft-repeated expressions of friendship for me, I baited a little trap for him. One of my soldiers, under my instruction, went to him one day and said he wanted to desert and would steal both of my horses and join the colonel's escort as soon as it should leave our lines. Had he violated his flag of truce by encouraging the soldier in any way to desert, I would have sent him and his whole party under arrest to Baton Rouge, and would have reported him directly to the Secretary of War. But to my pleasure, I must say, he not only refused to listen to the soldier but, cursing him soundly, ordered him to leave the house, nor did he stop there, but sent for me early the next morning by the sergeant of the guard and told me the whole story and offered to go with me to camp and identify the soldier. Of course, I was very much surprised and indignant that any of my men should be guilty of such conduct, but of course, he must be aware of the fact that I could not admit him to the fort, nor would it be proper for me to parade my entire force for the inspection, so thanking him for his friendly kindness and honorable conduct, and promising to endeavor to investigate the case, dismissed the subject. Before parting from him on that occasion, the old gentleman volunteered two promises to me, both as kind as unexpected, and pledged his word as a soldier to keep them. The first was, if I should ever be taken prisoner of war in his department, I should not remain a day in prison after he should hear of it, but should be paroled with full liberty to go where I pleased, and if taken, in the last he would use his influence with Colonel Ould (chief rebel commissioner for exchange of prisoners) to have me paroled or released; and the other promise was, if any of my soldiers should desert, and steal my horses and join his escort, he would immediately return the horses under flag of truce.[1] As he was quite sober at the time, I believed he was honest and sincere in all he said. I thanked him again and assured him that if occasion ever required, I should not fail to call on him to redeem his first promise.

At another time, as we sat together on the door step one evening engaged in general conversation, we touched on the war (a subject seldom attended to by either of us). He said, "This is the most unnatural and unnecessary war ever waged. The South never had the least occasion in the world to go to war. It was forced upon us by a lot of damned, hot-headed knaves who now take precious good care to keep out of the fire they have kindled. I voted against it and worked against it, but it was bound to come, and now we are in for it. It is a great and desperate game in which you and I have been forced to take parts. I will not say I think you are wrong and I am right, but this I will say to you my son, play against me as strongly as you may, but play honestly, and if you beat me I'll be your friend, and if I beat you I'll still be your friend." He spoke very earnestly, and severely denounced those of his army who had treated Union prisoners with neglect or cruelty. The prisoners he brought in spoke in the highest terms of his considerate treatment of them on the march, although he rode in a carriage while they were obliged to walk. He was a soldier in the Mexican War and has served in the rebel ranks in this war. He was quite humorous, and likes and can tell a good story, and it did me good to hear his big, hearty laugh.

I quote one of his stories as we sat in the moonlight that evening. "One cold, stormy night I was on picket on the Potomac up to my knees in mud and nearly frozen to death. On the opposite side of the river stood a Yankee picket similarly situated, each one using every endeavor to pick the other fellow off with his rifle. I thought this was all very foolish, as well as very disagreeable and dangerous, and was getting tired of it, so I called out, 'Hello Yank.' I was promptly answered, 'Hello Reb.' Said I, 'Don't you think if Old Abe and Jeff were obliged to stand here all night in the mud shooting at each other as we are, that we'd have peace before morning?' 'You bet your life,' came the Yankee's quick response."

The colonel was getting pretty dry by this time, so we returned to the parlor, where was assembled a lively little party of ladies and officers, both armies being represented by the latter. At the colonel's command, we all filled our glasses, when the old veteran proposed a toast: "May this cruel war soon be over, and may we <u>all</u> soon enjoy the blessings of a just and honorable peace." To which, of course, we could all, both blue and grey, respond most heartily. I have abundant reason to remember with pleasure the holidays spent at Highland Stockade.

At one time at the stockade, I had in my command a number of Mexican soldiers belonging to the 1st Texas Cavalry, to one of whom I took quite a fancy. He was a funny little fellow who could not speak a word of English, and replied to everything I said with, "Si señor." I was making considerable progress in domesticating him when they were all ordered to rejoin their regiment. On bidding me, "Adios, Señor Capitano," he presented me with a very fine horse hair "lariata" of his own manufacture. These Mexicans were all as expert in spinning lariats as they were in stealing hair from the manes and tails of their comrades' horses. They were also great gamblers and their whole time, when not spinning lariats, was occupied with monte.

An old negro also presented me, as a token of his friendly regard, with a young, full-blooded bloodhound pup, a very beautiful little animal, but for which I had about as much use for as I had for a pair of skates. He furnished me with entertainment for a while by tearing to pieces everything he could find in my quarters and howling in his peculiar melodious style every time he heard a bugle call.

I moved into town on January 10th and stayed that night with Mr. Knickerbocker, and the next day pitched my tent in the regimental camp. On the 12th, all of my 1862 recruits were mustered out.

Meeting Mr. Knickerbocker on Friday morning, January 13th, he said it was necessary for him to call on Madam Daigre that day on some legal business, and asked me to ride down with him. Being off duty that day, I accepted his invitation to lend him a horse and go with him. He was detained at his office longer than he expected to be, and it was noon when we started from Baton Rouge. He rode my running horse "Tom" and I rode a small trotting mare. I was already pretty hungry and told Mr. Knickerbocker that I meant to be at the madam's in time for dinner, which I knew from past experience was always served at two o'clock. He said he would try to stay with me, and I knew he would have to do so, for I knew he could not stop old Tom if he tried to. At half-past one we dismounted at the madam's, my little mare not once having broken her trot the whole distance of thirteen miles. Mr. Knickerbocker, who was not accustomed to cavalry riding, said he would accept defeat rather than another such victory.

We had, of course, an excellent dinner, and I had, of course, an excellent time with the young ladies, while my loyal friend was talking business with the madam. Major Craige and old Colonel Watts were also at Madam Daigre's. We stayed until nearly sundown, when we started to return by way of the stockade, where we stopped a few moments. During our call at Madam Daigre's, in a spirited little encounter with Miss Rodie at close quarters, I captured her photograph, which I carried off as a trophy, I told her, of our engagement. As I remember Miss Rodie, she was a fair blonde with light blue eyes and bright yellow hair, small and slender, but as active and muscular as a cat. She was a good musician, a fair singer, and a generally interesting young lady. Although she likes to be quoted "a saucy little rebel," she told me she was engaged to be married to a young Yankee lieutenant of infantry.

On Sunday, January 15th, our regiment moved camp from near the general hospital to a hill about a mile north from Fort Williams, where we have more room and are nearer the abatis from which we obtain our wood for fuel. Anticipating a movement of the regiment soon, I had not drawn a new tent, but had, since my return from the stockade, been using one belonging to Captain Rottaker of the 6th Missouri Cavalry, but as the weather was stormy and Captain Rottaker might want his tent at any time, Lieutenant Cayton and I commenced building a little board shanty.

I was this morning, January 19th, detailed on a commission to enquire into the cause of Lieutenant Irwin's (of our regiment) absence last summer. The evidence in the case showed that the lieutenant had a good time during his somewhat protracted absence, and that he reported back for duty as soon as, under the circumstances, he could conveniently do so. On his promise to not again offend in that way, the commission exonerated him.

Detailed for picket duty today, January 20th, but Cayton went in my place if I would work on the shanty, as he said he thought he could better serve his adopted country quarreling with the rebel women than he could at home building. Up to this time our regiment has used Cooke's single-rank tactics, but a late order from the chief of cavalry goes into effect today returning to the old regular army two-rank tactics. The order is not kindly received by our officers, as we have worked in both styles of drill, and for convenience and quick work prefer the single-rank formation.

We have officers' school every afternoon at two o'clock. Still raining, and our camp, especially the horse quarters, is very muddy and nasty.

On January 21st, after a brief call on our old landlady of the "Regulation Mess," I spent a pleasant evening at "Victor's" in company with Dr. Gray, Captain Rottaker, and others. Victor's is a little restaurant and saloon, the most quiet and orderly place of its kind in the city, and a general rendezvous for all the officers of the garrison.

Not being on duty today, January 22nd, and being tired of the mud and monotony of camp, I got a pass for the day from General Bailey and decided on a trip to the country. I invited Knickerbocker to ride with me to the stockade and vicinity, but he said he "had been there" once with me when the weather and roads were good, and declined to risk his life or limbs in the weather and roads of today. I didn't think the country mud could be any worse than that in camp, and I felt pretty certain that a warm and pleasant reception at the other end of the ride would compensate me for a cold and disagreeable ride, so accompanied by an orderly, I started down the Highland road.

I dined at the stockade with Surgeon Horn, Major Craige being out conscripting negroes to build a new fort. After dinner, I called at Duplantia's, where I found Major Craige. The major seemed to be doing well enough and said he thought Monday would be a better day to find darkies, and one day more wouldn't make much difference to the fort anyhow. After a brief but very pleasant call at Duplantia's, I rode to the river and called on Captain Keene on Gunboat Number 53. The steamer *Grey Eagle,* coming down, came alongside the gunboat and I went on board of her and was not a little surprised to meet Madam Daigre and family, who were on their way to New Orleans.

On returning Miss Rodie's photograph, she invited me to call on her when I might visit the city. After dinner with Captain Keene on the gunboat, I returned by the Highland road, reaching camp about 8pm; although the entire day was cold and stormy, I managed to put in my time to pretty good advantage. During my absence, Lieutenant Cayton had so far finished our shanty that we could occupy it, and found it a very good and comfortable shelter from the storm.

Went on picket the morning of January 23rd on the Clay Cut road. On account of the stormy weather, the reserve is stationed in a shed at Mrs. Bernard's (Magnolia Grove). Mrs. Bernard, in order to save her fences from being burned by the pickets, has a cartload of wood hauled to the reserve post every day. I took tea and spent the evening with Mrs. Bernard and her pleasant and interesting family, consisting of four daughters, one of whom is married, but her husband, she says, is in New Orleans. Mr. Bernard is an officer in the rebel army. If there are any sons, they are probably also in the rebel army, for there are no men about the place except hired servants. I frequently take them northern papers, which are full of war news, but the subject of war is never mentioned in our conversations.

I was relieved on picket this morning, January 24th, by a lieutenant of the 1st Louisiana Cavalry. The citizens all are far more partial and friendly towards officers and soldiers from the north than they are towards federal officers and soldiers from the southern states. I have always been treated with courtesy (by people of intelligence), and in many instances with very friendly consideration by the same people who treat with contempt and disdain loyal officers from their own or other southern states. It is no doubt perfectly natural that they, especially the women, should feel as they do. They call all loyal southern people "traitors." These loyal southern troops may be all right, but know we do not take them into full fellowship, and view them not without a shade of suspicion. I doubt if the Louisiana lieutenant who relieved me this morning will be honored with an invitation to tea by Madam Bernard this evening.

Today, January 25th, I made a wooden chimney to our shanty and a door of pieces of packing boxes, while Cayton lined the inside with shelter tents. Having now a safe place to keep it, I moved a lot of ammunition that I had stored at Knickerbocker's office to camp.

Our brigade commander, General Davis, seems to think we are green troops or that we have been wasting our precious time in idleness or ignorance, as recent orders from his headquarters require us to have two drills daily, one dress parade, four roll calls, officers' and noncommissioned officers' tactics classes, and all line officers to be present at all roll calls, stable, and water calls, and twenty-two bugle calls per day are ordered.[2] All this gilt-edged style will do very well for a time, while encamped in the city, but when we shall strike camp again, for some wild raid into the country, we will leave all such orders far behind us. We are all anxious for orders to march somewhere, anywhere.

The enemy, if there is any in this vicinity, seems to be taking a rest, and since the defeat of Scott at Clinton we have heard of no rebel troops nor guerillas in the country, and citizens and negroes coming to our lines have nothing to report. All scattering and irregular troops have probably been called in to prepare for the final exercises in their "last ditch." If the rebels don't locate that last ditch pretty soon, I fear they will not be able to find a place for it.

It was about this time that I had rather an interesting little adventure one day while on picket on the Greenville Spring road. A lady came to my post in a buggy and asked permission to pass in, stating that she wanted to get some medicine for her husband, who was sick. I was better posted in her domestic affairs than she thought, for I knew she had no husband, at least none at home. If she had one at all, he was probably in the rebel army. Under pretense of having to send a soldier to headquarters for a pass for her, I detained her some time and sat in her buggy, talking with her. After she had told me, in her most pleasant and bewitching manner, all about how sick her poor husband was and how anxious she was to get his medicine and return home, I took her hand and said, "Now madam, look me straight in the eyes and tell me the truth. I don't believe you have any husband at home, but I do believe you want to smuggle medicine or something else out of our lines." I expected and was prepared for a little scene of some kind, but she exceeded my fondest anticipation, for instead of doing the virtuous indignation act and giving me a red hot volley of rebel abuse, for which I was prepared, she began to cry, and the next moment was off in a paroxysm of hysterics. I was accustomed to being scolded and abused by rebel women at the lines, and in such cases knew just what to do, but here was an act not down in the bills. Alone in a buggy with a strange lady, and she in a fit, was a novel as well as an embarrassing situation for me, and I realized that I must change the situation of affairs with as little delay as possible. By means of some leaning and some carrying, I managed to get her out of the buggy and into a house nearby, where I left her in charge of the lady of the house. The good lady of the house, with whom I was slightly acquainted, but whose name, I regret, I have forgotten, at first declined to receive my patient and asked if she was often subject to such fits. I told her she appeared to be subject to one just then, which was about all I knew of the case, and that she <u>must</u> please take care of her for the present, and if the lady did not explain all satisfactorily, I would call another time and endeavor to do so, or to at least explain my connection with the unfortunate affair. I did call the next time I came on duty at that post, and was pleased to learn that my patient had recovered in a few hours and that the lady of the house was satisfied with her explanation of the affair.

Another lady, Mrs. B., a planter, used to pass in and out frequently on the Greenville Spring road, and always with a pass from General Herron, directing the officer on duty to pass her "without examination."[3] I had made up my mind that she was a rebel and a smuggler, and that General Herron knew it, and as I was not permitted to search her at the lines, I set a trap to catch her outside. I got all ready, and the next time she passed out, one of my men met her in the woods and offered to sell her his horse and arms, saying he had deserted. After some little parlaying, she bought the whole outfit and tied the horse behind her buggy. When a sergeant with a squad, who had secretly witnessed the whole affair, suddenly appeared and arrested her and the deserter and took them to the provost marshal, under the seat of the buggy were found six revolvers and a lot of cartridges. General Herron managed to get her released, and I heard no more of the case. That's the kind of a man General Herron is, and that's the way he fights rebellion.

On the evening of Tuesday, January 31st, all the officers of the regiment met at Lieutenant Colonel Marsh's quarters to give him a good send off, as he was going home the next day on a short leave of absence. He had provided liberally for a jolly good time, and that's just what we all had. Songs, speeches, and toasts followed each other in rapid succession, until they all became so mingled and confused that it was difficult to tell where one ended and another began. In our revelry, many toasts were drunk to the old folks at home and the girls we left behind us, as well as to the speedy success of our cause and the confusion of Jeff Davis, and it was nearly morning before we came to a good stopping place and dispersed to our quarters.

As I was on the regular detail for picket the next day, I hoped to get a little sleep and much needed rest, but I had scarcely lain down, it seemed, before the bugle sounded reveille. By good fortune, I secured the Clay Cut road post, which gave me an opportunity to spend a few very pleasant hours with the ladies of Mrs. Bernard's hospitable mansion. It was a very dark, rainy, and generally disagreeable night, and seemed to me to be about twice as long as it should have been.

Notwithstanding the continued heavy rains and the bad condition of the roads, a great many women continue to come to the lines with cotton. A few have passes and are permitted to enter, while those less favored stop at the outer lines with their loads and wait there for buyers. All day I have been annoyed by a lot of Jews and cotton speculators passing out and in with passes, "to the videttes and return." Our vidette posts have become regular cotton markets. This keeping women with their cotton outside, and permitting a lot of very doubtful speculators to pass out to trade with them, is a perfect farce and a great injustice. These women and negroes might just as well be allowed to come in and sell their cotton in open market, where buyers would come in competition with each other, and all have equal chances, instead of giving the business into the hands of a favored few who combine and buy at their own prices, and no more harm could be done by letting the women in to trade than by letting these unscrupulous operators out to trade with them. I do not know the market value of a pass entitling the bearer to buy and bring in cotton at the lines, but I think the traders can afford to pay pretty well for the monopoly. While our officers on picket use all diligence, I have no doubt but that a good deal of mail and contraband goods are constantly being smuggled out by these traders, and for which they can demand their own prices. Some of these traders seem to think that their "pass" from headquarters entitles them to do and talk as they please, and to treat us with disrespect as though we were a hindrance to their business. One little Jew today was so insolent to one of the soldiers on guard that I ordered him back to town with the promise of tying him to a tree if he came to my post again, pass or no pass. He showed his confidence in me by not coming again to any post where I was on duty.

I was honored by an invitation to dine at Mrs. Gummins' near the reserve fort on February 4th, where a very good dinner was seasoned with pleasant and entertaining company. About dark, Captain Sam Whitaker came out to wait at the lines for a squad he was going out in command of to lie in ambush on the Clinton road. At midnight, the videttes on the Clinton road discovered a squad of five or six horsemen approaching and fired on them without challenge. It was perhaps the party that Captain Whitaker was going out to lay for. The videttes, belonging to the 1st Texas Cavalry, must have been very much frightened or very stupid to fire on such a small party without challenge, for which I reprimanded them. It would have been the same if it had been a returning party of our own men. The field officer of the day, a captain of the 1st Texas, came up just after the alarm, but as I thought I had already given his men a good lesson in vidette duty, I did not report them to him. About two o'clock, Captain Whitaker's squad came up, when he moved out, but returned about daylight without having seen nor heard anything.

On Monday morning, February 6th, I received a special order from department headquarters to report immediately as a witness before a special commission at New Orleans. Lieutenant Austin Dement of Company B received a like order, and one came also for Tom Douglass, lately discharged from my company. Neither Lieutenant Dement nor I had any idea what case was being tried, nor what we were wanted for, but we were both glad to get out of muddy Baton Rouge for a time, as well as for the opportunity to visit the city.

The next day we secured transportation and got off at 5pm on the steamer *Belle Peoria*. The boat was laden with negro troops from Memphis, but as they were not admitted to the cabin, we had no difficulty in securing comfortable state rooms. We passed my old friend, Gunboat Number 53, at anchor near Madam Daigre's plantation, and arrived at New Orleans about midnight. Owing to a dense fog, the boat experienced considerable difficulty in landing, but finally tied up near the foot of Canal Street. We went on shore about seven o'clock, and after breakfast at the St. Charles Hotel, reported at the office of the provost marshal and were given passes until the 14th instant.

After a long search we found the rooms of the special commission, of which General "Baldy" Smith was president, on North Street.[4] We were examined separately, Lieutenant Dement being called first. In addition to the usual witness oath to "true answers given to all questions concerning the case now being tried," I was sworn to "not divulge any questions that might be asked me, nor my answers to them, nor the case being investigated." I began to think it must be a very serious case and that I had, perhaps, been getting into trouble of some kind myself, and was not a little surprised to learn at the first question that was put to me that my evidence was required concerning the notorious irregular conduct of General A. L. Lee at Baton Rouge, some particulars of which I have already given. All I knew was soon told, and we were dismissed. Both Dement and I, of course, respected our obligations, and the subject of the trial was not mentioned. In fact, I don't think either of us considered it worth a second thought or talking about.

We now had six days to run, if we wished to remain in the city, with nothing to do but to look out for ourselves. Fortunately, perhaps, for us both, our financial resources were very limited and no paymaster in sight, and everything in New Orleans at the top of war prices. But as we were bound to see the sights and go as far as we would, we commenced by posting our cash and starting out on economical principles. After dinner at the Saint Charles, which depleted our finances about three dollars, we contracted with "Alec" to drive us around and show us the city in his cab. As we could not stand the Saint Charles prices, we selected a smaller and less expensive hotel for our quarters.

The next morning I met my old friend Dr. Crutts, formerly surgeon of our regiment, in the rotunda of the Saint Charles, and also met Captain Hawk of the 12th Illinois Cavalry, and in the evening we all went to the varieties theater. Amongst the few points of interest to us are the bronze statues of General Andrew Jackson and Henry Clay. The former is equestrian, and is said to be one of the finest in the world. Every mark and line on both man and horse is perfect and true to nature, and the immense statue is so accurately balanced that the horse stands on its hind feet without support. In all other equestrian statues I have seen, the horse either stands on three feet, or his tail reaches to the ground to balance and support him. On the stone pedestal of the Jackson statue is this inscription: "The union must and shall be preserved," and there it has stood all through this long war, a prophetic warning from the spirit of brave old Jackson to the rebels who would destroy that union he fought to create.

On the pedestal of the Clay statue, which stands in the middle of Canal Street, is this quotation from one of his speeches: "If I could be instrumental in eradicating from the character of our country this deep stain, Slavery, I would not exchange the proud satisfaction I would enjoy for all the honor ascribed to the most successful conqueror." I was told that this inscription was not originally thus, but was placed there by order of General Butler soon after he took command of the city.

I called this afternoon on Miss Rodie, and had the pleasure also of seeing Mrs. and Miss Daigre, who were visiting in the city. I met General Lee at the Saint Charles, with whom I shook hands and spoke a few words. He seemed rather depressed in spirits, and I thought not very glad to see me, as he doubtless knew why I was in the city. I also saw Major Generals Herron, Steele, "Baldy" Smith, and Brigadier General Benton, and a score or more of other generals with whom I was not acquainted. The Saint Charles Hotel seemed like a beehive of general and field officers. Others besides Lee may have been there on "official business" connected with the special commission. I know I saw several who were justly entitled to an investigation. It was a current saying amongst the boys of the town "you can't throw a stick at a dog without hitting a Yankee general."

In the afternoon we rode out to the Halfway House on the shell road and at night went to the circus.

About the most interesting place in the city, to me, was the "French Market." It is a large, low building in and around which are displayed, in little stalls, almost anything and everything of a small or light character that can be thought of. The coffee, cake, and fruit stands kept by pretty French or Creole girls are the chief attraction, and were largely patronized by the soldiers. The coffee is made and kept in large silver tanks or urns, heated by spirit lamps. What kind of coffee is used, or how made, I know not, but I do know it is the strongest and richest coffee I ever drank, and the cheapest in the city. Here one can get a cup of coffee, a cake, or a piece of fruit and a smile from the pretty little French girl for twenty-five cents. The cups, the cakes, the smile, and the "thank you sir" are all small but sweet, and in such perfect harmony that the omission of any one would break the combination. As I had no use for fans, dolls, canes, spectacles, jewelry, nor any other of the thousands of little things for sale there, I confined my business to the coffee stands and always considered a quarter spent there well invested.

By February 10th, we were already getting pretty tired of idle city life, so we decided to return home to camp, and after attending a matinee at the Saint Charles Theater, obtained transportation and went on board the steamer *Saint Cloud*. The steamer started at 5pm, but soon stopped at Carrolton to land some troops, where she tied up for the night, returning to the city the next morning for wood and coal, and did not leave again until sundown, reaching Baton Rouge about noon on Monday.

In a day or two after my return to duty, orders were received for the regiment to embark as soon as transportation could be secured for Carrolton. Several companies went down the river on the 16th, and the next day Companies F, G, and L embarked on the little steamer *Jennie Rogers*. All on board bid a last goodbye to Baton Rouge at 10:30pm. Being unwell and very tired, I retired to my stateroom as soon as I had my company and stores on board, and did not rise until we reached Carrolton, about eight o'clock the next morning, where we pitched our camp near the river and just outside the town.

Just before leaving Baton Rouge, I traded off my racehorse "Tom," which had become foundered and unserviceable, to Mr. John Dougherty, a citizen, for a perfectly wild three-year-old stallion. The colt had never been handled at all and was not only wild, but vicious and full of fight. After considerable difficulty, he was corralled, lassoed, and enough horses attached to him to lead him to camp, and on board the boat. He resisted the draft to his utmost, but finally gave up, and in a few days I was master of the situation. The balance of the regiment came down from Baton Rouge the next day, and on Tuesday we were inspected by Captain Allen, Assistant Inspector General, who also inspected and condemned our surplus stores. General A. J. Smith's 16th Army Corps passed down the river today, February 19th. The avalanche is moving towards Mobile.

The only demonstration in honor of Washington's birthday was a salute of heavy artillery at this post. The peacetime military parade was omitted, as it would have been neither novel nor interesting. While in the city this afternoon, I saw Captain Keene of Gunboat Number 53, under orders for Pensacola.

On February 23rd, a special commission consisting of Lieutenant Lee, 3rd Massachusetts Infantry, Lieutenant Chase, 2nd New York Cavalry, and myself, was convened at my quarters to investigate the cause of the absence of Captain Hitch, 1st Louisiana Cavalry, from his command for nineteen days. As all the evidence in the case went to show that his absence was unavoidable, or nearly so, the commission acquitted him of blame

It has been raining, and raining hard, nearly ever since we landed at Carrolton, and the storm of last night was about the hardest I ever witnessed. The ground here is very flat and the water cannot flow off as fast as it falls; consequently everything that cannot float is under water and mud, and the worst kind of black, grimy mud that sticks like pitch. The common roads and unpaved streets are next to impassable, but from Carrolton to the city is a good shell road. I have made frequent visits to the city, seven miles from our camp, and have seen about all I can find of interest.

I have again made application to be mustered out and granted an honorable discharge on the grounds of expiration of term of service, and that my company has become so reduced in numbers that it contains less than the regulation number for a captain. I am not desirous of leaving the service; I want to see the play out and be in at the finish, which is evidently not now far distant, but I do want to get out of the regiment and out of the Department of the Gulf. Our old regiment has seen its best days. The old, original soldiers, with the exception of a few veterans, have all served out their time and gone, and the feeling of dissatisfaction amongst the line officers is very general. "The farther we go the worse we get." It was bad enough at Baton Rouge, but is very much worse at New Orleans. Contention and misrule amongst and by our general and field officers is causing a great deal of dissatisfaction in the line officers and in the rank and file of the army.

The *New Orleans Times* of the 26th instant has an account of the occupation of Fort Sumter and Charleston by our troops.[5]

February 28th was Mardi Gras Day, the great gala day of the year in New Orleans. The streets are full of masqueraders in carriages, on horseback, and on foot, and mask balls are announced for tonight at all the theaters and public halls. The grand parade, so far as I could judge, seemed to be made up of sports, courtesans, and generally disreputable characters. The better class of the population looked on from the sidewalk and windows, but took no part in the display. New Orleans is at this time full to overflowing with sports and disreputable characters of all kinds. I had ridden to the city in company with several of our officers to see the parade. At night some wanted to go to the theater and others to the mask balls, but I thought I had seen enough of the nonsense for one day, so I rode back to camp alone.

It was about this time that I had a little adventure that came very near a serious termination. I was walking along one of the main streets in New Orleans late one night in company with Captain Mower (with whom I had a close call and narrow escape once near Baton Rouge last August), when our attention was attracted by sounds of music and dancing in a hall over a saloon. Entering the saloon, we inquired of the barkeeper what was going on upstairs, and were told there was "a nice quiet little dance," and we were politely asked to buy tickets and "go up and have some fun." So we took tickets and went up a flight of narrow, crooked stairs into a hall, where were assembled about twenty-five of about the toughest and roughest looking men I ever saw, and about the same number of gaudily and scantily dressed women. A set was on the floor dancing, so that our entrance was unobserved, and being wet and chilly, we went to a corner of the room near a stove where we could see the dancing without ourselves being much seen.

Soon after that set was finished, the floor manager commenced calling off numbers, and the men answering to the numbers called selected partners and took places on the floor. This dancing by numbers was something new to me, and I was getting quite interested, hoping to learn something new in the act. "Numbers 28 and 29," called the floor manager, but there was no response. After repeating the call several times and receiving no answer, he came to where we were standing and asked the numbers of our tickets. We did not know, but on showing them, they were numbers 28 and 29. "Why didn't you answer? Go and git your gals and dance," he asked and commanded rather roughly. We told him we did not want to dance; besides we had our heavy riding boots and were wet and cold and in no condition to dance if we wanted to. He said he didn't care what we wanted, we had dance numbers and must dance. I replied that we did not want to dance and would not, and that he might go on with his business. With an oath, he caught me by my shoulders with the evident intention of pulling me out on the floor and giving me a forcible introduction to one of the waiting belles at the other end of the room. Quicker than I can tell it, Mower and I sprang away from the stove towards the door, but seeing our way blocked by the roughs, we backed up against the wall, so that we should not be flanked, and drawing our revolvers, threatened to shoot the first man that touched us. The girls began to squeal and run to the farther end of the room, while the roughs massed their forces on our front, and we saw several knives and pistols ready for action, and I felt sure we were in for a bloody row. We told them we did not come there for a row, and if they would let us alone, we would go away quietly, but if they pushed us, we would fire, and give them more row than they wanted. With our pistols cocked, we sidled along the wall towards the door and went down the stairs backwards, determined to shoot the first man that should attempt to follow or molest us. It was my first and last adventure with New Orleans roughs, and if that was "a nice, quiet little dance," I have no desire to see a rowdy one.

My application to be mustered out has been returned "disapproved." Colonel Sturgeon, chief mustering officer of this department, decides that my term of service will expire August 11th, <u>1866</u>. Worse and more of it. If I shall apply again for a discharge, I will perhaps be sentenced to a <u>life</u> <u>service</u>. The resignation of Lieutenant John Cayton of my company, tendered about two months ago, was accepted March 1st, and he was honorably discharged, by order of General Canby.[6]

I have been hard at work all day, March 3rd, trying to dispose of a great lot of condemned ordnance and other stores that were inspected and condemned by Major Cowan at Baton Rouge, but whose report has not yet been returned to me, and the absence of which causes much trouble in turning over or disposing of the stores. However worthless the stores may be, they are supposed to be in as good condition as when received by me, and I must keep and care for them until relieved of the responsibility by the report of an inspecting officer, or the receipt of a military storekeeper.

Many of the clerks and military storekeepers here are civilians, appointed through the favoritism or patronage of some general, and their insolence and independence is very trying to the nerves and patience of officers obliged to do business with them, and no satisfaction can be had by reporting them at headquarters. The ordnance officers and quartermasters here are the most unaccommodating of any I ever had to deal with. Their "office hours" are from 9am to 3pm, and no matter how urgent your business may be with them, there seems to be no power here that can or will oblige them to sign a paper, nor do any business out of their regular hours. While we in the field are obliged to work from twelve to twenty-four hours a day, exposed to all dangers and privations, and burdened with responsibilities, these dandy staff officers and citizen clerks live at their ease in the city, work six hours a day, and draw their pay every month. We don't mind the hard work, rough fare, and danger in the field; we expect all that and are willing to take things as they come, but it is unpleasant, to put it mildly, to us who have been in the rough and tumble for nearly four years to be snubbed and insulted by dainty staff officers and clerks who never smelt burnt powder, nor slept a night in camp in their lives. I have cursed, complained, reported, and offered to fight a whole office full of them, and the same has been the experience of every line officer in the regiment. They have become so accustomed to abuse that they seem to feel lonesome and neglected without it, and if an officer having business with them does not get mad right at the start, they will soon say or do something to make him get there.

The firemen of New Orleans celebrated inauguration day, March 4th, by a grand parade today and ball tonight. The parade was very fine, consisting of twenty-five fire companies with their machines.

I had the pleasure of seeing General Ben Grierson today. He has recently been made Brevet Major General, and is in command of all the cavalry in the military division of West Mississippi. It is really refreshing to meet a real field general once in a while, and I told General Grierson that he looked lonesome and out of place amongst the dandy generals of New Orleans. He said he felt a good deal that way, and should get out of town again as soon as possible. I also saw Generals Canby, A. J. Smith, Osterhaus, and Lee. I am afraid the verdict of the special commission will be against Lee, and result in his dismissal, and which he undoubtedly deserves, and yet with all his faults, I rather like him for his ability and cool bravery.

Lieutenant Cayton started for home at four o'clock this afternoon in charge of a squad of discharged soldiers. Before leaving, he gave me his ambrotype. When I bid him goodbye on board the steamer *Glasgow*, I felt that I had parted with almost my last friend. We enlisted at the same time in Quincy and have served together almost constantly ever since, and we had become intimate and fast friends. During all this time, not an unpleasant word has passed between us. As a soldier, John was true and trusty, and as a subordinate officer at all times courteous and obedient. Of a naturally restless and impulsive nature, he was sometimes quick to give and take offense, and his resignation was the result of a personal difficulty with our colonel. I was very sorry to lose him, for to me he was a firm friend and valuable assistant. He never violated his word to me, and I never hesitated to trust him with the most important or dangerous duties.

Although an Englishman by birth, he was a patriotic and loyal American soldier. He was an excellent singer, with a rich, strong voice, and was always foremost in all fun and frolics in camp. He was a good horseman and a reckless rider, and often when I have seen him on his fine black horse leading the men in drill or on some wild, breakneck chase, I could not keep from thinking of "Mad Anthony Wayne."

Of Company L's original 100, five only now remain besides myself. They are Sergeants Paris, Ralph, Patton, and Carter, and Private Bell, all veterans. All the rest are recruits, transfers, and drafted men or substitutes. Lieutenants Tipton and Clark of our regiment have also resigned and start home today.

On Tuesday afternoon, March 7th, Captain A. Whiting and I called to pay our respects to Adjutant General Lorenzo Thomas at his headquarters on board the little steamer *Rocket*. We found the general sitting on the upper guards alone, enjoying his after dinner cigar, and a very pleasant, affable old gentleman, glad to hear all we had to say and to answer all questions <u>unofficially</u>, but would attend to no <u>business</u>. He said his business office was in Washington and that he was now making a tour of pleasure and unofficial observation and inspection. I wanted to talk about being mustered out or transferred to some other command or duty, but he said he had left his official spectacles in Washington, but if I would forward my papers through the proper channels, they would receive attention in due time. Not very encouraging in view of my late efforts in that direction, so we talked about something else: the late rains, the rapid rise of the river, negro troops, etc. He was evidently seeking rather than giving information and asked our opinions and experiences on many subjects connected with the service. After a very pleasant hour with General Thomas, we went up town and spent the evening with Quartermaster Hunt. Captain Whiting having another engagement, I went alone to the theater, returning to camp on the 11pm train.

I went down to Schroeder's on March 10th with Colonel Bush to call on Major Larrison, who is going home, his resignation having been accepted. Like Victor's in Baton Rouge, Schroeder's in Carrolton is a general rendezvous and resort, and whenever an officer is wanted and can't be found in camp, it is, "Go to Schroeder's, you'll most likely find him there."

Lieutenant Irwin has also resigned and received his discharge. The great number of officers being daily discharged and no new promotions or appointments made must indicate that those high in authority anticipate a speedy termination of the war.

Companies H and I leave today, March 12th. Only three companies, K, L, and M, now remain, but we are carrying the weight of nearly the whole regimental field and staff, having the colonel, adjutant, quartermaster, commissary, and assistant surgeon; enough to run these little companies into the ground. I relieved Lieutenant Prather, Company H, on fatigue duty, unloading hay from a boat at noon, so he could leave with his company. About 4pm, I was relieved by a detail of negro troops from Camp Parapet.

Having received no marching orders yet and wishing to make the best of my time here, I went down to the city again this evening, March 13th, with Adjutant Moore and went to the Academy of Music. The performance was of the variety order, but very good, including a fine double trapeze act by Shappe and Whitney.[7] When we returned to Carrolton on the twelve o'clock train, the rain was falling in torrents and everything was flooded. Our camp was over a half-mile from the depot and our accommodations there not very attractive, having only little shelter (dog) tents; and the night being very dark, we concluded we could not do better than to camp right where we were, so we crawled into an empty freight car on the side track and, lighting our pipes, laid down on the floor until about four o'clock, when the storm having passed off, we walked to camp. I had but just gotten into my little shelter tent when the rain commenced falling again faster and harder than before, so that the ditches around my tent and the camp drains were soon full and overflowing, and when I crawled out, about daylight, I was soaked through and covered with mud and slime.

As our camp had become quite untenable, we moved in the afternoon to an old machine shop nearer the levee, where we found good and dry quarters for men and horses. The river has risen about a foot in the last twenty-four hours and is now so near the top of the levee in some places that there is great danger of its breaking over. The river is now about ten or twelve feet higher than the land outside the levee. Nearly all the troops, both white and black, and many laborers, are kept constantly on the levee guarding and repairing it. As a crevasse here would flood not only all the camps, but also the cities of Carrolton and New Orleans, and as there are fears that someone may break the levee and cause a crevasse, the soldiers have orders to arrest every man not there on duty or working under orders, and to shoot down anyone attempting to break the levee. Two crevasses are reported on the west side of the river above here, and one near Baton Rouge.

Late news from Baton Rouge is to the effect that a wagon train was captured by guerillas a few days ago between Baton Rouge and Clinton, and four soldiers of the 4th Wisconsin Cavalry killed, and that General Bailey has occupied and established a camp at Clinton.

After coming off duty on the levee this afternoon, I had a good solid old Dutch dinner at Schroeder's. Old Marm Schroeder, as a caterer to the appetites of hungry soldiers, is a booming success. A better, or at least a much more satisfying, meal can be had at her house for seventy-five cents than for $1.50 in the city.

Our grist has at last come from the slow grinding mill of the gods of war, and tonight we have orders to embark in the morning. I have very few pleasant recollections to record of our one-month's encampment at Carrolton. Nearly all of that time the weather has been stormy and very disagreeable, and having turned over all our heavy stores, and being in light marching order, I have had no good tent or cot, but have slept on the ground in a little, almost useless, shelter tent. Fuel has been scarce and I have been wet and covered with nasty black mud nearly ever since I have been here. Many of our best officers have gone home, and a general feeling of discontent and dissatisfaction has prevailed in the regiment. We have had no scouting nor picket duties, and I have had no opportunity to ride in the country. We have had a good deal of hard work to do, but of a disagreeable kind, and unsuited to our cavalry tastes, such as loading and unloading steamboats and working on and guarding the levee, and my personal, official intercourse with the officers and department clerks in the city has not been of a nature calculated to command my respect nor inspire a desire to ever see them or the city of New Orleans again.

Concerning the city of New Orleans, I must say I have been greatly disappointed. When I say that Canal Street is very wide, very clean, and very pretty, I have said about all I can in favor of the city. Canal, Saint Charles, and a few other principal streets are all, thanks to martial law, kept very clean, being swept by great horse-powered brooms every night, and frequently flooded and washed, and being paved with shells and kept so clean, are all white and free from dust. I saw very few large or handsome buildings, the houses generally being not over two stories high.

Canal Street is very wide and straight, and on both sides between the roadway and the sidewalks are rows, about six feet wide, of little garden plats filled with small shrubbery and many colored flowers. The ground on which the city is built is very low and flat, and the drainage is <u>from</u> the river towards Lake Pontchartrain. In times of high water, as at present, the water in the river is above the level of the city. In consequence of the ground being so low and wet, there are no basements or cellars to the houses, and for the same reason the graves in the cemeteries are nearly all above ground and built of masonry. So low is the ground and so near the level of the levee that I have seen, in the eastern part of the city, little fish swimming in the street gutters that were driven in by high water and winds from the lake.

"French Town" in the lower part of the city is occupied, almost entirely, by French and Creoles, is very crooked, very dirty, and the shops and houses are of the poorest kind. The narrow streets are often so full of domestic animals, burros, goats, pigs, and fowls, as to almost obstruct travel. I have heard much of the "fashionable gaiety" of New Orleans, but so far as I could observe, I thought the gaiety was of a very questionable character. About the only really good thing I saw or experienced was the baths at the Saint Charles Hotel. They were very fine and I took frequent opportunities to enjoy them.

But it may be that, under existing circumstances, I am not competent to give a fair and impartial opinion of the city; under more favorable conditions I might have seen things in a very different light. If we had had a more pleasant camp and better quarters, if the weather had been dry and favorable, if our duties had been more suited to our tastes and abilities, etc., I might possibly have seen another and more attractive side of the picture. But as it is, New Orleans is associated in my mind with no pleasant recollections. It is one of the very few places I have visited in the army that I leave without the least desire to see again. I fancy I must feel, on leaving New Orleans, something like Tom Moore felt when he said to London, "Dear, damned, distracted town, farewell."[8]

After bracing up on one of Marm Schroeder's best breakfasts, enough to last me all day, I left our quarters in the old machine shop and marched out on the shell road to Hickox's Landing on Lake Pontchartrain, about five miles from New Orleans, where we were to take a boat for Pensacola. Some five or six river steamers were at the wharf taking on infantry and light artillery for Mobile, but no seagoing vessel for us. The river steamers do not venture so far out as Pensacola. It is sometimes hard work for them to get to Fort Gaines in Mobile Bay.

Hickox's Landing has evidently been a very pretty place, and was a favorite resort for the sports and fancy of New Orleans, but it is sadly out of repair now. The shell pavements are broken and cut up by army wagons and artillery, and the trees and shrubbery destroyed by horses. The fences, sheds, and outbuildings of all kinds have been used for fuel. The piers and wharfs are rotting and falling into the water, and the bathhouses have lost their doors and floors and are now occupied by little squads of soldiers.

As we may possibly have to remain here several days, we have secured accommodations at an abandoned hotel near the landing. Our horses occupy the first floor and porch, Company M is in the second story, and Company L is comfortably located in the sky parlor, or as the men call it, "the first floor from the roof."

The day being quite warm, I took for the first time in my life a sea bath in one of the old bathhouses. The soldiers are putting in good time catching and boiling crabs and crawfish.

The distance from New Orleans to Pensacola by the way of the lake is about 150 miles shorter than down the river and out on the Gulf. I was in hopes we would go by the river route, as I was anxious to enjoy(?) a trip on the Gulf.

There is a fine swinging bridge over the canal here; vessels of light draught can go up the canal to "the basin" in the city. The *Polar Star*, a river steamer, passed up the canal to the city today. She was caught in a storm a few days ago on the lake, and her chimneys, steam pipes, and wheelhouses were blown away, and the boat otherwise damaged; about forty artillery horses were blown or washed overboard. A strong wind is blowing tonight and I fear the boats that went out this morning may have a rough time on the lake. I don't see how the river steamers with their high cabins and wheelhouses and wide decks can live at all in such waves as are running tonight on the lake. There is a lighthouse here on the end of the canal pier, and a revolving light can be seen a few miles distant on the coast.

A very hard storm of wind and rain all last night. The wind yesterday blew towards the lake, but after dark, it turned and blew from the lake, driving the water far up on the beach. Captain Jones, who would not come into the old hotel because he thought there might be bugs or "grey backs" in it, camped with Company K on the shore close to the water, and of course was drowned out.

I strolled out on the pier early this morning before breakfast. The wind was blowing fresh and cold, and the waves breaking over the pier gave me a shower bath for which I was unprepared. Being thoroughly wet and cold, I thought a glass of hot brandy would be the correct thing before breakfast, so I went up to the "Lake House" for a "brace." On approaching the bar, my attention was attracted to a gilt sign, conspicuously displayed, which read, "Plain drinks 25 cents. Hot or mixed drinks, 50 cents," which was very discouraging to a man who had only a quarter and expected to get a hot drink for fifteen cents. "Are those your quotations for today?" I asked the gilt-edged, bald-faced bartender. "Yes sir, what'll you take?" "I think I'll take a walk down to camp," and to camp I went and braced up with a tin cup of black coffee.

Later in the day, I tried my hand at the prevailing popular sport of crab fishing, but soon got out of patience and quit. I had better success catching crawfish in the bayou. I have tried to eat boiled crabs and crawfish, but don't like them. Some of the men are cooking and eating them continually.

March 17th. Our delay here is becoming tiresome. The lake, which was very rough yesterday, is as smooth as a pond today. For want of better occupation, I tried crab fishing again. After an hour or two of hard work, sitting on the wet pier and holding a stick in my hands, I succeeded in captured two poor little crabs. After working another hour and catching nothing, I concluded I was wasting a good deal of government time and getting very little to show for it. Those two crabs had cost the United States government, counting ten hours a day's work, about $1.25, and which in view of the fact that they were worth nothing at all, was rather a high price. Besides, my duties as a cavalry captain did not require me to catch crabs, so quite out of patience, I threw my two crabs and stick into the lake and quit the business. If I could catch the things, and they were fit to eat after being caught, I might find the sport more interesting.

I borrowed an old skiff this afternoon and rowed about two miles out on the lake. Two small ocean steamers, the *Clyde* and *General Banks,* came up this evening and anchored off the canal pier.

I borrowed a skiff from the provost marshal this morning, March 18th, to which I rigged a shelter tent for a sail and put out to sea alone. The lake was quite smooth and I sailed out a few miles with a very light wind and had to row back.

The steamer *General Banks* came into the canal, and about noon I went on board with my company and one company of the 31st Massachusetts Mounted Infantry. When we left towards evening, Companies K and M were embarking on the *Clyde,* which on account of her deeper draught, could not come into the canal, and the troops had to go out to her in a small steamer. We left Hickox's Landing about sundown and stopped a few minutes at Lake Port to take on a cask of ice.

The captain of the ship at first refused to give the officers staterooms, but offered us berths in the second cabin. The second cabin and the berths were very nice and clean, but if there was anything better to be had, we meant to have it, especially as the vessel was in government service and there were no other passengers on board. So we told the captain if we could not have staterooms and occupy the first cabin, we would remove the guard at the stair and let the soldiers occupy it. That made him more accommodating, and we were assigned to very good rooms. The ship, though small, was a fast sailing passenger steamer (propeller) and was finished and furnished throughout in very good style. The cabin was nicely carpeted and provided with sofas and easy chairs and the beds in the staterooms were as good as could be desired. I watched the light at Hickox's Landing until it sank out of sight when, being very tired, I went to bed and was soon asleep. On going on deck about sunrise the next morning, I found we were in Mississippi Sound, having passed through Lake Borgne during the night.

The sea was running high by reason of the late storm, and the wind being right against us made our little ship pitch and toss like a duck. I soon began to feel dizzy, and fearing I would be seasick, I went to my stateroom and slept an hour or two, and when I got up again I felt all right, and was not again troubled with seasickness, but some of the soldiers caught it pretty badly. After eating heartily, they would sit on the edge of the deck with their feet hanging over the side, looking down into the water. The inevitable result soon followed. Getting very dizzy, and afraid or unable to get up, they would fall backwards or roll over on the deck, while beans, bacon, hard tack, and coffee came to the surface in a partly digested condition and mingled freely with the groaning, suffering soldiers rolling on the deck. Many were so sick they were afraid they would die, but were soon so much worse they wanted to die and were afraid they wouldn't. The sympathizing(?) sailors prescribed drinking sea water, swallowing a piece of fat pork with a string tied to it and drawing the piece up again, climbing the rigging feet foremost, and various other equally good remedies. The only satisfaction the soldiers had was in seeing the sailors obliged to clean the deck of the mass of spoiled commissary stores.

We passed the mouth of Mobile Bay just before noon. Up to this time we had been running between the main shore and a line of islands and in sight of both. After passing the islands, we caught the full force of the waves from the open sea, and our vessel pitched worse than before.

After passing Mobile Bay, we could plainly see a long line of smoke rising above the forest on shore, which we knew marked the line of march of our army advancing on Mobile, and the rebel troops at Mobile could see in that steadily advancing column of smoke their certain doom. I was in hopes we would reach Pensacola in time to join this expedition in either Granger's or Grierson's command, but I feared now we would be too late.[9] It would be necessary for some troops to remain at Pensacola, and as we would probably be about the last to arrive there, I feared we would be kept there for garrison duty, and such proved to be the case. Passing close under the great guns of Fort Pickens, we entered Pensacola Harbor and reached the wharf at Barrancas about 5pm. Our horses, which were suffering very much from heat, confinement, and seasickness, were first taken out and allowed to roam and roll on the sand. Our wagons had been all taken to pieces, and with our other goods stored in the hold, but we finally got all ashore and pitched our camps about a mile from the wharf. The night being warm and pleasant, I did not pitch my tent (it was only a little shelter tent anyhow), but slept on the sand.

I learned from Captain Whiting this evening that our Lieutenant Colonel Marsh had been appointed colonel of a new regiment. If such is the case, it is a good thing for him and the new regiment, but bad for us and our old regiment.

On March 20th, all of our companies, except for Companies L and M, are ordered to go forty miles up the bay and there to land and go off on some kind of a raid, we to remain here until further orders. The country about here does not seem very attractive, but it is out of the city, and that is worth a good deal.

Today Adjutant Moore and I made a little tour of observation, visiting in turn the lighthouse, Fort Barrancas, the Redoubt, and the navy yard. The lighthouse is near the entrance to the harbor and is built of brick; the top, which is 150 feet above the sea, is reached by a circular iron stairway of 187 steps. The lantern, which is about six feet in diameter, is made of plate glass set in copper frames or sashes. The lamp is very large, and is a beautiful piece of workmanship of glass prisms and brass. Outside the lantern is a light iron balcony. The wind was blowing quite strong, and as we stood on the balcony, we fancied we could feel the tower swing. We could not get much information from the light keeper himself, but his wife was much more communicative and seemed proud of her superior knowledge in lighthouse affairs, and willing to give information to those knowing less than she did. She said on very stormy nights it was necessary for her husband to stay at the top of the tower, for at such times the glass was liable to be broken by the wind or by sea birds flying against it, and as she was afraid at such times to stay below alone, she would frequently spend the night up there with him. She also told how a soldier once went out on the balcony, and on looking down became so frightened that he lost his senses and had to be carried, screaming and struggling, down the long stairs; and also how a daring, foolhardy soldier once climbed to the top on the lightning rod.

Fort Barrancas and the Redoubt are both casemated forts, built of brick. Both are bombproof, being built principally underground with subterranean passages. The quarters for the garrison are underground, as are also the magazines and storehouses. At Fort Barrancas, I accidently came upon the chaplain, who had his office and quarters in one of the magazines of the fort. He said he was engaged in collecting and compiling a history of the old fort, which was built many years ago by the Spaniards. The bricks of which it is built were doubtless brought from Spain.

On the extreme western end of the Santa Rosa Island, at the entrance to the harbor, stands Fort Pickens, and opposite it, on a small bar or reef, are the ruins of Fort McRee. At the commencement of the war all the forts here except Fort Pickens were besieged by the rebels. Lieutenant Slemmer, then commanding Fort Pickens, refused to surrender, and a bombardment ensued in which Fort McRee was nearly destroyed. Fort Pickens was badly battered, but did not surrender. It is now being repaired. At the navy yard, a few buildings are yet in good condition, but the most of the works and quarters were destroyed by the rebels when they evacuated.

There are two little towns here near the navy yard, Warrington and Woolsey, both very small places inhabited by fishermen and their families, whose general reputation is as unsavory as the smell arising from the great heaps of decaying fish heads in the streets of the two villages. Barrancas, a little farther from the shore, is better and cleaner.

Our old friend, General Asboth, the "Flying Dutchman" of Columbus, is here in command of the post. All the forts here and the navy yard are garrisoned by negro troops.

I tried my luck fishing again today, March 22nd, but with the usual results, caught nothing, got tired, and threw my line into the water. As a fisherman, I appear to be a lamentable failure. After a bath in the harbor, I went up to call on General Asboth. He said he was glad to have me with him again and expressed the hope that we might have some of our old-time rides together again. I told him I had lost my best horses and was not so well mounted as I was at Columbus, but I would try to keep up with the procession.

Heavy cannonading has been heard today in the direction of Mobile, which indicates that the ball has opened there and that another of the rebel strongholds will soon be ours. From the looks of things now, Mobile must be nearly the last place that will require bombarding.

On Friday, March 24th, I crossed the harbor in a fisherman's boat in company with Adjutant Moore and Sergeant Paris of my company and visited Fort Pickens. The fort is garrisoned by the 25th United States Colored Troops, the major of that regiment being in command. We were shown over the fort by the officer of the day. The fort is built of brick, with bombproof casemates. It has capacity for over 200 guns, but there are only eighty-seven guns and two mortars at present in position. Workmen are now engaged in building the foundation for a 200 lb. barbette gun. The fort was considerably damaged by the rebel bombardment, but the breaches have been nearly all repaired. I did not learn the dimensions of the fort, but it is very large, being only second in size and strength to Fort Monroe. I did not find the officers here very entertaining; courtesy toward visiting officers seems to have been omitted from their military education. I was obliged to rely solely on my own observations, and their reticence to give me any information must account for my brief description of this very important and interesting fort. After strolling around a while, I thanked the officer of the day for his polite attendance on us, regretting that we had caused him so much apparent trouble and annoyance, and passed out over the drawbridge, and crossed the bay with "Sandy" in his fast sailing little dispatch boat.

On Sunday morning, March 26th, after company inspection, Captain Musser, Adjutant Moore, and I crossed over in "Black Charley's" fishing boat to Santa Rosa Island in search of shells. Landing at the wharf, we crossed over to the south side of the island and walked two or three miles up the beach, but could find nothing but small common shells; the large and fine ones are picked up by the soldiers at the fort as fast as they are washed ashore. A good opportunity presenting here, we took a bath in the surf, which breaks with great force on the south side of the island. It was my first experience in the surf. I managed to get out through the breakers and found very easy and pleasant swimming in the deep water beyond, but on coming ashore I was thrown with such force on the beach that I could not stand up nor walk for a while.

A good many porpoises were swimming about, and two came so near the shore that I shot them with my revolver. From the way they floundered about and lashed the water with their tails, the bullets must have stung them, but probably did no very serious injury. The porpoises seemed to be playing in the water, and on coming to the surface, would roll over and utter snorts not unlike the noise made by young horses at play. On the north side of the island, we found a dead porpoise that had been washed up on the sand; it seemed to be about as large as a horse.

When we crossed over to the island, the water was very rough and our little boat danced like a cork. Dr. Jones started to go with us, but on seeing the waves running so high, said his professional services were too valuable to the sick soldiers to permit him to take any such rash chance and went back to camp.

It is provoking to hear the bombarding at Mobile, and we here with so little to do. If we had been allowed to start as soon as we landed, we could easily have overtaken the slow-marching infantry and heavy artillery. I have always wanted to be at the last ditch when the dying came off. If there was more life and "get there" at regimental headquarters, I don't think we would be here in the rear. Nine companies were sent off on a raid soon after arriving here, under command of a major, while the colonel was ordered to remain here with three companies.

This afternoon, I started with Captain Musser, Lieutenant Garrett, and several soldiers, to go to Fort McRee, but could not cross the bayou between the mainland and the fort on account of the breakers, which were running very high, and on account of the rising tide, we could find no shells on the shore; but our trip was not altogether without interest, and Lieutenant Garrett furnished entertainment for the party, which to some extent recompensed us for our disappointment. First, he got himself and horse into a quicksand bed and had to be hauled out. He then ran foul of a big rattlesnake, which we all joined in killing, and finally, rode off a bank into about six feet of water, from which it required our combined efforts to pull him and his horse. We then told him we thought this thing had gone far enough, and that our time was too valuable to the government to be wasted in taking care of him and getting him out of trouble, and if he couldn't take better care of himself, we would consider it our duty, and an act of kindness to his family and friends, to tie him up in some safe place until we were ready to return to camp. We then went into the surf and enjoyed a delightful, though very rough, bath. The surf, by reason of a late storm at sea and the rising tide, was very rough, the waves breaking from six to eight feet high. I got such a terrible pounding and swallowed so much saltwater that I was sore and sick all night.

On March 29th, I went up to the mouth of the Escambia River, twenty-one miles, to meet General Asboth, who had gone up on the steamer *Matamora* to try to get her over the bar at the mouth of the river with supplies for General Steele's army.[10] The boat could not get over, but stuck fast on the bar, so General Asboth came ashore and returned with me to camp. If the boat could have passed over the bar, I was to have gone with a part of the escort on to General Steele, to notify him to send his wagons to the river. So here again the fates have played against me. One foot more of water on that sand bar would have sent me booming to Mobile, and I would have been there in time to participate in the fall and capture of that great stronghold.

The way to the mouth of Escambia River runs through level pine forests. The sand is dry and loose and is cut up and tunneled by "salamanders," a kind of gopher or ground mouse. These salamander holes and frequent "sink holes" of quicksand render travel difficult and somewhat dangerous. I saw many tracks of wild turkeys, but saw only one small flock of the birds. All the houses along our line of march were deserted.

About two or three miles from camp we crossed Bayou Grande. The bayou is very deep, but a sandbar has formed at its mouth on which we can cross, with a guide. The bar is in the form of a half-circle, the bend of the arc running far out into the bay. The bar is about one mile in length, and the water in it, when the tide is out, is not more than two feet deep. We got over all right, going up, but when we reached the bar on our return, which was after dark, the tide was rising and flowing very swiftly. We were getting along all right, and had passed the middle of the bar, when my horse became frightened at something floating on the water and began to rear and plunge. As I was riding with my stirrups crossed in front of me and holding my feet up out of the water, I had little or no control over him. After making several ugly plunges, he threw his head up and struck me over the left eye, knocking me perfectly limber. I remember seeing about a million of stars (there may have been a few more, I didn't stop to count), letting go all holds, and pitching head first into the water. The shock of the cold water revived me, and I was on my feet in an instant. My horse was soon caught, but could not be brought near me in the water. Hearing the splash, the general, who was riding just ahead of me, turned back, and seeing me in the water, exclaimed in his peculiar fractured English, "Vy my tear captain, do you like to walk better as to ride?" "No, General, but my horse wanted to have his own way, and as I don't understand the navigation of a horse at sea, I got off to go ashore." The weight of my arms, my top boots full of water, and the force of the tide, made it impossible for me to walk. A soldier offered to dismount and give me his horse, but I told him he could not walk in the water any better than I could, and neither could I mount behind him. So, with a soldier on either side holding my hands, I was walked ashore, where I emptied my boots and remounted my horse.

At the navy yard, the general stopped to see the commandant, and I had to wait an hour in my wet clothes and became very cold. When the general came out he told me he had just received news of a hard battle at or near Mobile, that the rebels had come out of their works and given battle in the field, with heavy loss on both sides and not much gain to either, and that the rebels had retired to their works. He also said that a French ironclad in Mobile Bay had attempted or threatened to oppose the further advance of our fleet. If it was an English war vessel, I would be more inclined to believe the commander was acting under instructions, but the French are and always have been our friends, and I must think if the commander of a French vessel has taken sides with the rebels, he has done so on his own responsibility. The old general seemed rather pleased at the prospect, however faint, of a war with France, and was ready to commence killing Frenchmen on sight.[11]

Our Lieutenant Colonel Marsh, to the surprise of everyone, arrived in camp this morning, March 31st, from his leave of absence. We had heard that he had been appointed colonel of a new regiment. He is most welcome and all are glad to see him back again. He says the Copperheads at home are all torn up the back and generally discouraged on account of the steady advance of our armies and the near and certain final success of the Union cause.

I have drawn good tents and have a very pretty and comfortable camp in a grove of small pines near a small stream or bayou of good water. My quarters are now some three or four miles from the beach, but the roar of the surf can be plainly heard at night, which mingling with the sighing of the pines, makes a strange, weird, and ghostly sound.

General Asboth visited my camp today. He asked me if I wanted to go to sea again on horseback and seemed to enjoy my little mishap very much. The old man is almost helpless by reason of a wound in his left arm, received some months ago, I do not remember in what action, but he is as fierce a rider as ever.[12]

I was on a board of survey yesterday with Captain White, 4th Tennessee Cavalry, and Lieutenant Kirby of our regiment, to decide the responsibility for the loss of a box of quartermaster's stores for which Captain Jones of our regiment was responsible. Under the circumstances, we decided that Captain Jones was responsible for the loss, and that he could by proper care have prevented it. The captain took it for granted we would clear him, and when the papers were returned to him, he swore and blustered a good deal and declared it was a clear case of conspiracy to ruin him. But he got over it in time and settled with the next paymaster for his carelessness.

My little rebel horse "Creole" that I brought from Baton Rouge had become so apparently tame and docile that I had somewhat relaxed my accustomed vigilance while riding him, and today he took advantage of my confidence. While riding through the village of Warrington, a little dog rushed yelping at his heels, and without stopping to inquire the cause of the little disturbance, nor the consequences of his own improper conduct, he just humped himself and bucked me over his head onto the sand and then, turning around, kicked at me. I tried to catch the little dog for the purpose of explaining to him the difference between impulse and reason, but he thought he saw blood in my eye and took refuge under a house, where it was so dark I could not see to shoot him. Lieutenant Kirby, with whom I was riding, caught my horse and had a good laugh at my expense.

On duty today, April 2nd, as field officer of the day. My guard today is a very mixed outfit, being made up of detachments from the 1st Florida Cavalry, 2nd Maine Cavalry (dismounted), and 25th U.S.C.T. The parade at guard mount looked very much like a burlesque at a variety theater. The darkies are fairly drilled and went through the evolutions pretty well, but the awkward maneuvers of the others would have made old Falstaff tired and sorry he had learned the trade. The 1st Florida Cavalry is made up of deserters from the rebel army, refugee tar heels, and scalawags generally. They say, "We uns has jined you uns kase the Confederates wouldn't let we uns live to home." There may be some truth in their statement, but I think they are with us for the sake of something to eat and clothes to wear. The 2nd Maine are pretty good soldiers, but having no horses, are doing infantry duty. I don't know why they have been dismounted. There must have been some good reason for it.

The 25th U.S.C.T. is a Pennsylvania regiment made up mostly of free negroes, many being from the city of Philadelphia.[13] They are an intelligent lot of fellows, and good soldiers, but like all of their class, are extremely superstitious. One of the infantry picket posts is on the shore of Bayou Grande at a point where are the ruins of an old bridge, called "Bragg's Bridge" because General Bragg (rebel) destroyed it when he retired from Barrancas. Nothing remains of the bridge except the burnt tops of the piles. The negroes stationed at this post declare that nearly every night a phantom cavalry company is heard crossing the old bridge. Of course, they cannot see the ghosts, but can distinctly hear the tramp of the horses on the planks and the rattle of the spirit soldiers' sabers. No darkey on the reserve at that post can be caught napping for an hour before and after midnight; all are wide-awake and on the qui vive. I have frequently, when on field duty, endeavored to hear the sounds the darkies declare they often hear, but have never been able to do so. I always make it a point to visit this post as near midnight as possible, hoping to learn something of these mysterious noises. If the guard reported, "Deys done crossed," I knew it would be of no use to wait, for spooks cross only once in a night. But if they had not been heard when I reached the post, I would wait until after one o'clock, but no ghosts ever crossed while I was present.

If I ridiculed the darkies' belief in spooks and told them they had heard only owls or coons in the trees or alligators in the bayou, they would be horrified at my wicked unbelief in spirits and most solemnly declare, "Fore God, Captain, we'se done heard them cross that old bridge many times." "But boys, there are no planks on the bridge, how can horses walk on those few burnt piles?" "Spirit horses don't need no real planks, sir, they crosses on a spirit bridge." They must have heard some unusual sounds, for different men all told the same story, but what the sounds were, I could not find out. Other officers have had the same experience, but none ever heard the midnight march of the phantom troopers.

During the day of April 3rd, I called at General Asboth's headquarters and there met several officers of the war steamer *Richmond*, just from Mobile, who reported the loss of two gunboats, sunk by torpedoes in Mobile Bay. They say the harbor, as well as the land around Mobile, is full of torpedoes. Mobile is not yet taken, but these officers thought the defense could hold out but a few days longer. Even the alligators were deserting the rebels and were assisting our fleet by exploding torpedoes in the bay. Heavy firing has been heard all day from Mobile.

April 5th. The bombing yesterday and last night was fiercer than ever. Mobile must be experiencing a pretty hot time. The strongest defenses are not at the city of Mobile, but are at Fort Blakely on the opposite side of the bay, and in the harbor. A few days ago, I made another attempt to reach old Fort McRee, but found the bayou too rough to cross on horseback. I think I shall not try to get there again unless in a boat.

I rode up to Gun Boat Point and called on Lieutenant Powers of the 25th U.S.C.T. He was quite fresh from Pennsylvania and had seen very little service. He was quite enthusiastic over the darkies, and his conversation was confined chiefly to that subject. It is an acknowledged fact by all who have seen or had any experience with them that "the colored troops fought nobly," and that they make very good soldiers. I think well of them myself, and was at one time anxious to raise and command a regiment of them, but I don't approve of making pets and associates of them, nor can I think they are better or entitled to more consideration than white soldiers. Lieutenant Powers may be excusable on account of his youth and inexperience, and possibly previous association, but if he serves long enough with his highly aromatic "sogers," he may find a dividing line more agreeable.

On returning from Santa Rosa Island this evening, April 6th, I found Colonel Marsh had gone out on a scout with three days' rations, which leaves me in command of the cavalry camp during his absence.

April 7th. My birthday, am 27 years old.

April 8th. Colonel Marsh returned tonight with a herd of beef cattle from Black Water River.

April 10. Am on duty as regimental officer of the day. We have glorious news today, Richmond and Petersburg are ours, and Grant is in hot pursuit of Lee, and Spanish Fort near Blakely is evacuated. Very little bombing has been heard today.

Went up to Pensacola today, April 11th, with Colonel Marsh. The town of Pensacola is situated on the west side of the bay, about seven miles above Barrancas, and has evidently been quite a bright and busy little town in its day, but it is now almost deserted and in ruins. I saw no shops nor stores, nor evidence of trade nor business of any kind, but an old Spanish lady, at whose house I stopped a few moments, said the town was experiencing quite a boom at present, and that its population had largely increased, in fact nearly doubled, during the last few weeks by the arrival of several refugee families and deserters from the rebel army, and that there are now about twenty families in the town. The crossing of Bayou Grande today was not marked by any incident or accident of interest. The bombing has recommenced and has been very heavy all day.

A salute of 100 guns, fifty at Fort Pickens and fifty at Fort Barrancas, were fired at noon today, April 12th, in honor of our late victories in Virginia and Alabama. No bombing has been heard today, and there is a rumor in camp tonight that Mobile has surrendered.

The paymaster has evidently lost track of us, as we have seen nothing of him for six months. We have all lent to and borrowed from each other until I don't believe there is a dollar in camp. I can draw rations from the commissary, when he has them, but he is just now out of many things, including candles and tobacco. I managed to make a raise of a little tobacco today, and when that is gone, I suppose I will have to reform for a while, as there is none raised in this country. We can always get tobacco on the gunboats for cash, but they do not give credit to soldiers. For want of a candle, I am writing my notes tonight by the light(?) of a very primitive style of lamp, made of a tin cup filled with bacon grease, in which a twisted rag sputters, smokes, and stinks. It only seems to make the darkness a little more visible.

This is the worst country to forage in we have yet seen. Its only products, so far as I can discover, are fish, charcoal, and "tar pitch and turpentine." We consume a good many fish and oysters, but have not been able to find any use for the other products. We see many vessels passing, but very few touch here and our mails are very irregular.

On making grand rounds as field officer of the day on April 13th, I found the officer in charge of the left of the picket line either very ignorant or very neglectful of his duty. He did not turn out his guard for grand rounds in the day, but remained sitting in the guard tent, and was not present when his guard turned out at night. I asked for him and the corporal said he was in the guard tent with his wife(?). As I approached the tent for the purpose of routing him out, he sauntered out without arms or uniform. As I did not wish to prefer charges against him, for I knew a court martial would dishonorably dismiss him from the service, I reported him verbally to General Asboth's adjutant, and I think the old general will give him some hints on guard duty that he will never forget.

General Asboth has issued a congratulatory order confirming the report of the surrender of Richmond and Petersburg, and the capture of Spanish Fort and the evacuation of Mobile. The "Confederacy" is becoming a very small affair.

There is a rumor in camp today, April 16th, that the rebel general R. E. Lee has surrendered to General Grant, with 55,000 troops. Although such an event has long been anticipated, it seems almost too good to be true.

Good and glad news is coming in thick and fast. It is reported today, April 18th, that Johnston and Beauregard have surrendered to Sherman and that Galveston, Texas, is evacuated. The report of Lee's surrender is confirmed, also that Lee has issued a proclamation, warning all Confederate troops east of the Mississippi River to lay down their arms and return to their homes. This virtually closes the war, and the great object for which we have worked and fought for nearly four long years, and for which so many thousands have died, is at last accomplished. The Union has been preserved. Cannons are being fired from all the forts and gunboats, and there is great rejoicing in all the camps.

April 22nd. The day of our rejoicing has been brief and is followed by one of gloom and sorrow. General Asboth has just returned from Mobile with the sad intelligence of the death by assassination of President Lincoln and Secretary of War Seward on the 14th instant.[14] I had just come in from my first grand round, being field officer of the day, and was in my tent when I heard a disturbance in camp and a voice shouting, "Kill the damned rebel." Looking out, I saw a crowd of soldiers in front of my tent struggling and seemingly greatly excited. Three or four had hold of one man, whom they were shaking and pounding, while others were crying, "Kill him, hang him!" I rushed into the crowd just in time to prevent a soldier from running the man through with a saber. On demanding the cause of the disturbance, several soldiers answered at once, "The President is killed and this fellow says he is glad of it." That was the first I knew of the death of the President. The soldier, who did not belong to my company, appealed to me for protection, and I sent him under guard to the provost marshal. On turning to reenter my tent,

I was met by an orderly with a verbal message from General Asboth, stating that the President and Secretary of State had been assassinated.

The camps are very quiet, but the feeling amongst the soldiers is sadly deep and intense. I can learn no particulars at headquarters. All we know is the dreadful deed has been done and our shouts of victory have given place to tears of sorrow.

Official orders announcing the deaths of the President and Secretary of State were received early this morning, April 23rd, and read at roll call. I never saw men so deeply affected, and when I read the order, although all were prepared to hear it, many rough, wicked men shed tears and sobbed like children. I cannot describe my own feelings, nor those of the soldiers. Instead of feelings and expressions of hatred and revenge that might naturally be expected, a feeling of quiet, dead gloom seems to have settled on all. The camps, which for several nights have been full of lights and sounds of music and rejoicing, are tonight dark and quiet. Some of my men said to me today, "Of course, you could not do otherwise than protect that fellow yesterday, but if you had been one minute later, he would have needed a burying squad instead of a guard."

During the day, half-hour guns were fired from all the forts and gunboats and minute guns from noon to one o'clock. All flags on the forts and vessels were at half-mast, as was also the guidon in front of my tent.

We are in receipt of the very welcome orders to march at daylight tomorrow morning, April 28th. I packed up a jar of small fishes, snakes, lizards, and scorpions that I had collected here for my brother Chan, and some seashells in a cartridge packing box, and sent it by express to my father in Quincy. During the day I had occasion to visit Fort Pickens to turn over some surplus ordnance stores, and while there I was offered a live starfish, the first I had ever seen. But as I had no way of keeping it, and had sent off my box of specimens, I was obliged to decline it.

Leaving Barrancas about seven o'clock the morning of the 28th, we crossed Bayou Grande at Gun Boat Point, and there leaving the bay, marched westward through the pine forests. About ten miles from Barrancas, we struck the trail of General Steele's army, and a wide and well-marked trail it was. The heavy wagons and artillery had cut deep into the sand, and the turpentine trees had been fired. It was the burning of these turpentine trees that made the heavy smoke we saw from the ship. We marched about thirty miles and camped near a small spring. The night being warm and fair, we did not pitch our tents.

The next morning, we crossed three small streams, branches of "Piney Woods Barrens," and at night camped at a fine large spring where there was good grass. The streams crossed this day were deep, but very clear; the water seemed to possess peculiar magnifying powers, so that it was quite impossible to tell how deep it really was by looking into it. We had a little trouble crossing the teams at one of the streams, and wishing to get ahead of the team in the creek, I went a few steps above the ford to cross. A soldier called out, "Look out Cap, that water's deep." My horse seemed to think so, too, and hesitated to go in, but on looking down, I could plainly see the bottom and did not think it was more than about eighteen inches deep, and the bank was about that high above the water, so spurring my horse, he plunged into not less than four feet of cold water. Fortunately, my horse did not fall down and I escaped with only a good splashing.

The next day, Sunday, April 30th, we passed through an old rebel camp at Canoe Station on the Mobile and Great Western Railroad, and camped twenty-seven miles from Fort Blakely. We doubled guards and I went on picket with my whole company.

We reached Fort Blakely about the middle of the afternoon the next day and went into camp. This place is very strongly fortified, in many respects resembling Fort Pillow, Tennessee. I did not stay here long enough to see much of the place, as we crossed the bay the next day to Mobile.

I went over on the little steamboat *Crawford* that used to ply between Columbus and Cairo. A channel had been cleared of torpedoes and was marked by buoys. We reached Mobile about sundown and camped on Government Street about one mile from the bay.

The next day we moved camp to Three Mile Creek, about two miles north from the city. I here found a paymaster with a big box full of money and was paid for six months, to February 29th, receiving, after deducting my commissary account, $808.00, enough to keep the camp pot boiling for another six months.

Today terminates my three years' service as captain of Company L, counting from the date of my commission, May 6th, 1862. I accordingly made application to Lieutenant Baker, A.C.M. at Mobile, to be mustered out by reason of expiration of term of service. After considerable bluster and display of pretended authority, which came very near causing a personal rupture between us, he finally concluded that he would be safe in mustering me out on the colonel's certificate that my three years as captain had expired. This was altogether unnecessary unless he had reason to believe that my commission from Governor Yates of Illinois was a forgery. However, it would be very little trouble to me to get the required certificate and return to the mustering office in the morning, and I came just that near missing the easiest, pleasantest, and only really enjoyable part of my whole service.

Feeling pretty tired on returning to camp, I laid down in the shade of a tree with my mind fully made up to get the colonel's certificate in the morning, be mustered out, and go home. I had not been in camp more than an hour when an order came for an officer to go to East Pascagoula, and to report immediately to General Veatch, commanding District of Mobile, for orders.[15] As I happened, by chance, to be the only officer in camp at that moment, all the others having gone to the city, the colonel asked me if I would go. I reflected a moment to myself: "The war is nearly over. I will soon be discharged anyhow; if I can get a good detail away from the regiment, I would rather stay a little longer and see it out. If I don't like the duty, I can at any time demand my discharge." I said, "Yes, I'll go."

In a few minutes, I reported for duty to General Veatch. At headquarters, I met Captain Sorenson of the 27th Wisconsin Infantry, also under orders for East Pascagoula with seventy men. Being the ranking officer, I was ordered to command the expedition and was given an order at the quartermaster for seven teams. I drew ten days' rations and was soon ready to start early the next morning. My orders from General Veatch were to make my headquarters at East Pascagoula, repair and guard the telegraph line, repair bridges and piers, and protect all good citizens and their property. In addition to my written instructions, the general told me privately that he had reason to believe that Jeff Davis, who had left Richmond, might reach the Gulf Coast and endeavor to escape in a small boat to Cuba, and of course I needed no special orders to look out for him and catch him if I could. I thought the capture of the "ex president" would certainly be a very satisfactory finale to my long, though not very eventful, career as a soldier. I knew that Jeff Davis would, of course, be caught, and why should not I be the lucky one to catch him?

I struck camp and moved out with forty men (twenty-six of Co. L, and fourteen of Co. K) just as the sun was rising the next morning, May 7th. On my way out of the city, I met General Veatch, who was out for an early ride, and who shook hands with me and wished me success.

I had for a guide a city police officer, formerly a rebel soldier, Mr. Empries, a name I always knew by sight, but could never remember. I found Captain Sorenson ready with his command at his camp, two miles out on the shell road. Marching out on the telegraph road, we crossed Ellis Creek at noon, where we halted two hours to repair the bridge and eat dinner, and at 4pm camped at Mrs. Baker's farm, eighteen miles from Mobile. It was a very short day's march for us, but about as much as the infantry could do. We made an early start the next morning and reached Franklin Creek at noon, where we halted two hours. After eating my luncheon, I threw my hat between the forked roots of an old stump and, using it for a pillow, caught a few minutes' sleep. On getting up and picking up my hat, I was not a little startled to see curled up between the roots of the stump under my hat a large rattlesnake, which I massacred.

At Nine Mile Creek, nine miles from East Pascagoula, I found the bridge gone and the corduroy road much broken, but as the weather looked stormy, I decided to push on and try to reach our journey's end before night. I found a good ford about a mile above the old bridge, and after seeing the soldiers and teams all over,

I galloped ahead with my guide and three men to find a camp. Reaching East Pascagoula about 5pm, I found a large abandoned hotel on the beach, which I decided to occupy. The cavalry got in just after dark, and the infantry about an hour later, in the midst of a heavy storm of wind and rain. Early next morning, May 8th, I reported to General Veatch by telegraph and sent Sergeant Ralph to Mobile with a written report.

We have splendid quarters here. The hotel is clean and in good condition. It has accommodations for about 300 guests, and as my little command consists of only 110 men and four officers, we have room enough and to spare. The house is, of course, entirely empty, there being no furniture of any kind in it. But there being plenty of loose lumber here, the men will soon refurnish the house. I occupy the hotel office for my headquarters. The cavalry are quartered on the first floor, and the infantry in the second story. The hotel stands on the beach and about 200 yards from the water. This has doubtless been a favorite seaside resort, and the village of East Pascagoula has evidently been a very pretty and attractive place, but it now looks very "faded and gone." A line of islands about ten miles distant breaks the force of the winds and waves from the Gulf so that there is no surf here and the water in Mississippi Sound is usually smooth.

Having no use for so many teams, I sent six of them back to Mobile in charge of Sergeant Patton and sent Lieutenant Jolly with a fatigue party and load of lumber to make a bridge over Nine Mile Creek. I also commenced work repairing the pier head. The wharf, which extends out into the sound about a mile, I found in good condition, but the floor of the pier head had been broken up and washed away.

This afternoon, I rode out to Griffin's Mill, six miles up the Pascagoula River, with Captain Yates of the gunboat *Jackson,* which is lying at anchor off this place, and after our return dined with Captain Yates on board his vessel, where I stayed all night.

There being now no war, nor enemies, I keep out no pickets and keep only one sentinel on duty at camp. But I keep scouts out along the beach to welcome the possible coming of the "ex president."

On May 10th, I went with a little party of ladies from the village to Horn Island, on the *Jackson.* On the island, I met Colonel Boswell, late of the army, and his wife, where the colonel is engaged in making turpentine. After a walk across the island, about a half-mile, we dined on board the *Jackson* and I returned to camp about nine o'clock.

Early Sunday morning, May 14th, the steamer *Kate Dale* touched here, landing ten days' rations and forage and a light mail for this post. General Dick Taylor, the last survivor of the Confederacy, surrendered to General Canby at Mobile last week.[16]

I rode this afternoon out to Franklin Creek, thirteen miles, with Captain Sorenson, and on Monday, May 15th, participated in another picnic on board the *Jackson*, where I spent the night. During the night, the steamer *General Banks* from Mobile put several ladies on the gunboat, and the next morning we all came ashore and rode horseback.

On May 16th, I received news by telegraph that Jeff Davis and staff had been captured near Macon, Georgia, on the 10th instant by Colonel Wilson. The "last ditch" has been reached at last, and the sun of the Confederacy has gone down forever. The rebels have fought long and well, with courage, bravery, and sacrifice worthy of a better cause, but "right the day has won."

It is needless to particularize day by day. Ever since the occupation of East Pascagoula by my little garrison, it has been one round of pleasure and frolic. It has been a season of rest and recreation after a long, hard, and often disagreeable service of nearly four years, and the same may be said for the officers of the gunboat. Scarcely a day passes that some of the naval officers are not on shore for a horseback ride to the country with the girls. The girls here have no horses, but all have saddles that fit my cavalry horses remarkably well. As the navy officers live better on board than we do in camp, I agreed with them if they would furnish the dinner, I would furnish the horses, so it has been little else than feasting and flirting on board, and riding and flirting on shore.

Since the reported capture of Jeff Davis, I have not sent out any patrols, and the only military duties required of my men are to attend roll calls, Sunday inspections, and a guard at headquarters. The men put in the most of their time fishing, raking oysters, and bathing. They catch great numbers of very fine fish, eels, and oysters.

Some time ago I found an oyster boat in good condition, for which Captain Yates gave me a mast and sail, and I have had a great deal of pleasure sailing on the sound and up the river. On one occasion, I was sailing some two or three miles from shore with a young boy. In passing over an oyster bed, the centerboard touched bottom, and in attempting to raise it, the boy broke the line. There was little or no wind blowing, and at every rise and fall of the waves, the board struck the hard oyster bed, threatening at every bump to knock the bottom out of the boat. I had no oars and could not get off the oyster bed, and I was sure if the tide was falling, my boat would soon go to smash. So to be prepared for the shock when it should come, I took off my coat and boots and directed the boy to do the same. I did not expect to swim to the shore, but to hang to the wreck until assistance could reach us from the gunboat. The poor boy began to cry and said he never could swim to the shore, and he just knew the sharks would eat us up in five minutes. I had seen many sharks while sailing on the sound, and I did not know but that there was one then under my boat waiting for dinner. However, my boat did not go to wreck, nor did the sharks get their dinner, but after bumping around it seemed to me a very long time, a light breeze struck us, and we were soon safe on shore.

One of our favorite resorts is a fruit garden kept by an old Spanish lady, where we get delicious mulberries and pure, rich cream. Many of the citizens about here are very poor and without means of subsistence. When I reported their condition to General Veatch, he sent me a lot of corn for distribution, which I have been giving out to all who apply for it. Amongst the applicants are a good many returned rebel soldiers.

Lee's and Taylor's men are coming home, and the country is full of returned rebel soldiers who, with a few exceptions, are orderly and well-behaved. I have had to arrest a few lawless ones, but have released them on their promises of future good behavior. Their offenses were light, generally for quarreling or fighting amongst themselves. Recently, I arrested two young men for stealing, and General Veatch telegraphed me to send them to Mobile. As a vessel was then at the wharf bound for Mobile, I concluded to go with them myself. The boys had been home but a few days and were having a good time with their sweethearts, and when arrested, the girls declared they would go with them to headquarters or to prison. I told the girls I could not take them as prisoners, and I certainly should not pay their fare as passengers, but they managed somehow to raise money enough to pay their fares and went along. Notwithstanding I had been supplying them with food for several weeks, these girls never ceased to "make faces" at me, and call me all the hard names they knew, and they were well up in hard names, and abused me in every possible way from the time we went on board the steamer until we reached the provost marshal's office in Mobile. I only laughed at and teased them and told them when they got back home to come to camp and I would give them more corn to brace up on for the next arrest I might have to make.

A terrible explosion of powder had occurred in Mobile two days before my visit. I never witnessed such a scene of perfect and complete destruction. Eight solid blocks of heavy brick buildings were blown completely down, and not a house within a mile of the explosion escaped some damage. Between 200 and 300 people were killed, who could be accounted for, but it was supposed the number of lives lost would not fall far short of 600 or 800. A good many soldiers on duty at the storehouses were killed, but the great majority of those lost were negroes, refugees, and stragglers from the rebel army and of whom no record was kept. A great number of horses and mules were also lost, as well as a vast amount of government and captured property of all kinds that was stored in the large warehouses in that part of the city, and several vessels lying at the wharf were sunk or blown to pieces. Not less than 100 tons of powder, in barrels, shells, and cartridges exploded.[17]

When I visited the scene on Sunday morning, May 28th (the explosion occurred Thursday afternoon), dead bodies and fragments of bodies were being removed as fast as they could be found. The weather was very hot and the smell from the dead bodies was almost unbearable. As the fire was still burning and shells frequently exploding, it was difficult and dangerous for workmen to labor in or near the ruins. No particulars of the cause of the explosion could be learned, as no one who was present at the time lived to tell of it. During the short time I was at the ruins, I saw many bodies burned and crushed beyond all possible recognition, brought out and laid in the streets. I was glad to get away from the city, and took the first steamer back to camp.

On the 6th of June, I was ordered by telegraph from General Andrews to rejoin my regiment at New Orleans.[18] I accordingly turned over my command and all government property in my charge to Captain Sorenson, and the next day embarked with my company in the steamer *Iberville* for New Orleans.

On reporting at headquarters in New Orleans, I learned that my regiment had gone up to Vicksburg, and I was ordered to proceed at once to that place. A boat was then waiting to take me, and I had a great deal to do in a very short time, and experienced a repetition of my former annoyance with the citizen clerks and government storekeepers. I had both ordnance and quartermaster stores to turn over, and the different storehouses were as far apart as they could be in a city of the size of New Orleans. I hired a cab by the hour and paid the driver double fare to put me through on double-quick time. I finally got my papers all signed and my business closed up.

As I was passing a photograph gallery, I thought I would like to have my picture taken before leaving the South, and went in. A lady was just sitting down to the camera, and the artist asked me to wait, or call again. I told him I could do neither and turned to go out, when the lady kindly offered me her seat, saying she was in no such hurry as I seemed to be in. I told the artist I wanted one dozen cards and would call for them in one hour, and when I called for them in an hour they were ready, and in a few minutes more I was on the steamer and booming up the Mississippi River towards home.

I wished very much to stop at Baton Rouge and see some of my old acquaintances there, but the boat was under orders to proceed directly to Vicksburg, and we passed Baton Rouge in the night. At Vicksburg, I found the regiment under orders to go up Red River. The other officers of the regiment, who all knew my time had expired, wanted me to go with them, but I thought I knew what a trip up Red River meant: lots of hard, disagreeable work and camping in the swamps. The war was over and the rebel armies disbanded and sent home, and if there were any rebs up in the swamps of Red River, they would soon come down and surrender or go home, if we let them alone.

I was senior captain in the regiment and had been recommended for promotion to major, but there were serious objections, that I could not get over nor around, to remaining longer in the regiment, so the next day, June 14th, I went to the mustering officer at Vicksburg and received my discharge. Returning to camp, I turned over my company and property to Captain Ewart, and bidding my comrade officers and soldiers a last goodbye, I stepped down and out, after just three years and eleven months' service.

I cannot describe my feelings on realizing that I was no longer a soldier, with no command and subject to the orders of no superior officer. I wandered about camp and the old rebel fortifications like one lost, or with no object in view, and I sometimes half regretted that I was free. During the day, I visited the spot where the rebel general Pemberton surrendered to General Grant. The little tree that once stood there was all gone, but with my knife I dug up a piece of its roots as a memento of one of the longest sieges and greatest victories of the war.

As I lay in my tent that night for the last time, my soldier life passed in review with all its ups and downs, its pleasures and perils, in camp and field. My part in the great drama, on which the curtain had been rung down, had been a humble and insignificant one. However I may have failed, I have tried to play rightly the parts assigned me, and my conscience acquits me of any intentional wrong or neglect of duty. I have at all times tried to do my best and to the extent of my abilities, but after all how little I seem to have done, and compared with others, how feeble and insignificant have been my services. While I have required discipline and obedience from those under my command, it has been that I could make a good report to those in authority over me, and I look back with pride to the record of Delano's Dragoons and shall ever feel that it was an honor to have served with men so good and true.

In the foregoing diary I have endeavored to note some of the principal and more interesting scenes and events I have witnessed and experienced. Many of the incidents mentioned may seem trivial and of no consequence, and others, perhaps, had better have been omitted, but I have noted them down to illustrate the ever-changing daily life of a volunteer soldier, more than for any interest or importance that may be attached to them.

I realize that my narrative is very imperfect and incomplete, for many of my notes were taken hurriedly and under inconvenient circumstances, and with no thought at the time of making further use of them, but more than all, due to the fact that I am a very incompetent story writer.

Having now been reduced, or elevated, to the rank of citizenship, I of course thought that I was done with all that pertaining to the army, but the gods of war had not fully endorsed my discharge, and there were further duties and experiences in store for me.

The next day after my discharge, June 15th, I took passage on one of the large steamers (I think it was the *Belle Memphis* or *City of Memphis*) for St. Louis, taking with me my colored servant, Wash Dabney, who had been my constant and faithful attendant ever since I left Island Number 10 in 1862, and two horses. The boat was crowded with returning discharged soldiers, there being about 1,200 on board, but I was fortunate enough to secure a good stateroom. As we steamed up the river, I watched with much interest the many well-known places as we passed them: Memphis, Tiptonville, New Madrid, Island Number 10, Columbus, Fort Holt, Belmont, places that will ever be famous in the history of the war and associated in my mind with many interesting events that can never be forgotten.

Another boat also loaded with discharged soldiers left Cairo about the same time we did, and both boats soon engaged in a race. I did not like the idea of the boats racing with so many lives on board, but thought perhaps one or the other would soon go ahead and the race would be off. I had gone to my stateroom and was reading, when the sergeant of the guard came to me and said he had overhead the mate of our boat say he would beat that other boat or bust his own, and that the soldiers were getting alarmed, and asked me if I could not interfere to prevent perhaps an explosion or other accident, and offered to put his guard under my command. I told him I was out of commission and had really no authority to act. He said he and his guard would obey my orders all the same if I would command them, and all the discharged soldiers on board would stand by me. I had noticed another officer on board in the uniform of a lieutenant colonel, and I went to him and suggested that, in accordance with the wishes of the soldiers, he should take command and stop the race and a possible accident, but he declined to act, as he was not really an officer, but belonged to the sanitary commission or medical staff, I forget which, and knew nothing about commanding soldiers, so I decided to shoulder the responsibility myself.

After going out among the soldiers and receiving their assurances that they would all stand by me in my endeavor to stop the race, I went to the captain of the boat and remonstrated against his endangering the lives of so many men by racing, at which he insolently replied that he was the commander of the boat and would do as he pleased, and that if I was afraid of getting hurt, I had better go ashore. This made me mad and I told him I was afraid of getting hurt, and that if he did not stop the race at once, I would put him in irons and would put a soldier in the pilot house and another in the engine room to see that the pilot and engineers obeyed my orders, for by General Canby's orders, the ranking military officer on any government transport was really the commanding officer and entitled to respect and obedience.[19]

It was now his turn to get mad, and with an oath he charged me with mutiny and defied me to arrest him. By this time, a large crowd had collected in front of the captain's office, anxious to see the outcome of the affair. I knew I could rely on the soldiers, so directing the sergeant to parade his guard, I ordered him to arrest the captain. He was advancing to do so when the captain said, "Hold on, you're too many for me, I'll give up." He then gave the necessary orders to his crew, and the boat came down to her usual speed, while the other boat passed on. The captain told me later that he wasn't fool enough to buck against armed soldiers, but that he would report me for mutiny to the commander at St. Louis as soon as we reached there. On arriving at St. Louis, I proposed to the captain that we go together to headquarters and make a joint report, but he good-naturedly shook hands with me, saying, "I have no report to make. We were both pretty mad yesterday, but it's all right now. Goodbye."

I changed boats at St. Louis, and in due time reached Quincy. I recognized a number of old familiar faces on the wharf and in the streets, but no one recognized me and I spoke to no one, but rode directly to my father's office, determined that he should be the first person I would speak to. I was not expected home, as I had not written to him since leaving East Pascagoula. He was at his desk and looked up as I entered, but did not know me until I spoke. I wished to neither see nor speak to anyone else now until I had seen mother, so I rode directly out home, about two miles, where my old mother's welcome home to her soldier boy was more than recompense for all that was past.

FRANCIS MOORE, CIVIL WAR VETERAN

"It may not be just the fair thing to remember every incident connected with those four long years of soldiering, but I can't help it. They are so mixed up and interwoven together that the mention of one calls the memory of another. It's the same old story, often told, yet always new."

—Francis Moore in a letter to the Delano's Dragoons Reunion, 1873[1]

After spending four years in camp and field with Francis Moore, the abrupt end of his memoir leaves us wondering just what impact the war had on this young man. He was twenty-three when the war started, twenty-seven when it ended. While other men of his age were marrying and starting families even before the war, Francis began and ended it a bachelor. Married men and fathers might refocus their attention on reestablishing the bonds of family that had been stretched by war, or look to the future of their own households, but Francis found himself returning to his parents in Quincy, not yet established with a livelihood and a family of his own, but certainly no longer a dependent. The experience of departing the army one moment and walking into his father's office the next presents the reader with an appropriate disjuncture, one that Francis must have experienced acutely. How did the events and emotions he related in the pages of his memoir impact the man who arrived back in Quincy in June 1865, unrecognizable even to his own father?

Francis's life after the war was a story of the West, of veteranhood and patriotism, and of civics and service. There is little doubt that the war was the defining event of his life, and although it did not determine the man he would become, it certainly played a role in shaping his identity, his values, and his ambitions. He continually sought to reestablish or rediscover the adventure, sense of duty, and strong bonds of comradeship and patriotism he described in his memoir. Indeed, these may have been values that he wrote backward into his reminiscences of the war as he tried to embody them in his own later life. In any case, the life he lived as a veteran of the Civil War was at least as colorful, challenging, and significant as the experiences he recounted as a soldier.

Faced with uncertain prospects and an undoubtedly troublesome transition to a peacetime life he had not yet established, Francis initially stayed close to what he knew. In a pension deposition, he said: "The first 6 months after my return home, I just staid [*sic*] around my father's home attending to some of his business and my own and settling up my accounts with the government."[2]

Despite his low wartime opinion of Missouri and its citizens, Francis had spent some time in the town of St. Joseph before the war, most likely in courtship of Ms. Henrietta Gyles. He returned to St. Joseph in late 1865 or early 1866 and was married to Henrietta in November 1866. He tried again to work as a carriage maker and in his pension deposition gave the names of a carriage dealer and a saddler and harness maker in St. Joseph as references, possibly his business partners. But Francis became ill within the year and "sold out on that [account], and poor business." Francis returned to Quincy in late 1866—it is unclear whether Henrietta followed him—and in 1867 joined Post #32 of the Grand Army of the Republic. His sister later remembered that Francis worked on their father's farm for two or three years after returning from Missouri, supervising the hands and doing light chores.[3]

In 1870, Francis moved to Omaha, Nebraska, where his brother, Richard, was a physician. In his testimony for Francis's pension file, Richard stated that Francis lived in Omaha for several years in the early 1870s and was unable to work during this time due to health problems related to a kidney ailment. This is contradicted by Francis's own correspondence and his pension deposition, in which he claimed to have worked as a baggage master on the Union Pacific Railroad running between Omaha and Cheyenne, Wyoming Territory. This is in line with the note he made in the memoir about encountering one of his messmates on the Union Pacific in Nebraska. It is not known whether Henrietta accompanied her restless husband during this time.

By the spring of 1871 Francis was in Beloit, Kansas, where he "took up a Government Claim of 160 acres." Henrietta apparently joined him there, and they stayed through 1873, Francis sending postcards and letters to the annual reunions of Delano's Dragoons. He also finally started a family. In late 1870 or early 1871, Henrietta gave birth to son Francis, Jr., followed by daughter Susan in 1872, both of whom were later listed as born in Kansas.

Portrait of Francis Moore after he moved to National City. Probably taken after his election to the city council in 1904. Courtesy of National City Public Library

After the joyful events of the early 1870s, Francis and his family endured a tragic decade. Late in 1873, Francis, Henrietta, and their children moved back to Quincy to attend his ailing father, who died in February 1874. While in Quincy, Francis took a position as manager of the Quincy Opera House. Francis's mother moved to Omaha to live with Richard, while Francis, Henrietta, and their children remained in Quincy. Henrietta died in March 1876 after a ten-day bout of typhoid pneumonia; the next year Francis's mother died, and he buried them both in Quincy. In April 1878, Francis married Mary Bywater of Quincy, who also died suddenly, in childbirth in December of that year. The next June, mourning his mother, his two wives, and an unborn child, Francis clipped a poem, "Rock Me to Sleep, Mother," from the *Quincy Daily News* and underlined several of the melancholy stanzas.[4]

Twice a widower and with two young children, Francis remained in Quincy until 1880 when he again moved west, this time to Otero, New Mexico, where he worked for a short time as a storekeeper for a railroad contractor. It is unclear whether his children accompanied him on the move, but it seems unlikely, given their young ages. He then moved to Ratón, New Mexico, where he worked for six months as a bookkeeper and clerk before moving on to Trinidad, Colorado, where he became the superintendent of a street railway managed by his former employer from Otero.

In 1884, Francis moved to a cattle ranch in the eastern foothills of the Rocky Mountains, twenty-five miles from Trinidad, despite his brother's evaluation that he was a "confirmed invalid." His sister, Lydia, and her husband, Ferdinand, lived nearby, as did his longtime friend and Company L veteran Tom Woodruff. Francis was married for a third time in Denver on March 17, 1884, to Dr. Annie Norton, a homeopathic physician and surgeon from Burlington, Illinois, who had graduated from the Detroit Homeopathic College in 1872.[5] They first met when Annie treated Francis for malarial fever in Quincy in the winter of 1874. She treated him again after the death of his second wife in the spring of 1879. After that, Annie moved to San Francisco for several years, and then to Denver, where she again met and treated Francis. Eight years younger than Francis, Annie was thirty-eight and had never married. Their ages notwithstanding, it was two more years before the birth of their son, Thomas, in 1886.

In 1886, Francis came down with another bout of malarial fever, and he underwent a long period of bed rest. His health began to deteriorate, and he was seriously ill again in 1890. His increasing health troubles must have convinced Francis and Annie to relocate to a larger town. In 1890, Francis, Annie, and young Thomas moved to the town of La Junta, on the southern bank of the Arkansas River in southeastern Colorado. In his pension deposition, Francis called his enterprise there a furniture shop, while the letterhead he ordered said that he dealt in household goods, and one of his acquaintances there described his store as "a second-hand shop." His oldest children from his first marriage, Susan and Francis, were both probably on their own by then, and it is likely that the Moore household now consisted of only Francis, Annie, and young Thomas. Annie helped Francis run the shop, likely did some doctoring as well, and cared for their son.

La Junta was a boomtown, a railroad hub, and its surrounding farmland was fertile and well irrigated. It was likely a place the small family expected to stay for a while. Francis joined Kilpatrick Post #41 of the GAR and ordered special letterhead for his store at "Moore's Corner." But although he apparently made a good try at shopkeeping, Francis and his small family moved once more, this time to Southern California in late 1895, a move recommended by Annie so that Francis could seek relief from another attack of typhoid fever, as well as the chronic liver complaints and rheumatism that had plagued him since the war. The mild climate of San Diego and its nearby coastal communities made the region a popular destination for those seeking relief from a variety of ailments.

Francis, Annie, and Thomas settled in National City, south of San Diego. Francis was fifty-eight, Annie was fifty, and Thomas was just nine years old. Despite his poor health and advancing age, Francis immediately became active in his new community. He supplemented Annie's doctoring income with his carpentry skills and was listed alternately in city directories as a woodworker, furniture dealer, cabinet-maker, and carpenter. On a pension form, Francis said that he did "occasional jobs of repairing furniture" from his home. For a time Francis maintained his own shop, but one of his neighbors recalled that "he had to give that up, and he wasn't physically able to attend to the business."[6] Annie, who was listed in city directories as a physician and surgeon, apparently also worked from the couple's home on F Avenue at 5th Street.

In 1897, when a drought and water shortage threatened National City, Francis dug a deep well in his backyard and, with an enormous cask mounted on a buckboard wagon, delivered water to his thirsty neighbors for one cent per gallon. Thomas later recalled making deliveries with his father's water wagon after school.[7]

In 1898, with the outbreak of the Spanish-American War, at the age of sixty-one, Francis joined a local company of what the *San Diego Union* called "minute men" and was elected first lieutenant. Although he probably never expected to see military action, the fact that he remained willing to offer his services suggests that Francis believed his wartime experience could still be of some use.[8]

Indeed, Francis maintained a strong identification as a veteran throughout his postwar life and believed strongly in the implicit and permanent value of his service. In addition to his brief stint as a pseudo-military volunteer, he applied this patriotic and nationalistic ethic through a steady record of public service. He served as a federal census enumerator for National City in 1900, was elected to the city council in 1904, and was listed as both a city recorder and a justice of the peace in 1911, holding the latter two positions until his death on December 22, 1912. In 1903, Francis joined Heintzelman Post #33 of the GAR and was active in the community service order Knights of Pythias. His funeral was held at the Knights' hall in National City, and his burial in a special section of La Vista Cemetery was conducted with GAR honors.[9]

Before moving to Southern California, Francis was also an active participant in the annual Delano's Dragoons reunions, almost always sending a letter if he could not attend. The reunions were an even more tangible way than GAR membership for Francis and his former soldiers to recall and relive the thrilling events of the war, to reminisce and swap stories, to construct and reconstruct their collective memory of the great defining events of their generation. Through his letters and speeches to the annual company reunions, Francis made clear that veterans' living memories were a profound source of comradeship, and that veterans themselves were the true repositories of the wartime memory:

> The years of service, the many hardships and privations, the marches, raids, forays and frolics that we have endured and engaged in together, should endear each to the other and bind us closer as our numbers grow fewer.
>
> The marble "Memorial Monument" is raised and unveiled <u>once,</u> looked at by the curious crowd, and then forgotten; but the yearly calling of that old roll, is the yearly rearing and unveiling of the "Soldier's Memorial Monument" within the hearts of each of us, that can never be forgotten.[10]

If Francis had his own ideas about how veteranhood and patriotism should be articulated, and the virtue inherent in maintaining the sacred memory of the wartime experience, he also shaped his ideas based on cues taken from the larger culture's shaping of wartime memory. In his assembled newspaper clippings, we can see Francis constructing, and participating in others' construction of, what Civil War service and veteranhood meant. He clipped such poems as "The Dying Soldier," or editorials entitled "The Maimed Brigade," stories about GAR events headlined "Our Heroes" and "The Last March," speeches about the war from former generals, and items about "Blue and Gray" reunions. Significantly, he even saved a clipping entitled, "The Mistakes of History; Universally Accepted Records Are Not Always Reliable." For Francis, the construction of his own veteranhood was informed by a desire to truthfully carry forward his wartime experience, and to put it to some useful service. If he could participate, even in small ways, in the creation of a more reliable history of his war, he believed he could also faithfully honor the sacrifices of his comrades. In doing so, he walked a fine line between an accurate representation of his service and a useful narrative of nationalism.

In one clipping, Francis saved a letter from Lieutenant John Cayton, who regretted his inability to attend the company reunion of 1874. Cayton asked: "Boys, stand by the principles we fought to sustain; don't be beguiled by the song of dead issues. Remember Sawyer, Delano, Catlin, Garrett, Murdock, Wilcox, Hill, and others, whose lives were sacrificed that those principles should be maintained. These issues will not be dead until a man's principles are respected in Arkansas and Louisiana as they are in Illinois and Nebraska."[11] This was the only reference in all of Francis's postwar clippings and writings to the stalled progress of Reconstruction for black Americans.

Although he likely shared at least some of Cayton's frustration with the racial injustice still everywhere evident, Francis's postwar writings make clear that his war had not been fought against slavery for the sake of the slaves, and that he viewed the postwar progress or failure of black civil rights as a separate issue that had little bearing on his own wartime service. As we see in his memoir, Francis's war was for the preservation of the Union and the destruction of what he viewed as an antidemocratic aristocratic system of wealth and privilege. He was utterly unself-conscious in his selective application of the democratic ideals he had supposedly fought to preserve. Instead of lamenting the racial strife so evident in the 1870s, his postwar ire remained forcefully directed against Northerners who had tried, as he believed, to subvert the cause of the Union. At the company reunion in 1877, Francis failed to take his old comrade Cayton's advice to resist the song of dead issues:

> [W]e would be unworthy of the name of men and soldiers if we should allow the fire of patriotism once kindled within us to die out. There is also another spark, another fire, that was once red hot in our hearts that should also be nourished and kept alive. There were those, who in the dark and uncertain days of the war, rejoiced at our reverses, who declared that the war was a failure, and cried peace—peace, when there was no peace, and who are now so anxious to bury the hatchet and shake hands across the bloody chasm by discontinuing all army reunions and striking from the annals of our country all record of our victories. They are the same contemptible copperheads who during the war could find no name too foul to apply to us. . . . I can, and do, honor and respect the true rebel soldier, who honestly believing he was right, dared to put on his uniform, show his colors and come out and fight like a man, and I am always proud to meet and clasp hands with a brave, honest man, be he friend or foe, but a two-faced deceitful copperhead, I hope I shall never cease to despise and curse.[12]

He wrote much the same in other letters, extolling his comrades to keep alive the "flame of loyalty" for the nation equally with the "spark of hatred" for those whom he continued to label "copperheads." The stakes of this ongoing identification with the stark labels of wartime were made clear in one letter in which Francis implored his comrades to kindle the love of Union in their children, so that "they shall be proud to say 'my father was a Union soldier,' and they will so love and honor that flag that it will never fall for the want of strong arms and willing hearts to protect it, and our dead comrades will not have died in vain."[13] Even more forcefully, for the reunion of 1886, he wrote: "Tell them a rebel soldier may be forgiven but a copperhead never. . . . This country belongs to those who saved it."[14]

For all of the nationalistic rhetoric in his later writings, however, the nation itself took a backseat here, as Francis almost too forcefully tried to articulate the value of his own contribution in fellowship with others who had made similar sacrifices. Francis could have written these strongly nationalistic themes backward into his memoir, but he did not, retaining the personal focus of his wartime writings. Even as he articulated a vehement nationalism in his later life, his was not only a nationalistic vision of veteranhood and patriotism, but one tied to his own personal grief, his advancing age and ill health, and his fear that the defining events of his life were slipping away both from his own memory and from the memory of the nation. The assembly and construction of his memoir was Francis's tangible effort to place them permanently in the historical record, to make them real again.

Much has been written on the exercise and expression of Civil War memory in the postbellum decades of the nineteenth century and beyond. But there is also much that remains to be explored, especially with regard to veterans' studies. Just as Civil War historians have rediscovered the experiences of the common soldier, so too can we rediscover the experiences of the Civil War veteran. In doing so, we can find narratives that do not always fit neatly within the political or organizational commemorative rhetorics, or within historians' conceptual frameworks for memory and narrative studies.[15]

If the content of Francis Moore's memoir is best viewed through the eyes of a young carriage maker from Quincy, its purpose is best viewed through the eyes of a rheumatic old man trying to make some sense of a life that must have passed all too quickly, and which was overshadowed by wartime experiences that likely escaped even his very comprehensive memoir. Francis's memoir and his later life are reminders that Civil War veteranhood and memory not only were shaped by the broader currents of nationalism, race, and politics but were also shaped within individual veterans in response to their unique personal trajectories.

APPENDIX A

Roster of Company L, "Delano's Dragoons," Second Illinois Cavalry

Name and Rank	Age	Occupation	Residence	Date of rank or enlistment	Date of muster	Remarks
CAPTAINS						
Sterling P. Delano	30	Lawyer	Quincy	Aug. 24, 1861	Aug. 12, 1861	Died Apr. 27, 1862
Francis T. Moore	25	Carriage maker	Adams Co.	May 6, 1862	July 2, 1862	Mustered out June 14, 1865
FIRST LIEUTENANT						
James K. Catlin	33	Merchant	Augusta	Aug. 24, 1861	Aug. 12, 1861	Adjutant
SECOND LIEUTENANTS						
Joseph L. Sawyer	22	School teacher	Camp Point	Aug. 24, 1861	Aug. 12, 1861	Resigned Oct. 25, 1861
Francis T. Moore	–	–	Adams Co.	Nov. 15, 1861	Aug. 12, 1861	Promoted
John Clayton	23	School teacher	Ellington	May 6, 1862	July 2, 1862	Discharged Mar. 1, 1865
FIRST SERGEANT						
Frederick C. Turner	22	Farmer	Ursa	Aug. 5, 1861	Aug. 12, 1861	Mustered out Aug. 11, 1864, as Sergeant

Name and Rank	Age	Occupation	Residence	Date of rank or enlistment	Date of muster	Remarks
QUARTERMASTER SERGEANT						
John N. Wilks	26	Farmer	Camp Point	Aug. 5, 1861	Aug. 12, 1861	Died at Island No. 10, Sept. 29, 1862
SERGEANTS						
William H. Burke	23	School teacher	Clayton	Aug. 5, 1861	Aug. 12, 1861	Mustered out Aug. 11, 1864
John Clayton	–	–	Ellington	Aug. 5, 1861	Aug. 12, 1861	Promoted 2nd Lieutenant
Daniel D. Hill	25	Farmer	Ursa	Aug. 5, 1861	Aug. 12, 1861	–
Arthur T. Murdock	24	Farmer	Emerson	Aug. 5, 1861	Aug. 12, 1861	Killed at Island No. 10, Oct. 17, 1862
CORPORALS						
John C. Cox	22	Carpenter	Camp Point	Aug. 5, 1861	Aug. 12, 1861	Mustered out Aug. 11, 1864, as Sergeant
Warner D. Elliott	24	Farmer	LaPrairie	Aug. 5, 1861	Aug. 12, 1861	Died at Fort Holt, Ky., Dec. 4, 1861
William G. Gilpin	24	Florist	Ellington	Aug. 5, 1861	Aug. 12, 1861	Died at Island No. 10, Sept. 29, 1862
Benjamin H. Phillips	27	Painter	Quincy	Aug. 5, 1861	Aug. 12, 1861	Discharged Dec. 20, 1862
Edwin Sexton	47	Farmer	Augusta	Aug. 5, 1861	Aug. 12, 1861	Mustered out Aug. 11, 1864
Obediah Spence	25	Farmer	Clayton	Aug. 5, 1861	Aug. 12, 1861	Mustered out Aug. 11, 1864, as Sergeant
Franklin Turner	40	Conductor	Quincy	Aug. 5, 1861	Aug. 12, 1861	Mustered out Aug. 11, 1864, as Sergeant
John Watson	27	Carpenter	Fowler	Aug. 5, 1861	Aug. 12, 1861	Mustered out Aug. 11, 1864, as Sergeant

Name and Rank	Age	Occupation	Residence	Date of rank or enlistment	Date of muster	Remarks
BUGLERS						
Charles Craine	22	Railroad hand	Camp Point	Aug. 5, 1861	Aug. 12, 1861	–
Francis C. Weaver	24	Farmer	Lima	Aug. 5, 1861	Aug. 12, 1861	–
FARRIER						
Maurice Bywater	22	Farmer	Quincy	Aug. 5, 1861	Aug. 12, 1861	Mustered out Aug. 26, 1864
BLACKSMITH						
James Kinghorn	25	Farmer	Augusta	Aug. 5, 1861	Aug. 12, 1861	Discharged Feb. 14, 1862
SADDLER						
Mortimer B. Crandall	20	Shoemaker	Camp Point	Aug. 5, 1861	Aug. 12, 1861	Mustered out Aug. 11, 1864, as Private
WAGONER						
William B. Hayte	33	Moulder	Quincy	Aug. 5, 1861	Aug. 12, 1861	Discharged Aug. 11, 1862
PRIVATES						
Barnett, William	22	Farmer	Ursa	Aug. 5, 1861	Aug. 12, 1861	Discharged Sept. 5, 1862, disability
Barr, Brenneman	19	Farmer	Ellington	Aug. 5, 1861	Aug. 12, 1861	Mustered out Aug. 11, 1864
Bell, William	35	Laborer	Beverly	Aug. 5, 1861	Aug. 12, 1861	Re-enlisted as Veteran
Berrian, James T.	23	Farmer	Ellington	Aug. 5, 1861	Aug. 12, 1861	Mustered out Aug. 11, 1864, as Corporal
Bimson, Benjamin	18	Wagon maker	Quincy	Aug. 5, 1861	Aug. 12, 1861	Mustered out Aug. 16, 1864
Bowne, Samuel W.	27	Farmer	Ursa	Aug. 5, 1861	Aug. 12, 1861	Died Mound City, Nov. 3, 1861
Brooks, John F.	25	Farmer	Clayton	Aug. 5, 1861	Aug. 12, 1861	–

Name and Rank	Age	Occupation	Residence	Date of rank or enlistment	Date of muster	Remarks
Browning, Jeremiah	21	Farmer	Richfield	Aug. 5, 1861	Aug. 12, 1861	Discharged Sept. 5, 1862, disability
Buck, Harvey S.	22	Druggist	Augusta	Aug. 5, 1861	Aug. 12, 1861	Discharged June 21, 1862, disability
Bywater, George	22	Butcher	Quincy	Aug. 5, 1861	Aug. 12, 1861	Mustered out Aug. 11, 1864
Carter, Martin	37	Merchant	LaPrairie	Aug. 5, 1861	Aug. 12, 1861	Re-enlisted as Veteran
Chase, William J.	21	Farmer	Fowler	Aug. 5, 1861	Aug. 12, 1861	Mustered out Aug. 22, 1864 as Corporal
Childs, Thomas D.	19	Farmer	Camp Point	Aug. 5, 1861	Aug. 12, 1861	-
Cook, Hiram W.	41	Mason	Augusta	Aug. 5, 1861	Aug. 12, 1861	Mustered out Aug. 11, 1864
Cramer, Frederick	23	Railroad hand	Camp Point	Aug. 5, 1861	Aug. 12, 1861	Mustered out Aug. 11, 1864 as Bugler
Crawford, William H.	19	Farmer	LaPrairie	Aug. 5, 1861	Aug. 12, 1861	Discharged Feb. 24, 1862
Currier, Darius A.	30	Mason	Augusta	Aug. 5, 1861	Aug. 12, 1861	Mustered out Aug. 11, 1864
Davis, James M.	23	Farmer	Camp Point	Aug. 5, 1861	Aug. 12, 1861	Discharged Feb. 24, 1862
Dawson, Barton S.	23	Butcher	Quincy	Aug. 5, 1861	Aug. 12, 1861	Discharged Sept. 19, 1862
Delano, Decatur D.	20	Farmer	Walker	Aug. 5, 1861	Aug. 12, 1861	Died at Island No. 10, Nov. 18, 1862
Douglas, John F.	27	Farmer	Clayton	Aug. 5, 1861	Aug. 12, 1861	Mustered out Aug. 11, 1864
Douglas, Joseph F.	25	Farmer	Clayton	Aug. 5, 1861	Aug. 12, 1861	Mustered out Aug. 11, 1864
Easum, Charles W.	20	Farmer	Camp Point	Aug. 5, 1861	Aug. 12, 1861	Mustered out Aug. 11, 1864
Farlow, George	21	Farmer	Camp Point	Aug. 5, 1861	Aug. 12, 1861	Discharged May 17, 1862

Name and Rank	Age	Occupation	Residence	Date of rank or enlistment	Date of muster	Remarks
Floyd, George F.	22	Farmer	Houston	Aug. 5, 1861	Aug. 12, 1861	Mustered out Aug. 11, 1864
Garrett, Richard S.	23	Wool carder	Camp Point	Aug. 5, 1861	Aug. 12, 1861	Killed at Island No. 10, Oct. 17, 1862
Gibbs, James T.	26	Farmer	LaPrairie	Aug. 5, 1861	Aug. 12, 1861	Discharged May 5, 1862
Green, William	20	Farmer	Richfield	Aug. 5, 1861	Aug. 12, 1861	Mustered out Aug. 11, 1864, as Corporal
Harbison, Robert	23	Farmer	Clayton	Aug. 5, 1861	Aug. 12, 1861	Mustered out Aug. 11, 1864
Hawley, Giles C.	31	Farmer	Augusta	Aug. 5, 1861	Aug. 12, 1861	Discharged Nov. 14, 1861
Hawley, Orestes K.	28	Farmer	Augusta	Aug. 5, 1861	Aug. 12, 1861	–
Henderson, James B.	32	Farmer	Ursa	Aug. 5, 1861	Aug. 12, 1861	Mustered out Aug. 11, 1864
Hesler, Francis M.	24	Farmer	Augusta	Aug. 5, 1861	Aug. 12, 1861	Mustered out Aug. 11, 1864
Hicks, Francis M.	19	Blacksmith	Quincy	Aug. 5, 1861	Aug. 12, 1861	Discharged Feb. 24, 1862
Homan, John S.	19	Farmer	Ellington	Aug. 5, 1861	Aug. 12, 1861	Mustered out Aug. 11, 1864
Johnson, Jonas P.	21	Farmer	Fowler	Aug. 5, 1861	Aug. 12, 1861	Mustered out Aug. 11, 1864
Kamp, Thomas J.	22	Wagon maker	Camp Point	Aug. 5, 1861	Aug. 12, 1861	Mustered out Aug. 11, 1864, as Corporal
Kemp, James	22	Farmer	Clayton	Aug. 5, 1861	Aug. 12, 1861	Mustered out Aug. 11, 1864
Kendall, Reese P.	32	Farmer	Liberty	Aug. 5, 1861	Aug. 12, 1861	–
Kimball, Henry M.	27	Farmer	Augusta	Aug. 5, 1861	Aug. 12, 1861	Mustered out Aug. 11, 1864
Kirk, William H.	23	Farmer	Huntsville	Aug. 5, 1861	Aug. 12, 1861	Mustered out Aug. 11, 1864

Name and Rank	Age	Occupation	Residence	Date of rank or enlistment	Date of muster	Remarks
Lewis, Thomas	19	Farmer	Camp Point	Aug. 5, 1861	Aug. 12, 1861	Died at Andersonville prison Aug. 20, 1861, Grave No. 6,238
Lindsay, Charles G.	28	Farmer	Ellington	Aug. 5, 1861	Aug. 12, 1861	Discharged May 23, 1862
Lindsay, Llewellyn	20	3 months soldier	Ellington	Aug. 5, 1861	Aug. 12, 1861	Mustered out Aug. 11, 1864
Lonnsbury, Guy F.	24	Farmer	Newtown	Aug. 5, 1861	Aug. 12, 1861	Mustered out Aug. 11, 1864
McMurray, William F.	20	Farmer	Clayton	Aug. 5, 1861	Aug. 12, 1861	Mustered out Aug. 11, 1864, as Sergeant
Matthews, John W.	26	Painter	Camp Point	Aug. 5, 1861	Aug. 12, 1861	Mustered out Aug. 11, 1864, as Corporal
Moore, Francis T.	23	Carriage maker	Quincy	Aug. 5, 1861	Aug. 12, 1861	Promoted 2nd Lieutenant
Morrow, Henry C.	23	Blacksmith	Payson	Aug. 5, 1861	Aug. 12, 1861	Discharged April 11, 1864, disability
Paris, William H.	21	Farmer	Richfield	Aug. 5, 1861	Aug. 12, 1861	Re-enlisted as Veteran
Patton, John D.	19	Farmer	Fall Creek	Aug. 5, 1861	Aug. 12, 1861	Re-enlisted as Veteran
Peabody, John L.	28	Farmer	Ellington	Aug. 5, 1861	Aug. 12, 1861	Mustered out Aug. 11, 1864, as Sergeant
Petrie, John	25	Blacksmith	Clayton	Aug. 5, 1861	Aug. 12, 1861	Mustered out Aug. 11, 1864, as Blacksmith
Phillips, Henry F.	27	Painter	Quincy	Aug. 5, 1861	Aug. 12, 1861	Discharged Apr. 26, 1862
Ralph, Orlando J.	22	Farmer	Ursa	Aug. 5, 1861	Aug. 12, 1861	Re-enlisted as Veteran
Selden, Gideon	38	Engineer	Augusta	Aug. 5, 1861	Aug. 12, 1861	Discharged Jan. 16, 1862

Name and Rank	Age	Occupation	Residence	Date of rank or enlistment	Date of muster	Remarks
Spence, James	22	Farmer	North East	Aug. 5, 1861	Aug. 12, 1861	Mustered out Aug. 11, 1864
Stokes, William C.	40	Farmer	Augusta	Aug. 5, 1861	Aug. 12, 1861 1861	Discharged Dec. 30, 1862, as Sergeant
Stowe, Horace H.	29	Farmer	Quincy	Aug. 5, 1861	Aug. 12, 1861	Discharged Sept. 5, 1862
Swaze, Daniel W.	34	Plasterer	Augusta	Aug. 5, 1861	Aug. 12, 1861	Mustered out Aug. 11, 1864
Temple, William W.	30	Farmer	Quincy	Aug. 5, 1861	Aug. 12, 1861	Mustered out Aug. 11, 1864
Triplett, Andrew J.	21	Farmer	Ellington	Aug. 5, 1861	Aug. 12, 1861	Mustered out Aug. 11, 1864
Welsh, Benjamin H.	21	Farmer	Camp Point	Aug. 5, 1861	Aug. 12, 1861	Discharged Oct. 4, 1861
Welsh, Robert G.	25	Farmer	Camp Point	Aug. 5, 1861	Aug. 12, 1861	Mustered out Aug. 11, 1864
Wilcox, Charles O.	18	Farmer	Quincy	Aug. 5, 1861	Aug. 12, 1861	Mustered out Aug. 11, 1864
Wilcox, William A.	21	Farmer	Quincy	Aug. 5, 1861	Aug. 12, 1861	Killed at Island No. 10, Oct. 17, 1862
Woodman, Daniel W.	31	Photographer	Camp Point	Aug. 5, 1861	Aug. 12, 1861	Transferred to Invalid Corps, Feb. 26, 1864
Woodruff, Thomas T.	22	Accountant	Quincy	Aug. 5, 1861	Aug. 12, 1861	Mustered out Aug. 11, 1864
Working, Jacob M.	28	Millwright	Augusta	Aug. 5, 1861	Aug. 12, 1861	Discharged Nov. 5, 1862
Wren, William W.	19	Blacksmith	Ursa	Aug. 5, 1861	Aug. 12, 1861	Discharged Nov. 25, 1862
Wright, Thomas E.	24	Farmer	Bloomfield	Aug. 5, 1861	Aug. 12, 1861	Discharged June 30, 1862
VETERANS						
Bell, William	–	–	Beverly	Mar. 14, 1864	Mar. 14, 1864	Transferred to Company E, consolidated

Name and Rank	Age	Occupation	Residence	Date of rank or enlistment	Date of muster	Remarks
Carter, Martin	–	–	LaPrairie	Feb. 29, 1864	Feb. 29, 1864	Transferred to Company E, consolidated
Harris, James R.	–	–	Warsaw	Feb. 29, 1864	Feb. 29, 1864	Transferred to Company E, consolidated
Paris, William H.	–	–	Richfield	Mar. 14, 1864	Mar. 14, 1864	Mustered out June 24, 1865, as 1st Sergeant
Patton, John D.	–	–	Fall Creek	Mar. 14, 1864	Mar. 14, 1864	Transferred to Company F, consolidated
Ralph, Orlando J.	–	–	Ursa	Mar. 14, 1864	Mar. 14, 1864	Transferred to Company E, consolidated
RECRUITS						
Alfeman, Henry	18	Brick mason	–	Sept. 23, 1864	Sept. 26, 1864	Substitute. Mustered out June 13, 1865
Allen, Stephen A.	25	Farmer	Augusta	Mar. 1, 1862	July 17, 1863	Mustered out Jan. 12, 1865
Austin, Moses	26	Farmer	Mendon	Nov. 9, 1861	–	Transferred to Company G, 1st Illinois Cavalry
Bates, Augustus H.	25	–	Grand Detour	Sept. 16, 1861	–	–
Benfield, George	31	–	Liberty	Nov. 11, 1863	Dec. 31, 1863	Vet. Transferred to Company E, consolidated
Bradford, James H.	28	–	Carthage	Aug. 9, 1862	July 17, 1863	Mustered out Jan. 12, 1865
Bywater, George	27	Farmer	–	Sept. 28, 1864	Sept. 29, 1864	Substitute. Mustered out July 14, 1865
Bywater, John	26	–	–	Aug. 16, 1862	July 17, 1863	Mustered out June 13, 1865, as Corporal

Name and Rank	Age	Occupation	Residence	Date of rank or enlistment	Date of muster	Remarks
Clark, Lafayette O.	18	Farmer	Bear Creek	Dec. 1, 1864	Dec. 3, 1864	Transferred to Company E, consolidated
Cranston, John	28	–	Carthage	Aug. 11, 1862	July 17, 1863	Promoted Saddler Sergeant
Davis, Thomas J.	19	-	Augusta	Nov. 12, 1863	Dec. 31, 1863	Transferred to Company E, consolidated
Douglass, James A.	27	–	Carthage	Aug. 12, 1862	July 17, 1863	Mustered out Jan. 12, 1865
Douglass, Joseph W.	25	–	Carthage	Aug. 12, 1862	July 17, 1863	Mustered out Jan. 12, 1865
Douglass, Thomas C.	22	-	Carthage	Aug. 12, 1862	July 17, 1863	Mustered out Jan. 12, 1865
Easum, John H.	19	–	Carthage	Aug. 16, 1862	July 17, 1863	Mustered out June 13, 1865, as Corporal
Edlestine, Edward J.	22	–	Quincy	Feb. 11, 1862	July 17, 1863	Mustered out Jan. 12, 1865
Elwood, John	21	–	Liberty	Nov. 12, 1863	Dec. 31, 1863	Transferred to Company E, consolidated
Frazell, Cyrus H.	25	–	–	Aug. 7, 1862	July 17, 1863	Mustered out Jan. 12, 1865
Gibbs, James F.	28	Farmer	LaPrairie	Jan. 4, 1864	Jan. 7, 1864	Transferred to Company E, consolidated
Goulty, Henry	25	Farmer	Augusta	March 1, 1862	July 17, 1863	Died at Baton Rouge, June 3, 1864
Graff, David W.	21	–	–	Aug. 14, 1862	July 17, 1863	Mustered out Jan. 12, 1865
Gusseman, Thomas J.	21	Farmer	Keene	Feb. 23, 1864	Feb. 26, 1864	Transferred to Company E, consolidated
Harris, James R., Sr.	46	Farmer	Hancock Co.	March 1, 1862	–	Discharged Sept. 17, 1862
Harris, James R., Jr.	18	Farmer	Hancock Co.	March 1, 1862	July 17, 1863	Re-enlisted as Veteran

Name and Rank	Age	Occupation	Residence	Date of rank or enlistment	Date of muster	Remarks
Howard, Reason	24	Farmer	Keene	Feb. 23, 1864	Feb. 26, 1864	Transferred to Company E, consolidated
Howard, William A.	44	Farmer	Walker	Nov. 11, 1864	Nov. 12, 1864	Transferred to Company E, consolidated
Hubbard, Harmon R.	24	–	Mendon	Nov. 9, 1861	–	Transferred to Company G, 1st Illinois Cavalry
Kincheloe, Alexander	19	Farmer	Walker	Nov. 11, 1864	Nov. 12, 1864	Transferred to Company E, consolidated
Knight, Cassius A.	23	Farmer	Quincy	Jan. 13, 1862	–	Died at Quincy, Sept. 29, 1862, accidental wounds
Lee, William	23	–	Liberty	Nov. 11, 1863	Dec. 31, 1863	Transferred to Company E, consolidated
Littlefield, Samuel C.	35	Sailor	Melbourne	Nov. 11, 1861	July 17, 1862	Mustered out Nov. 9, 1864
Miller, Harvey	44	–	–	Aug. 15, 1862	July 17, 1863	Discharged Dec. 16, 1864
Nelson, Samuel	28	Laborer	Bear Creek	Dec. 1, 1864	Dec. 3, 1864	Mustered out June 22, 1865
Obert, Virgil A.	22	Farmer	Augusta	Jan. 5, 1864	Jan. 7, 1864	Transferred to Company F, consolidated
Pitcher, Andrew J.	32	Laborer	Bloomington	Dec. 30, 1863	Dec. 30, 1863	Transferred to Company E, consolidated
Pond, George P.	23	–	–	Aug. 14, 1862	July 17, 1863	Mustered out Jan. 12, 1865
Rainwater, A. Jacob	19	Farmer	Quincy	Jan. 4, 1864	Jan. 7, 1864	Mustered out May 17, 1865, to date May 11, 1865
Ray, Jacob	18	Farmer	Warsaw	Jan. 19, 1864	Jan. 21, 1864	Transferred to Company E, consolidated

Name and Rank	Age	Occupation	Residence	Date of rank or enlistment	Date of muster	Remarks
Shank, Christopher C.	–	–	–	–	–	Mustered out June 12, 1865
Sneed, John S.	20	Farmer	Quincy	Feb. 24, 1864	Feb. 26, 1864	Transferred to Company E, consolidated
Spear, Joseph A.	18	Farmer	Walker	Nov. 11, 1864	Nov. 12, 1864	Transferred to Company E, consolidated
Spence, R. H.	28	Farmer	North East	Jan. 4, 1864	Jan. 7, 1864	Died at Baton Rouge, July 14, 1864
Spence, Willis	25	–	Clayton	July 7, 1862	July 17, 1863	Died at Baton Rouge, June 6, 1864
Stevens, Augustus	45	Druggist	Camp Point	Aug. 21, 1861	–	Discharged Oct. 3, 1861
Stockton, Jerome D.	20	Farmer	Walker	Nov. 11, 1864	Nov. 12, 1864	Transferred to Company E, consolidated
Sweet, Abner B.	21	Farmer	Augusta	Jan. 4, 1864	Jan. 7, 1864	Transferred to Company E, consolidated
Thompson, John	24	Farmer	Keene	Jan. 19, 1864	Jan. 21, 1864	Transferred to Company E, consolidated
Thornton, James T.	–	–	–	–	–	Mustered out June 12, 1865

Sources: Compiled from Report of the Adjutant General of the State of Illinois; and Illinois Civil War Muster and Descriptive Rolls Database, Illinois State Archives.

APPENDIX B

Letter of Francis C. Moore to Mary Moore, October 5, 1862

When Francis C. Moore visited his son in camp in October 1862, he wrote at least two letters back to his wife, Mary, in Quincy. Francis Jr. pasted both of these letters into his memoir at the appropriate place in the narrative. In this first letter, Francis Sr. describes his journey and his arrival and the health of his son. The elder Francis was sixty-five years old when he made this journey but evidently remained lively and active. The letter below is largely unedited—as Francis Sr. wrote it.

Sunday aff:
2 o'clock 5. Oct. 1862

My Dear Wife

I wrote to you yesterday at Cairo. I left there yesterday at 5 p.m. I got here at 10½ last night on the fine steamer Forest Green, she carries the mail, and at the landing found several of the soldiers waiting for the mail, they had a lantern and escorted me to our son's quarters, at that time Francis was at New Madrid and got back a little after 11 o'clock. Today we have rode over the several batteries, the fortifications are formed chiefly (that is, the inner parts) by bags filled with sand and stand up as regular as a stone wall. The large cannon are laying around dismounted, the large trees show the effects of the balls and shells thrown by the gun boats. All the works are past decaying, the Forest Green continued down the river to Memphis, a regular packet plying between Memphis and St. Louis will probably pass up Tuesday and I intend taking passage on her to St. Louis tomorrow or Tuesday morning we will go over to Island No. 10 and see the ravages of war there. To my delight, I found Francis apparently about as well as usual, appetite good enough and looking as well as whenever you saw him. When I get home I shall have a deal to tell of strange sights.

I think Saturday will find me at home. Two nights rail road journey and no rest, about satisfied me, but yesterday, and last night, rest has set me about right. As I shall not have any rail road to have on my return, I anticipate comfort. 4 p.m. Francis has just opened the two boxes and thinks a good mother is a great blessing.

I may not have a chance to write again.

Yours affect.
F.C. Moore

APPENDIX C

Letter of Francis C. Moore to Mary Moore, October 7, 1862

Francis Moore Sr.'s second letter to his wife Mary was written during a visit to his son's camp at Island Number 10 in October 1862. This letter contains more significant observations about the Southern populace and the soldiers in the army. Of even greater significance are his remarks on the fugitive slave woman, his son's camp cook, who will accompany him back to Illinois. The Moore family employed a black servant in 1860, but it is not known whether the woman Francis Jr. refers to as "Gilly Blackburn" in chapter 2 also remained with the family in Quincy. The letter below is largely unedited.

Tuesday eve., 7 Oct. 1862, Island No. 10

My Dear Wife

Yesterday afternoon I rode on horse back to the lake five miles from here. It is about 30 miles in length by probably 2 miles in width, the ground sunk at the great earthquake in fall of 1811 it was a heavy forest, chiefly of cypress, the whited and totally stripped bodies of the immersed trees are yet standing in the water, it is the most gloomy and desolate spot I ever supposed probably. From there we rode about five miles to Tiptonville on the west side of this great bend of the Miss. river and from there, five miles back to this place, making of considerable extent for me. I felt no ill effects from it and slept better last night than any time since I left home. Today we rode 2½ miles and dined with Mr. Merriweather and his wife who the officers call Aunt Dolly. She is about your size, good open-hearted people and live in good old fashioned Virginia style. He has about 25 darkies of all ages, from an old woman who says she is over 100 years old and so down to little ones beginning to run about. All decently clothed and their log cabins, well provided with bedsteads, table, chairs, etc., apparently living more comfortably than the poor settlers formerly did when you and I journeyed. Many of the settlers have lost their best slaves. Five valuable ones left this Mr. Merriweather, but some of them got tired of freedom and have returned. He got a letter today from one of them in Minnesota, who says he will soon return to his master.

I intended to leave here sometime during tonight on the steamer Memphis which trades between Memphis and St. Louis but as Francis thinks my visit too short I have concluded to remain with him a few days longer and therefore shall not be home this week. The ride yesterday was more exertion than Francis should have taken and it has somewhat enfeebled him. Several of the soldiers are on the sick list, but only one is much sick and he is getting better. The Major in command of this military post is a son of Daniel McNeil formerly living at Monmouth, he is the oldest son, and when we were there, he was a boy and named Butler McNeil, when he became of age he changed his name to Quincy McNeil, he is about the size of his father, jolly and good natured, but totally void of religious principles. As a whole, the soldiers are very civil and moral, no rowdyism. There is an excellent black woman (real black) who now cooks for Francis' mess, she wants to go north, and probably she will go under my protection to Quincy. She is quiet and well behaved, is 27 years of age, has had no children. My interpretation is that she will suit you, but I shall make no bargain with her, until you think best. Major McNeil will give her free papers. She appears to have been brought in a respectable family.

All the men who are here from Quincy and vicinity are in good health.

I hope Mr. Sherman gets along pretty well without me, when I get home he can take his turn.

Good night dear wife
as ever affec. Yrs.
F.C. Moore

APPENDIX D

Captain Francis Moore to Adjutant-General Lorenzo Thomas Requesting Permission to Raise a Black Cavalry Regiment

Headquarters Co. "L," 2d Ill. Cavalry
Columbus, Ky., April 3rd, 1863

General

In accordance with your proposition to grant commissions to those wishing to serve in Negro regiments, I respectfully request that I be permitted to raise and command a regiment of Negroes. Should you be pleased to grant my request, I will guarantee 1st to raise a regiment of not less than eight hundred negroes, within two months from the time I shall be permitted to commence recruiting. 2ndly. To furnish from the noncommissioned officers and soldiers now under my command good trusty men who have seen nearly two years service—sufficient to officer the whole regiment. 3rdly to report the regiment thus raised, at any military post in the Southwest, organized and ready for duty, within two months from the time I shall be permitted to commence recruiting for the same.

Failing in any or all of the above propositions, I and the men that may be permitted to assist me, will return to our respective duties as officers and soldiers, and will consent to have the time so lost deducted from our term of enlistment.

I, and the soldiers under my command, have been in active service in the United States Army since the month of July 1861.

I make the foregoing request and propositions, General, believing that I may thus be of more service to my country and my country's cause. Hoping they may meet your approval,

I am General
Your obedient servant
Francis T. Moore
Capt. Comdg. Co. "L" 2nd Ill. Cav.

To
Brig. Genl. L. Thomas
Adj. Genl. U.S. Army
Columbus, Ky.

Source: Compiled Military Service File for Francis Moore, NARA

NOTES

Introduction

1. Although more focused on regimental histories than memoirs, Robert Hunt, *The Good Men Who Won the War: Army of the Cumberland Veterans and Emancipation Memory* (Tuscaloosa: University of Alabama Press, 2010) observes that western theater veterans tended to engage directly in criticism and analysis of their service.

2. For the antebellum and wartime views of Illinoisans with regard to race, see Thomas Bahde, "Race and Justice in the Heartland: Three Nineteenth-Century Lives" (Ph.D. diss., University of Chicago, 2009).

3. Clay Mountcastle, *Punitive War: Confederate Guerrillas and Union Reprisals* (Lawrence: University Press of Kansas, 2009). See also Daniel E. Sutherland, *A Savage Conflict: The Decisive Role of Guerrillas in the American Civil War* (Chapel Hill: University of North Carolina Press, 2009); Charles Royster, *The Destructive War: William Tecumseh Sherman, Stonewall Jackson, and the Americans* (New York: Alfred A. Knopf, 1991).

4. Recent work on the war on the Mississippi River includes Myron J. Smith, Jr., *Tinclads in the Civil War: Union Light-Draught Gunboat Operations on Western Waters, 1862–1865* (Jefferson, NC: McFarland, 2010), and *The Timberclads in the Civil War: The Lexington, Conestoga, and Tyler on the Western Waters* (Jefferson, N.C.: McFarland, 2008); Thomas R. Campbell, *Confederate Naval Forces on Western Waters: The Defense of the Mississippi River and Its Tributaries* (Jefferson, NC: McFarland, 2005); William L. Shea and Terrence J. Winschel, *Vicksburg Is the Key: The Struggle for the Mississippi River* (Lincoln: University of Nebraska Press, 2003).

5. In an undated clipping from a Quincy newspaper, probably written while Francis lived there between 1874 and 1879, he wrote a nearly word-for-word version of his account of the death of Captain Delano and the later death of Lieutenant Catlin at Okolona, Mississippi. F. T. Moore Collection, San Diego State University, Special Collections and University Archives (hereafter, SDSU).

6. There is no evidence that anyone outside of Francis's immediate family knew anything about his memoir, or the lengthy process he must have engaged in to accumulate the material that he pasted into its pages. We also do not know what happened to Francis's manuscript and other clippings and correspondence after he died. Today, these comprise the F. T. Moore Collection in the Special Collections and University Archives at San Diego State University, but there was apparently no donor information recorded at the time of acquisition. It is possible that upon his death in 1912, Moore's widow, Annie, passed along his papers to the local Grand Army of the Republic post before going to live with her son in Arizona.

7. On the wartime generation's use of memory and commemoration, see David W. Blight, *Beyond the Battlefield: Race, Memory, and the American Civil War* (Amherst: University of Massachusetts Press, 2002), and *Race and Reunion: The Civil War in American Memory* (Cambridge: Belknap/Harvard University Press, 2001); Gary W. Gallagher, *Causes Won, Lost, and Forgotten: How Hollywood and Popular Art Shape What We Know about the Civil War* (Chapel Hill: University of North Carolina Press, 2008), especially chapter 1; and Alice Fahs, *The Imagined Civil War: Popular Literature of the North and South, 1861–1865* (Chapel Hill: University of North Carolina Press, 2001).

8. Stuart McConnell, *Glorious Contentment: The Grand Army of the Republic, 1865–1900* (Chapel Hill: University of North Carolina Press, 1992), 16.

9. Tamar Katriel and Thomas Farrell, "Scrapbooks as Cultural Texts: An American Art of Memory," *Text and Performance Quarterly* 11 (1) 1991: 2.

10. Patricia P. Buckler and C. Kay Leeper, "An Antebellum Woman's Scrapbook as Autobiographical Composition," *Journal of American Culture* 14 (1) 1991: 1–8.

11. Answer of Richard C. Moore and affidavit of Lydia G. Sherman, March 6, 1897, both in Francis T. Moore Pension File, National Archives and Records Administration (hereafter, NARA).

Chapter One—1861

1. Colonel Silas Noble was mustered out February 16, 1863, for "inefficiency," according to the Illinois Civil War Muster and Descriptive Rolls Database, Illinois State Archives (hereafter, ISA). See Appendix A for Sterling Delano.

2. By including Maryland here, Moore is probably referring to the Baltimore Riot of April 19, 1861, when the arrival of the Sixth Massachusetts Regiment, en route to federal service in Washington, D.C., was greeted by citizens hostile to federal military intervention in the secession crisis.

3. Camp Flagg was one of several temporary mustering and training locations throughout Illinois, which were discontinued relatively quickly; the primary training camps became Springfield's Camp Butler and Chicago's Camp Douglas. See Victor Hicken, *Illinois in the Civil War*, 2nd ed. (Urbana: University of Illinois Press, 1991), 6.

4. Arthur T. Murdock, from Marion County, Missouri, just across the Mississippi River, was appointed sergeant shortly thereafter and was killed at Island Number 10 on October 17, 1862. *Report of the Adjutant General of the State of Illinois, Containing Reports for the Years 1861–1866*, vol. 7 (Springfield: H. W. Rokker, 1886), 520. For all subsequent mention of soldiers in Company L, see Appendix A.

5. Moore here included a roster of the noncommissioned officers appointed that day. Because it is the same as the roster included in Appendix A, it has been omitted here.

6. Ed Prince does not appear on the adjutant general's roster for the company or in the muster and descriptive rolls of the company. It is possible that this is the same Edward Prince who later became colonel of the 7th Illinois Cavalry.

7. Captain Benjamin F. Marsh commanded what would become Company G of the 2nd Illinois Cavalry. Marsh was subsequently promoted to major, lieutenant colonel, and colonel of the regiment.

8. The Sisters of the Good Samaritan apparently split from the city's first ladies' benevolent organization, the "Needle Pickets" in July 1861. See David Costigan, "A City in Wartime: Quincy, Illinois and the Civil War" (Ph.D. diss., Illinois State University, 1994), 67–68.

9. Alexander Capron was rector of St. John's Anglican Church in Quincy. The "Institute" referenced here was likely an educational and missionary institution established in Quincy by Rev. Dr. David Nelson, a Congregationalist minister and abolitionist. See Henry Asbury, *Reminiscences of Quincy, Illinois* (Quincy: Wilcox and Sons, 1882), 72–74.

10. Edwin A. Hurd, a farmer from Quincy, joined the 50th Illinois Infantry the next month and died of disease June 20, 1862, at Quincy. Illinois Civil War Muster and Descriptive Rolls Database, ISA.

11. Although Missouri never formally joined the Confederacy, Moore's observation that the state was rebel soil probably reflected his and other volunteers' perceptions of the extent of anti-Union activity in the state.

12. Benjamin M. Prentiss, promoted to brigadier general in May 1861 from his position as colonel of the 10th Illinois Infantry (three months). Prentiss was captured at the Battle of Shiloh but was exchanged and was later promoted to major general. Ezra Warner, *Generals in Blue: Lives of the Union Commanders* (Baton Rouge: Louisiana State University Press, 1964), 385–86.

13. Buell's Independent Battery, organized in St. Louis in July 1861, attached to the Department of Missouri until February 1862, then part of the Army of the Tennessee and Army of the Mississippi. Assigned to 1st Missouri Light Artillery as Battery I in August 1862. The Benton Hussars were organized in St. Louis in September 1861 and served independently until January 1862. The Hussars were consolidated with other independent cavalry commands to form the 5th Missouri Cavalry in February 1862. Frederick Dyer, *A Compendium of the War of the Rebellion*, vol. 3 (New York: Thomas Yoseloff, 1959), 1312, 1319.

14. Brigadier General Meriwether Jeff Thompson of the Missouri State Guard and formerly mayor of St. Joseph, Missouri. Thompson's command became well-known for its swamp-fighting tactics against Union forces in Missouri. See Doris Land Mueller, *M. Jeff Thompson: Missouri's Swamp Fox of the Confederacy* (Columbia: University of Missouri Press, 2007); Donald J. Stanton and Goodwin F. Berquist, "Missouri's Forgotten General: M. Jeff Thompson and the Civil War," *Missouri Historical Review* 73 (3) 1976: 237–58; and Stephen Davis, "Jeff Thompson's Unsuccessful Quest for a Confederate Generalship," *Missouri Historical Review* 85 (1) 1990: 53–65.

15. The adjutant general's roster gives the name as "Guy Lounsbury," while both Moore and the Illinois Civil War Muster and Descriptive Rolls Database give it as "Guy F. Lonnsbury." See *Report of the Adjutant General*, vol. 7, 521; and Illinois Civil War Muster and Descriptive Rolls Database, ISA.

16. Thomas Hollowbush later joined the 10th Illinois Cavalry, Company K, as a private but was dropped from the rolls as a deserter in 1865. Illinois Civil War Muster and Descriptive Rolls Database, ISA.

17. This drawing could be not located in a search of *Harper's Weekly* issues between August and December 1861.

18. Confederate Brigadier General William J. Hardee, formerly of the U.S. Army, and author of the widely used *Hardee's Tactics* drill manual. While Hardee was indeed at Greenville at the time, the size of his force was likely much smaller than the numbers Moore gives from the informants. Ezra Warner, *Generals in Gray: Lives of the Confederate Commanders* (Baton Rouge: Louisiana State University Press, 1959), 124–25.

19. Like many of his contemporaries, Moore uses the terms *Dutch* and *German* interchangeably. Brigadier General Franz Sigel of St. Louis was one of several German revolutionary immigrants to lead Union forces. Although his military career was mixed, he was extremely popular among German American soldiers, who proudly adopted the phrase "I fights mit Sigel." See Stephen D. Engle, *Yankee Dutchman: The Life of Franz Sigel* (Fayetteville: University of Arkansas Press, 1993).

20. Claiborne Jackson was the pro-Southern governor of Missouri and organized the antifederal force known as the Missouri State Guard, with which the 2nd Illinois Cavalry had frequent skirmishes while in Missouri. After turning the guard over to the command of General Sterling Price, Jackson maintained a pro-Confederate shadow government in Missouri during the war. Christopher Phillips, *Missouri's Confederate: Claiborne Fox Jackson and the Creation of Southern Identity in the Border West* (Columbia: University of Missouri Press, 2000). See also William E. Parrish, "Jackson, Claiborne Fox," *American National Biography Online*, http://www.anb.org/articles/home.html (accessed June 21, 2010).

21. "French leave" connotes taking leave without permission—alternatively, taking anything without permission. For a nineteenth-century definition, see E. Cobham Brewer, *Dictionary of Phrase and Fable*, 14th ed. (Philadelphia: E. Claxton, 1879[?]), 816.

22. Although Grant had served in the regular army during the Mexican War, he reentered the service as a volunteer and was colonel of the 21st Illinois Infantry. He was appointed brigadier general of federal volunteers in July 1861.

23. No reference to Fort Prentiss could be located, but General Benjamin Prentiss commanded at Camp Defiance outside of Cairo in the spring of 1861. See "The Camp at Cairo Illinois," *Harper's Weekly*, June 1, 1861.

24. Joseph Holt of Kentucky was President James Buchanan's last secretary of war and was later the army's judge advocate general, presiding over the trials of the Lincoln assassination conspirators. See Gayla Koerting, "For Law and Order: Joseph Holt, the Civil War, and the Judge Advocate General's Department," *Register of the Kentucky Historical Society* 97 (1) 1999: 1–25.

25. Francis gives the name as "Cayton" throughout the memoir, but it is given as "Clayton" on official rosters and muster rolls. Private Francis Hessler, in a deposition in Francis Moore's pension file, distinguishes "Cayton" as the correct form, and a letter appearing in the Quincy *Daily Whig and Republican* also gives his name as "Cayton." I have used that spelling throughout.

26. Colonels Leonard Ross, Jacob Lauman, and James Tuttle were all promoted brigadier generals in 1862.

27. The 19th Illinois Infantry, raised by Russian-born Colonel John Basil Turchin. Nadine Lvova Turchin accompanied her husband throughout his field service and reportedly even briefly commanded the regiment when he was ill. For Nadine Turchin, see Mary Ellen McElligott, "'A Monotony Full of Sadness': The Diary of Nadine Turchin, May 1863–April 1864," *Journal of the Illinois State Historical Society* 70 (1) 1977: 27–89. Colonel Turchin was later promoted to brigadier general despite his court-martial for allowing his men to sack the city of Athens, Alabama, on May 2, 1862. See George C. Bradley and Richard L. Dahlen. *From Conciliation to Conquest: The Sack of Athens and the Court-Martial of Colonel John B. Turchin* (Tuscaloosa: University of Alabama Press, 2006).

28. Fort Jefferson was built by George Rogers Clark in 1780 at the confluence of the Mississippi and Ohio Rivers to consolidate his forces in the region and to assert American control of the important confluence region. See Kathryn M. Fraser, "Fort Jefferson: George Rogers Clark's Fort at the Mouth of the Ohio River, 1780–1781," *Register of the Kentucky Historical Society* 81 (1) 1983: 1–24; and John E. L. Robertson, "Fort Jefferson," *Register of the Kentucky Historical Society* 71 (2) 1973: 127–38.

29. The battle of Lexington, Missouri, occurred September 11–20, between Confederate General Sterling Price of the Missouri State Guard and Colonel James Mulligan, commanding the 23rd Illinois Infantry, 13th Missouri Infantry, 27th Missouri Mounted Infantry, Van Horn's Reserve Battalion, and the 1st Illinois Cavalry. The command under Mulligan surrendered entirely, including the 1st Illinois Cavalry. The regiment was paroled, then discharged, and many of the officers and men reenlisted in 1862. See *Report of the Adjutant General*, vol. 7, 484–85. For the battle of Lexington, see *The Battle of Lexington, Fought in and about the City of Lexington, Missouri on September 18, 19 and 20th, 1861* (Lexington Historical Society, 1903).

30. Moore is being a bit disingenuous here by dismissing the "few battles in Missouri" that occurred before Belmont, among which were the significant actions of Wilson's Creek in August and Lexington in September, but he is correct in his evaluation of Belmont as an early significant action in the West. For a contextualization of the battle of Belmont within the larger operations in the West, see Nathaniel Cheairs Hughes, Jr., *The Battle of Belmont: Grant Strikes South* (Chapel Hill: University of North Carolina Press, 1991).

31. General Grant was aboard the *Belle Memphis,* not the *Aleck Scott.*

32. Of course, there is no way to confirm that Moore was the first Union soldier viewed by General Polk that day, but Polk was present on the field, according to his own report: United States War Department, *The War of the Rebellion: A Compilation of the Official Records of the Union and Confederate Armies,* series 1, vol. 3 (Washington DC: Government Printing Office, 1880–1901), 306–10 (hereafter, *OR*).

33. This conforms with Grant's claim in his own memoirs that the battle at Belmont was in part a demonstration to convince General Polk that he could not safely send large numbers of troops away from Columbus to reinforce other commands in the field. See Ulysses S. Grant, *Personal Memoirs of U. S. Grant* (New York: Charles L. Webster, 1885–1886), 94–98. Grant gave the same rationale for the Belmont action in his reports filed at the time; see *OR,* series 1, vol. 3, 267–72.

34. Estimated Union dead, 120; estimated Confederate dead, 105. Approximately 2,500 troops were engaged on the Union side (in line with Moore's estimate of 2,700), approximately 5,000 on the Confederate side. See David S. Heidler, Jeanne T. Heidler, and David J. Coles, eds., *Encyclopedia of the American Civil War* (Santa Barbara, CA: ABC-CLIO, 2000), 207–8.

35. Commodore George N. Hollins of Maryland, formerly of the U.S. Navy. An overview of Hollins's career is included in General Clement Evans, ed., *Confederate Military History,* vol. 2 (Atlanta: Confederate, 1899), 156–57.

36. An abscess of the tonsils.

37. Henry Van Rensselaer of the famous New York family was appointed brigadier general and chief of staff to General Winfield Scott at the outbreak of the Civil War but, upon Scott's retirement in November 1861, became an inspector general, with the rank of colonel. See "Hudson-Mohawk Genealogical and Family Memoirs: Van Rensselaer," Schenectady Digital History Archive, http://www.schenectadyhistory.org/families/hmgfm/vanrensselaer-3.html (accessed June 9, 2010).

38. Franklin Moore, a farmer from Upper Alton, Madison County, features prominently in Francis Moore's memoir. He was not related to Francis, although he was often confused with him, and even Francis's compiled military service file at the National Archives contains some material for Frank Moore. Illinois Civil War Muster and Descriptive Rolls Database, ISA.

39. This passage is difficult to verify, either as a wartime statement or as a postwar reflection. While it is certainly possible that Moore thought so insightfully on the issue at the time, it is equally plausible that he wrote this passage well after the "knotty" problem of emancipation and enlistment of former slaves had been resolved.

40. A "Gordian knot": a difficult problem solved by a bold action. References the knot tied by Gordius, king of Gordium, allegedly cut by Alexander the Great in response to the prophecy that whoever succeeded in loosening it would rule Asia.

41. Moore's caution in transporting fugitive or contraband slaves across the river into Illinois was probably unwarranted, given the circumstances, but was not entirely without reason, as the state law prohibited the emigration of either free or enslaved blacks and punished their entry with imprisonment, a large fine, and public auction if the fine could not be paid. See N. H. Purple, *A Compilation of the Statutes of the State of Illinois, of a General Nature,* pt. 2 (Chicago: Keen and Lee, 1856), 781.

42. "Getting the mitten" refers to the rejection of a marriage proposal; that is, getting the mitten and not the hand. See Mrs. Henry Freeman, "Our Grandfathers and How They Lived," *American Monthly Magazine,* vol. 8 (1896), 17.

43. Alexander Simplot of Dubuque, Iowa. See Edward E. Deckert and Constance R. Cherba, "Alexander Simplot: Civil War Artist," *American History* 41 (2) 2006: 16–70; and Richard D. Martin, "First Regiment Iowa Volunteers," *Palimpsest* 46 (1) 1965: 1–59.

Chapter Two—1862

1. On the 12th of January, Moore was formally commissioned Second Lieutenant by Governor Richard Yates of Illinois, rank to date from day of election, November 15, 1861.

2. Confederate Brigadier General Simon Bolivar Buckner and Union Brigadier General Don Carlos Buell were both graduates of West Point and veterans of the Mexican War. Warner, *Generals in Blue,* 51–52; and Warner, *Generals in Gray,* 38–39.

3. Brigadier General Eleazer Arthur Paine commanded at Cairo in January and February 1862. Warner, *Generals in Blue,* 355–56.

4. Fort Donelson fell two days earlier, on February 16, 1862.

5. Neither General Gideon Pillow nor General John Floyd held significant commands after their flight from Fort Donelson.

6. Illinois secretary of state Ozias M. Hatch and state auditor Jesse K. Dubois were both Republican politicians and longtime friends of Abraham Lincoln.

7. Brigadier General John Pope's success in capturing New Madrid and Island Number 10 earned him promotion to major general and transfer to the eastern theater's Army of Virginia in June 1862. His army was defeated at the Second Battle of Bull Run, and Pope was transferred to the Department of the Northwest. See Warner, *Generals in Blue,* 376–77. See also Peter Cozzens, *General John Pope: A Life for the Nation* (Urbana: University of Illinois Press, 2000), and John Pope, *The Military Memoirs of General John Pope,* ed. Peter Cozzens and Robert Girardi (Chapel Hill: University of North Carolina Press, 1998).

8. As in other portions of the memoir, Moore's estimates here are probably somewhat inflated.

9. Moore is slightly mistaken as to the origin of the name "King's Road," also known as "King's Highway," which was named by Colonel George Morgan, a veteran of the Revolutionary War and an Indian agent to the Continental Congress, who settled the New Madrid area prior to its acquisition by the United States as part of the Louisiana Purchase in 1803. See Eugenia L. Harrison, "Place Names of Four River Counties in Eastern Missouri" (MA thesis, University of Missouri-Columbia, 1943). The name "Spanish Grant" likely refers to the land granted to Morgan by the Spanish government. For George Morgan, see Gregory Schaaf, *Wampum Belts and Peace Trees: George Morgan, Native Americans, and Revolutionary Diplomacy* (Golden, CO: Fulcrum, 1990).

10. Moore's contradiction here regarding the population of the region may be the result of his merger of two types of documents (his diary and his letters) to form his narrative, or it may be that Moore is referring primarily to male inhabitants when he says above that the country is deserted.

11. Brigadier General William Strong, in command of the District of Cairo from March 1862 to December 1862. Warner, *Generals in Blue,* 484.

12. As noted in chapter 1, Moore's numbers for the size of the Confederate force at Belmont are inflated, there being only about 5,000 troops in the field during the combat.

13. The "party of marines" was actually composed of fifty men of the 42nd Illinois Infantry, along with fifty sailors from Admiral Andrew H. Foote's gunboats, under the command of Colonel George W. Roberts of the 42nd Illinois. On the night of April 1, 1862, the expedition succeeded in spiking the guns and returning safely to the gunboats, helping to clear the way for the passage of the *Carondelet* several nights later. See Larry J. Daniel and Lynn N. Bock, *Island No. 10: Struggle for the Mississippi Valley* (Tuscaloosa: University of Alabama Press, 1996), 120.

14. On the New Madrid earthquakes of 1811–12, see Jay Feldman, *When the Mississippi Ran Backwards: Empire, Intrigue, Murder, and the New Madrid Earthquakes* (New York: New Press, 2005); Jake Page and Charles Officer, *The Big One: The Earthquake That Rocked Early America*

and Helped Create a Science (Boston: Houghton Mifflin, 2004); Norma Hayes Bagnall, *On Shaky Ground: The New Madrid Earthquakes of 1811–1812* (Columbia: University of Missouri Press, 1996); and James L. Penick, *The New Madrid Earthquakes of 1811–1812* (Columbia: University of Missouri Press, 1976).

15. Hans Christian Heg, born in Norway, commander of the 15th Wisconsin Infantry, known colloquially as the "Scandinavian Regiment" due to a large proportion of immigrants from Norway, Sweden, and Denmark. Heg was killed in action in September 1863 at the battle of Chickamauga. See Waldemar Ager, *Colonel Heg and His Boys: A Norwegian Regiment in the American Civil War*, trans. Della Kittleson Catuna and Clarence A. Clausen (Northfield, MN: Norwegian-American Historical Association, 2000); and Theodore C. Blegen, ed., *The Civil War Letters of Colonel Hans Christian Heg* (Northfield, MN: Norwegian-American Historical Association, 1936).

16. Companies A, B, C, and D participated in the siege of Corinth, Mississippi, in April and May, while Companies G, H, I, and K went on an expedition to Fort Pillow, Tennessee. Later in July, the bulk of the regiment was chasing Confederate cavalry and guerillas in Tennessee. Dyer, *War of the Rebellion*, vol. 3, 1021.

17. The companies of the 15th Wisconsin Infantry remaining at Island Number 10 were Companies G and I, which remained until October 1862. Dyer, *War of the Rebellion*, vol. 3, 1679–80.

18. Brigadier General Isaac F. Quinby, commanding the subdistrict of Columbus, and later the District of Mississippi. Warner, *Generals in Blue*, 387–88.

19. It is not clear why Moore references this order from Major General John Pope, who was then commanding the Army of Virginia and had no authority over any command of which Moore was a part. The order (General Order Number 5, issued July 18, 1862) to subsist off the countryside was part of a suite of controversial orders issued by Pope when he arrived in the East. It was not issued specifically with regard to cavalry operations.

20. Francis's younger brother, Richard, was twenty years old in 1862. Julian Sherman, with whom Richard was a student in 1860, was the same age; neither joined Company L. Federal manuscript census for Quincy, Illinois, 1860.

21. Two letters written by Francis Moore, Sr., to his wife were pasted into the memoir; they are included as Appendices B and C.

22. William Clark Faulkner (or Falkner), great-grandfather to the author William Faulkner, was one of Company L's most consistent enemies. Faulkner commanded a partisan regiment known as the Mississippi Partisan Rangers and fought at least occasionally under Nathan Bedford Forrest during the time Moore and his company encountered them. See Victor Hoar, "Colonel William C. Falkner in the Civil War," *Journal of Mississippi History* 27 (1) 1965: 42–62.

23. Although Moore's dislike of Major Quincy McNeil is evident, Major McNeil's official report of the operation gives Moore full credit for the capture of Faulkner and the other officers. See *OR*, ser. 1, vol. 17, pt. 1, 460–61.

24. At the time, Confederate Major General Mansfield Lovell was commanding a corps in General Earl Van Dorn's Army of West Tennessee. See *OR*, series 1, vol. 17, pt. 2, 729–30.

25. Brigadier General Thomas Alfred Davies commanded the District of Columbus in the District of West Tennessee and the Department of the Tennessee. See Warner, *Generals in Blue*, 113–14.

Chapter Three—1863

1. The proposed legislation referenced here was most likely a House bill introduced by Thaddeus Stevens on January 12, 1863, which called for the enlistment of 150,000 black

troops, or 150 regiments. The bill passed the House in early February but stalled in the Senate's Committee on Military Affairs, which concluded that sufficient means to authorize black regiments had already been granted. See Dudley Taylor Cornish, *The Sable Arm: Negro Troops in the Union Army, 1861–1865* (New York: Longmans, Green, 1956), 98–99.

2. Brigadier General Alexander Asboth, a former Hungarian revolutionary who had already accumulated an impressive record of service for the Union, was wounded at the battle of Pea Ridge in March 1862. See Earl J. Hess, "Alexander Asboth: One of Lincoln's Hungarian Heroes?" *Lincoln Herald* 84 (Fall) 1982: 181–91.

3. The Mississippi Marine Brigade, organized specifically to fight guerillas on the banks of the Mississippi River, was itself a novel experiment, but one plagued by problems of leadership and discipline. See Anne J. Bailey, "The Mississippi Marine Brigade: Fighting Rebel Guerillas on Western Waters," *Military History of the Southwest* 22 (1) 1992: 31–42.

4. Captain Albert W. Cushman, part of Colonel Robert V. Richardson's Tennessee partisan command, was captured March 14, 1863. See *OR*, ser. 1, vol. 24, pt. 3, 106.

5. Adjutant General Lorenzo Thomas, a career military officer, was responsible for raising black troops in the Division of the Mississippi between 1863 and 1865. He was acting under broad orders from Secretary of War Edwin Stanton, who sent Thomas on a tour of the western theater in late March. His speech on this occasion could not be located, but it was evidently successful. By the end of 1863, Thomas had succeeded in recruiting twenty black regiments, and by the end of the war had recruited 76,000 black troops, or 41 percent of the total number of black troops in Union service. For Stanton's directive to Thomas, see *OR*, ser. 3, vol. 3, 100–101. See also Michael T. Meier, "Lorenzo Thomas and the Recruitment of Blacks in the Mississippi River Valley, 1863–1865," in *Black Soldiers in Blue: African American Troops in the Civil War Era*, ed. John David Smith (Chapel Hill: University of North Carolina Press, 2002), 249–75; and James M. McPherson, *Ordeal by Fire: The Civil War and Reconstruction*, 2nd ed. (New York: McGraw-Hill, 1992), 348.

6. Colonel Robert F. Looney commanded the 38th Tennessee Infantry and was sometimes identified as a brigadier general in Union correspondence. See *OR*, ser. 1, vol. 24, pt. 1, 428.

7. Brigadier General James C. Veatch, formerly colonel of the 25th Indiana Infantry and a veteran of both Fort Donelson and Shiloh, commanded the District of Memphis from March 1863 until January 1864. Warner, *Generals in Blue*, 525–26.

8. Brigadier General John Sappington Marmaduke, formerly of the Missouri State Guard, had completed a raid into southeastern Missouri in April. Warner, *Generals in Gray*, 211–12.

9. Brigadier General James R. Chalmers commanded the Confederate District of Mississippi and East Louisiana in 1863. Warner, *Generals in Gray*, 46.

10. Reports from a number of officers, including Francis Moore, involved in the Coldwater/Hernando action are included in *OR*, ser. 1, vol. 24, pt. 2, 484–507. Confederate Brigadier General James R. Chalmers, then in command of the District of Mississippi, later became one of Forrest's generals. Warner, *Generals in Gray*, 46.

11. On June 30, 1863, Moore was formally mustered as captain to rank from the date of election, May 6, 1862.

12. The Union victory at Helena, Arkansas, was overshadowed by Union victories at Gettysburg and Vicksburg but finally secured eastern Arkansas and its ports on the Mississippi. See Mark Christ, *Civil War Arkansas 1863: The Battle for a State* (Norman: University of Oklahoma Press, 2010), especially chapters 3 and 4. See also Gregory J. W. Urwin, "'A Very Disastrous Defeat': The Battle of Helena, Arkansas," *North & South: The Official Magazine of the Civil War Society* 6 (1) 2002: 26–39.

13. Brigadier General Benjamin Henry Grierson's famous raid, of which the 7th Illinois Cavalry was a part, actually took place between April 17 and May 2, 1863. At the time of the raid, Grierson was colonel of the 6th Illinois Cavalry; he subsequently received a promotion to brigadier general. See Warner, *Generals in Blue,* 189–90; and Tom Lalicki, *Grierson's Raid: A Daring Cavalry Strike through the Heart of the Confederacy* (New York: Farrar, Straus and Giroux, 2004).

14. Confederate Colonel Robert V. Richardson, a partisan leader in Tennessee, joined Nathan Bedford Forrest's command in late 1863 and was later promoted to brigadier general. Warner, *Generals in Gray,* 256–57.

15. It is not clear what Moore means by a "film." The term could not be located in contemporary medical dictionaries.

16. Colonel John F. Newsom of the 18th Tennessee Cavalry and Colonel Tyree Harris Bell, originally of the 12th Tennessee Infantry, and later a brigadier general of cavalry, fought as part of William C. Faulkner's partisan command and were later among Nathan Bedford Forrest's lieutenants in Tennessee. For Newsom, see, for example, *OR,* ser. 1, vol. 23, pt. 1, 629. For Bell, see Warner, *Generals in Gray,* 25.

17. Colonel James S. Martin, 111th Illinois Infantry. Illinois Civil War Muster and Descriptive Rolls Database, ISA.

18. On September 25th, secretary of war Edwin Stanton wrote to Major General Stephen A. Hurlbut, commanding the XVI Corps at Memphis, asking for removal of Martin from command of the garrison at Paducah and "assignment of some officer there who will not permit the surrender of slaves to rebel masters, nor oppose the policy of the Government in organizing colored troops." *OR,* ser. 1, vol. 30, pt. 3, 844. Martin had apparently not been removed by mid-October, when Moore arrived, but was probably relieved shortly thereafter and resumed command of his regiment in early November. See *OR,* ser. 1, vol. 31, pt. 3, 25.

19. The antiwar Democrat Clement Vallandigham was the face of the Northern "Copperhead" threat. His run for governor of Ohio was conducted from exile in Canada. In this passage, Moore has mistaken Indiana governor Oliver P. Morton for Vallandigham's successful opponent in Ohio, prowar Democrat John Brough. For Vallandigham, see Frank L. Klement, *The Limits of Dissent: Clement L. Vallandigham and the Civil War* (Lexington: University Press of Kentucky, 1970).

20. Colonel E. H. Wolfe of the 52nd Indiana Infantry reported the incident on October 21 to Captain J. Hough, assistant adjutant-general at Memphis. *OR,* ser. 1, vol. 31, pt. 1, 692.

21. George E. Waring of the 4th Missouri Cavalry. Waring wrote a colorful reminiscence of his wartime experiences in *Whip and Spur* (New York: Doubleday and McClure, 1897), which discusses many of the same actions and locales mentioned in Moore's memoir.

22. Brigadier General Andrew Jackson Smith commanded cavalry in the Departments of Missouri and Mississippi and in Tennessee. Warner, *Generals in Blue,* 454–55.

23. Lieutenant Cayton wrote an account of this action, which appeared in the *Quincy Daily Whig and Republican,* December 11, 1863.

24. General W. T. Sherman's General Orders Number 4, issued October 28, 1863, was intended to fill the depleted ranks of existing regiments with conscripted or impressed citizens at the discretion of enrolling officers. It was not mandatory for all able-bodied citizens to report for service, but if conscripted, they could not refuse. See *OR,* ser. 1, vol. 31, pt. 1, 767.

25. Solomon "Sol" Street, a Confederate partisan commander under Colonel R. V. Richardson, was captured by Captain Frank Moore of Company D, 2nd Illinois Cavalry, near Union City on November 20, 1863. See Captain Frank Moore's report in *OR,* ser. 1, vol. 31, pt. 1, 570. For Street's military career, see Andrew Brown, "Sol Street: Confederate Partisan Leader," *Journal of Mississippi History* 21 (3) 1959: 155–73.

26. Confederate Brigadier General Philip Dale Roddey commanded cavalry under both Nathan Bedford Forrest and Joseph Wheeler, operating in both western Tennessee and northern Alabama. See Warner, *Generals in Gray*, 262; and Stephen Z. Starr, *The Union Cavalry in the Civil War*, vol. 3 (Baton Rouge: Louisiana State University Press, 1985).

Chapter Four—1864

1. Brigadier General Hugh Thompson Reid commanded at Cairo from October 1863 to March 1864. He entered service as colonel of the 15th Iowa Infantry. Warner, *Generals in Blue*, 392–93.

2. Brigadier General William Sooy Smith, chief of cavalry for the Division of the Mississippi. Warner, *Generals in Blue*, 464–65.

3. See chapter 3, n. 13

4. Lieutenant Colonel Harvey Hogg was actually killed at the Battle of Bolivar, Tennessee, August 30, 1862, according to the adjutant general's roster of the 2nd Illinois Cavalry. *Report of the Adjutant General*, vol. 7, 486.

5. Colonel Lafayette McCrillis of the 3rd Illinois Cavalry.

6. The casualty returns list Lieutenant James K. Catlin as killed, while General Grierson's report lists him as captured. See *OR*, ser. 1, vol. 32, pt. 1, 194, 261. In his memoir, however, Grierson provides a detailed account of Catlin's death in this action. See Bruce J. Dinges and Shirley A. Leckie, eds., *A Just and Righteous Cause: Benjamin H. Grierson's Civil War Memoir* (Carbondale: Southern Illinois University Press, 2008), 222.

7. Colonel George Waring of the 4th Missouri Cavalry, commanding one of the expedition's brigades, offered substantially the same negative evaluation of the raid in *Battles and Leaders of the Civil War*, vol. 4 (New York: Century, 1884, 1887, 1888), 416–18. Grierson also gives a detailed account of the expedition and its failure in his memoir, Dinges and Leckie, eds., *Just and Righteous Cause*, 215–24. General Smith was supposed to push his column through to Meridian to join Sherman's army there but delayed his march, giving Forrest time to intercept and repulse him. For Union and Confederate reports and correspondence from the entire expedition, including the actions described by Moore, see *OR*, ser. 1, vol. 32, pt. 1, 164–391.

8. General Orders, No. 376, issued November 21, 1863.

9. On March 25, Forrest raided Paducah, issuing a similar order to that Moore speculates was received in Memphis. For the raid and skirmish at Paducah, see Brigadier General Mason Brayman's report, *OR*, ser. 1, vol. 32, pt. 1, 510.

10. General Cooke commanded the District of Baton Rouge from October 1863 to May 1864. See Dyer, *War of the Rebellion*, vol.1, 558.

11. Moore misidentified the steamer as the *Ohio Belle*. The attack took place on May 3, 1864, during General Nathaniel Banks's failed Red River campaign. Colonel John J. Mudd took command of the 2nd Illinois Cavalry in February 1863. See *OR*, ser. 1, vol. 34, pt. 1, 622; and "The Red River Campaign," *New York Times*, May 29, 1864, for contemporary accounts of the incident.

12. For the Red River campaign, see Gary Dillard Joiner, *Through the Howling Wilderness: The 1864 Red River Campaign and Union Failure in the West* (Knoxville: University of Tennessee Press, 2006); and Ludwell H. Johnson, *Red River Campaign: Politics and Cotton in the Civil War* (Baltimore: Johns Hopkins Press, 1958).

13. Major General Daniel Sickles, surrounded by controversy after the destruction of his Third Corps at Gettysburg, had been removed from command after the battle and was on a tour of the occupied South. See W. A. Swanberg, *Sickles the Incredible* (New York: Charles Scribner's Sons, 1956), 261–68.

14. Wood took the field as colonel of the 137th Illinois Infantry, mustered on June 5, 1864, for one hundred days. The regiment was posted to Memphis and was assigned to picket duty along the Hernando road. The regiment was mustered out on September 4, 1864. *Report of the Adjutant General*, vol. 7, 90–107.

15. Confederate conscription was considerably more complicated than what Francis Moore knew of it. For an overview, see William L. Shaw, "The Confederate Conscription and Exemption Acts," *American Journal of Legal History* 6 (4) 1962: 368–405.

16. It is not clear whether Moore is referring to the Illinois Democratic convention in Springfield or the national Democratic Convention in Chicago, at which Clement Vallandigham was named as probable secretary of war under Democratic presidential candidate George B. McClellan.

17. Brigadier General William P. Benton, commanding the District of Baton Rouge, June–December 1864. See Dyer, *War of the Rebellion*, vol. 1, 558.

18. Confederate Major General and later Lieutenant General Richard Taylor routed General Banks's Red River campaign and later commanded the Department of Alabama and Mississippi. His was among the last Confederate commands to surrender in 1865. Warner, *Generals in Gray*, 299–300.

19. Brigadier General Albert Lindley Lee, recently appointed chief of cavalry for the Department of the Gulf, had commanded the cavalry in General Banks's unsuccessful Red River campaign. Although the campaign was unsuccessful, General Lee's reputation amongst the cavalry in his new department does not seem to have suffered. Warner, *Generals in Blue*, 278.

20. Colonel John S. Scott (sometimes misidentified as a general) of the First Louisiana Cavalry, headquartered at Clinton from at least May 1864. *OR*, ser.1, vol. 34, pt. 1, 907.

21. Brigadier General Henry Warner Birge. Warner, *Generals in Blue*, 33–34.

22. Major General Francis Herron commanded the District of Baton Rouge and Port Hudson from August to October 1864. See Warner, *Generals in Blue*, 228–29; and Dyer, *War of the Rebellion*, vol. 1, 556.

23. Brigadier General John Davidson, chief of cavalry for the Division of West Mississippi, led a raid from Baton Rouge against the Mobile and Ohio Railroad from November 27 to December 13, 1864. Dyer, *War of the Rebellion*, vol. 2, 756.

24. Brevet Brigadier General Joseph Bailey, formerly an engineer, was breveted for his successful damming efforts to refloat the boats of Banks's Red River expedition after the level of the river fell. Warner, *Generals in Blue*, 14.

25. Lieutenant Colonel N. G. Watts, Confederate commissioner of exchange at Mobile, Alabama.

26. Brigadier General George Leonard Andrews, commander of the District of Port Hudson as of December 26, 1864, immediately preceded in that position by General Benton. See Warner, *Generals in Blue*, 9; and Dyer, *War of the Rebellion*, vol. 1, 556.

Chapter Five—1865

1. Colonel Robert Ould, Confederate chief of the Bureau of Exchange.

2. Edmund Jackson Davis was promoted to brigadier general in November 1864, but Dyer's *War of the Rebellion* lists him as colonel of the 1st Texas Cavalry during his time in Baton Rouge in early 1865. He held several commands in relatively short succession while in Baton Rouge, and there is some discrepancy between Moore's dates and the period in which Dyer states the 2nd Illinois was under Davis. See especially Dyer, *War of the Rebellion*, vol. 1, 558–62.

3. This is very similar to Moore's earlier description of Mrs. Blakeman, who earlier traded in Baton Rouge with General Benton. Whether this is another woman, or if Blakeman had arrangements with both generals, or if Moore is confused as to which general was involved, is not known.

4. Major General William Farrar "Baldy" Smith was relieved of command of the XVIII Corps in July 1864 after failing to take Petersburg, Virginia. Smith was appointed special commissioner by Lincoln on December 10, 1864, "to investigate and report . . . upon the civil and military administration in the military division bordering upon and West of the Mississippi." See *OR*, ser. 1, vol. 41, pt. 4, 817. See also Warner, *Generals in Blue*, 462–63.

5. Charleston and Fort Sumter were occupied by federal forces on February 22, 1865.

6. Major General Edward Richard Sprigg Canby was then in charge of the Military Division of West Mississippi, and was in the midst of a prolonged campaign against Mobile Bay and the city of Mobile, Alabama, in conjunction with Admiral David G. Farragut. Warner, *Generals in Blue*, 67–68; and Dyer, *War of the Rebellion*, vol. 1, 257.

7. The partnership of Samuel Shappe and H. J. Whitney, gymnasts and acrobats, performed under the auspices of several traveling circus companies between 1863 and 1873. See William L. Slout, *Olympians of the Sawdust Circle: A Biographical Dictionary of the Nineteenth Century American Circus* (New York: Borgo Press, 1998); and "Olympians of the Sawdust Circle," Circus Historical Society, http://www.circushistory.org/Olympians/Olympians.htm (accessed June 15, 2010).

8. The poem is actually "A Farewell to London in the Year 1715" by Alexander Pope (1688–1744), and the line is "Dear, damned, distracting town, farewell!" See Pat Rogers, ed., *Alexander Pope, The Major Works* (New York: Oxford University Press, 2006), 118.

9. Major General Gordon Granger, commanding the Thirteenth Army Corps, Department of the Gulf, and Brigadier General Benjamin Grierson, commanding the Cavalry Corps of West Mississippi, were both operating against Mobile. See Dyer, *War of the Rebellion*, vol. 1, 568, 571.

10. Major General Frederick Steele was then commanding a division under General Canby operating against Mobile. Warner, *Generals in Blue*, 474–75.

11. No other reference to a French ironclad in Mobile Bay could be located.

12. General Asboth was wounded in the left cheek and arm at the battle of Marianna, Florida, September 27, 1864. Warner, *Generals in Blue*, 11.

13. The 25th U.S.C.T. was organized in Philadelphia in January and February 1864. They were garrisoned at Barrancas and at Fort Pickens from July 1864 to December 6, 1865, when they were mustered out. For full regimental history, see Dyer, *War of the Rebellion*, vol. 3, 1727; and Samuel P. Bates, *History of Pennsylvania Volunteers, 1861–1865*, vol. 5 (Harrisburg, PA: Singerly, 1871), 1026–46.

14. It was widely believed and reported at the time that Seward had died from a related assassination attempt carried out the same night John Wilkes Booth shot Abraham Lincoln.

15. According to Dyer, General Veatch was then commanding the 1st Division of the 13th Corps. Dyer, *War of the Rebellion*, vol. 1, 568.

16. Lieutenant General Richard Taylor, commanding the Department of Alabama and Mississippi, one of the last significant Confederate commands to surrender, in May 1865. See Warner, *Generals in Gray*, 299–300.

17. The explosion occurred on May 25. Moore's figures for the loss are probably generally accurate. In his report on the explosion, Captain James Patton, acting assistant inspector general at Mobile, estimated that five hundred people were killed or wounded, and estimated six acres of ruined buildings. Patton estimated twenty tons of powder exploded, whereas Moore reported one hundred tons, and contemporary newspaper accounts claimed as much as two hundred tons of total ordnance stores were involved. See *OR*, ser. 1, vol. 49, pt. 1, 565–67; *Report of the Secretary of*

the Navy . . . December 1865 (Washington, DC: Government Printing Office, 1865), 388–89; "The Fearful Explosion at Mobile," *New York Times*, June 4, 1865; and Mrs. Hugh C. Bailey, "Mobile's Tragedy: The Great Magazine Explosion of 1865," *Alabama Review* 21 (1) 1968: 40–52.

18. Brigadier General Christopher Columbus Andrews, then commanding a division of the 13th Corps. Dyer, *War of the Rebellion*, vol. 1, 568.

19. General Canby's order could not be located, but a similar directive had been issued in March 1865 by Colonel Lewis B. Parsons, chief of rail and river transportation in the Quartermaster-General's Office in Washington, D.C. See *OR*, ser. 3, vol. 4, 1239–41.

Epilogue

1. Clipping from the *Quincy Whig and Republican*, F. T. Moore Papers, SDSU.

2. Francis T. Moore Pension File, NARA.

3. Moore's acceptance into the Quincy GAR post is pasted into his memoir, at the break between the two numbered ledger books. F. T. Moore Papers, SDSU. See Lydia Sherman deposition in Francis T. Moore Pension File, NARA.

4. Certificates of death for Henrietta Moore and Mary Moore in Francis T. Moore Pension File, NARA. Newspaper clipping in F. T. Moore Collection, SDSU. Francis listed only three children in his pension application, Francis Jr., Susan, and Thomas, and no record of any other children could be found.

5. Annie graduated in the first class from the college after only a four-month course of instruction. See *Thirty-sixth Annual Report of the Superintendent of Public Instruction of the State of Michigan* (Lansing: W. S. George, 1872), 242–43.

6. Deposition of Alfred L. Leonard in Francis T. Moore Pension File, NARA.

7. National City Public Library, Morgan Local History Room, "Echoes of the Past" photograph exhibit.

8. "Local Intelligence," *San Diego Union*, May 9, 1898.

9. Grand Army of the Republic Collection, San Diego History Center; see also obituary for Francis Moore, *National City News*, December 28, 1912.

10. Letter of Francis Moore to 4th annual Delano's Dragoons reunion, September 28, 1871. Undated and unidentified newspaper clipping, F. T. Moore Collection, SDSU.

11. Unidentified newspaper clipping in F. T. Moore Collection, SDSU.

12. Unidentified newspaper clipping in F. T. Moore Collection, SDSU.

13. Unidentified newspaper clipping in F. T. Moore Collection, SDSU.

14. Unidentified newspaper clipping in F. T. Moore Collection, SDSU.

15. For a review of the recent literature on Civil War memory and commemoration, see Thomas J. Brown, "Civil War Remembrance as Reconstruction," in Thomas J. Brown, ed., *Reconstructions: New Perspectives on the Postbellum United States* (New York: Oxford University Press, 2006).

BIBLIOGRAPHY

Primary Sources

Archives & Repositories

Illinois State Archives (ISA)
Illinois Muster and Descriptive Rolls Database
National Archives and Record Administration (NARA)
Compiled Military and Pension Files for Francis T. Moore
National City Public Library, Local History Room
Photograph Collection
San Diego History Center
Grand Army of the Republic Collection
San Diego State University Library & Information Access, Special Collections & University Archives (SDSU)
F. T. Moore Papers

Published Works

Asbury, Henry. *Reminiscences of Quincy, Illinois*. Quincy: D. Wilcox and Sons, 1882.

Avery, Phineas Orlando. *History of the Fourth Illinois Cavalry Regiment*. Humboldt, NE: Enterprise, 1903.

Bates, Samuel P. *History of Pennsylvania Volunteers, 1861–1865*, vol. 5. Harrisburg, PA: Singerly, 1871.

Blegen, Theodore C., ed. *The Civil War Letters of Colonel Hans Christian Heg*. Northfield, MN: Norwegian-American Historical Association, 1936.

Directory of San Diego City and County. San Diego: Olmsted and Company Printers, 1897.

Fletcher, Samuel H. *The History of Company A, Second Illinois Cavalry*. Published by the Author, 1912.

Grant, Ulysses S. *Personal Memoirs of U. S. Grant*. New York: Charles L. Webster, 1885–1886.

Grierson, Benjamin H. *A Just and Righteous Cause: Benjamin H. Grierson's Civil War Memoir*. Edited by Bruce J. Dinges and Shirley A. Leckie. Carbondale: Southern Illinois University Press, 2008.

Hall, Winfield Scott. *The Captain: An Eighth Illinois Trooper*. Riverside, IL: W. S. Hall, 1994.

Johnson, Robert Underwood, and Clarence Clough Buel, eds. *Battles and Leaders of the Civil War*. 4 vols. New York: Century, 1884, 1887, 1888.

Pope, John. *The Military Memoirs of General John Pope*. Edited by Peter Cozzens and Robert Girardi. Chapel Hill: University of North Carolina Press, 1998.

Purple, N. H. *A Compilation of the Statutes of the State of Illinois, of a General Nature*. Chicago: Keen and Lee, 1856.

Report of the Adjutant General of the State of Illinois, Containing Reports for the Years 1861–1866, vol. 7. Revised by Brigadier General J. W. Vance. Springfield, IL: H. W. Rokker, 1886.

Report of the Secretary of the Navy . . . December 1865. Washington, DC: Government Printing Office, 1865.

San Diego City and County Directory for 1899–1900. San Diego: Baker Bros., 1899.

San Diego City and County Directory. San Diego: San Diego Directory, 1901–1920.

Sanford, W. L. *History of Fourteenth Illinois Cavalry.* Chicago: R. R. Donnelley and Sons, 1898.

Thirty-sixth Annual Report of the Superintendent of Public Instruction of the State of Michigan. Lansing: W. S. George, 1872.

United States War Department. *The War of the Rebellion: A Compilation of the Official Records of the Union and Confederate Armies.* Washington, DC: Government Printing Office, 1880–1901.

Waring, George E. *Whip and Spur.* New York: Doubleday and McClure, 1897.

Wills, Charles Wright. *Army Life of an Illinois Soldier . . . Letters and Diary of the Late Charles W. Wills, Private and Sergeant 8th Illinois Infantry; Lieutenant and Battalion Adjutant 7th Illinois Cavalry; Captain, Major and Lieutenant Colonel 103rd Illinois Infantry.* Washington, DC: Globe Printing, 1906.

Secondary Sources

Ager, Waldemar. *Colonel Heg and His Boys: A Norwegian Regiment in the American Civil War.* Translated by Della Kittleson Catuna and Clarence A. Clausen. N.p.: Norwegian-American Historical Association, 2000.

Bagnall, Norma Hayes. *On Shaky Ground: The New Madrid Earthquakes of 1811–1812.* Columbia: University of Missouri Press, 1996.

Bahde, Thomas W. "Race and Justice in the Heartland: Three Nineteenth-Century Lives." PhD diss., University of Chicago, 2009.

Bailey, Anne J. "The Mississippi Marine Brigade: Fighting Rebel Guerillas on Western Waters." *Military History of the Southwest* 22 (1) 1992: 31–42.

Bailey, Mrs. Hugh C. "Mobile's Tragedy: The Great Magazine Explosion of 1865." *Alabama Review* 21 (1) 1968: 40–52.

The Battle of Lexington, Fought in and about the City of Lexington, Missouri on September 18, 19th and 20th, 1861. Lexington Historical Society, 1903.

Blight, David W. *Beyond the Battlefield: Race, Memory, and the American Civil War.* Amherst: University of Massachusetts Press, 2002.

———. *Race and Reunion: The Civil War in American Memory.* Cambridge: Belknap/Harvard University Press, 2001.

Bradley, George C., and Richard L. Dahlen. *From Conciliation to Conquest: The Sack of Athens and the Court-Martial of Colonel John B. Turchin.* Tuscaloosa: University of Alabama Press, 2006.

Brown, Andrew. "Sol Street: Confederate Partisan Leader." *Journal of Mississippi History* 21 (3) 1959: 155–73.

Brown, Thomas J., ed. *Reconstructions: New Perspectives on the Postbellum United States.* New York: Oxford University Press, 2006.

Buckler, Patricia P., and C. Kay Leeper. "An Antebellum Woman's Scrapbook as Autobiographical Composition." *Journal of American Culture* 14 (1) 1991: 1–8.

Campbell, Thomas R. *Confederate Naval Forces on Western Waters: The Defense of the Mississippi River and Its Tributaries.* Jefferson, NC: McFarland, 2005.

Christ, Mark. *Civil War Arkansas, 1863: The Battle for a State.* Norman: University of Oklahoma Press, 2010.

Cimbala, Paul A., and Randall M. Miller, eds. *Union Soldiers and the Northern Home Front: Wartime Experiences, Postwar Adjustments.* New York: Fordham University Press, 2002.

Cornish, Dudley Taylor. *The Sable Arm: Negro Troops in the Union Army, 1861–1865.* New York: Longmans, Green, 1956.

Costigan, David. "A City in Wartime: Quincy, Illinois and the Civil War." Ph.D. diss., Illinois State University, 1994.

Cozzens, Peter. *General John Pope: A Life for the Nation.* Urbana: University of Illinois Press, 2000.

Daniel, Larry J., and Lynn N. Bock. *Island No. 10: Struggle for the Mississippi Valley.* Tuscaloosa: University of Alabama Press, 1996.

Davis, Stephen. "Jeff Thompson's Unsuccessful Quest for a Confederate Generalship." *Missouri Historical Review* 85 (1) 1990: 53–65.

Dearing, Mary R. *Veterans in Politics: The Story of the G.A.R.* Baton Rouge: Louisiana State University Press, 1952.

Deckert, Edward E., and Constance R. Cherba. "Alexander Simplot: Civil War Artist." *American History* 41 (2) 2006: 16–70.

Dyer, Frederick H. *A Compendium of the War of the Rebellion.* 3 vols. New York: Thomas Yoseloff, 1959.

Engle, Stephen D. *Yankee Dutchman: The Life of Franz Sigel.* Fayetteville: University of Arkansas Press, 1993.

Evans, Clement, ed. *Confederate Military History.* Atlanta: Confederate , 1899.

Ezell, Margaret J. M., and Katherine O'Brien O'Keeffe. *Cultural Artifacts and the Production of Meaning: The Page, the Image, and the Body.* Ann Arbor: University of Michigan Press, 1994.

Fabian, Ann. *The Unvarnished Truth: Personal Narratives in Nineteenth-Century America.* Berkeley and Los Angeles: University of California Press, 2000.

Fahs, Alice. *The Imagined Civil War: Popular Literature of the North and South, 1861–1865.* Chapel Hill: University of North Carolina Press, 2001.

Fahs, Alice, and Joan Waugh. *The Memory of the Civil War in American Culture.* Chapel Hill: University of North Carolina Press, 2004.

Feldman, Jay. *When the Mississippi Ran Backwards: Empire, Intrigue, Murder, and the New Madrid Earthquakes.* New York: New Press, 2005.

Fellman, Michael. *Inside War: The Guerilla Conflict in Missouri during the American Civil War.* New York: Oxford University Press, 1989.

Filbert, Preston. *The Half Not Told: The Civil War in a Frontier Town.* Mechanicsburg, PA: Stackpole Books, 2001.

Fraser, Kathryn M. "Fort Jefferson: George Rogers Clark's Fort at the Mouth of the Ohio River, 1780–1781." *Register of the Kentucky Historical Society* 81 (1) 1983: 1–24.

Gallagher, Gary W. *Causes Won, Lost, and Forgotten: How Hollywood and Popular Art Shape What We Know about the Civil War.* Chapel Hill: University of North Carolina Press, 2008.

Hall, Jacquelyn Dowd. "'You Must Remember This': Autobiography as Social Critique." *Journal of American History* 85 (September) 1998: 439–65.

Harrison, Eugenia L. "Place Names of Four River Counties in Eastern Missouri." Master's thesis, University of Missouri-Columbia, 1943.

Heidler, David S., Jeanne T. Heidler, and David J. Coles, eds. *Encyclopedia of the American Civil War*. Santa Barbara, CA: ABC-CLIO, 2000.

Hess, Earl J. "Alexander Asboth: One of Lincoln's Hungarian Heroes?" *Lincoln Herald* 84 (Fall) 1982: 181–91.

Hicken, Victor. *Illinois in the Civil War*. 2nd ed. Urbana: University of Illinois Press, 1991.

Hoar, Victor. "Colonel William C. Falkner in the Civil War." *Journal of Mississippi History* 27 (1) 1965: 42–62.

Hughes, Nathaniel Cheairs, Jr. *The Battle of Belmont: Grant Strikes South*. Chapel Hill: University of North Carolina Press, 1991.

Hunt, Robert. *The Good Men Who Won the War: Army of the Cumberland Veterans and Emancipation Memory*. Tuscaloosa: University of Alabama Press, 2010.

Johnson, Ludwell H. *Red River Campaign: Politics and Cotton in the Civil War*. Baltimore: Johns Hopkins Press, 1958.

Joiner, Gary Dillard. *Through the Howling Wilderness: The 1864 Red River Campaign and Union Failure in the West*. Knoxville: University of Tennessee Press, 2006.

Jones, Andrew. *Memory and Material Culture*. Cambridge: Cambridge University Press, 2007.

Katriel, Tamar, and Thomas Farrell. "Scrapbooks as Cultural Texts: An American Art of Memory." *Text and Performance Quarterly* 11 (1) 1991: 1–17.

Keenan, Jerry. *Wilson's Cavalry Corps: Union Campaigns in the Western Theatre, October 1864 through Spring 1865*. Jefferson, NC: McFarland, 1998.

Kionka, T. K. *Key Command: Ulysses S. Grant's District of Cairo*. Columbia: University of Missouri Press, 2006.

Klement, Frank L. *The Limits of Dissent: Clement L. Vallandigham and the Civil War*. Lexington: University Press of Kentucky, 1970.

Koerting, Gayla. "For Law and Order: Joseph Holt, the Civil War, and the Judge Advocate General's Department." *Register of the Kentucky Historical Society* 97 (1) 1999: 1–25.

Kwint, Marius, Christopher Breward, and Jeremy Aynsley. *Material Memories*. Oxford: Berg, 1999.

Lalicki, Tom. *Grierson's Raid: A Daring Cavalry Strike through the Heart of the Confederacy*. New York: Farrar, Straus and Giroux, 2004.

Logue, Larry M., and Michael Barton, eds. *The Civil War Veteran: A Historical Reader*. New York: New York University Press, 2007.

Martin, Richard D. "First Regiment Iowa Volunteers." *Palimpsest* 46 (1) 1965: 1–59.

McConnell, Stuart. *Glorious Contentment: The Grand Army of the Republic, 1865–1900*. Chapel Hill: University of North Carolina Press, 1992.

McElligott, Mary Ellen. "'A Monotony Full of Sadness': The Diary of Nadine Turchin, May 1863–April 1864." *Journal of the Illinois State Historical Society* 70 (1) 1977: 27–89.

McPherson, James M. *Ordeal by Fire: The Civil War and Reconstruction*. 2nd ed. New York: McGraw-Hill, 1992.

Mountcastle, Clay. *Punitive War: Confederate Guerrillas and Union Reprisals*. Lawrence: University Press of Kansas, 2009.

Mueller, Doris Land. *M. Jeff Thompson: Missouri's Swamp Fox of the Confederacy*. Columbia: University of Missouri Press, 2007.

Nichols, Bruce. *Guerilla Warfare in Civil War Missouri*. Jefferson, NC: McFarland, 2004.

Page, Jake, and Charles Officer. *The Big One: The Earthquake That Rocked Early America and Helped Create a Science*. Boston: Houghton Mifflin, 2004.

Penick, James L. *The New Madrid Earthquakes of 1811–1812*. Columbia: University of Missouri Press, 1976.

Phillips, Christopher. *Missouri's Confederate: Claiborne Fox Jackson and the Creation of Southern Identity in the Border West*. Columbia: University of Missouri Press, 2000.

Robertson, John E. L. "Fort Jefferson." *Register of the Kentucky Historical Society* 71 (2) 1973: 127–38.

Rogers, Pat, ed. *Alexander Pope: The Major Works*. New York: Oxford University Press, 2006.

Royster, Charles. *The Destructive War: William Tecumseh Sherman, Stonewall Jackson, and the Americans*. New York: Alfred A. Knopf, 1991.

Schaaf, Gregory. *Wampum Belts and Peace Trees: George Morgan, Native Americans, and Revolutionary Diplomacy*. Golden, CO: Fulcrum, 1990.

Shaw, William L. "The Confederate Conscription and Exemption Acts." *American Journal of Legal History* 6 (4) 1962: 368–405.

Shea, William L., and Terrence J. Winschel. *Vicksburg Is the Key: The Struggle for the Mississippi River*. Lincoln: University of Nebraska Press, 2003.

Slout, William L. *Olympians of the Sawdust Circle: A Biographical Dictionary of the Nineteenth Century American Circus*. New York: Borgo Press, 1998.

Smith, John David, ed. *Black Soldiers in Blue: African American Troops in the Civil War Era*. Chapel Hill: University of North Carolina Press, 2002.

Smith, Myron J., Jr. *The Timberclads in the Civil War: The Lexington, Conestoga, and Tyler on the Western Waters*. Jefferson, NC: McFarland, 2008.

———. *Tinclads in the Civil War: Union Light-Draught Gunboat Operations on Western Waters, 1862–1865*. Jefferson, NC: McFarland, 2010.

Stanton, Donald J., and Goodwin F. Berquist. "Missouri's Forgotten General: M. Jeff Thompson and the Civil War." *Missouri Historical Review* 73 (3) 1976: 237–58.

Starr, Stephen Z. *The Union Cavalry in the Civil War*. 3 vols. Baton Rouge: Louisiana State University Press, 1985.

Sutherland, Daniel E. *A Savage Conflict: The Decisive Role of Guerrillas in the American Civil War*. Chapel Hill: University of North Carolina Press, 2009.

Swanberg, W. A. *Sickles the Incredible*. New York: Charles Scribner's Sons, 1956.

Vernon, Alex. *Arms and the Self: War, the Military, and Autobiographical Writing*. Kent, Ohio: Kent State University Press, 2004.

Warner, Ezra. *Generals in Blue: Lives of the Union Commanders*. Baton Rouge: Louisiana State University Press, 1964.

———. *Generals in Gray: Lives of the Confederate Commanders*. Baton Rouge: Louisiana State University Press, 1959.

INDEX

Page numbers in italics refer to figures.

4th U.S. Cavalry, 170
7th Confederate Cavalry, 185
Aberdeen (Miss.), 172, 173
Adams County Dragoons. *See* Delano's Dragoons
African Americans, 32, 33, 83–84, 86, 103, 116, 120, 147, 162, 178–79, 189, 199, 205, 207–8, 212; on riverboats, 81; wedding and dance, 201. *See also* contrabands (former slaves); slavery
Aleck Scott, 44, 46
Allen, Pvt. Steven, 107
Alley, Miss Lou, 186, 199–200, 202
Alton (Ill.), 26
ambrotypes, 58, 229
Andrews, General Christopher Columbus, 252
Andrews, General George Leonard, 213
arms, 20, 26, 27, 30, 36, 59, 107–8, 119; Colt's revolvers, 27; Colt's revolving rifle, 96, 101; Henry repeating carbines, 197; sabers, 27, 36, 42, 138; Smith and Wesson revolver, 76
Army of the Potomac, 160, 164, 189
artillery, 34, 46, 49, 50, 56, 84, 99, 100, 109, 112–13, 127, 136, 137, 139–40, 159, 174, 189, 197, 211, 233, 245; "Lady Polk," 112; "Long Tom," 57, 58
Asboth, General Alexander, 122, 125, 129, 133, 243, 245, 246; attitudes toward black enlistment,130; corruption of, 201, 238, 240; reputation of 123–24; wounding of, 241

Bacon, Mrs., 203
Beauregard, General P.G.T., 147, 245
Bailey, General Joseph, 210, 219, 232
Baker, Capt. H. B., 203, 207, 208, 210
Baltimore Riot, 284n2
Banks, General Nathaniel P., 185, 186, 189, 190
Barrancas (Fla.), 229, 237, 242, 246, 294n13
Batchelor, Capt., 81
Bates, Pvt. Augustus H., 132
Baton Rouge (La.), 188, 189, 209, 210, 211, 213, 215, 216, 218, 223, 224, 225, 226, 227, 228, 232, 252, 293n23; description of, 185
Bayou Grande (Fla.), 240, 242, 244, 246
Bell, William, 36, 230
Bell, Col. Tyree Harris, 148, 149
Belle Memphis, 46, 254
Belle Peoria, 254
Belmont (Mo.), battle of, 46–53
Benton Hussars, 28, 34, 38, 39, 41, 42, 285n13
Benton, General William P., 191, 210, 213, 214, 225; involved in cotton speculation, 194
Berrian, James T., 107, 125
Bimson, Pvt. Benjamin, 140
Bird's Point (Mo.), 35, 38, 45, 56, 57, 58, 64, 71, 82
Birge, General Henry Warner, 196
"black flag," 155
Black Water River (Fla.), 244
Blackburn, Gilly, 103
Blandville (Ky.), 43, 61, 65, 67, 122, 125, 126, 167
Boardman, Col. Frederick, 185, 188
Bolivar (Tenn.), 182, 292n4
"bounty jumpers," 19
Bowling Green (Ky.), 67
Boydsville (Tenn.), 154, 156, 158, 161
Bronson, Fanny A., 115, 121

Brookhaven (Miss.), 208
Brooks, Pvt. John F., 136, 141, 142
Brownsville (Tenn.), 143, 148
Buckner, General Simon Bolivar, 67
Buell, General Don Carlos, 67
Buell's Battery, 18, 28, 30, 285n13
Buford, Col. Napoleon B., 44, 47, 48, 51
Burke, Sgt. William H., 62
Bush, Col. Daniel, 190, 230
bushwhackers, 4, 7, 20, 32, 71, 88, 90, 95, 96, 97, 198, 207. *See also* guerrillas
Butler, General Benjamin, 142, 215, 225
Bywater, Pvt. John, 95
Bywater, Pvt. Maurice (farrier), 125

Cairo (Ill.), 35, 44, 56, 57, 58, 67, 69, 81; description of, 45; military corruption in, 94; military importance of, 34–35; street fight in, 77
Caldwell, Mr. L., 186
Caledonia (Ky.), 154, 155, 156
Camp Butler (Ill.), 3, 18, 20, 22, 25, 26
Camp Crittenden (Ky.), 38, 39, 40, 43, 65, 67
Camp Flagg (Ill.), 3, 18, 20, 21, 22, 25, 43, 93
Camp Paine (Ky.), 69
Camp Parapet (La.), 231
Camp Point (Ill.), 20, 22
Canby, General Edward Richard Sprigg, 228, 229, 249, 294
Cape Girardeau (Mo.), 32, 34
Capron, Reverend Alexander, 22
Carondelet, 84
Carrolton (La.), 225, 226, 230, 231, 232
Catlin, Lieut. James K., 20, 21, 26, 36, 46, 49, 60, 62, 63, 67, 69, 88, 91, 95, 96, 97, 101; aid-de-camp to General Grierson, 168; death of, 176, 292n6; detailed as regimental adjutant, 102; duties of, 21, 45, 53, 54, 59; election of, 20; illness of, 57, 58; involvement in death of Captain Delano, 76, 77, 85–86
Cayton, Lieut. John, 36, 54, 91, 102, 105, 106, 115, 132, 133, 134, 162, 169, 193, 205, 206, 210, 218, 219, 220, 263; detailed as quartermaster, 102, 157; elected lieutenant, 86, 93; resignation and discharge of, 228, 229–30
Chalmers, General James P., 139, 140
Chancellor, 46
Charleston (Mo.), 70, 71, 72
Chase, Joe, 107
Chattanooga (Tenn.), 160
Christmas, 62, 162, 211, 212
church. *See* religious services
City Belle, 188
City of Memphis, 254
Clayton (Ill.), 23
Clear Lake (Ill.), 25
Clinton (Ky.), 123–24, 129, 130, 131
Clinton (La.), 188, 193, 196, 197, 198–99, 202, 203, 205, 208, 223, 232
Clyde, 235
coffee, 75, 170, 202, 225
Cold Water River (Miss.), 137, 139, 140
Collierville (Tenn.), 168, 169, 170, 178, 180
Columbus (Ky.), 34, 37, 38, 41, 42, 46, 53, 57, 61, 65, 66, 67, 70, 113, 122, 129, 133, 159, 160, 166, 167, 168; capture of, 73, 74, 83, 124; described, 122, 131; forces engaged in battle of Belmont, 47, 49, 50
Comite River (La.), 196, 197, 200
Como (Miss.), 154, 156
Confederates and Confederacy, 5, 69, 136, 146, 154, 155, 183, 189, 245
conscription, 19, 95, 145, 128, 131, 160, 191, 205, 230; Confederate, 91, 101, 129, 191, 293n15
contrabands (former slaves), 59–61, 120, 136, 143, 153, 160, 184, 209; as troops/soldiers, 6, 120, 129–30, 136, 181–82, 136, 143, 176; as source of information, 21, 44, 59, 71, 72, 110, 140
contraband (goods), 32, 61, 119–20, 129, 155, 223
Cook, Col. John, 28, 33, 58, 68
Cooke, General Philip St. George, 186, 219
Cooke's Tactics, 186
Copperheads, 6, 18, 24, 56, 128, 129, 205, 241, 263, 264
Corinth (Miss.), 103, 110, 111, 134, 159

cotton, 139, 173, 178, 184, 185, 188, 215; speculation in, 7, 182, 194, 201, 222–23
Covington (Tenn.), 135, 136
Cox, Sgt. John C., 117, 131, 159
Craine, Pvt. Charles (bugler), 62, 117
Crawford, 247
Crawford, Lieut. Henry B., 139, 140
Creoles, 7, 187, 189, 203, 225, 233
Cumberland River, 34, 57

Dabney, Wash, 135, 193, 254
Daigre, Madame, 213, 214, 218, 219, 225
Dallas (Mo.), 32
dances and dancing, 79, 80, 81, 117, 124, 162, 165, 201, 227–229; "stag" dancing, 62
David Tatum, 26
Davidson, General John, 210, 212, 293n23
Davis, Capt. (guerilla chief), 100, 101
Davis, General Edmund Jackson, 220, 293n2
Davis, Jefferson, 142, 222, 248, 250
Dawson, Pvt. Barton S., 62
Degolzer, Capt., 100, 101
Delano, Capt. Sterling P., 10, 18, 21, 23, 26, 27, 36, 38, 39, 41, 43, 46, 54, 62, 65, 66, 69, 73, 74; attempt to raise a regiment or battalion, 58–59; elected captain, 20; wounding and death of, 3, 26, 76–79, 85
Delano, Decatur, 77, 79, 107
Delano's Dragoons, 23, 26, 31, 95, 253, 258, 262
Dement, Lieut. Austin, 143, 168, 176, 223, 224
Denmark (Tenn.), 143, 148
Diadem, 124
Diligent, 82
discipline, breach of, 115, 118, 126–28, 168, 190, 194–95, 201. *See also* punishments
Donaldson, Bud, 161
Donaldson, Lieut. (guerrilla), 105
Donaldson, Mrs. Dick, 103
Dougherty, Col. David, 32, 33
Douglass, Pvt. Thomas C., 223
Dove, Capt., 68
draft. *See* conscription
Dresden (Miss.), 155–58
drill, military, 18, 20, 21, 25, 34, 36, 45, 54, 59, 106, 114, 118, 219, 220; proficiency of black soldiers, 136, 242
Dubois, Jesse K., 69, 288n6
Duff, Lt. Col. W. L., 69
Dukedom (Tenn.), 154, 156
Dunn, "Major," 186, 199
Duplantia, Alfred, 211, 212
Durhamville (Tenn.), 143, 145, 146
Dyersburg (Tenn.), 144, 146, 149, 151

earthquakes, 88, 132, 147, 163
East Pascagoula (Miss.), 247, 248, 249, 250, 255
Edwards, Joe, 87
Egypt (Miss.), 171
elections, 153; of officers, 20, 54, 86; presidential, 192, 201–3
Elliott, Cpl. Warner D., 57
Elliott's Mill (Ky.), 38, 39, 41, 65
Ellis Creek (Fla.), 248
Elwood, Pvt. John, 193
emancipation, 5, 6, 120, 130, 136, 179
Emma Duncan, 81
Empries, Mr., 248
Escambia River (Fla.), 240
Ewart, Capt. James, 131, 168, 253

Farmington (Mo.), 29
Faulkner, Col. William Clark, 104, 108, 135, 139, 140, 148, 149, 154, 155–60, 165, 289n22; capture of, 105, 108; described, 108
Feliciana (Ky.), 156
Felter, Capt. John H., 134
flags, 22–23, 114; Confederate, 36, 37, 69, 43; at death of Captain Delano, 78
fleas, 97, 150
Florida military units: 1st Cavalry, 242
Floyd, General Richard, 69, 288n5
Floyd, Pvt. George F., 140
Foley, Madame, 200, 201
Forked Deer River (Tenn.), 149, 151, 155, 162
Forrest, General Nathan Bedford, 4, 161, 162, 164, 165, 178, 289n22, 290n10,

291nn14–15, 292n26, 292n9; alleged attack on Memphis, 182; skirmishing in Mississippi, 171, 172, 174, 177
Fort Barrancas (Fla.), 237, 242, 244
Fort Blakely (Ala.), 243, 244, 247
Fort Defiance (Ill.), 35
Fort Donelson (Tenn.), 69, 73, 83, 110, 119, 134
Fort Gaines (Ala.), 233
Fort Halleck (Ky.), 122, 124
Fort Henry (Tenn.), 69
Fort Holt (Ky.), 37, 38, *46, 48, 55,* 58, 60, 65, 72, 73, 84
Fort Jefferson (Ky.), 38, 39, 40, 41, 43, 64, 65, 67, 286n28
Fort McRee (Fla.), 237, 239, 243
Fort Pickens (Fla.), 236, 237, 238, 244, 246
Fort Pickering (Tenn.), 141, 180, 181
Fort Pillow (Tenn.), 128, 133–36, 143, 146–48, 151, 155
Fort Prentiss (Ill.), 35, 56. *See also* Fort Defiance
Fort Sumter (S.C.), 17, 227
Fort Thompson (Mo.), 73, 74, 89, 90, 111
Fort Williams (La.), 185, 193, 204, 218
Franklin Creek (Fla.), 248, 250
French Creoles. *See* Creoles
Fredericktown (Mo.), 28, 29, 31, 32
Fremont, General John C., 27, 28
furloughs, 166, 181

Garrett, Cpl. Richard, 105, 107, 109
Garrett, Lieut., 239
General Banks, 235, 250
German-Americans, 28, 29, 31, 32, 38, 41, 132, 151, 157, 160, 285n19
Gettysburg, battle of, 191, 290n12, 293n13
Gilpin, Sgt. William G., 22; escorts Captain Delano, 77, 79, 81; illness and death of, 102, 103; participation in stag dance, 62
Glasgow, 230
Gooding, Col., 214
Goulty, Pvt. Henry, 166
Graham, Commodore, 46, 287n31
Grampus, 44
Grand Army of the Republic (GAR), 9–10, 258, 261, 262
Granger, General Gordon, 74, 236, 296n9
Grant, General Ulysses S., 33, 34, 45, 46, 60, 69, 141, 184, 253, 286n22; described, 67; in eastern theater, 189; strategy at battle of Belmont, 53, 287n33; surrender of General Lee, 245
Green, Cpl. William, 107
Greenville (Mo.), 31, 285n18
Greenville Spring (La.), 194, 206, 207, 221
Grey Eagle, 219
Grierson, General Benjamin, 168, 169, 172, 173, 174, 176, 178, 196, 229, 292nn6–7; movement against Mobile, 236, 294n9; raid to Baton Rouge, 143, 169, 291n13; reputation of, 144, 169, 173
Griffin's Mill (Ala.), 249
"Grimsley" saddles, 24
guerrillas, 4, 101, 136, 159, 185, 211, 212, 232; using bloodhound to hunt, 153; capturing, 96,164; in Denmark, 143; Faulkner's, 135, 155, 158; firing upon boats, 95; hunting in swamp, 87; pursuing at Horn Ridge, 97; relationship to Copperheads, 128; "Yankee guerrillas," 148. *See also* bushwhackers
gunboats, 75, 83, 84, 90, 127, 141, 142, 147, 188, 243, 288n13; arrival of, 58, 67; at battle of Belmont, 47, 51; Confederate, 38, 56, 65, 68; *Gunboat Number* 53, 214, 219, 223, 226
Gun Boat Point (Fla.), 243, 246

Hardee, General William J., 31, 285n18
Hatch, Ozias, 69, 288n6
Hays, Sgt. Jack, 212
Heg, Col. Hans Christian, 91, 92, 93, 288n15
Helena (Ark.), 141, 184
Hernando (Miss.), 136, 137, 140, 165, 293n14; battle of, 137–40
Herron, General Francis, 205, 221–22, 225, 293n22
Hickman (Ky.), 130, 134, 146, 153, 158
Hickox's Landing (La.), 233, 235

Highland Stockade (La.), 186, 191, 194, 210, 215, 217
Hill, Sgt. Daniel D., 41, 118, 121
Hogg, Lieut. Col. Harvey, 170, 292n4
Hollins, Commodore George N., 56, 287n35
Hollowbush, Tom, 30, 285n16
Holly Springs (Miss.), 169, 170
Homan, Pvt. John S., 167
Hope, 168
Horn Island (Ala.), 248
Horn Lake (Miss.), 136, 140
Horn Ridge (Tenn.), 97, 152
horse opera, 181
Hudsonville (Miss.), 169
Humboldt (Tenn.), 149
Hurd, Edwin A., 23, 284n10

Iberville, 252
Illinois military units: 2nd Artillery, 69, 127; 1st Cavalry, 20, 43, 60, 85, 286n29; 2nd Cavalry, 3, 26, 135, 136, 137, 155, 160, 162, 168, 172, 175, 176, 201, 206, 210, 284n7, 292n11; 4th Cavalry, 65, 134; 6th Cavalry, 291n13; 7th Cavalry, 142, 291n13; 10th Cavalry, 285n16; 12th Cavalry, 210, 224; 7th Infantry, 28, 58; 10th Infantry, 285n12; 16th Infantry, 73, 90; 17th Infantry, 29, 38; 19th Infantry, 28, 39, 286n27; 21st Infantry, 33, 286n22; 27th Infantry, 47, 48, 52; 28th Infantry, 28, 58, 65; 52nd Illinois, 67; 111th Infantry, 127, 291n17
illnesses, 57, 102–3, 118, 120, 132–33, 142, 143, 152, 166; ague, 57, 92, 144; malarial fever, 12, 102, 260; quinsy, 57; smallpox, 121
Illinois River, 23, 24
Indiana military units: 3rd Artillery, 161–62; 9th Artillery, 161–62; 7th Cavalry, 176; 52nd Infantry, 134, 291n20
Iowa military units: 2nd Cavalry, 71, 173; 2nd Infantry, 28, 30, 38; 7th Infantry, 38, 52; 40th Infantry, 161
Ironton (Mo.), 28, 29
Irwin, Lt. Samuel, 218, 231
ironclad boats, 38, 57, 48, 64, 65, 66, 68, 147, 241
Island Number 10, 34, 57, 67, 73, 74, 75, 84, 85, 91, 113, 134, 147

Jackson, 249, 250
Jackson, Claibourne, 32, 285n20
Jackson (Mo.), 32–34
Jackson (Tenn.), 148, 149, 161, 162
Jacksonville (Ill.), 24
Jeannie Deans, 79
Jennie Rogers, 225
Jews, 222
"jiggers," 193
Johnson, Col. A. K., 28, 58, 65
Jolly, Lieut., 249
Jones, Capt. Thomas, 234, 241
Jones, Willis, 93

Kansas military units: 1st Infantry ("Jennison's Jayhawkers), 132
Kate Dale, 249
Keene, Capt., 214, 219, 226
Kendall, Reese P., 41, 51, 62, 67, 102, 103, 143; involvement in death of Captain Delano, 76–77
Kentucky military units: 15th Cavalry, 118; 19th Infantry, 205
Keystone, 46
King's Road (Mo.), 74, 288n9
Kirby, Lieut., 241, 242
Knickerbocker, Mr. R. W., 210, 215, 218, 219, 220

La Grange (La.), 142, 143
La Junta (Colo.), 261, 262
Lake Borgne (La.), 235
Lake Ponchartain (La.), 232, 233
Landis, 187
Landrew, Col., 196
Landrum, Col. William J., 205
Larrison, Maj. Thomas, 130, 140, 230
Lauman, Col. Jacob, 38, 286n26
Lee, General Albert Lindley, 196–202, 205, 206, 208, 293n19; capture of Clinton,

Louisiana, 196–99; competence and loyalty questioned, 209, 224, 225, 229
Lee, General Robert E., 244, 245
Lexington, 46, 48
Lexington (Mo.), battle of, 43, 285n29
Liberty (La.), 198
Lincoln, Abraham, assassination of, 245–46
Locke, Revered William, 63
Lonnsbury, Pvt. Guy, 29, 185
Looney, General Robert, 135, 290n6
Loose Hatchie River (Tenn.), 135
Louisiana military units: 1st Cavalry, 220, 226; 2nd Infantry, 210, 211
Louisville, 68
loyalty oath. *See* Oath of loyalty or allegiance
Lyon family (Paducah), 114, 117, 153

Madrid Bend (Tenn.), 7, 93, 152, 161
Magnolia Grove, (La.) 195, 208, 220
Maine military units: 2nd Cavalry, 242
Mardi Gras, 227
Marmaduke, General John Sappington, 136, 139, 290n8
Marsh, Col. Benjamin F., 20, 201, 222, 236, 241, 244, 284n7
Marshall, Col. Thomas A., 60
Marshall, Judge, 60
Martin, Col. James S., 122, 124, 153, 201
Massachusetts military units: 3rd Infantry, 226; 31st Mounted Infantry, 214, 235
Matamora, 240
Mayfield (Ky.), 126, 154, 155, 158
Mayfield Creek (Ky.), 18, 65, 66
McClernand, General John A., 46
McCrillis, Col. Lafayette, 175, 292n5
McKeene, Pvt., 212
McLemoresville (Tenn.), 154
McMasters, Reverend Dr., 44, 116
McMurray, Sgt. William F., 42, 118, 121, 142, 195
McNeil, Maj. Quincy, 93, 97, 105, 108, 110, 112, 289n23
Mead, Capt. Charles W., 18
medical evaluation, 26
Memphis (Tenn.), 90, 134, 135, 138, 140, 141, 143, 144, 159, 161, 167, 168, 180, 181, 183, 184; Gayoso House Hotel, 168, 180, 181; hippodrome, 181; New Memphis Theater, 140
Mercer, William, 38, 43, 60
Meredosia (Ill.), 24
Merriweather family, 93, 152
Merriweather, Cpt. Robert, 105, 108, 149
Mexican soliders, 217
Milliken's Bend (Tenn.), 184
Mississippi military units: Marine Brigade, 7, 127, 290n3
Mississippi River, 3, 7, 29, 32, 34, 35, 38, 46, 63, 67, 69, 71, 73, 74, 80, 81, 113, 134, 146, 164, 186, 210, 252, 283n4, 286n28, 290n3
Mississippi Sound, 235, 249
Missouri military units: 1st Artillery, 136, 285n13; 1st Cavalry, 140, 285n13; 4th Cavalry, 31, 131, 151, 155, 156, 157, 291n21, 292n7; 6th Cavalry, 203, 218; 11th Infantry, 77; 21st Infantry, 120, 130; 24th Infantry, 161; 25th Infantry, 161; 26th Infantry, 71
Mobile (Ala.), 193, 226, 233, 236, 238, 239, 242–45, 247, 249, 251; explosion at, 251–52
Mobile Bay (Ala.), 233, 236, 241, 243, 294n6, 294n11
mockingbirds, 96, 195
Montgomery, 46
Moore, Annie (Norton), 260, 261, 283n6, 295n5
Moore, Francis C., 3, 103, 255
Moore, Capt. Frank, 59, 93, 99, 101, 134, 135, 140, 144, 145, 152–55, 158, 159, 160, 287n38, 291n25; dispute with Francis Moore, 190–91, 193
Moore, Lieut. George, 203
Moore, Henrietta (Gyles), 258, 260
Moore, Mary (Bywater), 260
Moore, Mary (Grant), 3
Moore, Richard Channing "Chan," 3, 12, 95, 246, 258, 260
Moore, Thomas, 260, 261

Moore, Lieut. W. B., 205, 231, 236, 238
Morganza (La.), 191
mortar boats and mortars, 58, 67, 75, 238
Morton, Oliver P., 153, 291n19
mosquitoes, 86, 88, 92, 150, 193, 195
Mound City (Ill.), 57, 64, 70
Mount Pleasant (Miss.), 178
Mount Sterling (Ill.), 23–24
Mount Sterling Horse Guards, 23
Mower, Lieut. Samuel, 186, 188, 299, 227, 228
Mudd, Col. John J., 185, 188, 292n11
Murdock, Sgt. Arthur T., 20, 22, 42, 59, 110; capture of Colonel Faulkner, 105; death of, 105, 107, 108, 109, 110
music and singing, 21, 31, 43, 44, 62, 80, 81, 115, 116, 117, 141, 213, 214, 222, 227; "Carry Me Back to Virginia," 65; "Dixie," 47; "rogue's march," 34
Musser, Capt., 238, 239

Natchez (Miss.), 185
National City (Calif.), 8, 261, 262
negroes. *See* African Americans
New Albany (Miss.), 170
New Madrid (Mo.), 34, 75, 85, 88, 89, 91, 288n7, 288n9, 289n14; siege of, 73–74
New Orleans (La.), 7, 61, 181, 213, 215, 223, 224–25, 227, 228, 229, 231; described, 232–33; "French Market," 225; St. Charles Hotel, 224–25
New York military units: 2nd Cavalry, 226; 14th Cavalry, 208; 17th Infantry, 161
Newburn (Tenn.), 149, 151
Newsom, Col. John F., 148, 149, 291n16
newspapers, 53, 56, 57, 64, 94–95, 108, 128, 146, 151, 164; *Cincinnati Gazette*, 65; *Harper's Weekly*, 31, 63, 121; "special correspondents," 63; camp newspaper, 72; *War Eagle*, 128; *New Orleans True Delta*, 215; *New Orleans Times*, 227
"Nigger Wool Swamp" (Mo.), 90, 193
Nine Mile Creek (Fla.), 248, 249
Noble, Col. Silas, 18, 102, 113, 115, 284n1
Normandy Creek (Miss.), 138, 141
Norton, Annie, 272

O'Brien, 134
oath of loyalty or allegiance, 4, 33, 88, 95, 97, 98, 101, 119, 144, 145, 146
Obion River (Tenn.), 104, 110, 111, 112, 151, 152, 159, 160
Ohio military units: 5th Cavalry, 136, 137
Ohio River, 34, 35, 38, 45, 58, 61, 67, 69, 119, 168, 286n28
Okolona (Miss.), 171, 175, 283n5
Ould, Col. Robert, 216, 293n1

Paducah (Ky.), 7, 45, 70, 113, 114, 117, 118, 122, 125, 131, 153, 167, 168, 182, 292n9; described, 116; winter quarters at, 113–14, 117
Paine, General Eleazer Arthur, 69, 70, 71, 72, 288n3
Painter, Lieut. Charley, 202, 203
parakeets, 95
Paris, Sgt. William H., 205, 230, 238
Pascagoula (Miss.), 210
Pascagoula River (Miss.), 249
Patton, Sgt. John D., 97, 230, 249
payment of soldiers, 90, 119, 244, 247
Peabody, Sgt. John L., 125
Pemberton, General John C., 141, 253
Pennsylvania military units: 19th Cavalry, 160, 170; 25th U.S.C.T., 242, 243, 294n13
Pensacola (Fla.), 226, 233, 236, 244
Peters, Claus, 132, 161
photographs, 218, 252, *See also* ambrotypes
Phul, Mrs. Von, 213
Pillow, General Gideon, 34, 37, 69, 134, 288n5
Pilot Knob (Mo.), 27, 28, 29–30
Pioneer Corps, 169, 176; "First African Pioneers," 176
plantations, 7, 120, 148, 178, 213, 214, 223; abandoned, 150, 184, 187, 88; forage from, 32, 151; Northerners leasing, 184–85
Platte Valley, 111, 136
plays. *See* theater
Polar Star, 234
Polk, General Leonidas, 4, 47–48, 61, 287n32, 287n33

Pontotoc (Miss.), 171, 176
Pope, General John, 73, 75, 79, 85, 94, 288n7, 289n19
porpoises, 239
Port Hudson (La.), 142, 143, 188, 198, 199, 208, 209, 293n22, 293n26
Portersville (Tenn.), 135
Powers, Lieut., 243
Prairie Station (Miss.), 173
Prentiss, General Benjamin M., 28, 31, 32, 33, 285n12, 286n23; superseded by General Grant, 33, 34
Prentiss, Lieut. George, 210
Price, General Sterling, 43, 53, 101, 285n20, 286n29
Prince, Ed, 20, 142, 284n6
prisoners: captured Confederate, 33, 41, 53, 69, 96, 107, 119, 159, 199, 208–9; courts-martial, 126, 127, 159, 161, 168, 190–91, 205, 206, 210, 245, 286n27; exchange of, 43, 58, 102, 128, 142, 159, 196, 212–13, 215, 216; paroled, 108, 140, 142, 144, 145, 146, 213, 216, 286n29; punishments, 34, 118, 157–58, 177, 195; questioning of, 105, 130–31; uselessness of, 95, 102

Quinby, General Isaac, 93, 289n18
Quincy City Guards, 19
Quincy (Ill.), 3, 5, 18, 19, 20, 22, 78, 79–80, 95, 255, 257, 258, 260, 284nn8–9

railroads, 29, 71, 72, 73, 78, 164; destruction of, 171–72, 173, 178; Hannibal and St. Joseph, 20; Mobile and Great Western, 247; Mobile and Ohio, 171, 293n23; Union Pacific, 210, 258, 260, 261
Ralph, Sgt. Orlando, 117, 230, 259
Ralston, Capt. Virgil, 70
Red River (La.), 186, 188, 189, 252, 292n11, 292n12, 293nn18–19, 293n24
"red tape," 6, 8, 58, 67, 133, 186, 189, 201, 206
Red Wood Bayou (La.), 188, 196
Redland (Miss.), 171
Redoubt (Fla.), 237
Reelfoot Lake (Tenn.), 104, 109, 111, 152
Reid, General Hugh Thompson, 166, 167, 168, 292n1
religious services, 21, 44, 63, 67, 110, 116, 140, 183, 184
Richmond, 243
Ripley (Tenn.), 145, 149, 151
Rocket, 230
Roddey, General Philip Dale, 160, 292n28
Rodie, Miss Lou, 213, 214, 218, 219, 225
Ross, Col. Leonard, 38, 286n26
Rottaker, Capt. Herbert H., 203, 218, 219
Rowland, Maj. J. G., 123
Russell, Lieut., suicide attempt of, 111
Ryan, Col., 89

Saint Cloud, 225
Santa Rosa Island (Fla.), 237, 238, 244
Sawyer, Lieut. Joseph L., 20, 28, 45, 54
Schmidt, Capt. William, 52
Schroeder, Marm, 230, 231, 232, 233
Scott, Col. John S., 196, 197, 198, 199, 202, 203n20
scouting, 36, 38–39, 42, 45, 58, 86, 88, 90, 98, 100, 104, 161, 186, 193, 196, 211
seasickness, 235–36
Seldon, Pvt. Gideon, 41
Sexton, Cpl. Edwin, 87
Shappe and Whitney (trapeze act), 231, 294n7
shelter (dog) tents, 133, 135, 169, 180, 220, 231, 232, 235, 236
Sherman, Julian, 95, 289n20
Sherman, Lydia (Moore), 3, 12, 260
Sherman, General William T., 160, 178, 245, 291n24
Shipley, Lieut. William, 52–53
Sibley stove, 69
Sibley tents, 68, 69
Sickles, General Daniel, 191, 293n13
Sigel, General Franz, 31, 53, 285n19
Sikeston (Mo.), 34, 37, 74, 75, 76, 82, 85, 89; described, 72–73
Simplot, Alexander, 63, 288n43
Sisters of the Good Samaritan, 21, 26, 41, 57, 284n8

Slemmer, Lieutenant, 237
slavery, 86, 120, 130, 263; as cause of war, 9, 145; effect on slaves, 136; effect on Southern society, 5, 144–45, 163, 189; abolition of, 163. *See also* African Americans; contraband (former slaves); emancipation
Smith, General Andrew Jackson, 160, 161, 163, 164, 166, 228, 231
Smith, General William Farrar "Baldy," 224, 225, 294n4
Smith, General William Sooy, 168–69, 170, 171, 176, 292n7
Smith, Maj. Thomas, 77, 113, 161
smuggling, 119, 221, 222, 223
snowball fights, 121, 165
songs. *See* music and singing
Sorenson, Capt., 248, 250, 252
Southerners: disloyalty of, 98–99; ignorance of, 5, 45, 86, 88, 144–45, 163; immorality of, 189. *See also* women, Southern
"Spanish Grant" (Mo.), 74, 288n9
Spence, Private James, 36, 42
Spence, Sgt. Obediah, 62, 104, 110, 132, 180, 187, 188
Springfield (Ill.), 3, 25, 26, 192n16
St. Francis River (Mo.), 28, 29, 31, 90, 91, 100
St. John, Philip, 187
St. Joseph (Mo.), 258
St. Louis (Mo.), 26, 27, 78, 80, 81, 255; Lafayette Park, 81; Washington Market, 81
Steele, Andy, 211
Steele, Maj. General Frederick, 225, 240, 246, 294n10
Stokes, Sgt. William C., 43, 44, 57, 67, 102, 103, 116
Street, Solomon, 160, 161, 291n25
Superior, 184
sutlers, 6, 27, 75–76, 151
Swank, Lieut. (guerrilla), 71–72

Tallahatchie River (Miss.), 170, 177
Taylor, General Dick, 195, 249, 251, 293n18, 294n16
Taylor's Battery, 28
Tecumseh, 99
Temple, Private William W., 157
Tennessee military units: 4th Cavalry, 241
tents. *See* shelter tents; Sibley tents
Texas military units; 1st Cavalry, 217, 223, 294n2
Thomas, General Lorenzo, 6, 129–30, 230, 290n5
Thompson, Merlwether Jeff, 4, 28, 32, 37, 71, 73, 74, 75, 88, 89, 93, 285n14
Thompson, Polly, 93
theater, 7, 67, 132, 140, 168, 180, 225, 227, 230; varieties, 81, 224. *See also* horse opera
Three Mile Creek (Ala.), 247
ticks, 86, 87
Tippah River (Miss.), 170, 177
Tiptonville (Tenn.), 93, 111
tobacco, 27, 30, 76, 90, 122, 173, 178, 244
Tombigbee River (Miss.), 172
Travis, Bill, 121
Trenton (Tenn.), 97, 149, 158
Troy (Tenn.), 151
Turchin, Col. John Basil, 28, 286n27
Turner, Sgt. Frederick, 42, 54, 63, 129, 130, 131, 132, 140
Tuttle, Col. James, 38, 286n26
Tyler, 46, 112

uniforms, 21, 25, 26, 58, 67, 136, 190; as disguises, 43, 207–8
Union City (Tenn.), 151, 153, 154, 155, 167, 168

Vallandigham, Clement, 153, 192, 291n19, 293n16
Van Rensselaer, Henry, 58, 287n37
Vance, Miss Kate, 181
Veatch, General, 135, 247, 248, 249, 251, 290n7, 294n15
Vicksburg (Miss.), 127, 134, 141, 145, 146, 184, 195, 252, 253
Vicksburg, siege of, 141, 142, 184, 290n12

Walker, Judge, 214–15
Walker, William, 214

Waring, Col. George E., 131, 155, 162, 167, 172, 174, 201, 291n21, 292n7; involved in arrest of Francis Moore, 157–59, 161, 165, 166
Warrington (Fla.), 237, 242
Washam House Hotel, 180
Watson, 184
Watts, Lieut. Col. N.G., 212, 213, 215, 218
Weaver, Francis (bugler), 62, 70, 107, 115, 117
West Point (Miss.), 173
White River (Tenn.), 184
White, Capt., 241
White, Lieut. Col., 47, 48, 52
White, Reverend Dr., 140, 181, 182, 183, 184
White's Bayou (La.), 188
Whiting, Capt. Augustus, 230, 236
Wilcox, Charley, 91
Wilcox, Pvt. William. A., 105, 107, 108, 109, 264
Wilks, Pvt. William C., 120
Wilks, Quartermaster Sgt. John N., 22, 25, 102
winter quarters, 45, 54–56, 113–14, 117, 159–60
Wisconsin military units: 13th Artillery, 193; 4th Cavalry, 185, 186, 191, 193, 200, 201, 203, 215, 232; 15th Infantry, 92, 93, 111, 289n15, 289n17; 27th Infantry, 130, 248
Wolf River (Tenn.), 180
Wolfe, Col. Edward H., 134, 291n20
women, Southern: attractiveness of, 45, 66, 183, 203, 225; disloyalty of, 99, 103, 114, 144, 145, 198, 220, 221–22; fear of Yankee soldiers by, 66, 172, 173, 183, 197–99; marriages of, 183, 204, 218; mourning attire of, 183; trading activities of, 222–23. *See also* Southerners
Wood, John (former Illinois governor), 69
Woodruff, Pvt. Thomas, 39, 54, 57, 63, 67, 260; detailed away from company, 93, 112
Woolsey (Fla.), 237

Yates, Capt., 249, 250
Yates, Governor Richard, 69, 86, 93, 247
Yellow Bluffs (Tenn.), 151
Yorkville (Tenn.), 149

www.ingramcontent.com/pod-product-compliance
Lightning Source LLC
Chambersburg PA
CBHW030256100426
42812CB00002B/459

* 9 7 8 0 8 7 5 8 0 4 4 1 5 *